Confluence

150 years of service 1863-2013

This book is dedicated to all employees and directors of the Company, past and present, who have shaped and guided it through its evolution.

Written by Malcolm Toogood

Design and layout by GetSet Graphics

Bright Pen

A Bright Pen Book

Malcolm Toogood has asserted his right under the
Copyright, Designs and Patents Act 1988 to be identified as the author of this work.

British Library Cataloguing Publication Data.
A catalogue record for this book is available from the British Library

ISBN 978-0-7552-1581-2

Bright Pen is an imprint of:
Authors OnLine Ltd
19 The Cinques
Gamlingay, Sandy
Bedfordshire SG19 3NU
England

This book is also available in e-book format, details of which are available at
www.authorsonline.co.uk

Contents

Acknowledgement

With grateful thanks to the many people without whose help this book could not have been produced. They know who they are and we hope they enjoy reading this book to which they contributed so generously.

Foreword

The word 'confluence' has particular resonance for us – literally and figuratively. Our business is based on the waters of the rivers Avon and Stour which come together in Christchurch. This meeting of the ways is reflected in the union of the Bournemouth & District Water Company with West Hampshire Water. Just as the two rivers wend their way inevitably towards each other, the two companies, fiercely independent and equal in every way, finally come together after a century of existing side by side.

This history, written within the wider social context, celebrates 150 years of serving and being part of our local community. It is written with all the warmth and humanity you would expect to find in the telling of a family story. And in part, this is what it is. It is a story about the company, told through its people – people who are rooted to the local community and many of whom are indeed family. One hundred and fifty years later, many of our people still have familial ties within a company that has welcomed generation after generation of family members. Through years of innovation, modernisation and changing corporate cultures, we have maintained this family feel. We are proud of our history and our heritage.

Roger Harrington

The Royal National Sanatorium, Bourne Avenue, Bournemouth 1865
One of the earliest photographs of the National Sanatorium from a stereoview by the photographer Frank Mason Good

A Nice Place to Live

Looking at the metropolis that is the modern County Borough of Bournemouth, it is difficult to imagine that a little over two hundred years ago the area it occupies between the small Dorset harbours of Poole and Christchurch was nothing more than miles of open heathland, much like the New Forest is today.

The natural sheltered harbour at the mouth of the Hampshire Avon to the east had been discovered in the seventh century and provided a living, mainly in fishing, for the inhabitants of the sleepy, isolated country town of Christchurch that grew-up around it. A thousand years earlier, the larger inlet of the River Frome to the west provided access for ships arriving from Rome and beyond, but a settlement did not fully-develop there until the eighth century. The town of Poole itself did not emerge until around four hundred years later.

A raid on Poole in 1574 by a combined French and Spanish force highlighted how easy it would be for an invasion to be launched upon England in the area. This prompted Queen Elizabeth to commission the Earl of Southampton to produce a survey, which revealed that the mixture of steep cliffs and shallow shoaling coastline provided *'dangerous landing places upon the sea coste from Bornemouthe, within the hundred of Westover, adjoyning to Dorsetshire.'*

Once the danger from the Armadas had passed, it wasn't long before that ease of landing was put to less-reputable usage, and by the mid-eighteenth century smuggling had become the main source of income for those living on the heaths and moorlands at the southern edge of the New Forest. It was the policing of those activities, together with the ever-growing threat of invasion from Bonaparte's France, that created the need for a local militia. The Dorset Volunteer Rangers were formed in 1796, under the command of Captain

Lewis Tregonwell. He successfully patrolled the clifftops with his men for more than fifteen years with some notable successes that reduced the smuggling operations to a mere trickle.

Captain Lewis Tregonwell by Thomas Beach, 1798

This activity was assisted by the passing of the Enclosure Act of 1802, which allowed several local landowners to acquire large tracts of the heathland, the borders of which they demarked with hedges and ditches. They also constructed roads to provide better access, and this opening-up of the area tended to drive-away the more questionable occupants. The strips of land along the coastline were shared between three landowners, William Dean, Sir George Iversen Tapps and a Mr Norris. Dean owned most of what is now Westbourne, Tapps most of what is now Southbourne.

By 1810, the invasion threat had receded considerably, and Tregonwell decided to retire from his military duties. He had long since decided that the area around the mouth of the small Bourne stream would make a fine place to build a residence where he could settle with his family and, after organising a picnic for them at the spot he had chosen, his wife was in full agreement with his decision. So he purchased 8½ acres from Tapps, for the grand sum of £179, and built his retirement home, Exeter House, at the centre of an estate which he christened Bourne Tregonwell. Today, that 8½ acre estate forms the entire town centre of Bournemouth, and his house is part of the Royal Exeter Hotel on the clifftop opposite the Bournemouth International Centre. The Tregonwell family moved into their estate in 1812, and, although there were other sporadic developments in the surrounding area, even forty years later it was still little more than a village with ninety dwellings scattered around the Bourne.

Tregonwell's House in 1883, when it was Newlyn's Hotel. The original building is the right-hand part.

Bourne Mouth from the Water c1850, showing the Bourne Stream flowing from the left side of the Belle Vue Hotel (in the centre), across the sands into the bay.

It was the selection of the area in 1855, by the Queen's physician Sir James Clark, for the establishment of the first National Sanatorium for the treatment of tuberculosis and other respiratory diseases that was to be the catalyst for the expansion of the town. This simple decision highlighted to the entire country the benefits of the clean and natural air, coupled with a climate more akin to the Riviera than the River Thames. Once the Sanatorium opened, visitors from the fashionable classes were attracted to the area. To service them, grand hotels and boarding houses began to spring-up, followed by large villas and terraces of rentable accommodation. The age of the seaside holiday had arrived.

In order to service the majority of this influx of visitors, Bournemouth would rely heavily upon the amenities and commercial services of Poole and Christchurch for many years whilst it established its own infrastructure. Still separated by open land from the new resort, these neighbouring towns had developed in starkly different manners. To the east, Christchurch remained a sleepy rural backwater where life was little changed from the previous centuries. Most of the roads were dirt tracks, there was no public lighting and water was still collected by hand from the pump in the town square. In 1835, a Royal Commission reported that: *'Christchurch is not a place of much consideration or importance, nor do there appear to be any causes in operation which are likely to produce any increase in prosperity or population.'*

Bournemouth Pier in 1855

To the west, Poole had developed into a thriving industrial port and by 1850 had a local municipal corporation which had organised a piped water supply to many parts of the town, funded by the levying of a rate. In 1851, the Poole Gaslight & Coke Company was formed, and within five years its gasworks near the quay was producing millions of cubic feet of town gas to illuminate most of the streets, as well as the majority of businesses and higher-end residential properties.

Although the new upstart rising between them boasted buildings that were probably grander than those of its western neighbour, Bournemouth's infrastructure was little better than that of its sleepy companion to the east. This was a particular embarrassment when city-dwellers from the capital began to arrive in their droves, expecting such a modern town to at least possess similar conveniences to those of their homes. So, on 14th July 1856, the Bournemouth Improvement Act was passed by Parliament, providing for the appointment and incorporation of a Board of Commissioners, armed with powers to create, amongst other things: *'the more efficient paving, sewering, drainage, lighting, cleansing, watching and otherwise improving the district, the provision of a pier and of a market and the levying of tolls.'*

But they were given no powers with regard to water supply, and in the matter of lighting they were restricted to *'entering into contracts for a period not exceeding three years, with any person or company for the supply of gas, oil, and other means of lighting the streets and public buildings.'*

It was not long before a steady stream of businessmen began calling at the newly-erected town hall to offer their services in these developments. Chief among them were numerous engineers, with glowing testimonials illustrating their successes elsewhere, offering to build a gasworks to illuminate the town. But the Commissioners had a different priority; they recognised that the medicinal nature of the town's attraction dictated the need to maintain a clean and healthy environment, and for that they needed running water.

However, at that time water was not seen by engineering entrepreneurs as a route to vast riches. And with many lucrative opportunities available in other towns and cities, once faced with the apparent onerous nature of the combination of the short-natured terms of the Act plus the Commissioners' additional requirement, the gas engineers quickly moved on. It would be a proposed Royal visit by Queen Victoria to the town, which thankfully for them did not materialise, that would finally bring the wake-up call for the Commissioners to do something about this.

They created the superbly-titled post of Surveyor and Inspector of Nuisances which was filled by Mr Christopher Crabb Creek, surveyor and advisor to one of the main local landowners. He first looked at providing street lighting using portable appliances, then at obtaining a supply 'without the nuisance of gas works' from the Poole Gas Company. During the discussions with Poole, an additional company was projected under the title of the Poole and Bournemouth Waterworks Company, the idea being to establish an undertaking to serve the joint purposes of both towns. Four sources of supply were considered, but when the Bournemouth Commissioners ultimately passed a resolution that they *could not but view with serious misgiving any intention to*

connect the Bournemouth stream with a water supply to Poole and Parkstone' the burghers of Poole withdrew from any further negotiations regarding both utilities.

Creek then obtained agreement from a Mr. Wansbrocht to submit a scheme for providing gas, who was then informed by the Commissioners that unless he also undertook the supply of water the suggestion could not be entertained. Another scheme was put forward by a Mr. Bennett but the Commissioners regretted that the means at their disposal did not permit them to provide public lights for the district. The following year a draft agreement was prepared with Messrs. Stears, but the firm could not undertake the provision of water, and the opposition of the Commissioners led to that also being abandoned.

Creek must have begun to wonder whether the main 'nuisance' in his title were his employers, but any frustration incurred was soon to be eliminated.

Exeter Road, Bournemouth 1863

A Proposal

In 1863, two more gentlemen from London arrived in Bournemouth for a meeting with the town's Commissioners. Their names were William Cash and Edward Woods, and they had some experience with the construction of gas undertakings.

They first made a proposal to the Commissioners of a similar nature to many received previously - that in return for an agreement to purchase the gas produced for lighting the streets, and free rein to lay piping throughout the Borough to provide domestic and commercial supplies to every property, the two gentlemen would build a gasworks at their own expense.

The Commissioners listened to the proposal patiently and, once concluded, advised the gentlemen that gas was not their immediate priority; it was a piped water supply that they needed - and urgently. Once that was available to them, then they would be more than happy to consult on other matters. It was at this point that all previous visitors had politely made their leave, but Cash and Woods listened carefully to the response, and asked for a few days to consider the situation, after which they would return and advise whether they could assist.

Cash and Woods were no ordinary businessmen: William Cash was a leading City accountant who held numerous posts as a director or auditor of gas undertakings, mining and railway companies, for most of which he had been instrumental in raising their initial financing. The Cash family were Quakers and are noted among the leading entrepreneurial families within that religious society during the Victorian age. His father, also named William, was a founder and later chairman of the National Provident Institution, which is now part of the Phoenix Assurance Group.

Bournemouth Pier approach 1865

Edward Woods was one of Britain's most eminent civil engineers, with appointments in similar companies across the country and abroad. His experience told him that, although it had never been considered previously, there were engineering synergies between gas and water utilities, not least the interdependency in raising steam motive power for both works. In addition, both needed to lay miles of mains piping throughout a town, and the potential for digging one trench instead of two, and thus securing customers for both services together, made sound economic sense.

Having ensconced themselves in the Bath Hotel overnight, they returned to the Town Hall the following day with a revised proposal for the creation of a joint utility company that would provide both services to the town. Even though this solved two of the Commissioners' main problems in one fell swoop, they were still reluctant to accept. Although they were happy to have the waterworks in the town, they insisted that any gasworks must be located at least two miles from the town centre, to ensure that any danger of pollution of their clean atmosphere was mitigated. This added considerable potential cost, as it would involve the laying of two miles of gas

mains that were, effectively, redundant in terms of revenue creation. It was unsurprising, in the face of such stubborn requirements, that many previous proposers had run away from the town.

But Edward Woods was no ordinary civil engineer; in fact he seemed to thrive on resolving impossible problems - perhaps it was that very aspect that retained his attraction to this project. Whilst Cash returned to London to take soundings with potential investors, Woods embarked on a reconnaissance of the area surrounding the town. With the aid of Mr Creek, he inspected the previously-considered water sources, one of which was on the Branksome Estate, for which Creek was also the agent. This land included the Bourne and its two contributory streams, plus the source of those streams - a large area of bogland that absorbed water like a sponge.

A meeting was arranged with the owner, who agreed to provide a site upon which a pumping station, reservoirs and filter beds might be constructed, plus an adjacent site for the erection of a gasworks. The combined sites provided the ideal combination of being some two miles west of the town, and providing a source for water

Commissioners

abstraction sufficient to provide for the needs of the growing town for many years into the future. They also solved a major logistical problem, in that they were closer to the only railhead in the area, at Poole, with the capacity at that time to receive the thousands of tons of coal that would be needed to be brought in annually to manufacture the gas.

When Cash and Woods returned to meet the Commissioners for the third time, Cash had already secured promises for most of the money needed to meet Woods' initial estimates for the cost of erecting the works and laying the two miles of mains to bring both gas and water from the remote site into the town. The Commissioners accepted the plans unanimously, and thus on 1st September 1863, the Bournemouth Gas & Water Company was born, being incorporated as a limited company the following year. Among the first directors of the company were two Bournemouth

Commissioners, James Haggard and the company's first Chairman, James Phillips. William Cash took the post of Company Secretary and Edward Woods became the company's first Chief Engineer.

Sixty years later, James Druitt, who served as Town Clerk and Mayor of Christchurch in the latter part of the 19th century, and was also one of the early directors of West Hampshire Water Company, put his memories of the time on paper. He recalled being present at an early meeting in 1863 at the law offices of his father, then Clerk to the Bournemouth Commissioners: *"I was much struck as a boy with the personality of both Mr Woods and Mr Cash. Mr Woods had one of the finest faces I had ever seen, and both Mr Woods as engineer and Mr Cash as financier were eminent in their professions. It is largely due to them that the company made such a good start."*

Canford Heath

SHIRE

Bourne

Wallis Ford

BOURNEMOUTH GAS AND
WATER WORKS

Bottom

Retreat

Service Reservoir
Potteries

UTH RAILWAY

Christchurch
(Detached)

HAMP

PARKSTONE

Sandy Cote

THE

SETDORSE

Poole Heath

Herbert Home

CANFORD MAGNA

Branksome Dene

DORSE

Location of Bourne Valley Works from an 1873 plan drawn by Edward Woods

Edward Woods
1814-1903

Edward Woods was an outstanding civil engineer. At the age of twenty he became assistant to John Dixon, Chief Engineer of the pioneer Liverpool and Manchester Railway. Two years later, in 1836, he succeeded Dixon as Chief Engineer, and held the post until 1852. In 1838 he presented a paper to the Institution of Civil Engineers containing some of the earliest accurate details of the working of locomotives, for which he was awarded the Telford silver medal. In 1849, he obtained patents for turntable design.

In 1853 he moved to London and established his own practice as a consulting engineer and was a member of the London Metropolitan Board of Works from 1870. He collaborated on locomotive designs for the London and North Western Railway producing research that provided an invaluable insight into early locomotive design and performance, and influenced many of his contemporaries. He also tested various continuous braking systems for the 1874 Royal Commission into the causes of railway accidents, his recommendations leading to the adoption of the Westinghouse System that became the standard on all British railways.

He was consultant engineer for railway companies in Spain, Australia, Syria, Chile and Peru, and Chief Engineer for the Central Argentine Railway, where he was responsible not only for surveys and construction for the entire 250-mile length, but also for the design of bridges, locomotives and rolling stock. In 1872, he designed the Honduras Ship Railway to connect the Atlantic and Pacific oceans, then, in 1880, the Lancashire Plateway where steam locomotives hauled trains of wagons of varying widths along modified highways.

He designed mining installations in Peru and Spain, and was on the Board of the Patent Concrete Stone Company - the inventors of the concrete manufacturing process. As well as Bournemouth, he was Chief Engineer for the Roumanian Gas Light Co and Colombo Gas & Water; he also designed and built the entire water system for Montevideo.

He had been elected a member of the Institution of Civil Engineers in 1846, became a council member in 1869, Vice President in 1881 and President in 1886. He was elected to the Royal Institution in 1861, was President of the mechanical science section of the British Association in 1877, and President of the Smeatonian Society of Civil Engineers in 1884. He worked right up to his death, at the age of eighty-nine, and his obituary in 'The Times' concluded: *"His strength of character, soundness of judgment, and fertility of resource were largely aided by the singularly amiable disposition and quiet manner which distinguished him throughout his long, useful and active career, and made friends of all who enjoyed the privilege of his acquaintance."*

Bourne Valley Pottery 1925

Bourne Valley

Work commenced on the company's first site at Bourne Valley in early 1864. Water was obtained from the headwaters of Kinson Brook, the central arm of the Bourne stream, and collected in culverts that ran into reservoirs on the site.

After passing through sand filters the water was pumped, initially by means of pumps powered by steam-driven beam engines, up to a service reservoir on the high ground near the works of Sharp, Jones & Company, manufacturers of stoneware sewer and gulley pipes and known locally as the Bourne Valley Pottery. From there it flowed into the town under gravity.

By the end of 1864, the initial lengths of mains had been laid into the town and six customers had been connected, the first of these being a market garden in Cambridge Road nearly a mile and a half away from the works. Just two operational staff were employed at the inception of the company, the General Manager, Mr Maber, and a salesman named Rebbeck. Through the latter's efforts, the number of connections had risen to 185 by the time that the waterworks had become fully-operational five years later.

From that point, the rate of connections accelerated and by the time legislation was placed before Parliament for the Bournemouth Gas & Water Act in 1873, that figure had nearly quadrupled, necessitating a fourfold increase in service reservoir capacity at the site near the Pottery. As water demand increased, the water intake source from the Bourne Stream did not have the capacity to meet it, so a sixty-foot well was sunk at Bourne Valley, coupled to new pumps. This assisted for a short while, but the rapid enlargement of the town necessitated finding sources nearer the new developments. In 1876, a well was sunk at Springbourne, feeding a new 160,000 gallon brick water tower erected in Palmerston Road at Boscombe, the latter remaining in service for more than a hundred years. It was eventually sold in 1995 to a developer, who converted it into eight apartments.

Although the company was primarily established as a gas supplier, that side of the business was much slower in getting off the ground. When the 1873 Act was passed by Parliament, it was specifically noted in the documentation that in those first ten years of operation, the company had incurred great expense in laying down totally unproductive mains and works for distributing gas a distance of two miles in accordance with the requirements of the Commissioners. By raising the status of the operation to that of a Statutory Company, regulated by and answerable directly to Parliament, the owners were able to establish some degree of autonomy in their future developments. As a result, the Chairman James Phillips, who was also a Commissioner, resigned and was replaced by an independent Chairman, Robert Hudson FRS, Vice-president of the Zoological Society.

A site plan, reproduced from the company's minutes of the time, shows that the two operations were accommodated separately. Nevertheless, there was always a sharing of resources in that the boiler house fed the steam engines for both aspects and manual workers were allocated where they were needed. As demand rose, reaching forty-seven million cubic feet by 1880, so the number and sizes of the gasholders increased. The fourth, and largest of those shown on the plan is the only remaining structure on the site from this era.

Bournemouth's gas was produced by a process called carbonisation. When coal is heated to redness out of contact with air the constituent gasses are driven off, leaving behind a carbon-rich solid called coke. When the liberated gasses react with the residual carbon they form a mixture of primarily hydrogen, methane and carbon monoxide, known as town gas. This process was carried out at Bourne Valley in horizontal retorts, essentially a twenty-foot-long bench containing a number of tubular ovens that were loaded with coal then heated for eight hours whilst the gas was drawn off by an exhauster. It then passed through a condenser before being collected in the gasholder, from where it was delivered to the gas mains on demand. At the end of the process, the remaining coke was removed from the tubes and either reused for firing the ovens, or sold to both commercial and domestic users as a virtually-smokeless fuel for heating their premises.

Stoking horizontal retorts at Bourne Valley

Within the large retort house at Bourne Valley, there were four individual benches, all of which were hand-charged. Each tube only opened at one end, which meant heavy manual work to fill them with coal using just a shovel. Afterwards the spent coke had to be extracted with a hand rake from the same end that they had been charged. Although the overall process was continuous, the retort benches were phased at varying stages throughout a day, meaning each

District workers with their carts. A Horse and Dandy is shown on the left.

retort was only fully in production for a portion of the time. The army of stokers servicing them was either loading coal into the retorts or removing the still-hot coke after the process had finished, working twelve-hour shifts Monday to Saturday and eighteen hours on Sundays.

Additional workers were employed outside in the yard, unloading delivery carts, carrying fresh coal to the stoking areas and removing the coke to outdoor bulk storage facilities. Yard workers' hours were from 6:30am to 5:30pm weekdays, 2pm on Saturdays. In the winter, weekdays were reduced by an hour, 7am to 5pm, but Saturday finishes were extended to 4pm. Holidays consisted of one Saturday outing each summer at the company's expense.

In those early days, the thousands of tons of coal needed each year were delivered by rail to the sidings of the Southampton and Dorchester Railway at Poole, from where it was transported by road on a fleet of horsedrawn wagons. The company kept a stable of heavy draught horses at Bourne Valley which regularly won prizes for turnout at the local shows. When the London & South Western railway branch line was constructed to Bournemouth West Station in 1874, it ran past the southern edge of the Bourne Valley site enabling the coal to be delivered to sidings provided nearby at Branksome Station.

For the first few years, the entire administration was run from the office of the company secretary, William Cash, in London. By the mid-1870s, the amount of trade was sufficient to open a local office, and this was located in the front room of a small detached villa called Dene House at the foot of Poole Hill, where the local Secretary Mr Bryant lived. His staff consisted of two collectors, Mr Evanson and Mr Morrell and a small boy named Smith to run errands, including carrying business correspondence to and from Bourne Valley. In addition there was a small team of fitters managed by the company's only inspector, John Walker, who also worked out of that one room.

One of those fitters, Edward Hardy, worked for the company for more than fifty years, and recalled on his retirement: *"How things have changed since April 1877 when I first started work as a boy with my uncle William Budden looking after the lead pot. This was on the first 14 inch gas main from Bourne Valley works to County Gates. We had no motors to carry pipes and material but had to manage in the old way with horses and a Dandy. There were only two men and myself and the boy as workmen on the district and one turncock and a flusher. My job in the spring time was to help Mr Cutler to clear the Culverts which brought the water to the filters at Bourne Valley."*

Both collectors also worked for the company for more than forty years, retiring in the 1920s when they gave their recollections to Co-Partner magazine. Evanson explained: *"We did our office work on a large table which was also used as a counter. The company's collection area extended from Bourne Valley Pottery through Bournemouth, Boscombe, Springbourne and Southbourne to Tuckton. Both gas and water works were at Bourne Valley and Mr Monk was the manager. My duties were to collect the outside districts while Mr Morrell took the central district. We collected only gas, water and coke accounts as other charges were paid before the work was done."* Mr Morrell recalled: *"The difficulty was there were no numbers and scarcely any names to the cottages where new customers were located. I had to ask Mrs Jones where Mrs Brown lived and perhaps that was at the other end of the road which made it very difficult to a stranger. We had between us to do the work of the office as well as the collecting and many times had to work very late to keep things up to date."*

For a quarter of a century, Bourne Valley works continued to grow step-by-step with the growth of Bournemouth until it became evident that new means would have to be employed to cope with the ever-increasing demand, particularly for water.

People *A group of Gasworks employees of the 1890s. The young lad would have been an errand boy.*

J.H.WALLS   R.GOOD   W.H.B. W.H.QAKER

The Turncock

Edward Street was one of the oldest employees of the company. He came from Ringwood and entered the company's service as a stoker at Bourne Valley in 1869, transferring to Poole Hill when a post for a Turncock became vacant.

In those early days, the lower parts of Bournemouth were only supplied with water from noon until 3 o'clock and a Turncock had to shut down the water at night and turn it on in the morning, visiting hotels and boarding houses every evening to see that the cisterns were full. The beam engine pumped the water to Bournemouth and Boscombe Tower through the eight-inch main down Surrey Road and up the seven-inch main along Bourne Valley Road to the Pottery reservoir, from where it returned to the lower levels of Bournemouth under gravity.

When there was a fire, the Turncock was called out to shut down the mains in order to give an adequate supply at the required point for the work of the brigade. After a constant water supply was installed, some of these duties were no longer necessary and Edward Street was made Turncock for the whole district. He was highly respected by the company and a well-known figure to many of the older inhabitants of the Borough. His period of service extended over forty-five years to 1914 from which date he received a pension from the company.

Longham 1921

New Sources

By the mid-1870s, big changes were taking place not only in Bournemouth but also in the surrounding districts. Building activity at Springbourne, Boscombe, Winton and Pokesdown meant that the company's connections passed the thousand mark.

Although the gasworks at Bourne Valley could be expanded regularly to cope with these rapidly-rising demands, the existing water intake sources did not have the capacity to meet them, so Edward Woods turned his attention to the River Stour. Out of several possible sites along the banks of the river, he chose Tuckton for the sinking of the next well. This source initially looked to be the answer, so a remote pumping station was added there in 1881 feeding the water tower at Boscombe. However, problems began to arise with the consistency of supply due to the unstable sand in the area, renewing the need for further explorations.

Woods re-examined the options that had been rejected in favour of the Tuckton project, and the most promising of these was at Longham village, where an extensive deposit of water-bearing gravel existed in the river floodplain on the Wimborne Estate alongside a disused water-driven corn mill. So the mill buildings and adjacent land were leased and a test well was sunk in the gravel which proved capable of providing very ample supplies. It was decided to develop the site, by constructing underground collection conduits and to use the undershot waterwheels already installed alongside the mill house to power the pumping equipment.

In parallel, land at Alderney two miles away was leased from the Canford Estate for the construction of a reservoir and water treatment plant on a site which possessed the twin basic requirements of relative isolation and adequate elevation. This was the modest beginning of the site that was destined to

Longham

develop in such a way that, some seventy years later, Alderney Works would ultimately become the pivot around which the whole of the company's development in water supply was to be centred.

With Longham and Alderney fully on-line, the water supply from Bourne Valley was essentially closed down and demoted to a standby facility in 1885. But within a year, a dry summer proved the water wheels at Longham Mill were not up to the task at peak demand, and these needed to be rapidly replaced with turbines. This necessitated restarting Bourne Valley, and using the River Bourne in addition to the streams. But this also caused problems, as related by George Allen, who worked there at the time: *"The River*

Bourne was condemned for drinking purposes because of the soapsuds and the overflow from pigsties that trickled into it. But the summer of 1886 was very hot and dry and the only way of getting enough water was to use that flowing down the Bourne. In order to prevent an undue amount of added flavour in the water supply we had to scrub the whole length of the river from the works to the source with brooms! It was a very near thing although the water was, of course, carefully filtered, and we did it successfully for no complaints came through of any pig wash epidemic."

With the new turbines on-stream at Longham, it soon became obvious that too much reliance had been placed on the power obtainable from machinery driven by the fluctuating flow of water in the River Stour, so these were supplemented with Worthington Simpson steam pumping engines to add reliability. A year later, the redundant beam engines from Bourne Valley were moved to Longham to provide a further reserve of pumping plant.

All of these installations, together with the areas where new building was taking place, needed to be linked by new mains. The sizes of the water mains grew from eight to twelve and then fourteen inches, while gas mains were smaller. All were constructed by the same team of service layers, and all of their tools and materials had to be taken about on a hand truck, the usual load being about nine hundredweight, which was almost half a ton. One of the team, Sam Shepherd, remembered one occasion when he and his mate had to push a cart weighing fifteen hundredweight - *"a good start for a day's work!"* he remarked.

Another, James Budden, recalled: *"Gas mains in those days were puny affairs, two and three inches were common, seven and eight were huge. New mains were laid in all directions sometimes replacing, sometimes duplicating the old. No plans were kept, the men carried them in their heads. If any doubt arose as to the exact course a few holes were dug here and there in likely spots just like digging for rabbits. Any mains repairs meant no gas or water for the consumers in that neighbourhood until the job was finished and they received no notice! Cutting out a gas main was a haphazard job, no gas masks, no oxygen, neither was there any bypassing. As greater precautions had to be taken, backing became necessary but blowing up the bags was done by mouth, and gassing was a common experience under such conditions."*

The gas supply side increased even more rapidly than the water. In the year 1880, the gas made was forty-seven million cubic feet, and this had increased to 172 million in 1890. The price of gas in 1878 was 6s.6d (32.5p in today's money) per 1,000 cubic feet, but by 1887, this had reduced to 4s.0d. Water charges were fixed against the rateable value of the property, and where that did not exceed £12 per annum, the water charge was fixed at 2d per week. Above that, a percentage was levied rising to 5% on properties with a rateable value above £20 per annum. Revenue was, therefore, always more heavily-weighted towards the consumption-led supply of gas, which consequently produced in the order of 75% of the company's earnings.

39 Poole Hill

Whilst all this was going on, the expansion of the company's business meant that they were outgrowing their original administration

Workers at Longham 1921

office. During the 1920s, one of the collectors at that time, Mr W Evanson, recalled the location: *"we were housed in a detached villa on Poole Hill with a small garden in front, and part of the outer wall is now in the middle of Bayley and Sons ironmongers shop. The local secretary lived in the house and the front sitting room was the general office and I think another room was used as a private office. The land extended round the corner and was enclosed by a wall, the ground being covered with gas and water pipes and various other materials."* So, in 1884, the company opened new purpose-built offices together with a small showroom on a piece of land nearby at 39 Poole Hill, and the inspectors and fitters responsible for making the individual property connections moved to join the service layers at Bourne Valley.

There were also changes at Board level. The Chairman, Robert Hudson, died in 1883 and was succeeded by George Friend Whiteley, a Twickenham surgeon, who had been a director since 1867. When he died in 1886, his son, George Crispe Whiteley, a London barrister, author of a number of law books and past president of the Cambridge Union, replaced him. Then, in 1891, the secretary and one of the founders of the company, William Cash, also died. He was likewise replaced by his son, also named William, himself a very eminent accountant and partner in the family firm of Cash, Stone and Company.

At the turn of the century, Thorneycroft steam wagons replaced the horsedrawn drays for transportation of coal.

Collectors and Messengers used bicycles to get around.

The rapid expansion during the latter part of the century did not take place against a wholly-benevolent background. Public records show that, in 1880, the Bournemouth Commissioners were casting a closer eye over the company, and the profits it was making; proposals were introduced by James Phillips

District Staff used hand carts to transport their tools and materials.

to take the company into public ownership. Although these were dismissed, they resurfaced in 1884 when the publication of the company's intention to raise additional capital was challenged by the Commissioners because they *"thought it probable the town would shortly require to purchase the gas and water works."* This rumbled on until 1887 during which time one Commissioner even remarked in a public meeting that he believed *"we are paying for water almost three times as much as any town in the kingdom."*

Despite comparisons with other historical records that show this to have been a considerable exaggeration, several Commissioners decided that significant reductions in the local charges of up to a third could be made if they were running the company themselves. It would appear that negotiations took place over the next eighteen months, during which the directors offered to sell the entire company for £407,000, a truly

People *Wimborne Pumping Station 1902*

Wimborne

vast sum for such a small undertaking at that time. If this was a manoeuvre to put the matter to bed once and for all, they must have been astonished when the Commissioners agreed to this figure, and had an agreement drawn up. The matter was then put to two public meetings in July and August 1889, where a number of local ratepayers, led by a Mr Rebbeck, forced the matter to a public poll, essentially a local referendum. The vote took place in September, where the Commissioners' proposal to purchase was defeated by 1,861 votes to 1,661.

With their independence assured, the directors' attention returned to keeping at least one step ahead of growing consumption and, in 1895, this focussed on the possibility of obtaining water from the chalk which underlies the sweeping downlands of southern England. The advantage this offered was water which was purer at the source, and acting on eminent geological advice, three acres of land were acquired in the valley of the River Allen at Walford Bridge on the outskirts of Wimborne Minster.

Well-sinking operations commenced in 1896 and, in the Spring of 1898, a twenty-four inch main was laid to link the source into the trunk mains at Longham. By adding tunnels, called addits, driven outwards into the chalk from the bottom of the well, a yield of about one and a half million gallons a day was achieved, but this was by no means as much as had been hoped for. Nevertheless, the development of the source went ahead, and a second pumping main was laid from Longham to Alderney, with two additional reservoirs, together with their attendant filters, added at Alderney.

This allowed the company to dispose of their redundant pumping station at Tuckton, which was purchased by the newly-formed West Hampshire Water Company, who covered the supply area immediately to the east of Bournemouth's.

Pipe-laying, Bridge Street, Christchurch 1908

Christchurch

Whilst all of this was happening in the expanding town of Bournemouth, most of the residents of Christchurch were still obtaining their water from a variety of wells, including that serving the pump in the town square, or from the mill stream.

In 1875, the Public Health Act placed a duty on all sanitary authorities to arrange for the provision of 'wholesome and sufficient water' for the needs of the inhabitants in their areas of responsibility. Where a water supplier was not already fulfilling this function it devolved on the local authority.

Christchurch was not meeting this obligation and there were many petitions for a supply of clean, safe water. As most of the townspeople threw their sewage on to their gardens or down their cellars, with the swift rise in population many of the shallow wells intermittently became contaminated and, by modern standards, totally unfit for use. The Council, however, apparently did not take the risks too seriously because, in 1887, its own report stated: *"Five hundred persons obtain their drinking water from the pump at the lower end of the High Street. If water can be obtained from our own sources, there is no need to hoodwink any water company into the town and if a water system is necessary the Council can obtain it, at a little outlay, from the high ground to the east of the Borough. If we can use and keep pure the existing supply all the water of the town can be supplied, but it is absolutely essential that the pump should be put into an efficient state of repair and others erected to increase the supply."*

In 1893, a surveyor's report for The Square House, one of the largest and best built residences in the town, stated: *"The water used for domestic purposes is derived from two sources. For the bath and lavatory supply it is from a*

Sinking the first 147-ft well at Knapp Mill in 1893

well in the adjoining Mansion Brewery where the water is strongly impregnated with iron and cannot be used for cooking. The water for cooking and drinking is brought to the house by hand having been drawn from a public well in the street which is about thirty feet deep and, being drawn by an ordinary suction pipe, the water level cannot be lower than this. This arrangement cannot be regarded otherwise than with suspicion, as the extremely porous nature of the subsoil and the close proximity of the well to the surface drainage of the roads and the house-drains renders the water peculiarly open to attack from all sides."

Fortunately, in the previous year, a number of local businessmen, among them Mr John McMillan, had decided to take decisive action

before typhoid or cholera eradicated the people of Christchurch. They conferred with a London-based civil engineer, John Howard, on the possibility of bringing a piped supply of wholesome water to the town. Howard drew up a scheme to abstract water from the River Avon, pump it up to a reservoir on St Catherine's Hill and then feed it by gravity through pipes back to a point near the junction of High Street and Castle Street. This plan was supported by the Town Council and incorporated into a local Parliamentary Act which received Royal Assent on 24th August 1893, and thus the West Hampshire Water Company was founded.

McMillan, together with two local Aldermen James Druitt, a solicitor, and John King, was elected as director, and the Mayor of

Christchurch, Samuel Bemister, became the first Chairman. By the end of 1893, a lease had been taken out on land at Knapp Mill where the pumping works were to be located and Mr Howard commenced construction on the company's behalf by sinking a 147-ft well on the site which proved successful. The following year, plans for construction of the waterworks by the South West Suburban Water Co Ltd were approved, and later that year, the company appointed its first Chief Engineer, Mr R St George Moore. Two acres of land were purchased in 1895 from the Fourth Earl of Malmesbury, the largest landowner in the area, for the construction of the reservoir, and the laying of mains proceeded at a pace. On 13th August 1895, the Knapp Mill works was opened by the Earl of Malmesbury where, in the pumphouse, two triple-expansion steam engines powered the Worthington Simpson pumps that supplied water to the reservoir after it had been filtered through charcoal. Piped water had finally come to Christchurch, some thirty years after it had first been supplied in Bournemouth.

But the Act did not just cover the town; it empowered the West Hampshire Water Company to make supplies available to a rural area covering some seventy square miles stretching northwards to Ringwood, and east to a line drawn through Lyndhurst, Brockenhurst and Milford-on-Sea. This was a total contrast to the smaller, and more densely populated, urban area covered by the Bournemouth company, because the small towns and villages that needed to be served were widely spread apart. This was a major undertaking, not only logistically but financially as well, the latter not assisted by the statutory setting of charge rates that were the same as Bournemouth's.

The company was originally incorporated with a share capitalisation of £50,000, but when in September 1894 the first shares were allotted,

West Hampshire Water Company logo

only 15% had been taken up. The largest individual shareholders at that time were John Howard and the Earl of Malmesbury, and the company struggled for several years to raise the necessary capital it needed. This may have been due to the predominance of town councillors on the Board in those early years, most of whom were well-meaning and public-spirited, but did not possess substantial personal fortunes.

However, it wasn't just the financial constraints that prevented services being supplied to the more remote areas, in particular at Lyndhurst. There had been numerous proposals there over the preceding years, ranging from simple schemes for sewerage to a full-blown gas and water company, all of which had either been filibustered-away by the Parish Council or, when allowed, had rapidly become embroiled in legal battles over minor issues such as grazing rights. The Parish and District Councils, along with the New Forest Guardians, had opposed the inclusion of Lyndhurst in the West Hampshire Water Act, but when overruled by the legislation, they set about making it as difficult as possible for the company to comply.

The Earl of Malmesbury officially opens Knapp Mill Works on 13th August 1895

By involving the New Forest Verderers and the Commons Preservation Society, they brought about an amendment to the Act that forced the company to lay the twelve miles of mains from Christchurch to Lyndhurst within eighteen months of the date of the Act or, alternatively, to be pumping water from a local source within three years.

Both options would have involved the payment of substantial compensation to commoners and landowners and, even had the funds been available, the full co-operation of the local authorities was clearly never going to be forthcoming. So, the directors negotiated the sale of this impossible requirement to South Hampshire Water for £125 followed, a few years later, by a similar agreement for Brockenhurst.

These were lessons well-learned because subsequently more local landowners were attracted to take an interest in the company, primarily through the establishment of a good return on investment. This was an influence that would stand the company in good stead when the area of supply began to expand further east during the first half of the next century.

The first of those landowners, James Cooper-Dean, became a director in 1898. He owned the Littledown Estate to the west of Bournemouth and had inherited most of the land in Westbourne from a distant uncle. He became a major benefactor to the town of Bournemouth, including allowing the construction of the Grand Marine Drive and Promenade on the

Slow Sand Filters, Knapp Mill 1916

Building slow sand filters, Knapp Mill 1916

West Cliff as well as donating the East Common and the site of St Ambrose Church. He was followed onto the Board in 1900 by John Kemp-Welch, the squire of Sopley Park two miles north of Christchurch. His family owned the Schweppes Company, his father having acquired the patent for the process of creating carbonated water from Jacob Schweppe when he was a wine merchant in Bath during the 1820s. Both gentlemen served as directors for many years.

In 1897, encouraged by the quick increase in demand, the directors agreed to a scheme for a new engine, boiler, filter beds and clarifier, together with an extension to the pumping station at Knapp Mill. They also reached

agreement with the Bournemouth Gas & Water Company to take over the mains in Southbourne, as well as the Tuckton Pumping Station. As a result Southbourne Water Tower was built, but the pumping station at Tuckton was not a success, drawing up far too much silt. In 1899, an agreement was reached to make a bulk supply available to the Barton-on-Sea Water Company, after which the distribution mains network was extended to New Milton where a red brick water tower was constructed.

In the seven years leading up to the turn of the century, the company had created a water supply from scratch and connected more than a third of the existing nine hundred properties in Christchurch to it. The remainder were still

Southbourne Tower, originally constructed in 1897

using private or public wells, but the developers building the new estates surrounding the old town were making the connection of water supplies a major sales incentive, and commercial, industrial and agricultural concerns were taking a rapidly-increasing gallonage. Two years later, the Barton-on-Sea area was incorporated, due to the projected local company being unable to find a viable source of water in its area.

The West Hampshire Water Company was now well on the map.

Benjamin Read

This enterprising individual was essentially the first commercial water supplier in Christchurch. Known locally as 'Benny the Bucket', he drew water from the town pump into a wooden bucket and offered it from house to house for a ha'penny a time.

Benny would also join in May Day celebrations in the town by dressing himself up with all the ribbons he could collect from the drapers and go round the town cadging for coppers.

This portrait of Benjamin Read dates from 1841. It was originally thought to be by Thomas Musgrove Joy but is now attributed to a local artist named Curtis. The actual painting now hangs in the Managing Director's office in George Jessel House at Alderney.

H. W. WOODALL & A. MoD. DUCKHAM.
APPARATUS FOR THE MANUFACTURE OF GAS.
APPLICATION FILED JULY 1, 1904.

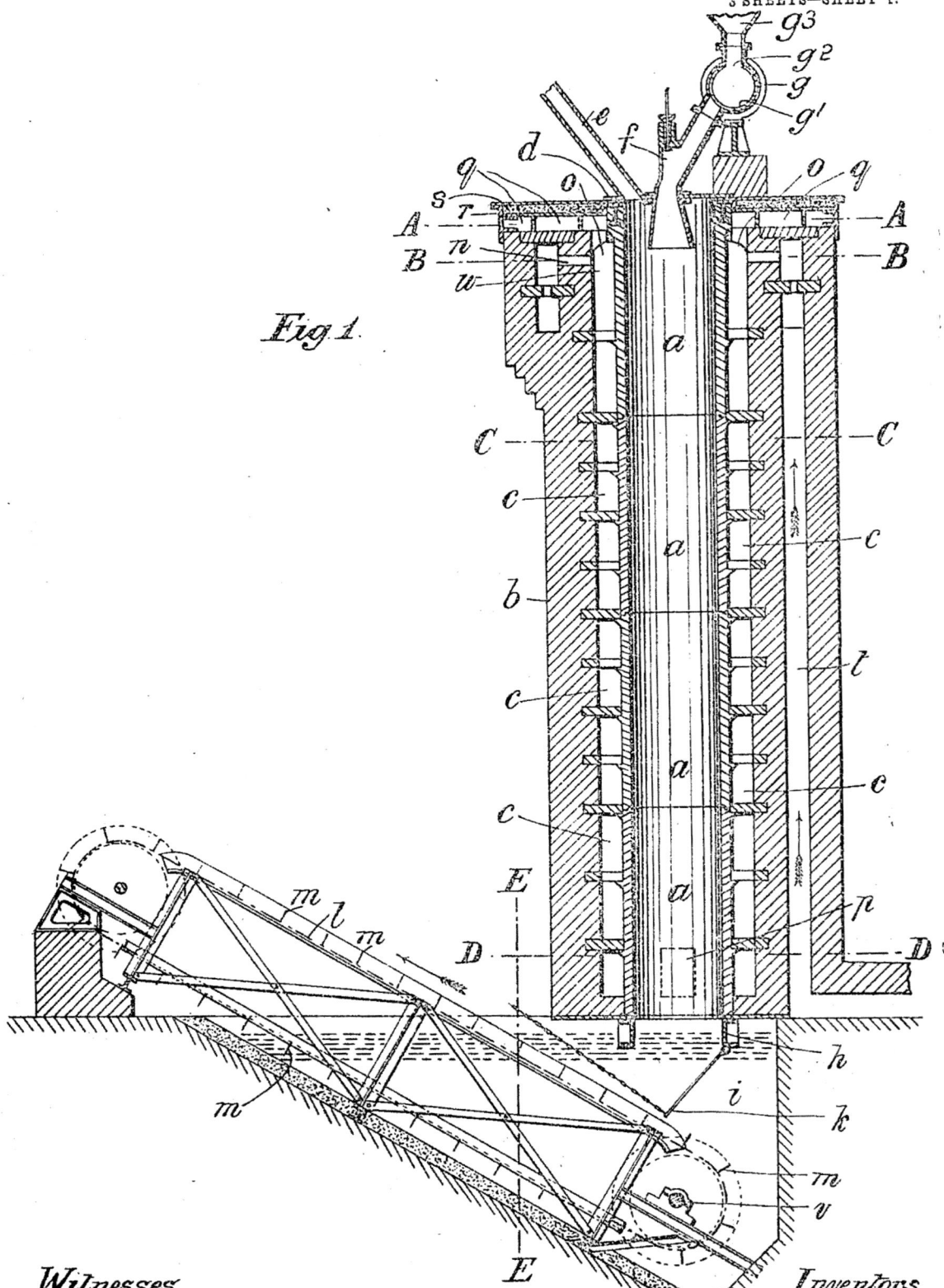

Fig 1.

Witnesses
WM. Kuchne
Edward Garton

Inventors
Harold Whitemore Woodall
Arthur McDougall Duckham
By Richards
ATT'Y

Vertical Retorts

By the turn of the century, Bournemouth Gas & Water Company had established their main water sources at Longham and Wimborne guaranteeing their ability to supply their area well into the future. However, the gasworks at Bourne Valley was now working at full capacity to meet the ever-growing demand caused by the rapid expansion of the town.

This expansion in the gas side of the business was not simply caused by the builders of new housing developments being persuaded to incorporate gas cooking ranges into their kitchens, the company had also become extremely successful in hiring gas heating equipment to businesses and households, and the new cheap, efficient and clean method of heating was being retro-fitted to many older properties as well. It was becoming increasingly-apparent that a major new gasworks would soon be needed, but could not be accommodated at Bourne Valley due to the restricted area available there, where the site had become surrounded by the new westward developments on the outskirts of the town. In addition, the Parliamentary Act governing

the company still included the restriction on the proximity of any new works to residential areas.

This problem fell into the lap of the new general manager of the company, Harold Woodall. He came from a family of gas entrepreneurs and his father, Corbett Woodall, was a director of several gas undertakings in addition to Bournemouth, including the London Gaslight & Coke Company, at that time the largest gas company in the world and of which he would become Governor in 1906.

Harold came up with an interesting solution - to buy the Poole Gaslight & Coke Company from Poole Corporation. Not only would this add a large area of supply, it included an established gasworks on a site outside of the area governed by the Bournemouth Commissioners, and therefore beyond any objections that they may raise as to location. Most importantly, the site had room to more than double the size of the works, plus it was next to the harbour, meaning that the huge increase in tonnage of coal needed to fuel the expanded capacity could be delivered in bulk by sea.

The purchase was completed in September 1902, and work commenced immediately on the erection of additional buildings, fully equipped with the latest machinery. This included new coal-handling facilities on Poole Quay, including an extension to the quay itself, for the economical and rapid handling of coal and other material delivered there. The acquisition also brought into the company ownership the imposing headquarters building in Poole High Street called Beech Hurst. This is an 18th century mansion built for the wealthy merchant Samuel Rolles, and it was retained as the local office and showroom for Poole.

In terms of staff, at the beginning of 1902, the company employed a total of around seventy covering all aspects of the business. The existing Poole gasworks was far larger than Bourne Valley, so by the end of the year after amalgamation, Bournemouth Gas & Water Company had more than doubled in size. Over the next four years, it doubled again as the Poole works was expanded and updated. In addition, new mains were laid through Poole and Parkstone linking the two sites at Poole Quay and Bourne Valley together, as well as allowing connections to be made to consumer properties in that area that had previously been considered uneconomical by the Poole company.

Despite this rapid expansion in production capacity, Harold Woodall was also very aware that the methodologies for the production

Harold Woodall on his retirement in 1949

of town gas were quite inefficient. The tried and tested process utilised structures called horizontal retorts, manned by armies of stokers who loaded the fresh coal manually and removed waste coke in a similar manner. He was aware of experiments with vertical retorts across the industry, where the coal could be gravity-fed from hoppers above the coking bed at a rate that would extract the maximum amount of gas before the spent coke fell to the base of the apparatus. However, the results of these experiments were constantly disappointing, mainly due to the continued utilisation of manual coal feed and coke extraction. A primarily-automated solution was needed.

In 1903, two things happened that would alter the direction of the gas industry forever. Firstly, Edward Woods, the Chief Engineer of the company since its inception forty years earlier, died.

Experimental conveyor at Bourne Valley with the team who produced it. Arthur Duckham is top right.

This caused the promotion of Harold Woodall to the role of Chief Engineer and General Manager, necessitating the requirement to take on a deputy to assist him in this dual role. That deputy turned out to be a fresh-faced twenty-four-year-old engineer named Arthur Duckham.

Duckham was not only highly thought-of, but also very ambitious, and Woodall recognised in this young protégé an intellect that might resolve the retort issues. So, in their spare time the two men examined the results of the experiments of others. It was those conducted by Settle and Padfield that produced the eureka moment, when Duckham turned to Woodall one evening and declared: *"Look, Harold, this is where these fellows were wrong! They should have kept the retort full and controlled the coal feed by the rate at which the coke was extracted, instead of trying to synchronise the coal feed and coke extraction so as to preserve a constant empty space at the top of the retort!"*

Woodall persuaded the Board to finance the building of an experimental installation at Bourne Valley, and having secured £100 to pay for the materials, Duckham set to work in the evenings constructing, testing and modifying this machine. The work proved so successful that, in 1904, the Board voted a further £50 towards the development and then, the following year, further funding to build a production prototype. When this also proved successful, Woodall and Duckham patented the process that became the Woodall-Duckham Continuous Vertical Retort.

Briefly, the continuous vertical retort is a sealed refractory brick funnel in which coal is heated and carbonised as it slowly and continuously descends under gravity. The gases and volatile by-products are driven from the coal during the descent and taken away from the top of the retort whilst the residual coke is extracted from the bottom. The speed of coal feed and descent is automatically controlled by the rate of coke extraction which can be adjusted to suit the type of coal being used. The heat in the coke in the lower portion of the retort is also utilised for producing water gas, mainly hydrogen and carbon monoxide, by admitting steam through the extractor box so that it reacts with the incandescent coke. The amount of steam determines the calorific value of the mixture of coal gas and water gas leaving the top of the retort by the gas offtake. The coke is finally quenched by water sprayed within the extractor box and is discharged cold without flame or smoke.

Because this new process took place vertically, as opposed to the previous horizontal configuration, the footprint of each retort was much smaller. This meant that it was possible to install vertical retorts in groups known as benches and, once productionised, it became possible to install up to sixteen vertical retorts on the same floor space previously occupied by just one horizontal retort. In addition, by utilising a conveyor beneath the outlets at the base of the retorts, coke extraction could be automated without the need to shut down the process, allowing it to run continuously. With coal hoppers added at the top, the only manual stoking required was to keep them topped up, and hence a team of half a dozen stokers could maintain a bench of sixteen retorts, whereas previously they would have tended just two.

But it wasn't just the huge reduction in manning levels that contributed to the increase in productivity of these new retorts; they were also far more efficient. A single vertical retort of these early patterns could carbonise double the amount of coal per day as one complete horizontal bench, and extract more cubic feet of gas per ton whilst doing so. A bench of sixteen vertical retorts was capable of producing more than thirty times as much gas as its horizontal predecessor. Of course, to do so it consumed larger quantities of coal, necessitating the development of evermore efficient coal-handling equipment. And eventually, following twenty years of continual development of both size and process efficiency, that production rate would triple.

To allow the commercial development of the process plant, the Board released Duckham from his employment and he left the company, with their blessing and a cheque for a hundred guineas, to found the Woodall-Duckham Company. In return, both Woodall and Duckham agreed to supply the very first commercial installation at Bourne Valley free of charge, and any future installations in Poole free of any patent royalties.

Although Sir Arthur MacDougal Duckham GBE became one of this country's leading industrialists during the nineteen-twenties and thirties, later histories reveal that, in those early days before the patents were fully granted, financing the infant company was extremely difficult, and Duckham even had to sell his car to raise the capital needed to keep the company going. Board minutes reveal that it was Bournemouth Gas & Water Company who bought that car, a 16HP Mercedes, from him for £350.

Those four production retorts delivered to Bourne Valley in 1907 were the first of thousands installed over the next forty years throughout the world, including eight further installations at Poole. They were all produced by the Woodall-Duckham Company, which became the world's leading manufacturer of gas-production equipment and is now part of the Babcock Engineering Group. Yet none of that could have happened without the vision of two engineers employed by the Bournemouth Gas & Water Company, with the full backing of their Board of directors.

Sir Arthur McDougall Duckham GBE, KCB 1879-1932

Known to his family and friends as 'Bob', Arthur Duckham was the middle of three sons of a civil engineer; the elder brother went into marine engineering and the younger founded the Duckham Oil Company. At seventeen, Arthur joined the South Metropolitan Gas Company where he studied carbonisation and furnace work, supplemented with evening studies in engineering at King's College London. Aged twenty, he was appointed assistant superintendent of the Old Kent Road Gasworks, then three years later, joined Bournemouth Gas & Water Company as deputy to Harold Woodall.

Having together invented the vertical retort and formed the Woodall-Duckham Company, it was Duckham who went on to manage the development of the new company, the success of which was due as much to his character and ability as a salesman, as it was to his technical expertise. He was a dominating figure, six feet tall and weighing eighteen stone, but with the knack of making and keeping friends and of inspiring others. In the early years of his company there were problems of cash flow, but a number of gas industry suppliers took shares in the company to ensure its survival. Later it expanded to produce plant for other chemical processes, as well as town gas.

When war broke out, Duckham was seconded to the Government's invention department, becoming Deputy Controller of Munitions Supply late in 1915. He adapted well to life in Whitehall, and progressed to become a member of the Munitions Council, Director-General for Aircraft Production and, in 1919, a member of the Air Council. His services were recognised by a knighthood in 1917. He was appointed to the Sankey Commission on the coal industry, and produced a supplementary report commending state ownership of mineral rights and a role for miners in the direction of the industry. He was instrumental in the creation of the Institution of Chemical Engineers and was elected its founder President in 1922. He was also a member of the Légion d'honneur, and became a patron for the arts. In 1928, he led a Government economic mission to Australia to advise on trade opportunities, following which he was created a GBE.

Duckham's status as a leading industrial statesman was endorsed by his election to President of the Federation of British Industries, a post he never took up due to his sudden death at the age of just fifty-two. His obituary in Bournemouth's Co-Partner magazine included this tribute: *"The men worked willingly for him because they liked and admired him. They gave back gladly what he had already given to them in full measure - friendship. He was genuinely interested in everybody who worked with him and soon knew all about their interests, families and daily life. Years afterwards on his frequent visits to the Bournemouth works, he would catch sight of an old friend then rush across the yard to greet him. His eager questions showed he had forgotten none of the details he had learned in the days of stress. Success had left the essential man untouched, and therein lay one of his greatest attractions: he was always the same - a friend for life."*

Knapp Mill, 1897

A New Century

Whilst the first few years of the new century were a time of consolidation on the water side of the Bournemouth company, the much younger West Hampshire Water Company was beginning a period of rapid growth and change.

The first Chairman of the company, Alderman Samuel Bemister, had died just after the turn of the century, part way through his seventh term as Mayor of Christchurch. He was succeeded as Chairman by John King, another ex-Mayor and also a serving Alderman. King was part of a long-established brewing family in the area, and had inherited the Mansion Brewery from his half-brother, which he subsequently sold in 1891 to Strong & Co, together with The Square House which he also owned. The Square House was a grand Palladian-style building, built on the corner of High Street and Wick Lane facing the Market Square, which gave it its name. It was built in 1776 for the brewer John Cook, who owned the Mansion Brewery next door, and was demolished in 1958 when the entire site was redeveloped as a shopping arcade. Today, on the corner where The Square House stood, is a Pizza Express restaurant.

From the proceeds, King purchased Iford House, near Holdenhurst, where he adopted the life of a country gentleman, becoming a shareholder and director in a number of businesses. However, he was not an inactive participant, and as Chairman of West Hampshire Water Company, a position that he would hold for the next thirty years, he brought a much more businesslike approach to the company. At that time there were just three permanent employees - Sambrooke Newlyn the Secretary/Manager, who had held the post since the company was established, Cox the engine driver, and a foreman. Much of the mains laying was subcontracted, and any other tasks were fulfilled by casual labour.

The works at Knapp Mill was on part of the land occupied by an 18th century corn mill, which was owned by the Mills family. It would appear that the corn mill was still in operation at the time, because a new lease was issued to two millers, Maidment and Barnes, in 1909. Around the same time, a new well was sunk near the works to a depth of 906ft, but was abandoned the following year as the water was unfit for use. It is not clear if this was to extract further supplies, or to find a purer source, because by that point the company was primarily extracting water directly from the River Avon. There were isolated complaints about the quality of water throughout those early years, and although the company's own analysis did not support these criticisms, the increased quantity of water being pumped led the directors to decide to increase the filter beds by two thirds. Regardless of the new filtering and other measures, an enquiry was held by Hampshire County Council during August 1906 into the purity of the company's water, but the results proved indeterminate.

On 11th October 1911, a special Board meeting was held with the object of immediately terminating Sambrooke Newlyn's engagement as Secretary because of *'a deficiency in his accounts at 7th October 1911.'* Newlyn had served as Mayor of Christchurch in 1906 and 1907, but had clearly fallen on difficult times, and was only saved from prosecution by his two sons attending the meeting and offering to put down the amount of their father's guarantee, an offer which the directors decided to accept without prejudice to any further claims. One of the sons, Mr J S Newlyn, then started working in the company's offices, presumably as part of the agreement that was reached.

The replacement recruited by the directors was David Llewellyn, who would serve in the combined roles of Secretary, General Manager and Engineer for more than forty years. He had barely got his feet under the table, however,

when a potential crisis hit the area at the beginning of 1912. Typhoid had broken out at Ringwood and although the town was within the company limits, it was not supplied at that time. The concern was that it was situated on the River Avon just twelve miles north of the water intake to Knapp Mill works. The Chief Medical Officer of Health for Bournemouth, Dr Edwards, suggested that the company should obtain a temporary supply of water for Southbourne from the Bournemouth Gas & Water Company and, after some deliberation, the West Hampshire directors agreed that the Southbourne mains be reconnected to those of Bournemouth for a minimum period of three months. At the suggestion of Dr Thresh, the company's analyst, a temporary chlorination plant was installed at the Knapp Mill works, and regular analysis showed that the water being supplied to the rest of their area was free of any contamination by typhoid, meaning any potential epidemic never developed.

At the same time, the Bournemouth company were in negotiations for the purchase of both the Wimborne Water Company and the Christchurch Gas Company. With their source at Walford Bridge fully on-stream, the former was a relatively easy decision as the small local undertaking was already being supplied from there. Agreement for the acquisition of the Christchurch Gas Company followed by the end of the year, and it was probably a logical next move for the Bournemouth Company to take over the West Hampshire Water Company as well.

Whether this was prompted in any way by the concerns of Dr Edwards is not known, but in January 1913, a formal offer was made to the directors of the West Hampshire Water Company. The only response recorded in the Bournemouth Board minutes was a letter that same month from West Hampshire giving the necessary notice to discontinue the temporary

Contact Tanks, installed at Knapp Mill in 1898

connection to Southbourne. According to West Hampshire records, the takeover suggestion was declined due to the offer being only to purchase shares at par value. However, the Bournemouth Board minutes show that the offer was made at market value, at that time 60% above par. Regardless, this was the first of many overtures that would be made between the two neighbouring companies, in both directions, and not the last time they would result in rejection.

Following this episode, David Llewellyn ordered the installation of four gravity pre-filters housed in a substantial iron building at Knapp Mill. The pumping station was now working around the clock, and extra staff were taken on to run the night shift permanently. The following year an additional filter bed and pure water reservoir were also constructed there, plus the company's small administration office in Stour Road was expanded with the addition of three clerks and a telephone connection.

Within months, however, the outbreak of war brought an entirely different set of challenges. One of the company's first employees, Mr W Bishop, a member of the Territorial Army, was immediately called up, the directors agreeing to make up his wages, as they did for all other employees who joined the Forces. By the middle of 1915, there were army camps in and around Christchurch and new mains were laid to supply them with water, fire hydrants were installed, plus considerable extensions were carried out at Barton-on-Sea and New Milton to the camps constructed there for the care of wounded Indian soldiers. The directors also had to decide whether it was necessary to guard the reservoirs against contamination *'by evilly disposed persons'*, whilst the Milton Volunteer Training Corps asked for use of New Milton Tower for their drills, followed by the Artillery Coast Defence School who used the top of the tower *'to enable them to take certain angles along the coastline.'*

Bournemouth staff who served in India with Lt Col Woodall during the First World War

In 1916, David Llewellyn, J S Newlyn, A Morris and W W Shaw were also called up. The company advised the authorities that in their opinion *'the business of a water company is of military as well as public importance'* and gave notice of appeal. This was successful in the case of Llewellyn and Morris.

Over at Bournemouth, the effects were felt more keenly, where 298 of the company's staff were called up, including their Chief Engineer and General Manager, Harold Woodall. He embarked for Peshawar in India in 1914 as a Major with a battalion of the Dorset Regiment, and was mentioned in dispatches as well as being made a Companion of the Indian Empire. He would return at the end of the war as a Lieutenant Colonel; twenty eight of his staff would not return with him.

Members of the colony at the printworks. Count Vladimir Tchertkov is standing second right.

The Tuckton Colony

When the source at Tuckton Mill, along with the pumping station known as the Iford Waterworks, was finally abandoned at the end of the 19th century, all of the machinery was sold to the Sheffield-based scrap merchants, Thomas W Ward Ltd. The empty building was subsequently leased to Count Vladimir Tchertkov, a Russian exile. He was a great friend of Tolstoy, and had fallen-out with the Tsarist regime causing him to flee to England in 1897, together with a number of other radicals, who established a colony at nearby Tuckton House, organised in line with Tolstoyan principles of domestic simplicity and non-violence.

It was a spartan existence, but it attracted plenty of media attention, the Daily Mail reporting in 1902: *'The inmates rise at six o'clock, beginning the day with a sea bathe at Southbourne. At about nine a mouthful of vegetarian food is snatched, followed by work till one when a light vegetarian lunch is eaten. Then work again until seven or eight when the meal of the day is partaken. At this, all members of the community sit down together, no-one serving, no-one acting as servant. The most striking point in the whole Tolstoy gospel is the equality of master and servant.'*

Tchertkov established a printworks in the old waterworks building, where the colony organised the reproduction of Tolstoy's works, the handwritten manuscripts for which were kept in a concrete strong room. He liaised with publishers, translators and distributors in the West, as well as smuggling the unexpurgated works to and from Russia. A newspaper was also produced, printed on rice paper so that it could be folded into a normal envelope to be posted individually to supporters in Russia.

After the 1917 revolution, Tchertkov was invited back to Russia by Lenin to publish the works officially. The printworks was closed in 1918, and the building sold to local motor engineers Frank Kiddle & Sons.

THE CO-PARTNER.

PUBLISHED BY

THE · BOURNEMOUTH
GAS · AND · WATER · Cº

PRICE TWO PENCE

No. 1.

SEPTEMBER, 1920.

As part of the scheme, the company produced a quarterly staff magazine named 'The Co-Partner'.

Co-Partnership

During the late Victorian and early Edwardian period the industrial landscape of Britain became littered with bitter industrial disputes, not least in the larger gas undertakings in the major cities.

One such occurred in 1889, when the newly-established Gas Workers' Union, under the redoubtable Will Thorne, threatened strike action at the South Metropolitan Gas Company, the second largest in the country. Having recently won an eight-hour day for stokers, the union then attempted to establish a closed shop. The Chairman of the company, Sir George Livesey, tried to defuse the crisis by proposing a workmen's profit-sharing scheme and offering the security of twelve-month contracts of employment. When three stokers applied to join the scheme, the union demanded their dismissal. Livesey refused, and a bitter two-month strike ensued, but the company was able to maintain gas supplies throughout and the union was forced to concede defeat. Following this, Livesey's ideas progressed from profit-sharing to co-partnership, conceived as a compact between manager and employee to recognise their common interests.

Described by Livesey as 'Christianity in business', co-partnership was expressed through fair employment practices, consultation, the encouragement of thrift and, ultimately, elected worker-directors. It quickly polarised political opinions. During the early part of the 20th century, industrialists who embraced the system, such as the shipping magnate Sir Christopher Furness, saw its objects as simply industrial peace, and a way to *"soften or obliterate the divisions between employer and employed."* Harry Quelch, a leading British socialist of the era, and editor of the Social Democratic Federation newspaper 'Justice' denounced it as *"a fraud upon the workers."* Today, one of the best examples of such a scheme survives in the John Lewis stores.

The first Co-Partnership meeting held at the Pavilion in 1938

Many gas companies introduced co-partnership schemes, and the innovation was fully justified by its success in creating superior industrial relations in the industry. By 1906, nearly 5,500 employees of South Metropolitan had, between them, more than £340,000 invested in the company, and there were three employees on the Board of directors. That same year, a record bonus of 9.34% was paid on wages and salaries. Also in 1906, a close friend of Livesey, Corbet Woodall, became Governor of the London Gaslight & Coke Company, the largest gas company in the world and South Metropolitan's neighbour north of the Thames. He immediately introduced co-partnership into that company, and proposed similar schemes among the other gas undertakings of which he was a director; one of those was Bournemouth Gas & Water Company, where his son Harold was General Manager.

The Bournemouth scheme allowed any employee to join once they had completed two years' service. It was not compulsory, but with an annual bonus on offer of the same percentage as the dividend paid to shareholders, it would be a bold man who ignored it. On 3rd October 1908, the scheme was laid before a meeting of the employees and approved by them. 348 eligible employees registered immediately to join the scheme and, at the November meeting, the directors approved the first six appointees to the new co-partnership committee. This was essentially a workers council, and consisted of four elected workers each representing a specific area of the business, together with the General Manager Harold Woodall and his deputy, Philip Moon, the person who had replaced Arthur Duckham after he left the company two years before.

In addition to the bonus scheme, which would consistently pay around 8% of annual salary at Christmas time over the ensuing years, a further percentage was invested into company shares to create a benevolent fund to be used to provide benefits to the families of workers who died in service or were forced to retire early through ill-health or accident. Members were also encouraged to purchase shares themselves at agreed discounted rates to assist them to provide for their retirement; these shares to be ultimately repurchased by the company at annually predetermined rates. In 1917, a pension scheme was added which provided very attractive returns, particularly for long-serving employees, and a few years later those benefits were extended to cover widows. With many of the staff making the Bournemouth Gas & Water Company a lifetime career, a high percentage retiring with in excess of forty years' service, and some more than fifty, this was another extremely desirable benefit.

In 1920, an expanded co-partnership works committee was created comprising twenty-four members. These included Harold Woodall and Philip Moon but, for the first time, it was chaired by an elected worker instead of one of the managers. That first Chairman, William James Haynes, was a fitter in the workshops at Bourne Valley, and had been a member of the team that worked on the development of the vertical retorts. His first Chairman's report not only sets a contemporary aspect to the attitudes within the industry just a couple of years after the end of the first world war, but also shows how articulate the ordinary worker of the times was, a factor so often misrepresented by modern social-historians:

"Our scheme has become a real-life power for good in the course of only twelve months. Our committee has totally justified itself and will continue to do so as long as the right men are elected to serve on it, men who have broad

The first enlarged Co-Partnership committee 1919-1920

minds which can take a long and wide view of things and see both sides of the question. As the first elected Chairman of the committee I am a staunch believer in it as a real-life factor in the task of helping workers to a better understanding of what is entailed in the management of a huge undertaking like ours and in bringing the employers and workers in close contact to their mutual benefit. The management of the company have entered into this scheme wholeheartedly and if we all pull together in the right spirit its possibilities are beyond calculation."

This eloquence was continued by their secretary, H T Symons, one of the showroom salesmen, who also wrote a short article for the magazine: *"There are big things to be done, loads to be lifted, wrongs to be set right and work, effort and energy are the only remedies for the troubles we see around us. Do not let us be discouraged by the babel around us from pressing-on with the work we have before us in endeavouring to obtain industrial peace. The Country, nay the whole world has need of live men, unselfish men, genuine men who are able to inspire mankind with the nobility of their example. Each of us in his sphere is able to set an example which will have some effect upon the world around us, and, if we all concentrate on that fact alone, we shall not have striven in vain."*

Each year there was an annual meeting of co-partners, where the Board of directors would present the company's annual report, together with a full explanation of how this translated into the benefits to scheme members. A separate co-partner's report was also produced, where all of the figures were supplied, providing full transparency in the company's dealings with their staff. These meetings were attended by the full Board; in fact it was often reported that directors had made special arrangements to be there. The report was presented personally by the Chairman, and at the 1928 meeting, celebrating the twentieth anniversary of the scheme, William Cash reported that: *"the bonuses have been at the satisfactory rate of 8½%, and for the whole year 1927 a total of £9861.18s.11d has been distributed to 707 members, taking the total bonus since the scheme started to over £80,000 which is I think a very satisfactory figure and shows the total amount the company has been able to provide in the co-partnership scheme since it came into being in 1908. In addition, the total invested in shares in the company stands at £32,000."* By 1949, total bonuses amounting to £355,498 had been distributed to members and the amount invested in stock by employees increased to £61,666; that same year the pension scheme fund, which during 1948 paid out pensions amounting to £21,433 to ex-employees and widows, held a balance of £692,446.

The annual meeting initially took place at Bourne Valley, during the summer on the morning of the annual sports day, but by the mid-1920s had evolved into an evening social event during March, as reported in the Co-Partner magazine: *"Members of the scheme were encouraged to bring their families along, and from 7pm they assembled as the works band played selections of lively music. At 7.30pm, the formal meeting began and lasted an hour until, punctually at 8.30pm,*

refreshments were served and the hour-long silence of the business meeting gave place to the merry rattle of cups on saucers and the buzz of general conversation as each guest was given a plate containing appetising sandwiches and cakes and offered the choice of tea, coffee or lemonade. After this, our own Rainbow Follies concert party under the leadership of Mr Lester rounded off a pleasant evening in a most enjoyable manner." By the 1930s, these meetings had grown so large that more than a thousand attended them, and they had to be held in the Bournemouth Town Hall, the only building available in the area at that time with the capacity to hold this number of attendees. However, even that accommodation became cramped as more staff joined the scheme, and the meeting moved on to the Pavilion when that building was opened in 1938.

The Rainbow Follies

The co-partnership scheme would provide the bedrock for the development of the company, and its relationship with its staff, through good and bad times, for more than eighty years right through to the latter part of the 20th century.

The Commissionaire

One of the first Head Office Commissionaires, J Thomas, retired in 1928 after fourteen years' service. He gave his recollections to Co-Partner magazine, which not only show his own interesting background, but also how much the co-partnership scheme could be of benefit, even in so relatively short a time.

"I was born at Amesbury, Wiltshire and the whole neighbourhood was agricultural, the only education I received being at the village night school. At the age of seven I was tending sheep on the Downs. For this seven-day week I received the sum of two shillings which small amount, added to my father's wage, helped to maintain a rather large family. My father was an engine driver entitled to 13 shillings a week. After a year or so with the shepherd I was sent to the carter and commenced working on the land, ploughing, sowing, reaping and mowing - a real farmer's boy. But farm work became irksome and I obtained employment on the Squire's estate which was considered a privilege. I eventually left to join a brother in Southampton, where I obtained work in a gentleman's garden. It was here that I first saw the smart young policemen of the Hants constabulary, who rather took my eye so I made up my mind to join the force.

Not having any testimonials with me I was given a form to be signed by friends in my village giving the period they had known me. They wrote across both columns 'all his life', so being 20 years of age I was armed with 20 years character. Within a short time I was a member of the Hants County force. I completed my 26 years service and was pensioned. I may say however that this period was pre-war and all pre-war pensions are small. I was obliged to obtain employment, and was taken-on as commissionaire at the gas company's office in July 1914 by Col Woodall the then general manager.

Soon after this the war broke out and being a member of the police reserve I was called upon to take up police duty in place of the men who had been called up for military service. At the conclusion of the war I returned to my duties at Poole Hill until March 1927 when we took over the fine new building in Old Christchurch Road of which we are all so proud. It was my privilege to hear many of the remarks of the customers on leaving the showrooms. Several said 'the best out of London' while a majority said 'what a beautiful place.'

I would advise all, especially the young men, to become co-partners. Had it not been for the co-partnership scheme, under which I was enabled to obtain several shares which the company purchased from me on my retirement, I should not have been residing in my own cottage today."

Telpher revolving coke crane installed at Pitwines in 1923

Pitwines

Although the Poole works had undergone major enlargement in 1906, as war approached it was already apparent that further expansion would be needed to cope with the ever-increasing demand from consumers in a coastal area ranging from the outer expanses of Poole in the west to Milford-on-Sea in the east, a distance of more than twenty miles as the crow flies.

For this, the directors had decided to build a completely self-contained new gasworks near to their existing Poole site on an area of reclaimed mudlands in the harbour known as Pitwines. A lot of the material used for the reclamation was waste coal ash and similar materials generated from the Poole works over many years and, in 1912, the company acquired some of this land for the erection of a large gasholder, together with a new purifying plant, the work on which was completed in 1915.

However, in 1914, the Harbour Commission had tried to obtain full control of more land around the harbour through amendments in Parliament to the Poole Harbour Bill. These changes had been vigorously resisted by all of the private and commercial landowners in the harbour area, including Bournemouth Gas & Water Company, resulting in the proposals being defeated, and Pitwines remaining outside of the area controlled by the harbour Board. When the company itself went to Parliament in 1919 with a bill to obtain powers to erect their new works on the Pitwines, they found themselves fiercely opposed by the Harbour Commissioners and Poole Corporation. The Corporation had, in a previous Act, prevented the company from obtaining powers to build additional gas manufacturing plant within the town and, as this included the area of land between Poole Works and Pitwines, they sought to maintain this restriction. In addition, the

Mitchell Coal Transporter installed at Poole Quay in 1922

Harbour Commissioners wished to prevent the company from purchasing an additional strip of reclaimed coastal land linking Pitwines to the sea, a piece of land that would enable the delivery of coal by ship directly at the new works, but was outside of their harbour area.

The company ultimately gained approval, but only by conceding to the demands of both bodies, meaning that the Pitwines site would effectively become an extension of the existing works, even though it was more than a quarter of a mile distant and the land between contained residences, as well as commercial properties. To transport the tens of thousands of tons of coal required annually to feed the new works, Parliament approved the installation of an overhead conveyor to take the coal across the rooftops of the buildings between the two sites, from the existing bulk silo on Poole Quay to the new coal store at Pitwines.

To prepare for the new works, upgrading of the existing facilities at Poole Quay was started in 1922. The bulk coal store on the quay was doubled in size and additional coal-handling plant installed, in the form of a Mitchell transporter of 100 tons per hour capacity to assist the existing Temperley transporter which only had a third of that capacity. Additional gravity bucket conveyors were also installed to match the speed of the transporters.

Bourne Valley Gasholder excavation

The overhead conveyor between the sites, with an overall length of 1,250 feet, was then installed, and this would not only transport the coal from the quayside to the new 12,000 ton capacity concrete coal bunkers at Pitwines, but also return spent coke to Poole works. To handle this, the original steel coke hoppers were dismantled and replaced by ferro-concrete hoppers of five times the capacity. These were equipped with mechanical feeders, the existing static lift being replaced by a revolving Telpher crane placed in a central position in the coke yard and capable of feeding coke directly into hoppers placed overhead of the water gas plant and boiler houses, from which the generators and boilers were fed by gravity.

The work on the major buildings at Pitwines eventually commenced the following year. The new works was based around a vertical retort house provided by the Woodall-Duckham company and consisting of twenty-four retorts, each capable of processing seven tons of coal a day to produce 2.75 million cubic feet of gas. This was delivered by three separate exhausters driven by vertical steam engines. At this end of the conveyor, vertical skip hoists elevated the coal at a rate of forty tons per hour to the coal hoppers on the top of the retort house, the discharge coke hoppers being fed by an endless Telpher track running through the retort house.

A relief gasholder was built for the new water gas plant that was housed in the main block of buildings to provide another 1.9 million cubic feet production capacity. This plant was powered by a waste heat boiler which also provided power for the steam engines. The coke was delivered by hydraulic charging apparatus, state-of-the-art equipment when installed. Electricity for the site was supplied by two 150kW British Thompson Huston generators powered by horizontal gas engines, fuelled from the water gas plant.

To cope with the increase in the amount of gas pumped from Pitwines to the main gasholders at Bourne Valley, additional boosting plant was added capable of delivering 360,000 cubic feet of gas per hour. At Bourne Valley a new steam-driven gas compressor was added to supplement the existing onward high-pressure gas supply to Longham and beyond. The supply of gas to the eastern end of the town was increased through a new twenty-four-inch main, which extended beyond to Christchurch gasworks, where a new half million cubic foot spirally guided gasholder was installed. To improve the local supply in Christchurch the old retort house there, which had been derelict from 1914, was pulled down and replaced by a new large booster and boiler house.

This all shows what a major project the company had undertaken. When the Poole Gasworks was acquired in 1903 their employees, including workmen, office and showroom staff did not number more than seventy. After completion of the Pitwines expansion in 1925, the company employed nearly a thousand, and annual production of gas had almost quadrupled to 1.7 billion cubic feet.

But this wasn't the only investment during those years. Water supplied annually had also virtually doubled in the same period to 1.2 billion gallons, and the facilities expanded

accordingly. In 1922, new Armfield turbines were installed at Longham to increase the pumping capability to Alderney, where additional reservoir capacity of three million gallons was provided during 1923, along with an increase in filtering plant.

An Armfield Turbine installed in 1922

An increasing number of commercial customers was utilising gas as the fuel for generating electricity. A regular stream of orders for the accompanying gas engines had been received during the immediate pre-war years, and these continued to flow in throughout the war. In the early 1920s, the demand was greatly stimulated as a result of the very reasonable hire purchase terms that the company offered, including the expansion and renewal of existing plant. One such installation was at Brights, one of the largest department stores in Bournemouth town centre, where a second installation was added in the basement to cope with the extension of the retail space above, which was lit by more than 500 separate bulbs.

5,000,000 cubic feet Gasholder interior steel tank

Stores at Bourne Valley

Electric Generators at Pitwines were driven by Gas Engines.

A motor tower ladder was used to maintain gas street lights.

On top of this, the company's retail business was virtually doubling annually, spurred on by the rapid expansion of house building in Bournemouth, illustrated by 632 brand new houses being connected in 1923 alone. In that same year, the company supplied and installed 804 cookers, 3,965 lights, 1,570 fires and 223 boilers to domestic customers.

The Bournemouth Gas & Water Company had clearly become a substantial undertaking.

Knapp Mill aerial view 1926

Knapp Mill

After the First World War, West Hampshire Water Company continued to expand its customer base, and the early 1920s witnessed extensive building of new estates around Christchurch, keeping the company busy.

In 1921, mains extensions were made to Sway and Boldre, bringing running water to properties there for the first time. All of this necessitated considerable capital investment, and the first was to purchase their Knapp Mill site from the owners, the Mills family.

Knapp Mill is the site of the oldest water mill in the Christchurch area, and is mentioned in the Domesday Book of 1086. What became the Hundred of Christchurch was divided into four districts, Sirlei, Rodedic, Egheiete and Bovre. That of Egheiete included Holdenhurst, Hurn and Chenep (or Knapp) where there was a mill belonging to Hugh de Port. He was one of the most prominent landowners in Hampshire holding more than fifty manors, some direct from the King, others from Bishop Odo of Bayeux, the King's half-brother. The actual entry reads: *'Hugh holds 1 hide in Chenep. Three allodial owners hold it in parage of King Edward and there were three halls. Then, as now, it is assessed at 1 hide. There is land for one plough, which is there with 1 serf and there are a mill worth 20 shillings and a fishery worth 50 pence and 16 acres of meadow; it is now worth 30 shillings.'*

The estates comprising the mill passed under William Rufus to Earl Richard de Redvers who gave them to the Priory Church in 1392, although the mill was no longer included in the Priory lands at the time of the dissolution of the monasteries. In 1522, it was still a corn mill but by the end of the 17th century it had become a fulling mill. At that time wool was the main industry in the area, being spun and woven in the many cottages in and around Christchurch from where it was

Early woodcut of Knapp Mill

taken to the Fuller, who cleaned and shrank the cloth using Fuller's Earth and plenty of clear water. Then it was put in a machine known as a gig which raised the nap on a revolving drum of teasels, machinery driven by water power. The mill, at that time in the ownership of the First Earl of Malmesbury, was badly damaged by fire in 1760; once restored it returned to being a corn mill. In the mid 19th century, it was leased to John Norman, a miller, who also had the lease for Mill House and garden, the osier bed, Mill Plain and the islands above.

In 1916, Miss Mary Frances Mills inherited the property. The Mills family were bankers, her great grandfather William Mills having joined Vere, Glyn & Halifax as a partner in 1770. In 1851, the bank changed its name to Glyn, Mills & Co, and was purchased in 1939 by the Royal Bank of Scotland, which merged it with another acquisition, Williams Deacons, to create Williams & Glyns Bank. Miss Mills lived

at Wolhayes, a rambling Victorian mansion at Highcliffe that she had inherited from her mother's side of the family, the Entwhistles. Wolhayes was modelled on the White House in Washington and, after, World War 2, became the Marydale Convent. It was demolished in the 1970s, and the land redeveloped into what is now known as the Wolhayes Garden Estate.

In 1919, West Hampshire Water Company bought the mill and nine acres of land, known as Holly Field, from Miss Mills for £2,000, together with the lease with the two millers, Maidment and Barnes, who they subsequently bought out. In addition, they agreed to pay £35 per annum to Miss Mills for the right of abstracting water from the upper intakes of the river. The Saxon foundations of the mill were demolished the following year to make way for the building of a hydraulic turbine house which pumped water to Christchurch reservoir using the river flow as energy. It was found that the

The new Turbine House under construction. Note the partially-demolished mill building on the left

foundations were laid on timber baulks, scarfed and bolted together with wooden dowels. These timbers were laid several feet below the bed of the river and the original builders successfully relied on these massive foundations to provide the building with its strength and stability. The baulks were black with age when taken up; within a few hours they began to crumble, but after a thousand years, and perhaps more, their centres were still in good condition and exceptionally hard.

The existing steam-driven pumps were retained as a supplementary facility, together with an electric pump that had been installed in 1920. In 1923, the first automatic chlorine dosing plant was installed, the first of its kind in the country. In contrast to their western neighbour, staffing was kept to a minimum and, at that time, the outside men worked 48 hours a week with no overtime until after 5.30pm, although seven days' holiday on full pay was given each year. Water prices, however, were dropping and in 1922, the wages of the workmen were reduced by 1s.6d a week to an average of £2.15s.

In 1924, additional land was acquired at Latch Farm alongside Knapp Mill to allow for further extensions to the works to cope with an expansion in the area of supply to include Burley. This was purchased from the estate of James Druitt, one of the original directors of the company. By the following year, office space at Stour Road, which was also the residence of the Secretary, had become very crowded, so David Llewellyn offered to move out and subsequently bought a house in Twynham Avenue, following which both numbers 19 and 21 Stour Road were purchased for the sum of £2,000. Also in 1925, it was decided to build an additional storage reservoir on St Catherine's Hill and in early 1926, five acres of land were purchased from the Earl of Malmesbury at £300 per acre, with an option on a further five acres at the same price.

However, the company was beginning to struggle in obtaining supplies of coal for its steam-driven plant due to a major coal strike. When this extended into the General Strike, its effects were felt across the region.

Demonstrators marching down a road during the General Strike, which was organised by the Trade Union Congress in support of the Miners' Strike to resist wage cuts.

Strike!

"Whether it is that coal affects character or whether it is that only men of a certain character are attracted to coal mining, the fact remains that both miners and mine owners taken in the aggregate are a grim dour dogged lot. Once they come to grips the fight goes on until one side or the other is down and out. They never admit defeat and, it seems, have no use whatever for sweet reasonableness."

These were the rueful words of the Chairman of Bournemouth Gas & Water Company, William Cash, when he summed up the events of 1926 in the Christmas edition of Co-Partner magazine. And what a year it had been for a company that depended on coal, not only as raw material for the production of its main product, town gas, but also for the motive power for most of the machinery that delivered its other product, water.

The General Strike of May 1926, like most major industrial action in Britain throughout the 20th century, centred on a coal-mining dispute. Similarly, it was a dispute that had simmered away for many years, in this case since the end of the First World War

eight years earlier. The mines had been under Government control throughout the war period, and the miners maintained the minimum wage rates they had won through their strike action of 1912. Fears of industrial action during the austere conditions of the immediate post-war period had delayed the return of the mines to private hands for three further years, during which time miners' wage rates were still retained. But losses being incurred through the combined effects of lower production rates and reduced exports meant that this only delayed the inevitable wage reductions when privatisation occurred. The result was a three-month miners' strike during 1921.

William Cash, Chairman from 1918 to 1949

The unsatisfactory conclusion to that strike rumbled on through the next four years, despite a general improvement in the industry through steadily-rising market prices. However, the hiatus from a sudden reversal in this trend during 1925 threatened another coal strike, this time supported by other unions, so the Government formed a Royal Commission and bought the time for it to make its report by providing a subsidy to the mine owners for a nine-month period. When the Samuel Commission reported in March 1926, their recommendations included a 13.5% reduction in wages. Following the refusal of the miners' union to accept this, the owners instituted a lock-out on 1st May. Two days later, an estimated 1.7 million workers walked-out in support of the 800,000 locked-out miners. The General Strike lasted just nine days before it was called off by the Trade Union Congress, but the miners held out for a further seven months, and it was the knock on effects of that longer stoppage which brought huge consequences to utility companies across the country.

Following the uneasy truce brought about by the Government's subsidy the previous year, the directors of Bournemouth Gas & Water Company had decided to cover the eventuality of the Royal Commission proving unsuccessful, and by 1st May 1926, the company had accumulated 20,000 tons of coal in their stores at Poole. This represented around three months' production, a period twice as long as any previous strike; in addition, a ship's cargo of 1,500 tons had been loaded at Goole before the end of April. This cargo was en route to Poole Harbour, but a Government embargo designed to avoid exacerbating the situation with the dock-workers meant it would be weeks before permission was obtained to discharge this coal into the store.

Having such a large supply in hand, and with summer coming on, there seemed every prospect of being able to last out. Strangely, the strike itself also provided some temporary relief, as the closure of the railways meant that many people intending to visit Bournemouth during May and June cancelled their holidays, leaving hotels and boarding houses empty for weeks. Reduced street lighting ordered through the State of Emergency imposed by the Government also brought down consumption, and the unexpected extent of the strike made the public more ready to heed Government warnings, bringing a good response to appeals for economy in the use of gas and electricity. However, when rail services were restored and general confidence returned, visitors once again poured into the town, sending gas consumption up to nearer normal levels.

As the months passed by without any improvement in the situation at the pits, and with stocks depleting into the autumn, it became very clear that if gas supplies were to be maintained by the company, foreign coal would have to be brought in. However, in order to minimise the effect on British industry, the

The 'William Cash' alongside Poole Quay

Government had quickly forbidden the export of British coal whilst the dispute continued, and consequently European countries that depended on those exports for their supplies had to go elsewhere, turning initially to the continental coal market and causing remaining stocks in western Europe to rapidly vanish. Looking further afield, the company obtained supplies of Silesian coal from Poland which was found to be quite good for making gas but had poor caking qualities, meaning the coke produced from it was unsuitable for onward use. When supplies of Silesian coal were exhausted, attention turned to Czechoslovakia, where the coal known as Ostrauer was not as suitable for gas making, but produced a much stronger coke.

In order to ship this Polish and Czechoslovakian coal into the UK, it had to be transported long distances by rail from central Europe to either Baltic or North Sea ports. However, there was insufficient coal-handling plant at those ports to cope with the unusually heavy consignments being rushed to the sea coast, so the port sidings became choked with filled wagons that could not be discharged into the waiting ships. As a result, although there was plenty of coal being produced in the eastern mines, plenty of ships ready to take it away and plenty of buyers ready and eager to get all they could, there developed a shortage of railway trucks to carry it to the ports. Towards the end of the summer, the congestion and delay became increasingly exasperating for the company, and as the general demand for coal sharpened, the situation became utterly hopeless as it was useless sending more vessels to hang about in European ports on the off-chance of receiving a cargo.

Cooker repair workshop at Bourne Valley

This difficulty had been foreseen during August when the company began to supplement the already irregular supply of continental coal by obtaining consignments from America. By the end of autumn, the company had made arrangements for depending entirely upon American coal for the maintenance of the town's gas service. However, this brought complications of another nature, as the oceangoing colliers could only unload at deepwater ports such as Southampton or Sheerness, meaning that every American cargo had to be transhipped into coastal vessels on arrival in England.

By the time autumn began to turn into winter, America was meeting a large part of the world's demand for coal. Eventually, precisely the same situation arose as had been experienced in Europe and the sidings and wharves became choked with coal wagons, the delays adding to the expenses of the waiting ships. Normally during autumn, the main cargo across the Atlantic from North America was corn, so the additional demand for coal tonnage sent freight costs soaring. The total result was the price of American coal delivered alongside at Poole was three times the amount that British coal would have cost in normal times. In the second half of 1926, the company had to purchase 40,000 tons of foreign coal and the extra cost compared with the similar quantity of English coal bought, under the contracts which were in abeyance owing to the stoppage, was over £70,000.

Whilst the supply of gas had been fully maintained during the whole period of the stoppage the same couldn't be said with regard to coke, the amount available for distribution to the company's regular customers being considerably reduced. There were several causes at work in bringing about the shortage. Firstly, less coal was carbonised week by week and consequently a smaller amount of coke was produced, plus the poorer caking capabilities of the European coal further reduced the net yield. Next, as the maintenance of the gas supply was the company's chief concern, a greater proportion of what coke was produced was being used to manufacture water gas. Finally, in view of the uncertainty of the outlook with regard to the continuance of coal supplies, a considerable stock of coke was accumulated so that it would be possible to continue producing gas even if the coal supplies should become exhausted. For some months during the summer, it was only with great difficulty that deliveries of coke were maintained to hospitals, bakers and other customers who were rendering public services.

In the autumn, the company was able to secure two cargoes of German foundry coke which, although unsuitable for ordinary use, could be used for making water gas. With these added to reserve supplies, home-produced coke was released for domestic and industrial purposes and, even after the introduction of a Government emergency permit system, the company was able to maintain its supplies. Nevertheless, the revenue obtained from the sale of coke, normally a very important line item in the annual accounts, fell-off considerably.

It was when the cold snap came in October and output took a sudden steep upward leap, that coal and coke became hard to come by on the retail market, and what was available was expensive and of poor quality. With gas available on tap, shivering householders gladly availed themselves of it; those, that is, who had taken a long view of the situation during the summer and already had gas fires installed. New customers for gas besieged the showrooms and queued up to sign orders for gas fires, cookers and geysers. In the six weeks of October into early November, the company took orders for 1,691 fires alone, and fitters had a hectic time when, in one single week, 357 gas fires were installed, establishing a record in the history of the company.

People *Bournemouth Gas & Water Company 1922*

During those busy weeks, appliance sales were up 60% on the corresponding period the previous year, whilst gas consumption shot up by nearly 30%, despite a 10% rise in price caused by the ever-increasing cost of foreign coal. Even though appliance manufacturers were able to cope with the increase in demand, the basic materials to install them became difficult to obtain. Iron foundries were shutting down their ovens because they were unable to obtain metallurgical coke, in turn closing the strip mills which turned out the wrought iron tubing used for gas and water services at the time. When the added demand caused supplies of wrought iron pipes to run out, the company switched to steel tubing instead. The greater part of new service mains was also laid using welded steel tubing, but even those supplies ran

out once the makers was unable to obtain the steel plate from which the tubes were made.

When the price of gas was allowed to rise at the end of September, it was hoped that the increase would be sufficient to meet the extra costs, and that imported coal prices would remain fairly steady thereafter. Unfortunately, the price of foreign coal continued to increase in leaps and bounds so that by November, it stood another 50% higher again. The directors decided that instead of raising the retail gas price again, they would maintain their current price over a longer period after things returned to normality, being of the opinion that consumers would find it easier to cope that way rather than to be faced with a further sudden hike in price. Their judgement turned

Gas cooker testing prior to delivery

Part of the wide range of gas appliances on display in the company's showrooms

out to be absolutely right, as they retained more customers gained during this period than gas companies in other parts of the country which had chosen the opposite course of action.

Of course, it wasn't just the directors who were responsible for that increased customer loyalty. Not for the last time, the staff of the company would work flat-out at a time of difficulty to do all they could to assist consumers who, of course, were also their neighbours and friends. When wild rumours flew about Bournemouth in early May 1926 that the company's men were coming out on strike, the positive reaction to an ensuing item in the local newspaper confirming that the men intended to stick to their jobs and carry on was palpable.

When the accounts for the year revealed that, despite a huge increase in gas supplied, the costs incurred meant that overall profits had sunk by nearly 50%, the directors decided to maintain their dividend unchanged, and hence also the co-partnership bonus, by not carrying forward any profit to the next year. They even managed to find an additional £5,000 to put into the pension fund, and to finish such a momentous year in a breakeven position without having to resort to raiding the reserves.

As the total losses to the country brought about by the General Strike and the coal stoppage were being estimated at between £250 and £300 million, this showed just how well-run Bournemouth Gas & Water Company was.

Whilst nearly ninety years on, the nine-day General Strike of 1926 is now depicted by history as a somewhat short-lived example of social rebellion, these contemporarily-recorded experiences of one company show that it was just one part of a long seven-month period during which the same story of difficulties, delays and vastly-increased expense was experienced in every walk of life. It is probably also fair to say that, by maintaining gas supplies at a time when electricity supplies were still far from universally available, utilities like Bournemouth Gas & Water Company played no small part in alleviating the discomfort of a long-continued shortage of solid fuel because, even if the coal cellars were empty, their customers could fall back on gas for heating and cooking.

Coastal Colliers

For more than thirty years, Bournemouth Gas & Water Company maintained dedicated ships, known as coastal colliers, to carry the bulk of its fuel supplies from the Yorkshire coalfields to Poole. These were loaded on Humberside, primarily at Goole harbour, and for the return trip the load was either coke or, if empty, water ballast. The round trip, including loading and unloading at both ends, took seven days.

All of the ships were leased from Stephenson Clarke, the oldest shipping line in the world and the owners of most of this type of vessel at the time, as they provided a similar service to most gas companies with access to local docks. The first company vessel, named SS Corbet Woodall, was unfortunately mined and sunk off the Sussex coast during the First World War. This was eventually replaced with the SS Pitwines and, in 1929, a second ship was added named the SS William Cash. Each vessel was about 230 feet long and could carry around 1,600 tons of coal.

During the Second World War, although maintaining their prime role as much as possible, the ships were often diverted to other requirements. All merchant ships were armed with a deck gun, and both were involved in wartime incidents. The William Cash was sunk in London's Royal Victoria dock during an air raid in September 1940, but was salvaged, repaired and returned into service. In March 1941, she encountered a German e-boat off the Norfolk coast, which was damaged by *'direct hits at short range'* from the ship's gun. The ship survived the war and continued in service until 1958.

All that remains of the SS William Cash is the ship's bell, which is on display in the company's engineering department.

In January 1940, SS Pitwines survived an attack during which she was bombed and machine-gunned by a German aircraft twenty-five miles off Flamborough Head. In November that year, she was involved in quite a famous incident off Yarmouth, when newspapers reported *'German bombers rained bombs on the British steamer Pitwines for nearly an hour. Though the ship was struck, she was taken in tow.'* A year later she was lost, not through enemy action but following a collision with the SS Gateshead near Hartlepool. She was replaced after the war by a new ship, the SS Branksome.

Mr Granville Martin Howard holding a 49lb salmon taken from the Royalty Fishery on the River Avon at Christchurch, 1952

The Royalty Fishery

The fishing in Christchurch Harbour and its feeder rivers is not only amongst the best in the country, but can also be traced back thousands of years, demonstrated by the discovery of a flint harpoon head in a back garden close to the Priory. Christchurch oysters were also a delicacy enjoyed by the Romans.

Archaeologists believe that Hengistbury Head nearby was populated as early as 9000 BC and have also found evidence of very early settlements at Wick, Stanpit Marsh, Latch Farm and St Catherine's Hill. There is the reference to a fishery at Knapp Mill predating the entry in the Domesday Book for Knapp Mill and, in the middle ages, landowners and tenants reaped considerable profits from the fisheries of the Avon and Stour, records showing that in 1299, eighty-three salmon were caught valued at £8.10s. The annual wages paid to fishermen at that time amounted to 3s.4d, whilst repairs to the weirs on the Avon and Stour represented an outlay of £1.7s.3d. By the 15th century, the annual value of the lamprey fishery alone was £1.12s.11d, the Prior paying

the Lord of the Manor £2.13s.4d for the right of fishing in the two rivers, although this did not include the salmon fishery which remained in the control of the landowner. By the end of the 16th century, what were known as *'the water, fisheries, ponds and fishponds within the site circuit and precinct of the Monastery of Christchurch, Twynam and also the waters of the Stowre and Avon'* had become the property of the Prior.

After the dissolution of the Priory in 1540, Henry VIII granted a lease of the Priory lands to his future Lord Chancellor Thomas Wryothesley, later the First Earl of Southampton and ancestor of the current Dukes of Bedford, to which five years later he added a salmon fishery. On the First Earl's death in 1550, the lands passed to a wealthy

Calais merchant Steven Kirton, then when he died three years later, to his uncle Robert White until 1565, when they lapsed to the Crown. However, the fishery, which had been awarded a Royal Grant during the reign of Mary Tudor, remained in the control of the Earls of Southampton from whom it passed by marriage through the eldest daughter of the fourth Earl, Lady Elizabeth, via the Digby family Barons of Geashill in Ireland, to the Mills family in 1750.

Records show that two hundred years ago in 1814, 1,600 fine salmon were taken in the Avon in one year alone, but by 1864, those imposing numbers had dwindled down to a few inferior catches. This was due to the placing of fixed nets at the mouth of the river, but fortunately the nets were condemned as illegal and removed, with the result that the numbers recovered, topping 1,300 in 1913. In 1880, a Mr Henry Ffenell related catching a salmon in the Avon *'weighing 53 pounds, and measuring 4ft 4in in length and 2ft 4in in girth.'*

In 1927, ownership of the Royalty rested with Miss Mary Frances Mills, eight times great granddaughter of Thomas Wryothesley, and the lady who, eight years previously, had sold Knapp Mill to the West Hampshire Water Company. In August that year, Miss Mills advised that the fishery may be put on the market, and the following year, it was resolved by the company to make an offer *'for the whole of the fishery now let to the Avon Salmon Association and the meadowland forming part of the fishery but now let to separate tenants.'* After some protracted negotiations with Miss Mills' agents, a sale was agreed at £16,000 and, to pay for the purchase along with other capital projects, a new issue of 20,000 5% preference shares was created. Those capital works included necessary piling work at the fishery house on the Avon, new steel hatches to replace the old wooden ones on the great weir and the erection of eel racks round the eel house. The

Royalty Fishery sea trout fishing

company formally entered into possession of the Royalty Fishery on 1st February 1929 and has administered it ever since.

The Royalty Fishery is one of southern England's most famous salmon and sea trout fisheries producing salmon and sea trout throughout the season in most water conditions. The season opens in February when the first of the Avon's famous spring salmon arrive, their average weight being around fifteen pounds. April sees the arrival of the first sea trout ranging between four and ten pounds, then in June, the first grilse and the start of the main sea trout run. The season closes at the end of August for salmon and October for sea trout. It is also one of England's most famous coarse fisheries and produces many specimen fish including carp, pike, perch, roach, bream, and

Salmon painting and original tackle

dace with regular catches making the angling press as headline news. The recently-set record for a barbel is sixteen and a half pounds, and other recent captures include four-pound perch, eight-pound chub, plus carp and pike up to thirty pounds.

This, then, was the jewel that the West Hampshire Water Company acquired, and over the years the company has exercised a continual duty of care and investment to maintain the fishing rights and general amenities. The majority of the Royalty Fishery is now leased to Southern Fisheries, apart from the Stour upstream to the lower limit of the Throop Fishery and a small section of the lower Avon to the confluence with the Stour, which is managed by the company in conjunction with Ringwood and District Anglers' Association, along with two thirds of Christchurch Harbour. Some years ago David Ransley, the Fisheries Manager at that time, provided an insight into the Royalty:

"The river is a living entity. The fishery staff are adept river watchers and know its moods well. In winter it is brown, heavy and bellicose, filling the banks to the brim, rooting out weed in the bed, tearing banks and tree roots away and slamming obstacles with a ponderous weight.

R

Royalty Fishery Emblem

Then is the time to be in the boathouse in the dry, giving the punt a thorough rub down and revarnish. In spring the water is lighter, it sparkles and clears and the fish may spawn safely on the patches of clear gravel. Only salmon fishermen are on the water in very restricted numbers, and that is the time to paint the fishery house, prepare the grass cutters and trim the reeds and banks. In summer the weed grows again in the bed, the water is clear and flows more slowly; the angler can see his quarry. On hot days the water is lifeless; there is no sparkle, the fish lie inert and uninterested and the fisherman becomes frustrated. The philosopher knows that there are good and bad days; fish are unpredictable and moody. The action man becomes belligerent and wants his money back, he does not possess the philosopher's peace of mind and endless belief in the one perfect day.

The bailiffs cope with all these moods with equanimity and, at the end of the day, we know that most of them will be back again another day, already waiting when we open the gates at 7.30am, festooned with rod covers and bags, bait boxes, landing nets, umbrellas, folding camp chairs and large box compendiums full of tackle. These are either slung from already sagging shoulders or towed along on wheels which bear a close resemblance to those shopping trolleys so beloved of elderly ladies that can fell a man in a supermarket queue. Permits purchased, the heavily-laden figures, many with turned down waders to hinder their progress, will break into the semblance of a canter and head once again for their favourite swims."

After World War 2 the company found that, as well as possessing a flourishing and popular fishery visited by anglers from all over the country, it was also in the middle of the steady expansion of recreational boating activity. Although the approach to Christchurch Harbour from the sea is not easy, due to the bar that creates a more restrictive depth of water than other harbours along the south coast, it nevertheless attracted a steadily-increasing number of boats. Ownership of a large proportion of Christchurch Harbour and the rivers leading into it meant that there were mooring facilities to be offered. Initially these areas were leased out to boatyards, clubs and local councils who provided rented moorings for the thriving population of private yachts, motor cruisers and catamarans.

Towards the end of the 1980s, the company felt that it should have a more direct control over the administration of a number of its moorings, and to that end as renewable leases lapsed or were surrendered, moorings were taken back under direct control, the boat owners benefitting from the cheaper rates possible without a 'middleman'. Another objective was to improve the appearance of the harbour and rivers by ensuring that moorings were well-maintained, smart and pleasing to the eye, and this was achieved through the introduction of new pontoons and trot moorings, as well as easily-identified mooring marker buoys. The boat park at Waterloo Compound was improved by adding parking bays, a number of bow-on moorings

Christchurch Priory and Royalty moorings

for smaller craft, an easier slipway access to the river and better security measures. All of this provided a more consistent service to boat owners using the Royalty facilities.

One of the longest-running leases was with the Christchurch Sailing Club. Formed in 1874 and one of the oldest non-royal clubs in the country, the club had leased some 120 moorings from the company since 1951 to accommodate its cruiser fleet. In 2007, negotiations were opened to sell those moorings, and two years later the club took freehold possession of a sizeable stretch of the river bed on the Bournemouth side of the River Stour from Wick to opposite their clubhouse, and downstream to where the river meets the open waters of Christchurch Harbour. At a reception to celebrate the handover, an inscribed plaque was presented to the club's commodore, Rick Thompson.

The Fishery House is now the home of a small museum, called the Rod Room, dedicated to the history of fishing in the Royalty, and among the exhibits is a cast of the official record salmon catch there, a massive 49-pounder caught in 1952 by a local bank manager, Granville Howard. Opened in 2008, the museum is run by its creator, local salmon specialist Tony Timms. He relates the story of the events surrounding this record catch: *"Mr Howard had survived the Somme during the First World War. He later lost a leg when he was hit by a train whilst attempting to retrieve a rugby ball from the tracks, but it never hindered his twin passions of shooting and fishing. On that day by the river he was playing this massive fish with his syndicate rod, when his artificial leg fell off in the mud. The gillie with him said 'let me get that for you Sir,' to which the reply came - 'Never mind the @*!* leg, just get the fish!'"*

GAS

THE BOURNEMOUTH GAS AND WATER COMPANY

707 TOBAC

Boscombe Showroom 1935

Showrooms

The Bournemouth Gas & Water Company headquarters building had been at 39 Poole Hill since 1884, supplemented by a showroom at 134 Old Christchurch Road, opposite Horseshoe Common, which was opened in 1911. The separation of the showroom at that time allowed Poole Hill to be largely reconstructed so that the district staff could be transferred from Bourne Valley to head office.

Following World War 1, the company developed a large volume of business in the sale of gas appliances, and the showrooms at Horseshoe Common became increasingly cramped, with neither window nor floor space allowing a full display of the actual extent of the company's resources, or of the continual improvements being made in gas appliances of every description. The increase in gas consumers in the area meant that the consequential increase in district staff created similarly cramped conditions at Poole Hill.

In 1925, the opportunity arose to purchase the building occupied by Godfrey's Music Emporium, at 136 Old Christchurch Road next-door to the showroom, following which both were demolished to enable a new combined headquarters and showroom building to be erected in their place. The adjoining premises on both sides had to be carefully shored-up whilst workmen dug down twenty feet below street level to create the foundations for the steel skeleton of the new five-storey building which, when completed eighteen months later, had a frontage of seventy-four feet. The quoted descriptions below, best read in a 'Mr Cholmondley-Warner' fashion, come primarily from an article written for the Co-Partner magazine by the showroom manager of the time.

The ground floor housed the main showroom, which extended to over 3,000 square feet. To our modern

The new headquarters building at Old Christchurch Road, opened in 1925. Photo taken from Horseshoe Common

eye, the large areas of oak block flooring, Cuban mahogany panelling covering the walls to a height of eight feet and the mahogany sheathing of the numerous pillars would feel quite claustrophobic, but at the time they were considered as giving *'a feeling of spaciousness with the rich colouring suggesting warmth and comfort,'* exactly what was needed to sell Mr and Mrs Smith a new heating system. The panelling scheme was cleverly arranged to form a series of fireplaces on two sides of the showroom, each containing an example of a modern gas fire with an appropriate surround of marble or art metal. Another, designed to form the focus of the whole scheme, made: *'a fitting shrine for our roll of honour flanking the bronze tablet on either side with panels containing the names of the company's men who also served. Here seats form an inglenook where the weary may rest awhile and pay tribute and thankful remembrance of those who fought and fell.'* The showroom was lit by

'a bewildering variety of fittings for artistic house lighting on ceiling walls and pillar. Whether it be brackets or pendants or shades or globes here they are in an endless variety of choice.'

Great ingenuity was used on the layout of this showroom, in that: *'The consumer in his coming and going from the main entrance has traversed well-nigh 150 feet of highly polished floor, and run the gauntlet of many alluring devices for lighting heating and beautifying his home. Happy the man, and thrice happy the woman, who has not cast longing eyes on some at least of these aids to the comforts and conveniences of home life, for those who can pass them by unmoved must either be cast in spartan mould or will have nothing left in life to long for!'*

The basement below had an area of 3,500 square feet and contained another large

The style of the new main showrooms reflected the traditional wood and leather of the 1920s

Another part of the main showroom at Old Christchurch Road

showroom devoted to the display of the more commercial or heavier gas apparatus. Below that again was a lower basement area of 1,100 square feet which provided space for a cycle store, as well as housing a small gas engine and vacuum cleaning plant. The central heating system was supplied from a coke-fuelled boiler and the general supply of hot water was obtained from a calorifier cylinder.

The upper floors were all used for company staff. Apart from the offices of the general manager and his assistant, the greater part of the first floor was occupied by the rental office which was *'closed in by a handsome screen of mahogany, the upper portion of which is filled with figured glass. The interior has very conveniently arranged ledger desks for 33 clerks being provided with ample space between them to allow easy passage from one part of the room to another.'* The offices of the chief clerk and the district superintendent were also on the first floor, along with a telephone exchange affording *'intercommunication between all the different rooms in the building and also with the widely scattered departments of the company from Poole Works and Pitwines to Ferndown and New Milton.'* The second floor housed the district department in an open-plan office with clear glazed partitions

Christchurch Showroom

dividing off the offices of the assistant district supervisor, the wage clerks and the complaints department. The correspondence department occupied a separate office: *'conveniently fitted with filing cabinets.'*

On the third floor: *'another large office is intended for the collectors and meter readers, and an ample range of large tables and benches has been provided so that they can carry out their duties without overcrowding when they meet at the close of the day's work after coming heavily laden from all parts of the district.'* They must have been delighted with having to lug all those pennies up three flights of stairs in order to count them! The drawing office was also on the top floor: *'Here hundreds of ordnance survey maps contain details of the exact position of the hundreds of miles of*

underground mains for gas and water with all the complicated arrangements for controlling and diverting the supply which are necessary in order to enable repairs and alterations to be made with the least possible inconvenience to consumers.' Finally, a well-fitted mess room was provided where: *'Those who fancy a hot meal in the middle of the day can exercise their culinary skill in the bungalow cooker and perfect themselves in the art of washing-up at the H&C sink.'*

Other than for a small corner of the first floor landing which was arranged as a waiting room *'where those who have appointed business with the officials may rest in comfort until they can be attended to,'* contact with the public was handled in the showroom at *'the long desk where the cashiers greet the consumer with a*

As public tastes changed, showrooms evolved to be more light and airy, like this classic Art Deco style at Boscombe in 1935

New Milton Showroom

welcoming and expectant look and speed him on his departing way with a neatly-executed receipt. The consumer who wants information or who wishes to report some defect will secure prompt attention at the counter which we find under the suspended legend 'Enquiries' and will doubtless be interested in the working of the pneumatic delivery tube which conveys details of the complaint or question to the appropriate department two or three floors above and returns an answer in less time than would be taken by a messenger running up and down stairs.'

It would be easy to misunderstand these, by today's standards somewhat-patronising, descriptions of their new buildings as being self-aggrandisement, but in fact they just communicate the pride that the staff of the company had in its, and their, continued success. The reality was that they were built simply to fulfil the expanding needs of the company and its customers. Such was the matter-of-fact nature of the undertaking, that there was no formal ceremonial opening of these impressive new buildings. Instead, notices were displayed during the last few days of Poole Hill that those premises would be closed on Saturday, 12th March 1926 on account of the removal and that the new offices would open for business at 9 o'clock on Monday morning 14th March. That the move was successfully accomplished in so short a time shows just how well the company's staff

Moordown Showroom

worked together, as *'an enormous amount of work had to be done that weekend by everybody concerned so that everything was ready for the reception of the public when the doors opened on the Monday.'*

The old Poole Hill building was sold by auction in 1927, where it was acquired by the Norwich Union Insurance Company. The insurance company's staff moved in during December that year, and their staff magazine described their new offices as: *'a large, lofty and exceedingly handsome room, the walls being panelled with dark mahogany, lined with marble above. Overall the new premises give an*

impression of dignity worthy of the status of the society.' Today, 39 Poole Hill is an arts and entertainment venue named 'The Winchester'.

This was the start of several years of extension and refurbishment of existing buildings, as well as adding new premises. Prompted by the increasing sales in appliances, a lot of this work focussed on showrooms, and the next to be changed were at Beech Hurst where the offices were refurbished and a completely new showroom added in an extension alongside. Today, the main building is home to a firm of solicitors, and the showroom extension is a branch of Café Nero. In 1933, a new showroom

Lecture Hall at Moordown Showroom

was built at Moordown, then the following year, another brand new building at Christchurch Road in Boscombe, probably the most iconic of them all. This was designed in the Art Deco style, and still catches the eye today, with the main showroom as a car and cycle accessory shop.

Beech Hurst at Poole, with new showroom alongside

These outlying showrooms were specifically intended to capture as much business as possible from residents in the new estates springing-up in those areas, which were some distance from the main showrooms in the centre of town. Competition from electricity suppliers was growing and, as electrical goods could be transported and plugged in without complex installation, their sales techniques were evolving into one-on-one demonstrations in consumers' own homes. So a feature of these new gas showrooms was the lecture hall, at the front of which was a slightly raised dais where demonstrations of equipment and techniques could be made to around a hundred customers at a time. The cookery demonstrations were extremely popular, as they still were in the main showrooms at Horseshoe Common; but instead of being a long bus-ride away, it was now possible to take them to within walking distance of the potential customer.

The crowd gathered by the famous question-mark display in 1929

A lot of work was put into the window displays, particularly at Horseshoe Common where Mr C W Cook was in charge for many years. The displays regularly won prizes and awards, both locally and nationally, and the regular changes to them created the necessary intrigue that would draw many shoppers to pass by just to see what the current theme would be. Any shopkeeper will tell you that the biggest task is getting buyers to stop and look into a window, whereas once that has been achieved something catching their eye will inevitably draw them through the front door. One of Mr Cook's most successful displays, in 1929, just featured question marks in one of the windows. When passers-by gazed deeper inside, they saw a lighted geyser delivering hot water through a curved pipe into a funnel. From the side of the funnel a short length of pipe projected horizontally, and on the other side of the window in line with this pipe was a tap from which hot water poured into a bowl. But there was no connection between them, just several feet of empty air. An article in Co-Partner takes up the story:

'Crowds collected and filled the pavement until passers-by had to step into the road to go around them. Those in the back rows asked what they were all looking at, whilst those in the front argued how it was done. Opinions varied considerably: one man maintained that

the water kept going round and round, another said it wasn't real water; but even the least observant could see the splashes leaping over the side of the bowl and falling on the floor. A more ingenious spirit said it was all done by mirrors, but at that moment a member of staff went into the window to wipe up the water that had splashed on the floor. As he walked all around the apparatus without difficulty, the mirror theory went flat. A taxi driver, who said his son was a hot water fitter, voiced the opinion the water was vaporised after leaving the geyser drawn across the vacant space and then condensed before getting to the tap; anyhow he was going to ask his son. The display led to considerable activity at the enquiries desk.'

Which, of course, was how it really worked.

People *Water Rates department taken on Horseshoe Common, 1949*

Sports day shenanigans

Up The Lights!

Bournemouth Gas & Water Company always had a thriving Sports and Social Club, with annual sports days attended by most of the staff, their families and friends, as well as the directors. There were sections for cricket, tennis, bowls, gardening and cooking, amateur dramatics, even a band. But the strongest part was the Football Club.

Founded in 1899 as a works team, Bournemouth Gasworks, nicknamed 'The Lights', joined the Hampshire League West Division in 1904, and over the next ten years they pulled together one of the best teams in the district, winning the Dorset Senior Cup four consecutive seasons and reaching the third round of the FA Amateur Cup on three occasions. They eventually attracted enough players to also field a regular reserve side in the Dorset League.

But after the outbreak of war in August 1914, and the enlistment of most of their players, no football took place for four years, and the ground at Eastlake where they rented a pitch was given up to allotments. After peace was proclaimed, the club had to start right from the beginning again, and initially they borrowed pitches wherever they could until the directors of the company managed to obtain a lease on their previous ground, meaning they had a home of their own for the first time. In that first post-war season, the club won the Dorset League, finished fifth in the Hampshire League West division, were runners-up in the Dorset Senior Cup, losing by the only goal of the final to the semi-professionals of Weymouth Town, and made it to the third round of the Amateur Cup before being beaten by Oxford City, again by the only goal. There was some consolation from that cup match, however, which attracted a ground record attendance paying total admissions of £129, a club record.

The tennis and bowls courts at Eastlake

The acquisition of a permanent ground brought the creation of a cricket club for the summer months, as well as allowing the company to stage its first sports day the following year, an event that would become a fixture in the company's calendar for the next twenty years. Over 1,200 people attended that August Saturday in 1920 to see a programme of events that included serious races like the hundred and two-hundred-yard sprints, as well as the more light-hearted egg and spoon, wheelbarrow and three-legged races. There was also an inter-departmental tug of war. A programme of music filled the intervals, provided by the newly-formed gasworks band under the conductorship of Mr Ambrose, who continued after the conclusion of the sports to provide the backing for a dance which was held on the green.

In 1923, tennis and bowls clubs were added, with their own dedicated playing areas but sharing a new clubhouse. When the sports day was held in May that year, a vegetable, fruit and flower show took place in conjunction with the sports and, after the prizes were awarded, all of the exhibits were sent to the Cornelia Hospital in Poole, an establishment regularly supported by the company's staff over many years. By 1926, the sports had grown to more than twenty different events, including separate races for ladies and children; and the fruit and vegetable show contained over forty classes. To the inter-departmental tug-of-war was added an inter-company competition that would grow to become a major feature of the day. On this first occasion, teams travelled from Portsmouth and Southampton Gas Companies, and Portsmouth emerged undefeated to be the inaugural winners of the specially-presented Shield.

The tug-of-war was a popular feature of every sports day.

Getting a drenching during the obstacle race

The Lights team that won through to the FA Amateur Cup Final in 1929/30

The Football Club had continued to progress, being promoted to the Hampshire League Division One in 1921 of which they were crowned champions two years later. In 1923, they changed their name to Bournemouth Gasworks Athletic FC, winning the Dorset Senior Cup on three further occasions. The later years of the twenties saw the club record some fine runs in the FA Amateur Cup, and their performance in that competition during the 1928/9 season gave a hint of things to come, when they won through all of the qualifying rounds to reach the competition proper. In the first round they beat one of the leading London clubs, Tufnell Park, but in the second round they had to make the long journey to another prominent club, Wycombe Wanderers.

The London News reported that: *'Bournemouth Gasworks delighted a large crowd with clever football in the first half when they scored twice, through Petty, to Wycombe Wanderers thrice. Afterwards however they found the heavy ground too severe a handicap and though their defence, especially Cobb at left back, fought valiantly to the end they were unable to prevent the home team from scoring two more goals. Wycombe's play on a deplorable pitch came as a revelation to the record crowd numbering 5,109, and it will take a strong side to beat them."* The club's own report surmised: *'our team were hardly up to their usual standard after the long journey, but we feel if we had met them at Bournemouth we would have proceeded further in the competition. We are hoping the success will enable us to get exemption from the qualifying rounds next season.'*

Although they may have been viewed as sporting bravado at the time, some of those words would prove prophetic, as the very next season, 1929/30, 'The Lights' went all the way to the final. This was no mean achievement, as the team did not get their second wish, again having to play their way through all four qualifying rounds before reaching the competition proper. However, in all four games they were drawn at home, resulting in convincing victories against Blandford, Royal Engineers, Royal Marines and Fareham.

Once through to the competition proper, the opposition again became much tougher, but the footballing Gods continued to favour them with home draws, the first of which was a rematch with their previous season's nemesis. This time they beat Wycombe by the odd goal in three, a performance made all the more impressive by that same Wycombe side winning the competition the following season for the only time in its long and distinguished history. Following that confidence-boosting win, 'The Lights' dispatched Welton Rovers and Barnet in quick succession. The quarter-final was also at home, and a two-nil win over Percy Main Amateurs from North Shields put them through to the semi-final, where they were drawn against one of the top sides in the country, Wimbledon. That match had to be played on a neutral ground, but the relatively short trip to Portsmouth's Fratton Park did not prove any disadvantage, with several thousand supporters travelling to see their works team progress to the final by two goals to nil.

The team's exploits even made it to the pages of 'The Times' which gave the match half a column. After expressing his opinion that Bournemouth were fortunate to win, their correspondent went on to explain that: *'Wimbledon's centre-forward Dowden was very well looked after by the Bournemouth defence, with the result that although Wimbledon did a lot of attacking, the tight marking and the comparative failure of Wadey at outside left, who made little of the many openings worked for him, and Christie, who although a good natural footballer had an off day, gave Joyce in the Bournemouth goal a far easier afternoon than he could have expected.*

The splendid play of Saunders and Cobb, the Bournemouth backs, was however even more responsible for Wimbledon's failure to score; their kicking and tackling was sure and as a pair they quite held their own with the more experienced opposition. Bournemouth, who played through all the qualifying rounds, have done remarkably well and even if they find their ultimate opponents in the final rather too much for them, they will at least have considerable consolation in looking back on their triumphant and convincing progress.'

Unfortunately for 'The Lights', that last sentence would also prove prophetic.

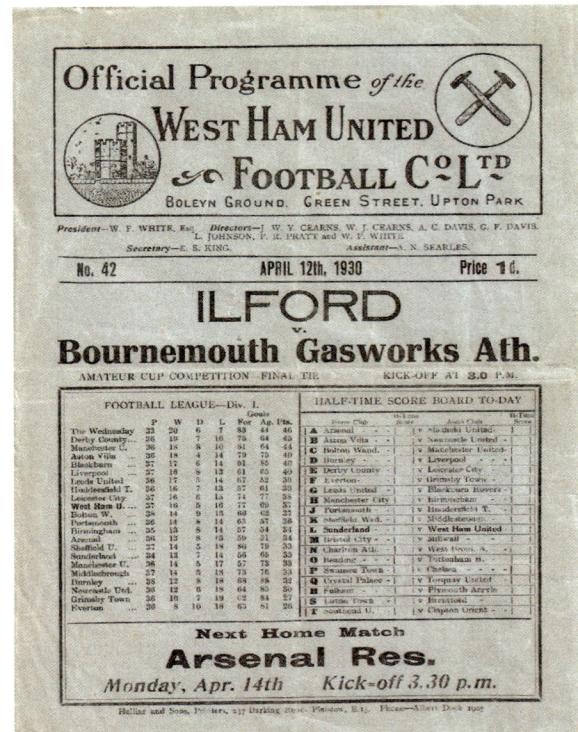

The official programme for the 1930 FA Amateur Cup Final.

The final was against Ilford, probably the top amateur side of the time, with half of their team current England amateur internationals. The match was played at West Ham's Upton Park ground in South London, and several

Another full house for a home game

trains were laid-on to take the thousands of supporters travelling from Bournemouth to cheer-on their mates, boosting the attendance to an imposing 21,800. Their manager afterwards wrote in the Co-Partner magazine: 'The special trains ran to schedule and a goodly number of supporters cheered on 'The Lights' in their encounter with Ilford. Hopes ran high during the first half of the match and our men held their own well as the score one goal each showed. In the second half the fates were distinctly unkind for though we were outplayed it was not to the extent indicated by the 5-1 scoreline.'

But there was a reward of an unexpected kind that came at the Co-Partnership meeting a couple of months later. During his speech,

Chairman William Cash announced: 'in connection with sports I should like to tell you that within the last three days we have agreed and signed to acquire a new sports ground. We did feel, especially at such a time as this, that the current facilities are not worthy of the company and the directors have decided to secure a piece of ground of about ten acres near the Alder Road. This new ground will provide a great deal more room but it will take some time to lay out and I cannot tell you when it will be available. There is a great deal of work to do but we hope you will enjoy your sports and leisure there.'

It would be two seasons before Alder Road was available, but the team's exploits in getting to the final exempted them from qualifying for

The Alder Road ground, opened in 1932

the competition proper the following season. However, their participation was short-lived, going out in the first round at Barnet, thus demoting them back to the qualifying rounds for 1931/2. Undaunted, they won through the qualifying games again to be rewarded with a long trip to the top team in the Spartan League, Chesham United, who they defeated by four goals to one. The second round brought the previous season's runners-up, Hayes Town, to Eastlake and after a very close game, 'The Lights' ran out the winners. In the third round, they were drawn away to Leyton Orient, who they outplayed for the first part of the game until their long-serving captain, Cornibeer, received a concussion in an unfortunate collision. There were no substitutes in those days, and although he bravely played on for the rest of the game, he could remember nothing of it afterwards, including the three-nil losing scoreline.

The new sports ground at Alder Road was opened in September 1932, just in time for the start of the season. This description in Co-Partner magazine provides a good idea of how much had been achieved in just two short years: *"It is difficult to realise when one looks at the broad green expanse of the new sports ground that only a couple of years ago it was a rough stretch of unkempt heath land, a bit of the primeval swamp in which the Bourne took*

its rise. There is a difference in height of 64 feet between the top corner on Alder Road to the bottom of the railway embankment which will give an idea of the amount of soil, 52,000 cu yd, which had to be dug out of the hillside and distributed over the low places in order to provide the 30,000 sq ft. of level surface. Turnstiles are provided at the entrance as well as a small car park with an exit on Sheringham Road, and the new grandstand and four-foot high banks around three sides of the football ground provide spectator areas. The stand has a steel framework and the breeze blocks from which the walls of the stand are constructed, as well as the walls around the whole ground, were made by the company from refuse ashes. There is a large canteen at the back of the building with a serving counter for making tea and coffee, above which is the committee room. In the centre of the ground is the cricket pitch with a circle practically as large as that on the County Ground at Dean Park. Beyond that again are the tennis courts and a large space for the bowling green. Every employee will be given a ticket bearing his own name allowing him use of the ground at any time and he can also apply for a further ticket for his wife and children, although this does not allow entrance for football matches."

In the next issue, the football club's reporter gave his views on the new facilities: *'Bournemouth Gasworks started a new era in their history this season with the removal of the club's headquarters from Eastlake, the scene of so many of 'The Lights' triumphs, to the luxurious new stadium in Alder Road. The playing pitch is 5 yards wider and 5 yards longer than at Eastlake and the goalposts are of the latest rounded type more prevalently used on league grounds. The idea of a practice pitch which has been made to save the turf on the ground proper is a latest Arsenal scheme so that 'The Lights' are not behind the times. So luxuriously appointed is the pavilion that* it is worthy of a first division club. Nothing has been spared and the result is a building both attractive to the eye and practical. There is seating accommodation for 602 available to the public and in addition a centre portion holding 120 which is reserved for officials. The dressing rooms are the latest word in luxury and no distinction is made between the accommodation for the visiting and home teams. They are more spacious and airy than many possessed by league clubs and the tiled bath is big enough to take the whole team. Many amateur clubs have to be content with a dressing room no bigger than the apartment provided for the referee at Alder Road, while there is one novel device which might well be adopted on other grounds - a bell which rings in both dressing rooms and gives the signal for the teams to go out.'

Although these new facilities immediately inspired the team to more FA Amateur Cup heroics in the season 1932/3, the luck of the draw didn't go with them, their only home game on their new ground coming in the quarter-final. The previous rounds found them chasing all over the country, travelling over 1,500 miles for games ranging as far away as Guiseley in Yorkshire and Stowmarket in Suffolk. Nevertheless they won through, even when the weather threatened to prevent them from playing that quarter-final after torrents of rain fell during the entire thirty-six hours preceding the match. Despite the soft turf, play was possible and a two-nil win over Erith & Belvedere took them into the semi-final, where they played Stockton on Millwall's old ground at New Cross. The match was lost on an unfortunate penalty for accidental handball early in the first half. The Gasworks team raided the Stockton goal time after time and pressed continuously, but the score at half-time remained unaltered at the end of the match.

Bournemouth Gasworks Athletic F.C. colours

In the remaining years up to the war, the club made the occasional foray to the second or third round, in addition to winning the Hampshire League a further four times. But the 1938/9 title would be the last hurrah for what was clearly an exceptional works side, because it must be remembered that this team was composed entirely of employees of the company - stokers, fitters, salesmen and inspectors who were paid nothing for their heroics on the sports field. Only two games would be played at the start of the 1939/40 season before a contest of much higher stakes broke up the squad.

People

The sports days, abandoned when war broke out, were revived during the late 1950s and continued to be a popular social occasion.

The Band

A company band had long been the desire of George Whiteley when he was Chairman, but it would not be until 1919 when *'the opportunity occurred to purchase a set of instruments at a reasonable price and the great difficulty which had hitherto stood in the way having been removed, a band was promptly formed. Under the able leadership of Mr F Ambrose it has made great strides and is now one of the best in the district. It is ever to the fore in the aid of charity and has never refused to play for a deserving cause.'*

The band made its first public appearance at the 1919 Sports Day where *'an excellent programme of music was rendered in a truly surprising manner considering the short time the band had been in existence,'* and was a fixture at every company event thereafter. They also performed Sunday concerts in Poole Park, turned out for fêtes and sporting events across the region and competed in competitions around the country. In 1924, the band made its first live broadcast from the BBC studios in Bournemouth, supplying the entire afternoon programme on 28th May.

The section was very well supported by both staff and management, both making generous donations to purchase more instruments and then uniforms, and they were obviously led by a keen enthusiast: *'Certainly Mr Ambrose spares no pains to bring on his men as there are two full practices every week, attended by the 32 bandsmen and in addition to this 12 candidates have been selected from amongst the younger men anxious to join the band and these receive instruction from Mr Ambrose twice-weekly also.'*

The band with William Cash at the BBC in 1924

They performed in all winds and weathers.

But it wasn't always plain-sailing, as this appeal from 1921 shows: *'we are badly in need of a first-class cornet player. Mr A E Longman our present solo cornet has had the misfortune to lose his teeth and we have grave doubts as to whether he will be able to tackle his instrument as in the past.'* The band also attended football matches on Saturdays where it came in for a certain amount of risk and excitement: *'On one occasion lately the ball was kicked into the grandstand by a hefty back and came in contact with a frail clarionet. We found the ball intact but only pieces of the instrument. Harmony remained undisturbed, for the football club has kindly promised to pay for the damage done.'*

Alderney No.5 reservoir

Ringwood

It seems strange in these modern times to think that, less than eighty-five years ago, a large English market town with a population of five thousand, that had existed from mediaeval times, still had no piped water supply. But that was the case in Ringwood until, with great pomp and ceremony, the wife of the Chairman of Ringwood District Council, Mrs Keeble, turned on that supply on 6th December 1930.

Although Ringwood had been part of the original area designated in the 1893 West Hampshire Water Act, it had been more than thirty years before the sixteen miles of pipeline could be laid to supply the town from Knapp Mill. Four additional slow sand filters were also constructed at Knapp Mill to handle the increased demand, and the following year an acre of land was purchased to the east of the town at Picket Hill for the construction of a reservoir, which was completed in 1932, together with a new chlorinator and ammoniator that were also installed at the works there. The following year, just three years after turning on the supply, more than a thousand houses in the town had been connected, and a hydrostat pump was added to the local installation to maintain mains pressures.

With the wide expansion of the mains network being fed by just the one source, from the Avon at Knapp Mill, there were regular increases in pumping capacity at the works there. Although the effects of the upheavals of 1926 had less effect on the West Hampshire Water Company, their exposure to the use of coal as the fuel for part of those pumping operations was not lost on the management, who decided to look at alternatively-fuelled equipment to supplement the river turbines and steam-driven pumps already in service. They subsequently placed an order with Sulzer Brothers for new

Ringwood in the 1950s. Apart from the increased traffic, this scene is little changed from 1930. The Regal Cinema on the right was previously the Town Hall.

diesel-driven pumping plant and generators, which were installed during 1928 in a new Diesel House. This installation was also regularly extended over the next seven years to cope with the continuing increase in demand.

In 1933, an extension to the mains east of Milford-on-Sea was put in hand to serve Pennington, and new mains were commenced in a north-easterly direction to make the connection to Bransgore. In 1935, a second hydrostat pump was added at Ringwood to enable work to start on an extension of the

mains to Fordingbridge. This was due to the adding of a huge area to the company's responsibilities, extending northwards from Ringwood to beyond Downton, west to Highbourne and east to Nomansland. The following year, the old steam pumping house at the works was demolished and in 1937, was replaced by a new low-lift pumphouse.

That same year, the company's engineer, David Llewellyn, reported that the company had exceeded 300 miles of mains covering its area of supply, which had expanded to

page 106

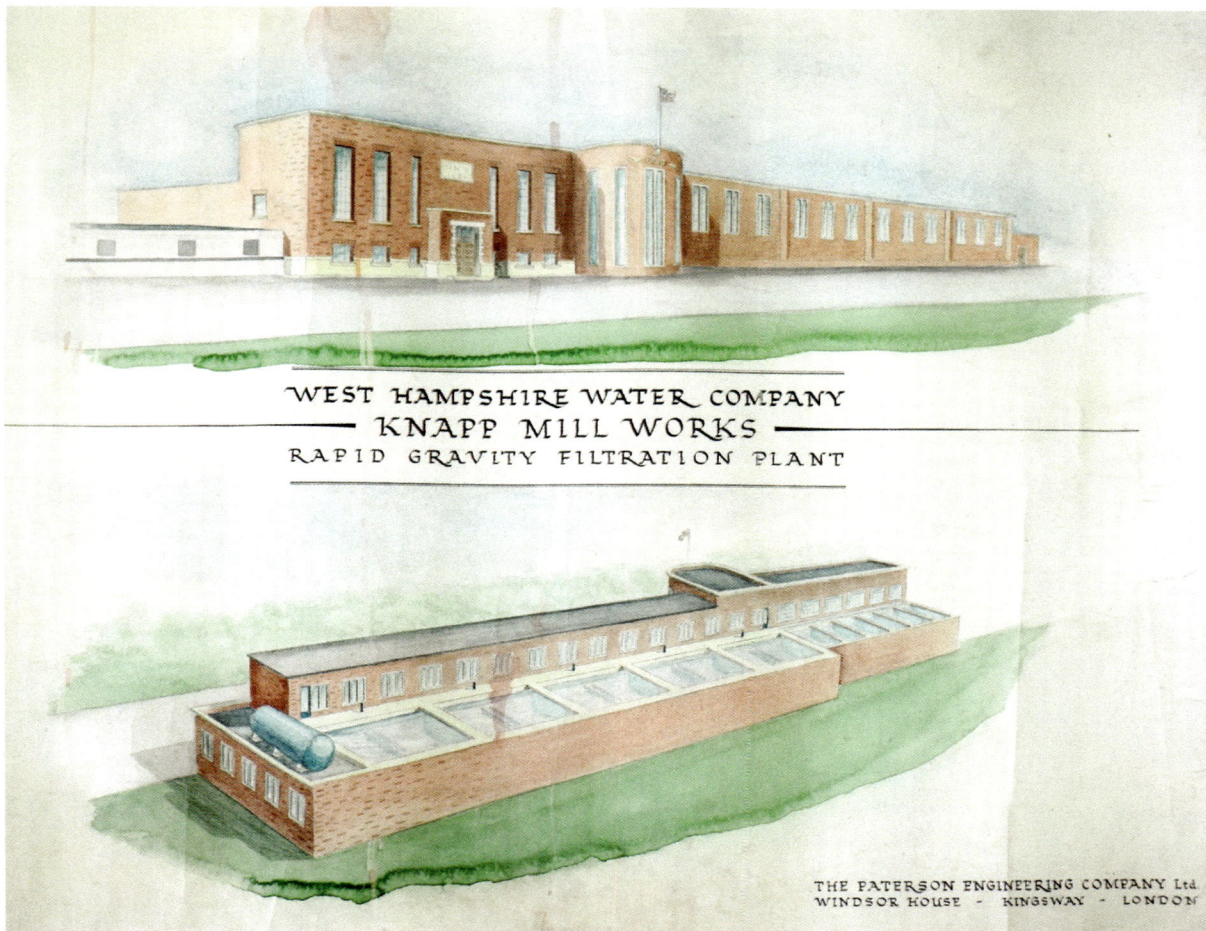

WEST HAMPSHIRE WATER COMPANY
KNAPP MILL WORKS
RAPID GRAVITY FILTRATION PLANT

THE PATERSON ENGINEERING COMPANY Ltd.
WINDSOR HOUSE · KINGSWAY · LONDON

Original watercolour illustration of Knapp Mill Works

225 square miles. However, with the rapidly growing demand for connections, maintenance of supplies to existing areas brought its own problems. A considerable difficulty had been experienced during hot weather in supplying the upper area of Sway, largely due to the heavy consumption of water in the lower parts of the district. This was because the original eight-inch main to New Milton Tower was no longer large enough and, after examining several alternatives, it was decided to lay an additional larger main to the Tower, via Bashley Cross.

To finance all of this development, John Kemp-Welch proposed, in October 1935, the issue of a further £200,000 of share capital and, following the approval of the Board, a quarter was taken-up within weeks. Kemp-Welch, a director since 1900, took over the Chair at the beginning of 1931 following the death of John King, who had been Chairman of the company for over thirty years; a few months later his son, Hubert Kemp-Welch, also joined the Board. At the annual general meeting that year, the company reported a 20% increase in the gallonage supplied to consumers in the previous year alone. A comparison to ten years earlier, in 1921, showed that although expenses had doubled, receipts had trebled in that same period, resulting in a fourfold increase in profits.

Reservoir No.5 under construction at Alderney in 1938

Although this showed that West Hampshire had become a substantial company, with a capitalisation in 1931 of over £300,000, its total pumped capacity that same year of 300 million gallons was still only a quarter the size of the water part of its neighbour in Bournemouth. At that time, water was responsible for less than a tenth of the Bournemouth company's total annual revenues, and this brings into stark focus, perhaps, why West Hampshire viewed any overtures from Bournemouth as potentially a serious threat, particularly as the latter was regularly absorbing other smaller gas and water undertakings in the area.

During the 1930s, the water side of the Bournemouth company continued to grow steadily, but the major investments made during the latter part of the 1920s ensured that the year-on-year increases in demand were handled with only small demands on the capital budget. Other than the addition of two sedimentation tanks at Longham, and three new diesel-powered Allen pumps at Alderney to improve distribution pressures, the expenditure was confined to the continued expansion of the mains pipe network until, in 1939, a fifth reservoir was added at Alderney in anticipation of another expansion in demand.

Philip Moon OBE, Chief Engineer from 1906 to 1946

In 1938, Bournemouth Gas & Water Company's chief engineer, Philip Moon, had reviewed the viability of the existing sources of water supply over the next ten years. His report highlighted a narrowing margin between maximum yield and increasing demand. The most obvious source available to bridge this gap was the River Avon, so discussions were held with West Hampshire Water Company to ascertain whether it could supply Bournemouth's requirements. Although the River Avon was capable of supporting such an increase in abstraction, estimated at up to ten million gallons a day, it would have meant a many-fold increase in pumping capacity at Knapp Mill. Although West Hampshire had the capabilities of financing such an expansion, the ultimate result would have meant a new major customer taking more than three-quarters of its annual production, and when Bournemouth suggested that, in return for this extra business, they should have a seat on the West Hampshire Board, the whole scheme was politely declined.

The Bournemouth company then indicated that its only alternative course of action would be to apply to Parliament for powers to erect a pumping station of its own on the banks of the Avon, upstream of Knapp Mill between Christchurch and Ringwood. West Hampshire Water Company decided not to object to such a scheme, providing that its interests were given reasonable protection and the company was compensated for the loss of river power resulting from the abstraction. Bournemouth then confirmed its intention of proceeding with that plan, and began preparing changes to its own legislation to obtain the powers needed, as well as negotiating with local landowners to find a suitable site for the works, and permissions to lay around five miles of supply mains piping across the open countryside to Longham.

However, these plans were already being overshadowed by the looming political crisis in Europe, and the possibility of war with Germany, which had been casting its shadow for several years before. In January 1936, a letter had been received by both companies from the Town Clerk of Bournemouth suggesting the appointment of representatives to serve on a joint civil defence committee of Poole, Bournemouth and Christchurch Corporations for the purpose of precautionary schemes for safeguarding the population and public undertakings in the event of air raids. It would not be long before that committee would have need to test its work.

The aftermath of the raid on the Metropole Hotel

For the Duration

The first visible indication that the public received of the imminent outbreak of hostilities was the imposition of the blackout in July 1939. This was to make towns invisible to enemy aircraft at night time, so across Bournemouth all windows were sealed at night with lightproof material. Street lights, the majority still gas-powered, were extinguished, car headlamps were masked and even traffic lights were switched off, except at key locations.

However, preparations had started far earlier with the formation of a local civil defence committee in 1937, which included representatives from both companies. Planned methods of communication between the companies and the authorities during air raids were devised, and these were put in place within days of the declaration of hostilities. They primarily utilised telephone systems, and were dual-purpose, because not only did the works of both companies need to obtain early warnings to protect their staff, all now classed as essential workers due to the need to maintain supplies, but also the service staff and fitters needed to be on alert to assist in damage repairs should they be needed.

First priorities were the provision of shelters, and these varied considerably. The entire ceiling of the cellar of the Bournemouth Gas & Water Company's headquarters in Old Christchurch Road was strengthened providing space for all of the staff, with sufficient spare to house any civilians in the vicinity at the time of a raid; similar precautions were taken at West Hampshire Water Company's headquarters in Stour Road. At Knapp Mill a separate shelter was constructed with capacity for the works staff, a pattern repeated at Bourne Valley and Pitwines.

The other main Bournemouth water sites at Longham and Alderney, and the West Hampshire reservoirs at St Catherine's, were considered less likely to attract direct attacks, but were camouflaged in any case.

Special equipment, including protective clothing and breathing apparatus, was provided for the use of all repair gangs, and a single-decker Bournemouth Corporation bus was requisitioned and converted into a mobile first aid and decontamination unit by the Bournemouth company, to be stationed in Poole. West Hampshire had been involved in 'war work' since June 1939, when the War Office advised there would be 10,000 men under canvas at Hatchett Pond, Beaulieu and 6,000 more at Burley. The company laid a temporary four-inch pipe on the ground from Bull Hill to the proposed camps, which in reality were never fully occupied.

The first female gas fitters at Bourne Valley in 1939

By August 1939, eleven West Hampshire Water Company employees who were Territorials had already been recalled to the Army. By the end of December, more than 200 Bournemouth Gas & Water Company employees had enlisted, a number which would rise to 570 by the end of hostilities. Some were replaced by women

One of the Home Guard units from Bourne Valley in 1940 - the real 'Dad's Army'

operatives, and at one point there were twenty-two female gas fitters operating from Bourne Valley. With the imminent collapse of France raising the spectre of invasion, in May 1940 the call went out to defend the homeland shores, and corps of Local Defence Volunteers were formed from the workers at Bourne Valley and Knapp Mill. These were later organised into units of the local Home Guard Battalion, who guarded all of the main installations of both companies throughout the rest of the war. Scaffolding appeared in the water of Bournemouth Bay, together with barricades along the seashore, all covered in barbed wire. Pillboxes sprouted on the cliff tops and the western chines were mined.

With more than half of the mains layers and fitters either serving in the armed forces overseas, or assigned to Home Guard duties, and with outside work reduced to essential maintenance only, the remaining gangs were diverted to civil defence duties, such as building blast walls around schools and hospitals. Arrangements were then ordered to interconnect the various water suppliers so that, in an emergency, water could be switched from area to area. Locally, West Hampshire Water Company, Bournemouth Gas & Water Company and the Borough of Lymington were grouped together in this way.

The first bomb was
a direct hit on this
stores building

This is where the
canteen was located,
hit by the second bomb

This is where the third
bomb, the UXB, was
located and defused

This aerial view of Bourne Valley shows just how large a target the gasholders were.

All that remained of the workshop block containing the canteen after the raid

In September 1940, water mains were laid by West Hampshire Water Company to various new airfields. The first was to Ibsley Aerodrome enabling it to become a satellite of Middle Wallop early in 1941. Originally home to 32 Squadron's Hurricanes which were later replaced by the Spitfires of 118 Squadron, it was later handed over to the Americans in the lead-up to D-Day. The next airfield to be connected was Hurn where, in view of anticipated post-war developments, a twelve-inch main was laid. Also opened in 1941, it was home to the Special Duty Flight of Halifaxes and Mosquitos moved there from Christchurch.

During the Battle of Britain, at the height of the blitz, Bournemouth was a strategic location because one of the main radio beams used by the Germans to guide bombers to their targets was transmitted from Cherbourg and passed directly over the town, the reason why local people still remember the swarms of German bombers passing overhead on the nights of big raids on the Midlands. The Air Ministry rapidly realised that if they could pinpoint the exact direction of the beam, they would be able to identify the planned target, and their specially-equipped aircraft from Boscombe Down became a familiar sight flying back and forth over Bournemouth to detect and intercept the beam.

Although considered, at the start of the war, a safe-enough area to house evacuees from the more obvious targets of Southampton and Portsmouth, by the height of the blitz all towns along the entire south coast had become secondary targets for daylight air raids when there was dense cloud cover over a prime target inland. To maintain the element of surprise, such raids were normally made by small numbers of aircraft, and as a result, the sound of sirens became increasingly familiar in the town, more often than not followed shortly after by an 'all clear'. When they sounded just after midday on 27th March 1941, most of the workers at Bourne Valley were gathered in the canteen having lunch.

At 12.20pm, a lone Dornier 215 appeared flying low down Kinson Road and within seconds deposited three bombs on the site, aiming for the large gasholder. The first bomb hit the storeroom, and the explosion shook the canteen about fifty yards away, sending its occupants diving for cover. The second was a direct hit on the canteen, where it hung by its fins from the ceiling for a few moments before it also exploded, killing thirty-three and injuring many more.

One survivor from the canteen, Tony King, who was only twenty years old at the time of the raid, was playing cards with his mates. He gave his account to the Bournemouth Echo in 2005: *"The amazing thing was that I normally never stayed for lunch because I only lived up the road, but I'd had my papers to go into the Army so I said to my mum 'Pack me some sandwiches and I'll have lunch with my pals and say goodbye to them.' The first bomb pitched about fifty yards away and shook the building. Everyone shouted 'Down!' Immediately above us was a badminton court with an eighteen-inch reinforced floor, and there was another 500lb bomb caught by its fins in the ceiling. As we started to get up, it went off five feet away from us, and the whole building came down. I don't remember much after that. I was upside down, I know that much because there was all the pressure on my head. I didn't think I was going to get out of the rubble. The man who found me found my foot first. l remember being pulled out and yelling 'fresh air,' then l saw my arm was hanging off. There were eight on my table and six were killed. I don't know how I got away with it, all of us who survived were lucky."*

The third bomb landed close to the railway viaduct, which survived because that bomb failed to detonate and was later disarmed. The damage did not interfere with the supply of gas but the loss of so many skilled men at one works was a serious handicap. But it could have been far worse as, had any of the bombs hit one of the gasholders, the devastation would have been widespread in the surrounding housing estates. At the same time, some houses were hit by further bombs in Lowther and Methuen Roads, near to the train station, while others were evacuated in Alma Road afterwards because of another unexploded bomb, all of which suggests that there was probably another aircraft involved as the Dornier could only carry four bombs of that size.

Interior shot of the rebuilt canteen at Bourne Valley

Reporting restrictions at the time meant that neither the names nor number of those killed could be mentioned, even in the company's own Co-Partner magazine. A short piece in the July 1941 issue did give some details of a memorial service held shortly after the raid: *'the Vicar of a large parish church most kindly offered to make all the necessary arrangements for such a service. When it became generally known, so many applications for admission were made that it soon became clear that the church would not hold all who wished to be present, so a neighbouring hall was provided with loudspeakers so that those who could not find seats in the church could still join in the service. Amongst the large congregation there were representatives of civic authorities,*

1914   1918

IN MEMORIAM

BUGDEN, R.	GLOUC. R.
BREWER, H.F.	HAMPS. R.
COOK, G.W.H.	R.E.
CROFT, H.C.	H.A.C.
GIFFORD, L.F.	HAMPS. R.
HOARE, R.J.	HAMPS. R.
HAWKINS, S.G.	DORSET R.
HALL, A.H.	R. SUSS. R.
HAMES, H.W.	DORSET R.
LOADER, E.C.	DORSET R.
MASTERS, H.C.	DORSET R.
MILLS, A.	HAMPS. R.
MASON, E.H.	D. CORN. L.I.
NEW, A.	DORSET R.
NICKSON, P.B.	HAMPS R.
PEAKE, J.	R. NAVY.
PULLEYBLANK, W.S.	HAMPS. R.
SMITH, A.O.	DEVON. R.
SHORT, S.E.	R. NAVY.
STOUT, G.N.	R.G.A.
TUCKER, W.J.	HAMPS. R.
TROKE, E.J.	NOTTS. & DERBY. R.
TRICKETTS, G.	DORSET R.
THORNE, W.A.L.	DORSET R.
WARE, W.	R.E.
SHIPP, C.	STAFF. YEO.
WHITTLE, W.	DORSET R.
WILSON, F.J.	DORSET R.

PRO PATRIA

ROLL OF HONOUR

KILLED AT BOURNE VALLEY
WORKS DURING AIR RAID
MARCH 27TH 1941

The memorial plaques now located at St Aldhelm's Church in Branksome. The one on the left records the employees who fell in the First World War, and was originally displayed in the Old Christchurch Road showrooms. The one on the right lists all who fell in the Second World War, including those lost in the Bourne Valley raid.

our directors and many of the chief officials accompanied by their wives. There were home guards amongst the casualties and the members of our staff who are in the home guard asked to be allowed to take part as a tribute the memory of their fallen comrades. Few of those present will forget that united Act of Memorial. Perhaps the last scene of all will remain longest in the memory, for when the final Blessing had been given the men of the home guard stepped out into the aisle turned inwards and stood at attention. So by instinct the whole great congregation followed their example facing inwards and standing in solemn silence whilst the mourners slowly made their way to the west door. That spontaneous expression of sympathy, too deep for utterance, formed a fitting conclusion to a service in memory of the fallen.'

Memorial plaques engraved with all of the names of the victims, together with those staff members who also fell in the armed forces during both world wars, were later erected in the offices at the Bourne Valley works. When some years later those offices were scheduled for demolition, the plaques were rescued by members of the British Gas Retired Employees' Association and stored until a new home was found for them in St Aldhelm's Church, Branksome, where they remain to this day.

At the time of this raid, experiments in the manufacture of hydrogen gas for the Government were being conducted at the Pitwines works, where the company converted one of its water-gas benches into a large-scale plant to supply hydrogen for the balloon barrage. The company's Chief Engineer, Philip Moon, was seconded to the Ministry to oversee the project, and so important did the results of his work prove to be that he was later awarded the Order of the British Empire. He was replaced as the company's chief engineer by John Haynes, who had a distinguished career in gas engineering almost as long as his predecessor. Another change in the senior management at Bournemouth at this time was caused by the death of the deputy Chairman Sir Charles Morgan, who was succeeded in that role by the very popular figure of Lt Col Harold Woodall.

Over at West Hampshire, Edwin Plummer had taken over the Chairmanship after the death of John Kemp-Welch shortly before the start of the war. The company continued to lay mains to supply the ever-increasing number of airfields in the area, and towards the end of 1941, it was the turn of Beaulieu Aerodrome, first used in 1910 when the New Forest Flying School was opened, and then during the First World War. The following year, the mains were extended to a new airfield built further to the west on Hatchet Moor. Holmsley Airfield soon followed, the home to successive bomber squadrons until its closure in 1946, then Bisterne on the estate owned by the Mills family, which was set up in 1943 to receive aircraft as plans for the invasion of Europe began to take shape. Christchurch, just north east of the town, which had opened in 1935 for private planes, was also expanded extensively to become a De Havilland factory airfield. Lymington was another airfield built for the invasion of Europe plus Stoney Cross, set in the New Forest, which was originally planned as a secret airfield but later developed as an advanced base for both fighters and bombers. Most of these airfields involved considerable runs of mains and often the installation of booster pumps, paid for by the War Office.

As the intensity of the attacks on these shores diminished as the end of 1942 approached, attention switched to the other fronts with

letters from Bournemouth staff serving overseas being printed in the Co-Partner magazine, although obviously heavily-censored, along with reports of decorations received. Mixed among these, however, the poignant tributes to those workers who had fallen, along with others listed as missing in action or held as PoWs became more regular. With regard to the latter, the company maintained contact wherever possible and arranged for Red Cross Parcels to be sent to them regularly whilst interned; one such recipient was Corporal Cyril Scott, the football team's left back, taken prisoner in Belgium prior to the evacuation of Dunkirk.

In 1943, the Knapp Mill works had a lucky escape when a 500lb bomb was dropped on the island between the two hatches. Fortunately it did not explode and was successfully removed by a bomb disposal unit. Two other installations belonging to Bournemouth were not so fortunate; the New Milton Gas showroom received some blast damage and then the only gasholder at the Wareham distribution site was destroyed by a direct hit. As the frequency of air raids increased, both companies constructed large emergency water tanks known as Static Water Supplies around the area to feed the fire pumps. The full-time fire brigade was supported by the volunteer Auxiliary Fire Service which had been created just before the war, and the Bournemouth area was split into seven AFS zones. In addition, each large works, including all of those run by the two companies, had its own fire crews, made up of volunteers from the workforce, and as well as the regular drills there were area competitions. Bourne Valley crews proved particularly successful in those.

But there were other occasions when they were called-out to incidents in the town, and one of those was on 23rd May 1943, when Bournemouth suffered its worst air raid of the war. Right on one o'clock on a Sunday lunchtime, 26 Focke Wulf FW190s flew in from the sea on what was known as a tip and run raid. This type of raid was primarily designed to undermine civilian morale, hence the time usually chosen for an attack being lunch or tea time when most everyone was eating or relaxing. South coast towns were the main targets due to the ease with which these Luftwaffe units, flying out of Cherbourg and Caen, could reach them almost undetected.

One of the Bourne Valley volunteer firecrews with some of the trophies won in inter-company competitions

Because they flew in at low level, the air raid siren only sounded five minutes before they were over the town. They flew down Holdenhurst Road dropping bombs and machine-gunning indiscriminately until they reached the centre of the town, where they achieved direct hits on the Metropole Hotel and Beales department store, before turning out to sea again. One aircraft was shot down by an anti-aircraft unit positioned on top of Bournemouth Central Station; it landed in Grove Road. Casualties were high although not officially disclosed, but have since been estimated at around 120 civilians killed, plus over 50 serving air force personnel who were in the Metropole Bar, a popular place for airmen billeted in the town during their training at airfields in the area. Fifteen of those were Canadian and seven Australian, and it has been speculated that they were the intended targets,

as they had only arrived in the town during the week before.

One of the bombs fell in the road in front of Beales fracturing water and gas mains, including a 24-inch boosting pressure main. The company's workmen from Bourne Valley, together with one of their firecrews, were quickly on site and, once the fires had been extinguished, set to work repairing the mains. Some black humour was unintentionally added on that occasion when the Corporation's highway workmen arrived to place red danger lamps around the crater, but as these were paraffin lamps, they reignited the escaping gas, and the firecrew had to deal with the fire all over again!

In the run-up to D-Day in 1944, thousands of troops were stationed in and around Bournemouth making their final preparations for the Normandy landings. Military vehicles were parked head to tail around Queens Park where American troops were temporarily camped, taking advantage of the cover provided by tree-lined avenues. Once they had all embarked in June, and German forces were

In the early part of the war, all district workers were provided with protective clothing and breathing apparatus.

Dealing with the aftermath of the bomb in front of Beales

steadily driven away from the French coastline, the air raids ceased and life began to return to some semblance of normality.

As the threat receded, Home Guard units were disbanded and workers returned to the task of maintenance, badly needed after five years of other priorities. Plans that had been shelved when the war began were dusted off, and some were immediately put into action, whilst preparations were made to start others when hostilities ceased. At West Hampshire Water Company David Llewellyn, now a director of the company, began to examine what use could be made after the war of the miles of mains laid to the various wartime airfields, some of which were being returned to agriculture, while others, such as Hurn, were being earmarked for industrial development.

Over at Bournemouth Philip Moon, having been released from his secondment to the Air Ministry, had also been promoted to a Board position, where he too examined the post-war picture. At Pitwines a steam purifier house was built and Christmas 1944 saw the commissioning of retort house number six. Parliamentary authority had been obtained in 1940 for the extraction of up to ten million gallons of water a day for Bournemouth from the River Avon, and having looked at a number of sites, one was selected at Matchams to feed a new cross-country pipeline to Longham. The route for this pipeline had been identified during the early part of the war, and agreements signed with several landowners to enable it to be laid as soon as circumstances allowed.

All that remained was to await the end of the war, and the return of those serving elsewhere. Twenty-seven workers from Bournemouth

Memorial Service at Alderney

Gas & Water Company did not return. They served in all three arms and included Battery Sgt Major Crouch of the Royal Artillery, who had joined the company as a boy in 1929 and died in Normandy. Flight Engineer Sgt James Jeffrey was a fitter on the Parkstone District. His Stirling bomber captain had been seriously injured in a raid over Austria, but stayed at the controls to fly the aircraft close enough to England to enable most of the crew to successfully bailout and be rescued. He then attempted to bring it back to base, but it ran out of fuel and ditched into the sea. The captain, Flt Sgt Middleton of the Australian Airforce, was subsequently posthumously awarded the Victoria Cross; James Jeffrey had elected to stay with the aircraft and help his captain, but died with him.

Leading Stoker William Brenton, a fitter on the New Milton District, was originally posted as missing, and it was eight months before the worst was finally confirmed to his family. He had volunteered for a combined operations attack on St Nazaire, and was assigned to a skeleton crew aboard HMS Campbeltown, a destroyer specially modified to ram the dock gates. The ship was accompanied by a commando landing party in smaller launches, whose job was to disable the dock powerhouse then evacuate the crew of the Campbeltown. The operation was a complete success, but only a third of the raiding party returned, the remainder being either captured or killed in the fighting; William Brenton was one of the latter. The 1952 film 'Gift Horse' was based on this raid.

RAF Ibsley Control Tower

West Hampshire Water Company purchased the disused airfield at Ibsley in 1991. The three runways had long-since been removed by quarrying activity, along with most of the perimeter tracks that had been used as a racetrack during the 1950s by the likes of Mike Hawthorn, Roy Salvadori and Ron Flockhart. What did remain, however, was a piece of World War 2 heritage - the disused control tower.

The 'Type 518/40 Watch Office with Meteorological Section' is one of around fifty of these iconic buildings constructed by the Air Ministry during the early years of the war, but the one at Ibsley is believed to be the only surviving unaltered example whose floors and balcony were formed entirely from concrete. And in case that isn't enough of a distinction, there's always the fact that it's a movie star, featuring in the Leslie Howard classic film 'First of the Few' telling the story of how R J Mitchell developed the iconic Spitfire fighter, filmed at Ibsley in 1941 with the help of the aircraft and pilots of 501 Squadron, who were stationed there at the time. It was also from this very control tower that the scramble command was given in 1943 to the Spitfires of 616 Squadron to intercept the Luftwaffe FW190s that attacked the Metropole Hotel.

In August 1992, a group of enthusiasts was granted permission by the company to stage an RAF Ibsley Exhibition at the site as part of a wider Bygone Days event being held in aid of charity. Such was the interest shown, particularly by ex-Ibsley personnel who came from all over the country to attend, that it resulted in the formation of the RAF Ibsley Historical Group. Over the intervening years, they have helped comrades who were based there to be put in touch with each other again, as well as with surviving relatives of others.

Mockbeggar Lakes and Ibsley Water from Ibsley Common, New Forest

The group conducts research into historical details connected with the airfield when it was operational, between 1941 and 1952, as well as staging an annual exhibition of photographs and memorabilia concerning the history of RAF Ibsley and the local district. These regular meetings at the site also attract veterans travelling from the USA, Canada, Australia, Poland and Czechoslovakia whose squadrons were stationed there during the war.

One of the long-term aims of the group has always been to preserve and restore the control tower, to house a permanent display of the collection of memorabilia they have assembled to mark those who served at Ibsley. That goal took a significant step forward in 2010, when Sembcorp Bournemouth Water granted a lease to the RAF Ibsley Airfield Heritage Trust, a body formed to work alongside the Historical Group and take responsibility for the restoration of the building.

BGWCo

1922

1947

POOLE

BOURNE VALLEY

Presented to

J. H. Mills

in recognition of Twenty Five
Years continuous service with
The Bournemouth Gas
and Water Company

Signed on behalf of the
Board of Directors

Chairman

Date

March 31: 1948

EUSTACE NASH

LONGHAM

Bournemouth Gas & Water Company Twenty-Five Years' Service certificate

Nationalisation

After six years of war, and the accompanying austerity, Bournemouth Gas & Water Company must have been looking forward to returning to a semblance of normality, albeit following a period of recovery. They could not have imagined that, within weeks, they would be pitched back into the uncertainty of another battle, this time with their own Government.

Within days of announcing the German surrender, a general election was called. Although Churchill was expected to win, the outcome was a political earthquake and the Labour Party swept to a landslide victory. Their manifesto pledged wholesale nationalisation of primary industries, including fuel and power which, of course, covered gas. Water, however, was considered of secondary importance, although that too should ultimately be nationalised, but in a later parliament. Over the next few years, one by one those industries key to the post-war economy fell into public ownership. Unsurprisingly, one of the first was coal mining, in 1946, followed by electricity in 1947 and then the railways in 1948.

The next cab off the rank was to be gas, and the proposals by the Minister of Power at the time, Hugh Gaitskill, were summarised in a recently-released cabinet minute from 1948: *'Gas is an old industry and its structure is Victorian. There are over a thousand undertakings with great variations in efficiency and size, which range from the London Gaslight and Coke Company, the largest in the world, to numerous small country gasworks. Development of gas grids will never be nationwide, as in electricity, and geographical reorganisation is most difficult with the present structure, but is highly desirable in the interests of the supply of cheap and abundant gas to industry as well as to domestic*

Matchams

consumers. *The unsatisfactory structure of the industry has long been recognised and in 1942 the Gas Industry were invited to submit suggestions for reorganisation. The inadequacy of those Proposals led to the Heyworth Report which recommended what was, in effect, a scheme of nationalisation under ten Regional Boards, to the ownership of which all existing undertakings were to be transferred. The industry is in fact dead ripe for nationalisation.'* That same year, the Gas Nationalisation Bill was passed into law.

In essence there was little any gas company could do, other than negotiate the settlement it received. The industry cost the Government £200 million, which it raised through bond issues, and during 1949, the 1,064 local gas undertakings were absorbed into twelve area Gas Boards, each an autonomous body with its own Chairman and Board structure; the gas part of Bournemouth Gas & Water Company, including the works at Poole, Pitwines and Bourne Valley, the outlying stations at Christchurch, Wimborne, Wareham, etc, the showrooms and office buildings, plus all of the mains piping and the staff, became part of the

Southern Gas Board. Even the Alder Road sports ground became part of the public utility, although not for too many years as it was eventually closed during the 1950s and sold-off for development; it is now covered by the houses and bungalows of Yarmouth Road.

However, unlike the majority of gas companies which were dedicated to that one purpose, absorbing Bournemouth was not completely straightforward because it was a dual utility. Identifying the actual individual assets was relatively easy, as most of the gasworks were on dedicated sites, as were the waterworks at Alderney, Longham and Wimborne. But a lot of what the company owned or had legal access agreements for, serviced both aspects, including the mains trenches, many of which contained water pipes as well as gas. The Bourne Valley site was also dual-purpose, as was the headquarters building in Old Christchurch Road. Teasing all of those apart took some time, and it wasn't until 1952 that the details, and compensation payments, were eventually finalised, and what remained of the company was renamed the Bournemouth & District Water Company.

Sir William Cash, grandson of the founder and Company Secretary from 1931 to 1964

It is hard to imagine quite how traumatic the nationalisation of gas was to the company. Probably the starkest indication of just how much the company changed can be gauged from the accounts. Those for 1948, the last year as a gas and water company, show that total sales were £1.8 million. In 1950, the first full year after nationalisation, they were just £180,000. In effect, some 90% of the company's trade, its plant and equipment and, of course, its staff had been passed into public ownership. Along with the sports ground also went the football team, the band and the company sports day.

Shortly before all of this happened, Philip Moon, the General Manager, Chief Engineer and, latterly, resident director of the company died suddenly. He had been with the company since 1906. His place on the Board was taken by another William Cash, the son of the long-serving Chairman and grandson of the founder. He had been the Company Secretary since 1931, and it was to him that the task of negotiating with the civil servants what value would be left when the final form of the water company took shape.

Then there were the staff, most of whom were in the company's co-partnership and pension schemes. Leaving that aside, it was relatively straightforward that those working exclusively within the gas operation would transfer to the new publicly-owned Gas Board, and those on the water side would stay. However, there were many staff who covered both, whether they were district workers or office staff. For them, particularly those with many years of service, deciding where they would go became an agonising choice, because this had always been a career company, and not only would they be separated from long-standing work colleagues, many of the staff worked with, or were part of, second and third generations of their own family.

Bournemouth & District Water Company Twenty-Five Years' Service medal

Beaulieu RAF Tower

Expansion

Being solely a water company, and thereby freed of the immediate distraction of being nationalised, West Hampshire Water Company was able to hit the ground running as soon as hostilities ceased on 8th May 1945. As well as the programme of maintenance that had been set in motion at the end of 1944, its first priority was to deal with the urgent need for replacement equipment.

At the top of that list were additional pumps for Knapp Mill, as well as new ammoniating and chlorinating equipment to replace the existing plant which was so badly corroded it was no longer serviceable. New mains were also needed to service major housing schemes at Ringwood, Fordingbridge, Barton-on-Sea, Ashley and Christchurch. As part of this requirement, a twelve-inch steel main was laid to Fordingbridge to link-up to the pumping station being constructed there, which came into operation in March 1948. To pay for all of this, £50,000 of additional capital was raised by a new issue of debenture stock, but the harsh winter of 1947 not only delayed work on the new

housing estates, it also resulted in expenditure on many burst mains. As labour was in short supply the company was allowed to supplement their own staff with prisoners-of-war working at 1s.6d per hour.

In November 1947, Philip Moon of the Bournemouth Gas & Water Company approached David Llewellyn regarding the possibility of amalgamating the two water undertakings. There were some fears at that time regarding potential nationalisation of the water industry, and at its annual conference the Water Companies' Association inaugurated a fighting fund against such moves. In addition, it was suggested that some rationalisation should be considered among the smaller companies as a further defence strategy. Both gentlemen attended that conference, and Philip Moon was most likely concerned about the relative strength of the water part of the Bournemouth company after gas nationalisation, and so was examining alternatives to going it alone. The suggestion was considered by the Board of West Hampshire but, once again, they advised that they were not in favour of entering into negotiations.

Hubert Kemp-Welch, Chairman of West Hampshire Water from 1948 to 1968, with his wife

There were a number of changes to senior staff in 1948. Hubert Kemp-Welch became Chairman after the death of Edwyn Plummer, and would hold that post for more than twenty years. The vacancy on the Board was filled by Major John Mills, a cousin of Mary Mills the original owner of Knapp Mill. Two new senior managers also arrived in Norman Chaplin, who was appointed Chief Accountant, and Philip Ogden who joined as Deputy Chief Engineer, and was then promoted to Chief Engineer four years later when David Llewellyn retired after forty-one years of service. This included many years as a senior officer of the Water Companies' Association and, following his retirement, David Llewellyn was awarded the OBE for his services to the water industry.

In 1949, a new West Hampshire Water Act added Beaulieu, Landford, West Wellow and Plaitford to the company's area. These were relatively small additional areas at three different extremities of the existing territory, and therefore would require separate new mains. One of the company's staff back then, Alan Cafe, recalled the times:

Philip Ogden
Chief Engineer

"Having just returned from army service I was asked if I would be interested in a few days work at New Milton Water Tower and it was start next day. At the time the West Hampshire Water Company was small but its growth was already underway. With the new houses and estates that were popping up all over the place the company laid on services and mains water supply to thousands of homes, almost all are still served by the original mains inside the gate and new mains outside, good workmanship still going strong. The company had an office in Stour Road with a coal fire and a small window for people to pay - a bit like a railway station, without the trains. After joining the staff Frank Cox asked if I could do some labouring - he was a service layer. I stayed with Frank and his driver for a long time; he taught me to drive and I took the test at Bournemouth - the instructor assured me that my driving would improve over time. My time with the company involved numerous jobs and up-skilling, like all things in those happy bygone days we just did it and carried on. There was one Christmas on a call out to a house in Holmsley where the table was laid with food and drink and we could help ourselves - in those days folk were more friendly towards tradesmen. One of the perks was the company had many coach outings

The first post-war company staff outing was well supported.

where we grabbed our wives and had a jolly good day out, and the women had a chance to natter and catch up on the gossip."

At the next annual general meeting, the Board submitted estimates of capital expenditure for the following ten years totalling £690,000 to cover the expanded area, plus other projects including the erection of a steel water tower at Redlynch to serve Downton. With the plans approved, work commenced on Beaulieu in 1950, and the following year on Landford, Plaitford and Wellow. Also in 1951, the twelve-inch trunk main was extended from Fordingbridge to Standlynch, the northernmost extremity of the company's area, to serve a new reservoir being constructed there. At the same time a new rapid-gravity filter house was constructed, the steel for both projects having to be imported from Italy because of British steelworks being hampered by yet another coal strike, which unfortunately also brought mains-laying to a halt because of shortages of pipe. This year also saw the founding of the company's Sports and Social Club.

In 1952, the vehicle fleet was replaced with twelve new cars and two vans all equipped with radio telephones, some of the first to be used in vehicles. The vans were three-wheelers, which Alan Cafe also recalled: *"at one time the West Hants had a couple of three wheel vans that had plastic windows, too much weight in the back and you had very light steering - strangely enough they vanished as mysteriously as they arrived."* The first Allen high-lift pump was installed at Knapp Mill, where a residence was also constructed for the new chief engineer. Mains-laying commenced in Downton and, the following year, a booster pump was installed there to supply Whitsbury, allowing the Redlynch Water Tower to be dismantled and moved to Beaulieu Hilltop.

A waste detection scheme was started in 1953 as a result of the difficulties in meeting demand the previous summer when record outputs were recorded on seven consecutive days. This had caused the level of St Catherine's reservoir to fall rapidly and, during one day, New Milton Tower emptied leaving parts of the area without water for several hours. The objective of the scheme was the prompt detection and repair of mains leaks, with a special squad of workmen formed for this purpose. Waste detection meters were installed and proved very successful; in the New Milton area alone thirty-one leaks to communication pipes, ten leaks on main valves and thirty-six leaks on supply pipes were discovered. By the end of 1954, water leak detection had resulted in a saving of 102 million gallons of water per year.

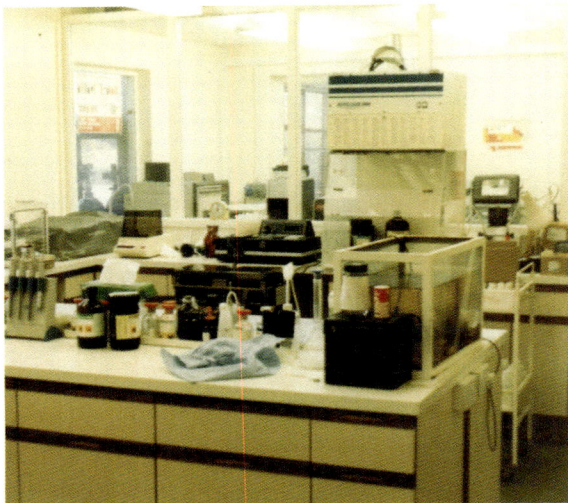

West Hampshire Water set up its own laboratory at Knapp Mill in 1954.

1954 proved another busy year, with new bulk supplies being provided to New Forest Rural District Council for the areas of Bramshaw and Minstead and also to Salisbury and Wilton Rural District Council for Alderbury, Grimstead, Pitton, Farley and Whiteparish. A water tank was erected at Whitsbury, and additional employee houses built in Knapp Mill Avenue. The company also took a considerable step forward by setting up a chemical and bacteriological laboratory under Eric Hodges as Chief Chemist and, in conjunction, investigations for new underground sources of water were also put in hand.

Perceptions of water quality had always been a thorn in the side of the company, due to its only source being water taken from the River Avon. From the start, there was no doubt that water supplied through the mains was far safer than well-water because water companies applied various forms of filtration, so the paramount responsibility rested on their shoulders to ensure that the water supplied to the customer remained 'pure and wholesome'. In the archives of the West Hampshire Water Company there is a considerable volume of correspondence on this subject in the early years of the last century between Dr Edwards, the Medical Officer of Health for Bournemouth, and David Llewellyn as Secretary of the Company.

Part of Dr Edwards' duties included regularly taking random samples of West Hampshire's water for analysis, which he often found unsatisfactory. The company's own analyst, Dr Thresh, would then take a sample, and find it clear. Because the samples were never taken simultaneously, the matter rumbled on until April 1912 when the Bournemouth Sanitary Committee declared samples to be unsatisfactory, this time citing contamination of the river source and inadequate filtering. After investigations, pollution of the river was identified and traced to a farm which was intermittently discharging untreated sewage. The company then introduced chlorination, one of the first to do so, but this measure did not meet with Dr Edwards' approval, who declared it *"a new-fangled idea neither approved by Parliament nor the local authorities."* However, after the adoption of chlorination the major conflicts subsided.

Nevertheless, there were always differences of opinion and odd failures, but over the years increasingly sophisticated methods of treatment coped better with the ever-fluctuating quality of the river water that arrived at Knapp Mill, whether caused as a natural result of drought or flood conditions or from the accidental discharge of organic material. But as the years passed, problems of chemical and metal particle contamination became more frequent and, in the 1950s, it also became necessary to monitor for radioactivity. Eric Hodges introduced a water quality regime comprising daily sampling at Knapp Mill and fortnightly sampling at the reservoirs. He also set up a continuous research programme on improved methods of filtration.

Laying the dedicated pipeline to Fawley during 1955

In 1955, work commenced on a new water resource for the northern part of the company's area. A test borehole was sunk at Hale and, once the supply was proven, additional boreholes were made and a pump house built on the site. Two more filter beds were installed at Knapp Mill, together with a new superchlorination plant, and mains were extended to the Breamore area. Major repairs were carried out on the Fishery following a breach under the great weir.

1955 also brought the most important addition to the company's customer book, one that would ultimately secure its commercial future for the next forty years. The Esso Petroleum Company had decided to build a large refinery on the Solent at Fawley which, at that time, was situated in the area covered by Southampton Corporation Water Board. However, they were unable to make a supply available by the time Esso required it, on 1st January 1956. So when, late in 1954, the oil company looked around for alternatives, the senior officers of West Hampshire Water Company were able to present them with plans that would meet all of their requirements. This was no small commitment, because it would mean implementing a separate intake and pumping station at Knapp Mill to feed a new large diameter pipeline which would need to be taken twenty-five miles across the New Forest, including through land that was not within its area of supply - and all of this had to be achieved in less than twelve months.

The original contract was for up to four million gallons per day of rough-filtered water for industrial processes, but by 1961, this requirement had risen to eight million and the following year to ten million gallons per day of treated water. The company met this requirement by the construction of additional rapid-gravity filters and a booster station on the main at Adlams Lane. That the water began to flow right on time, even though the customer was not ready to receive it, is testament to the abilities of the engineers and workers on the project. But it wasn't just the physical work that brought this about, and for his work on arranging the finance and navigating the myriad of regulatory and legal paperwork, Stanley Hill of the company's accountants, Arthur Collins & Co, was made a director of the company. He served in that capacity for nearly thirty-five years, during which time he built a deserved reputation as a water finance expert and 'guru' within the industry.

Later in 1956, a burst on a major main left large numbers of customers in Highcliffe, Beaulieu

The new pumping station at Knapp Mill to serve the Esso refinery at Fawley

and Burley without water. This incident highlighted the lack of reservoir capacity in this growing area and it was decided to proceed with the construction of a one million gallon reservoir at Sway, which began the following year. Although nationalisation of the water industry was still a threat, it was decided to issue a further 240,000 shares to finance this, plus other schemes that included a booster station at Stem Lane and a new control room at Knapp Mill.

However, during the early summer of 1957, a water crisis developed which began with the reservoirs having to be filled overnight on Thursday, 13th June. The following day, levels in the contact tanks dropped dangerously low, and during the evening some complaints were received of lack of pressure in Southbourne and Burley. On the Saturday, the rates of flow reached record levels, 20% above the designed capacity of the works, and on the Sunday,

water was pumped from Hale to Christchurch reservoir so that, by Monday morning, all reservoirs were again full. However, that morning Whitsbury Tower quickly emptied and the levels in the reservoirs at St Catherine's, Milton and Beaulieu fell quickly. Throughout the day, many houses at Burley were without water, soon joined by Barton-on-Sea and Stanpit, and by 6pm, a large area of New Milton was also without water. Later in the evening, a little water was run in, but at the expense of other areas which then dried up, causing the Stem Lane booster to be stopped. Beaulieu Tower then emptied quickly, cutting off supplies to that area. More emergency transfers meant that on the Tuesday, the company just coped until heavy thunderstorms broke over most of the area in the evening bringing the output back to the normal levels.

This experience, however, demonstrated that the original measures adopted the previous

View up the river at Knapp Mill

The new headquarters building at Knapp Mill, opened in 1961

Plaque displayed in reception at Knapp Mill

year were insufficient to cope with the rapidly-increasing levels of summer demand, and resulted in the implementation of a five-year programme to increase storage capacity. This included the extension of St Catherine's reservoir by two million gallons, the construction of a storage reservoir at Burley, improvements to the Ringwood reservoir and a second reservoir at Sway.

1958 was another year of continued expansion and investment. Agreement for extra abstraction up to 25 million gallons per day was obtained from the Avon and Dorset River Board on the condition that one turbine was removed from the turbine house and a fish pass constructed with a fish fence down river. A new intake was then able to be constructed at Knapp Mill. The Beaulieu Airfield water tower was purchased from the Air Ministry and there were further extensions of the mains from

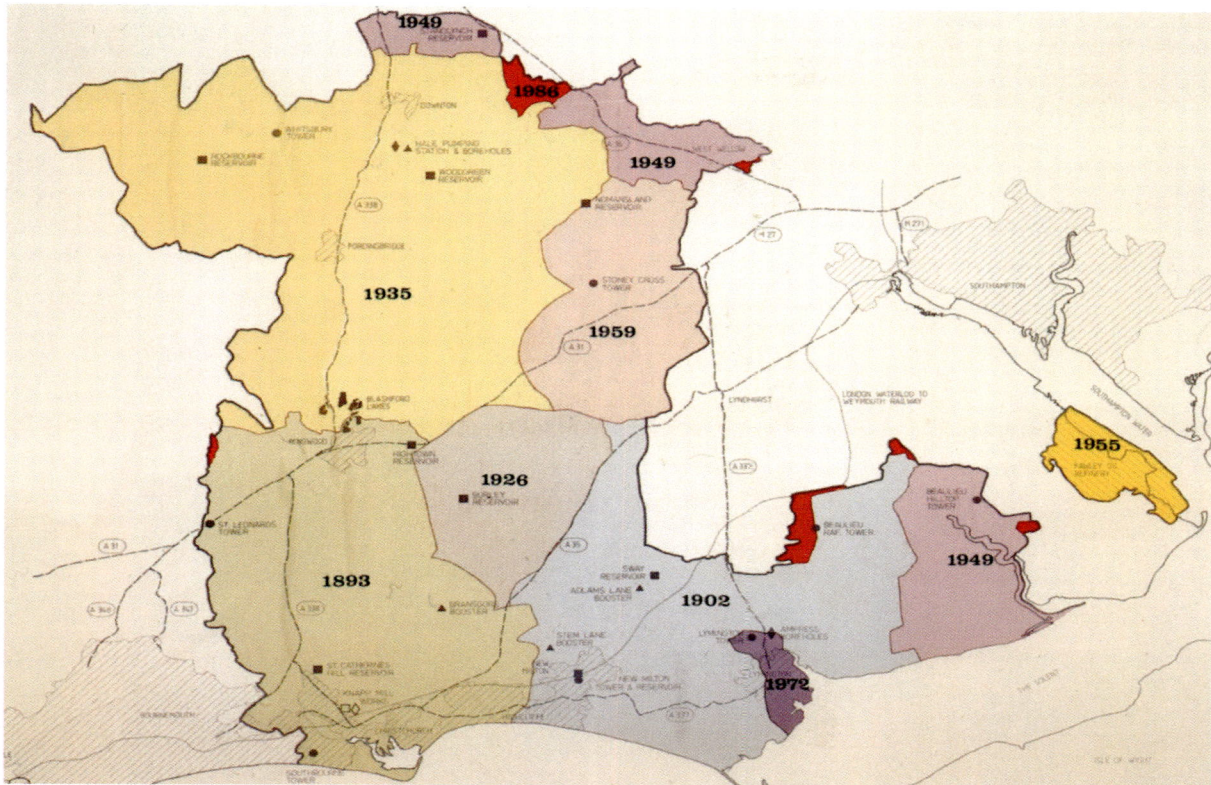

The extent to which West Hampshire's area of supply had expanded by the early 1970s.

Knapp Mill to Somerford, plus a link for Sway reservoir with the distribution network in the south. A fourth borehole was commissioned at Hale, where an aeration plant was also installed.

In 1959, Bramshaw and Minstead were transferred to the company's area of supply. The following year, Burley reservoir was completed, work on a new two million gallon reservoir at New Milton was started, and Stellar filters were installed at Sway to treat water from the Fawley main. In addition, a settling lagoon was built at Knapp Mill, a new contact tank was installed under the Rapid Filter House and an additional pump was installed in the Fawley pump house.

This concluded a decade of considerable investment and expansion for West Hampshire Water Company. In 1950, it had been supplying an average of 3.4 million gallons per day, but by 1960, this had risen to 7.2 million gallons per

day of treated water, plus the supply to Fawley amounting to another 8 million gallons per day. Storage capacity had also risen from 3.2 million to 6.6 million gallons, and some 180 miles of new mains had been laid.

In fact, both companies were now, statistically, of a similar size. Bournemouth's daily output was 8.5 million gallons, supplying 56,000 properties through 450 miles of mains in an area of 136 square miles. West Hampshire supplied a smaller number of properties, 38,000, but they were spread across a larger geographical area of 260 square miles covered by 600 miles of mains. The real contrast was in the turnover, £322,000 for Bournemouth compared to £410,000 for West Hampshire.

The giant may have been diminished by the loss of its gas business, but the neighbouring minnow had now grown into a prize fish.

Alderney in the late 1960s

Recovery

By contrast, Bournemouth & District Water Company started the 1950s in some disarray. Not only had the loss of the gas assets decimated their cashflow, but they had lost the best of their mobile equipment and a large portion of their leading staff to the Gas Board.

The remaining staff, numbering barely more than a hundred, were essentially spread to the four winds, some in the main works at Longham and Alderney, the rest in temporary accommodation on sites now controlled by the Southern Gas Board, including Bourne Valley and Old Christchurch Road. In 1989, Nina Bishop, an employee from that time, wrote to the company's magazine, Tic Tac, describing her experiences:

"I started at what was the old Bournemouth Gas & Water Company in 1946 just as the original employees were coming back from HM forces. These recently demobbed servicemen were like horses turned out to grass, getting up to all sorts of skylarks, probably relief at having reached home again but to an impressionable youngster it was

a strange introduction to office life. All waste paper was saved up to be thrown at favourite targets, one being the pilot officer prune moustache of that stalwart of the Westover Rowing Club, Henry Carr, and there were regular cries of 'I say you chaps' as his whiskers were pranged from behind.

Came the nationalisation of gas and all was changed. Having had it dinned into us all the time we worked for the old company that water didn't pay, in fact that it was a liability, those of us who went over to the water side were in some doubts as to how long this new job was going to last. We were allocated space in the old gas company attics at Old Christchurch Road and at one time were without a typist, the few letters requiring typing shared out between those who had a knowledge of that skill. Things were at a low ebb whilst those in the gas company talked of their glowing future as we had to pass through their offices to reach our attics.

Clearly something had to be done and social events were put in train. Whist drives were held in those attics, a football team was mooted and a cricket team was started, for which I embroidered the badges. Then there was the gardening club and, full of zeal, we invited the BBC's Gardeners' Question Time team along, but the club folded after a few years. Luckily it was resurrected in time for their acceptance of the invitation in 1965 under the Chairmanship of 'Jingles' Engleman with Bill Sowerbutts, etc, in the team. Anyway this programme of social events had the effect that was intended - we all felt more secure that water was going to carry on after all."

Long-standing Chairman, William Cash Senior, stood down on completion of the nationalisation and was replaced by Sir George Jessel, who had been a director for twenty years. Deputy Chairman, Lt Col Woodall, also retired and was replaced by Sir Geoffrey Shakespeare MP, who had joined the Board at the end of the war. With the loss of their Chief Engineer, John Haynes, to the Gas Board, and the sudden death of Philip Moon, the company needed a new engineer and general manager. The man they chose to steer the company through these difficult times was Norman Martin, who had been with the company since 1921, and was in charge of the Alderney works. He proved to be the perfect choice. He selected Alderney to be the site the company would be centred on, and

Norman Martin

set about pulling together all of the disparate operations from their various outposts. Although there were few buildings at Alderney, there was plenty of space, so it was relatively easy to set up temporary buildings to house equipment and stores for spare parts, most of which, apparently, suddenly appeared from Bourne Valley one day, unannounced, in a fleet of Gas Board lorries!

Although investment in the gas side had been curtailed whilst the spectre of nationalisation hung over it, this had not been the case with water. Work on the Avon extraction scheme had started before the end of the war, and the new intake and pumping works at Matchams were commissioned in 1949, together with the completion of the pumping main to Longham. With the new single supply on line, the company abandoned the sources at Longham, which had become increasingly troublesome to maintain. A similar situation existed at Wimborne, where the output had never reached the expected potential, so the search began for additional sources to improve supplies in the western part of the area.

In 1951, four additional filters were added at Alderney, followed by a new reservoir, the sixth on the site. The following year, the most symbolic indication of the company's renaissance appeared when a brand-new three-storey block of administration offices was opened at Alderney, the building that remains the company's headquarters to this day. Nina Bishop continued her recollections thus: *"Finally came the day that the offices were transferred out to Alderney which changed the lives of all of the females who loved shopping. Instead of wandering around the posh shops such as Beales and Bobbies (Debenhams to you) in our lunch hour, we had to work on Saturday morning leaving only the afternoon for the shops, and as all the good shops shut at 1pm it was a great drawback. Those of us without cars had to catch the only*

People
Senior Staff and Inspectors in 1951. Norman Martin is centre front in the darker suit.

People
Bournemouth Water Staff at Longham, 1958

Matchams, 1949

bus for Alderney via Bournemouth Square, walk from Wallisdown, or cycle all the way often in the rain with the wind against us. Then, joy of joys, one Saturday off per month was celebrated with coffee in Beales or by organising a day out in Southampton by train - going shopping again of course."

Although the threat of nationalisation of water companies had receded with the return of a Conservative government in 1951, their opposition to the idea was not as resolute as had been anticipated and, consequently, the spectre arose regularly throughout the decade. In 1955, a ministerial circular was received with little enthusiasm. Its stated aim

was to create fully unified water undertakings responsible for both supply and distribution, large enough for local resources to be developed to the best advantage, for major capital works to be financed and supervised, and an expert full-time staff, including engineers, chemists and accountants, to be employed *'which is needed for the safe and economic conduct of the undertakings'*. The Minister requested that all water companies, irrespective of size, should consider combining with their neighbours either by setting up joint Boards, amalgamating, or taking over one or more neighbouring undertakings.

Repairing a main near Boscombe Tower in the 1950s

This again prompted discussions with West Hampshire Water Company over a possible amalgamation, together with the Mid-Wessex Water Company, who made a similar suggestion on the grounds that it was desirable to form units of a size that could resist any threat of nationalisation and could economically employ the necessary specialists and maintain adequate safeguards over the purity of the water supply. Once again, these overtures came to nought. Then, in 1958, a resolution was passed at the Labour Party conference that: *This conference asks the next Labour government to set up a nationwide survey into the question of fresh water supply.*

The conference further instructs the National Executive Committee to give a promise that in view of the needs of the public in established rural areas, all our water supplies should be publicly owned as opposed to private company projects. This to become effective as soon as possible after our return to power.'

The 1959 election did not result in a Labour victory, but neither did it cause any slackening of the party's resolve to renew their nationalisation programme when the opportunity did finally present itself. Thus the decade ended with as much uncertainty as it had begun, and for similar reasons.

A view of Alderney in the 1950s, with the administration block in the background

Moling

Impact moling is a labour-saving technique that is particularly helpful when laying a pipe across ground where access is difficult, or where excessive disruption will result, such as installing a service pipe into a property without the need to dig-up an established garden or driveway. Instead of excavating a deep trench, two small pits are dug at the launch point and reception point, to a depth sufficient to avoid any surface features or foundations. A torpedo-shaped pneumatic device, known as a mole, is then aligned and used to drive through the soil between the pits, at the selected depth, using a percussive or hammer effect, with the pipe usually drawn in behind the mole. Used extensively by service crews all over the world, the device was actually invented over ninety years ago, by an employee of the Bournemouth Gas & Water Co.

Known originally as the Mangnall-Irving Thrust Boring Machine, it was featured in a 1922 issue of 'The Engineer', which observed: *"Who is not painfully familiar, be he cyclist or motorist, with the sudden ridge or depression across the road, marking the lurking gas or water pipe? Who has not noticed the humps and hollows which so quickly spoil the smooth surface of a newly laid wood pavement? By means of the thrust borer the centre of the road need never be disturbed, and the saving in reinstatement charges to the company responsible for breaking up the road is considerable. When the service has to be laid under a double tramway track with its bed of old rails and solid concrete, the saving in labour is enormous."*

It was named after its inventors, Roy Irving, Superintendent of Poole Gas Works, and Arthur Mangnall, a Yorkshire-born engineer working for The Hydraulic Engineering Co of Chester, that manufactured the machines.

Mangnall-Irving Thrust Boring Machine

Bournemouth Gas & Water Company purchased one of the first machines and Co-Partner gave examples of its usage, including when they loaned the machine to the Bournemouth Electric Light Company to lay two cables across Poole Road to the new Picture Palace at Westbourne: *"A sectional plan of the road showed that there were two large gas and water mains, electric cables and tramway tracks with deep reinforced concrete bed, the utmost clearance between the bottom of the tramway bed and the top of the mains being six inches. In spite of all the difficulties two parallel tubes were successfully laid, the job was completed in six hours and a net saving of £14 was made. Judging from present experiences, this machine will pay for itself in thirty borings."*

Today's machines are virtually unchanged from those first used all those years ago.

The ice on the sand filters was so thick, chainsaws were needed to remove it

The Big Freeze

The winter of 1962/63 was the coldest for nearly 200 years. On 22nd December 1962, the temperature plummeted by 12°F and remained below freezing point until February 1963. On Boxing Day there were heavy snowfalls, and three nights later, blizzards swept across the South West of England and Wales and, driven on by stiff easterly winds, snow drifted to over twenty feet (six metres) deep in places, blocking roads and railways, bringing down power lines and cutting off villages.

January 1963 was the coldest month of the 20th century, with an average temperature of 28°F (- 2.2°C). The country froze solid, with the lowest temperatures of -20°F (-28.9°C) recorded in Sutherland on the 11th January. Much of England and Wales was snow-covered throughout the month, and freezing fog was a constant hazard. Rivers froze over to sufficient thickness to allow skating, and at Herne Bay in Kent the sea froze for one mile out from shore. In February, more snow came accompanied by gale-force winds, and another thirty-six-hour blizzard caused further heavy drifting in most parts of the country.

Bournemouth and Christchurch did not escape this severe weather. West Hampshire Water Company's Chief Engineer, Philip Ogden, reported that: *"At the start of the month the temperature fell slowly, frost occurring each night. From 11th to 27th January the ground temperature was below 20°F every night, dropping to 10°F on 23rd January. The air temperature was only a few degrees higher during the period, the lowest reading being 11°F on 26th January. Ground ice appeared for a short time in the River Avon on 10th January after which the river surface above the Knapp Mill works froze over completely and*

Ground ice on the River Avon, January 1963

only a narrow channel remained below. The
river temperature was at freezing point but the
temperature of the water going into supply was
maintained at 33°F."

Ground ice is a rare phenomenon, and occurs in
only a small number of rivers across the world,
of which the Hampshire Avon is one. It is not
a common occurrence, the previous occasion
having been in 1954, and before that all the way
back to 1929. Effectively, the river freezes from
the bed upwards rather than from the surface
down. Ice formed at the bottom is somewhat
different in character from surface ice, and
appears more like frozen snow masses. After a
time it loosens and rises to the surface, often
bringing weeds and stones with it, forming into
floating masses coming down the stream. Such
masses, of course, are a major problem for river
intakes and pumps.

With both companies deriving a lot of their
source water from the Avon, this could
have caused severe problems. However, the
refreezing reported at Knapp Mill kept the
occurrence to a minimum, and upstream at
Matchams, following the previous experience
of the phenomenon in 1954, Bournemouth had

installed permanent steam raising and injection
plant to prevent this granular ice clogging the
intake screens. But that wasn't the only factor
affecting both companies, by any manner of
means. Underground sources were unaffected
because the water temperature was above
freezing, and pump houses were also kept at
positive temperatures. However, ice forming
on the external slow sand filters was a major
problem and additional excavators were brought
in to assist in clearing it. An employee at the
time, Dave Dufall, recalls:

Large chunks of ice had to be removed from reservoirs.

'I will not forget the first weeks I was employed
by the company in the Winter of 1962. It started
snowing on Boxing Day and continued into
1963 and then it froze. It was the third week
in January when I was stood off from the job
I was doing as the ground was too frozen to
work on; so I was sent to Alderney works. I had
to make my own way there from Wimborne on
a motorbike, the roads were barely passable.

De-icing operations went on day and night.

We had to get long crow bars to break the ice on the filters which was about a foot or so thick. We had to put the broken ice over the edge. This went on for quite a few weeks until it started to thaw in early April and then we were able to start cleaning the sand in the filter beds. The ice we took off took until the end of May to completely disappear.'

For a while, West Hampshire could not obtain supplies of coal for their steam boilers, but managed to borrow two truckloads from the local yard of British Railways as a stop gap. There were numerous mains bursts and pipes leading up to water towers at Stoney Cross and Beaulieu also froze then subsequently burst. When they were repaired, larger heating appliances were installed to prevent repetition.

As the frost continued, it struck deeper into the ground and service pipes began to freeze below ground. The number increased rapidly and both companies were at times almost overwhelmed with telephone calls. Many of the pipes, especially those laid in the earlier part of the century, were too shallow and in many cases the freeze up was on the company's side of the stopcocks. Portable generators were used to thaw underground service pipes, many of which promptly froze again. The gradual process of lowering these pipes in the ground went on for over a decade afterwards.

Throughout the whole area a full-scale emergency was in force, and control rooms were set up at both company headquarters which were manned around the clock. A priority

Working on a frozen main in St Clements Road in January 1963

scheme for emergency supplies was adopted where the first priority went to hospitals, nursing homes, houses where serious illness was present and older people living alone. The second priority went to doctors' and dentists' surgeries, and business premises where supply of mains water was essential for health, such as cafés and farms. For everyone else, standpipes were erected on fire hydrants and water tanker vehicles were hurriedly pressed into service. Mobile teams worked around the clock to help consumers in difficulty, particularly where pipes inside their houses were frozen or bursting.

At West Hampshire, Philip Ogden reported to his Board that by the end of January they were: *"having to use eight defreezing units, 93 one-hundred-gallon tanks, 153 standpipes on hydrants, 13 mobile tanks varying in capacity from 200 to 800 gallons, 300 jerry cans, seven hired lorries or vans and ten 250-gallon tanks from the civil defence store. The extra cost of*

this operation is currently £1,600 per week." These conditions lasted well into March, when he reported that: *"while we have thawed out 1,040 houses, there are hundreds of supplies still frozen."*

Over at Bournemouth, Norman Martin advised the conditions were worse than at any time within his memory: *"Almost every house has suffered from frost in some way, many thousands of houses have been completely without water and literally thousands of calls have been received by the company throughout the day and night requesting help in one emergency or another. It has been necessary to make many stopgap arrangements and to call upon the services of any members of staff at any moment when they happened to be available. Everyone has willingly done their utmost in every manner possible, whatever their normal employment might have been, to assist the public and help maintain the company's tradition of service, often working in conditions of extreme difficulty."* At the end of March, the Board minutes record that they had approved *'recommendations made by the general manager for the payment of special bonuses to those members of the staff who have not been recompensed in any way for long hours of arduous overtime work often in extreme conditions.'*

Ray Cherrett, at that time the manager of the Print Department at Alderney, recalled how the staff coped: *"The pipes should have been two-foot-six down, but a lot of them weren't, and so many were frozen that we had to buy special devices that we fixed on the stop-cocks and the electrical charge gave just enough heat to thaw the pipes. Of course, quite often the pipes had cracked, so when they thawed we had a burst to repair. All the expense, the company swallowed it all - no charge was made for any of this, cost the company thousands of pounds. We all helped out, regardless of our usual job.*

A slight problem delivering a new de-icing boiler at Matchams in 1962, just months prior to the big freeze

We would finish our normal work for the day, then join one of the crews out on the road for a few hours. Didn't see home much in those months, other than my bed!"

The Bournemouth & District Water Company accounts for 1963 show an exceptional item cost of £19,181 covering this period. To put that into perspective, it amounted to an 18% increase on the entire distribution costs for that year. The directors recorded in their annual report: *'this was a period of exceptional strain upon the company's resources both of manpower and equipment. The staff responded magnificently and were quite unsparing of themselves in their efforts to assist and serve the consumers. The task of organising emergency supplies in the town and taking supplies to outlying areas made tremendous demands both upon men and transport in cruel conditions and called for the exercise of very considerable ingenuity and improvisation. The cost of all this is no real criterion of the nature or magnitude of the task. Your directors are proud of the company's achievements in this emergency and though the cost was high, the service was maintained despite the most adverse circumstances.'*

Telegraph Cottage on Chalbury Hill, demolished in 1968

Politics

Radical change came to the industry with the passing of the Water Resources Act of 1963. This co-ordinated water resources on a regional basis for the first time in England and Wales. This was achieved by creating twenty-seven River Authorities with areas related to the main river basins, whose duty was to conserve, redistribute and augment the water resources of their area, advised by a Water Resources Board whose role was to investigate and plan the country's future requirements on a national scale.

These changes brought considerable potential benefits to the twenty-nine statutory companies, which provided about a quarter of the water supply in England and Wales and included both West Hampshire Water Company and Bournemouth & District Water Company. They had become hard-pressed to find increased sources of supply to meet demand but, under the new framework, the local River Authorities were able to grant licences for new sources to be taken from their rivers. It would, however, take nearly ten years before the legislation evolved to the point that the effects began to materialise.

The 1960s was a decade of consolidation for West Hampshire Water Company, which commenced with their moving from the cramped headquarters at Stour Road they had occupied since the early years of the company, into long-awaited new offices constructed on the Knapp Mill site. Throughout the next ten years, the plant and facilities were regularly upgraded and extended, the only major construction projects being the completion of the second St Catherine's Reservoir in 1962 and the new Rockbourne Reservoir commissioned in 1968.

Drilling trial boreholes at Stanbridge in the early 1950s

In 1963, West Hampshire's total income exceeded £500,000 for the first time, and average daily output was in excess of twelve million gallons. Following the introduction of the new legislation, their directors again considered the possibility of mergers. Alternative plans were laid before them - to remain independent; to regroup with local authority undertakings such as Salisbury and Wilton or Amesbury; that old chestnut of merging with Bournemouth; or regroup with them all. There was even a potential name for that merged undertaking - The Avon Valley Water Company. But the Ministry was not impressed with the proposed merger with the South Wiltshire authorities, although they did urge West Hampshire to open negotiations with Lymington, which in fact it had been trying to do for some time. However, once again as the threat of compulsion receded, so did the negotiations.

They were revived again, briefly, after the 1966 general election, when a larger majority for the Labour government once again raised the threat of nationalisation, this time accompanied by the potential drain on the company's assets caused by proposals for a new capital gains tax. With many of their senior staff also due for retirement in the near future, the potential for a merger with Bournemouth became somewhat attractive, and approaches were made accordingly. This time any reluctance was on the part of Bournemouth, and the discussions were short-lived. This was probably because, having survived the upheavals of gas nationalisation and come through the previous decade intact, Bournemouth & District Water Company had recovered its equilibrium and confidence.

Under the steady stewardship of Norman Martin, later joined by an equally-able deputy in Peter Campbell, the company was beginning to reap the benefits of having essentially built a new company from the discarded parts of the

Peter Campbell

Stanbridge Mill Pumping Station

old. They had even re-introduced the annual staff sports days on the recreation ground constructed at Alderney in 1953, although they were more social events than athletic, the latter being dominated by fun events for the families as well as the staff.

Norman Martin had instituted the Sports Club primarily to help revive the company football team. He was a very keen supporter, from the successful days of 'The Lights', right the way through to his retirement, and beyond. Several staff members still with the company remember how he rebuilt the teams partly through his apparent preference to employ men who had some footballing prowess. In fact, recruitment processes were generally far more relaxed than they are these days. Les Brown, who retired as Supply Manager in 1995, remembered his first encounter with Norman Martin in 1968:

"I had just left the RAF, and applied to join the company as a Radio-Electronic Technician. Mr Martin used to come up to Alderney to watch the company's football team play, and they said he will see you after the match. So I had to turn up here

at half-past four on a Saturday afternoon to meet him and have my interview. A week or so later, I was walking down the road in Wallisdown when this Austin 1100 pulled-up and the window wound down. It was Mr Martin, and he said 'Ah Mr Brown, can you start on Monday? I'll send you a letter.' Then he wound his window up and drove off!"

Although the water company teams never quite matched the exploits of 'The Lights' before the war, the two sides regularly won silverware in district leagues and county cup competitions. Their pitch was considered one of the best in the area, so good in fact that the England Amateur team used it as their training ground prior to an international match held at Dean Park in 1958. But football didn't dominate, the cricket team was also very successful and there were tennis courts plus sections for gardening, fishing and darts.

In 1963, Bournemouth & District Water Company celebrated its centenary in somewhat muted circumstances, due to the prolonged effects of the hard winter and the uncertainties caused by the new regulatory system. Among the directors who

George Jessel House 1960s

lifted their glasses to toast the event was one who represented the third generation of the family that had served in a senior capacity throughout the company's entire history - Sir William Cash. He had been knighted in 1958 for his services to the gas and water industries and charities including the Girls' Public Day School Trust, of which he was Chairman. He died the following year.

Having three generations of a family, each with a history of long service within the company, was not just confined to the upper echelons. There are many examples throughout company magazines of retirement presentations to staff with more than forty years' service who mention their father and grandfather having worked for the company before them, far too many to be unusual enough for an individual mention in this history. It is a tradition that continues to this day.

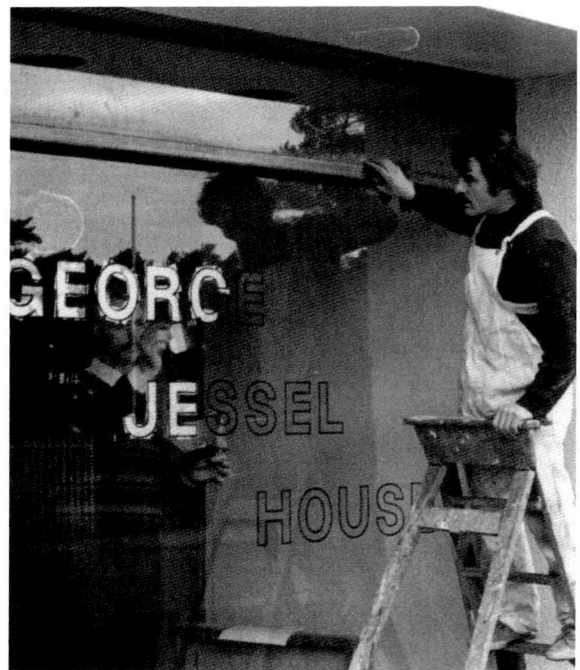

George Jessel House window decal being fitted

Canteen at George Jessel House 1960s

Norman Martin retired in 1969 after twenty years as general manager out of a total of forty-eight with the company. Not one for the limelight, his contribution to the company cannot, however, be understated, as his achievements in reconstructing it in the 1950s probably stand on a par, in corporate terms, with the engineering skills of Woods and Moon, the innovation of Woodall and Duckham and the administrative prowess of the three generations of the Cash family. The

overall stability engendered by these leading lights is illustrated by his being succeeded as chief engineer and general manager by Peter Campbell, a person with many years' service in the industry and the company already under his belt, and only the fifth man to hold that post in 106 years.

The major focus of the Bournemouth company during the 1960s was the development of a new underground source. In October 1959, the

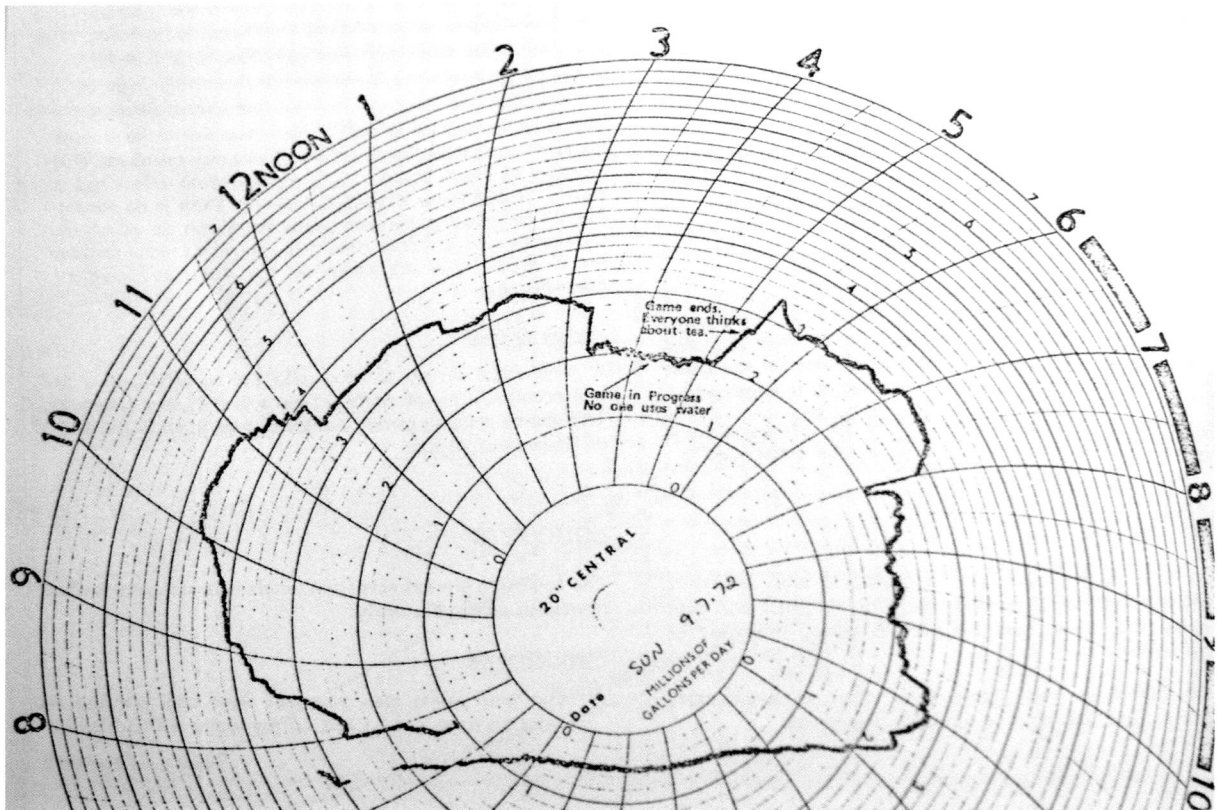

Consumption chart on the day of the Wimbledon Men's Final in 1972. Note the sharp rise in demand after 5.15pm.

company had taken over the water undertaking owned by the Wimborne and Cranborne Rural District Council, resulting not only in a considerable increase in its area of supply, but also the acquisition of a source of supply in the chalk downs eight miles north of Wimborne at Stanbridge Mill. This had been developed by the council in the early 1950s by sinking two boreholes accompanied by the construction of a small pump house. The quantity being pumped was in the region of half a million gallons each day but tests indicated that it had considerably more potential. An application to the newly-established Avon and Dorset River Authority resulted in a licence being obtained for five and a half million gallons per day, followed by the drilling of two larger additional boreholes in 1966.

The commissioning of the expanded Stanbridge Mill source in 1970 was an important milestone in the history of the Bournemouth company, as for the first time it had a substantial source of supply producing water capable of being introduced directly into the distribution system. Previously all major sources had produced raw water which had to travel to Alderney for treatment before being distributed. The savings in capital expenditure were therefore considerable, and provided a key advantage in profitability over other companies that had to source entirely from local rivers, as indeed Bournemouth had been since abandoning its previous underground source at Longham.

The water from Stanbridge entered the system via a service reservoir on Chalbury Hill, on the site where Telegraph Cottage once stood until it was demolished in 1968. The cottage was one of the points on the Murray Telegraph system which was established in 1795 to link the port of Plymouth with the Admiralty in London by means of a string of such stations sited on high ground. The type of signalling was by a shutter and frame so arranged that it incorporated into a two-roomed wooden hut in which the telegraphers lived. In a trial during 1806, a single signal was transmitted from London to Plymouth and back again in just three minutes.

Stanbridge Mill was brought on line at a time when large-scale housing projects were underway in Ferndown and planning policies were evolving to establish a community of 60,000 people around Verwood. In addition, the development of tower blocks of flats and offices in Bournemouth itself was proceeding rapidly. Continuous improvements in standards of living brought attendant increases in water consumption per head, but it wasn't just the effects on overall consumption. Monitoring equipment at Alderney began to show that peaks and troughs could be caused when a major sporting event was on TV. When bad weather meant that the Wimbledon men's singles final was postponed until Sunday in 1972, the TV viewing audience was consequently much higher. Consumption of water dropped to a very low value during the afternoon while the match, a thrilling five-setter, was in progress. But when it finally ended with the American Stan Smith hoisting the trophy skywards at 5.15pm, there was an almost instant increase in demand of one and a half million gallons of water within the space of ten minutes as kettles were filled and toilets flushed.

Public objections to the continuance of large-scale flooding of valleys to provide increased water reserves encouraged a heightened interest in conservation. Part of the licence from the River Authority required the company to make available compensation sources in the case of the local River Allen becoming compromised by their abstraction from the underground source,

and in 1971, this was established at Gussage. A second compensation source at Crichel was commissioned in 1974 to provide regulation of levels in Crichel Lake, which overflows into the River Allen.

It was clear that identifying new ecologically-viable sources of supply was to play an even greater role in the development of water companies. So the company turned back to their original underground source at Longham created in the 1880s, the old workings for which were abandoned in 1928 but were found to be still in remarkably good condition. Through the early part of the 1970s, a system of well-points was put down in the meadows alongside Longham works and test pumping was carried out to reassess the value of the gravel source there, with early tests producing an encouraging 400,000 gallons a day. In addition, in 1973, a borehole was sunk in the chalk on a site in the village of Horton following geological surveys suggesting that it might provide an underground source, similar in characteristics to Stanbridge Mill. However, from test pumping the quantity obtained did not come up to expectation.

In 1974, the original Mill House at Longham was demolished. During the process a mummified cat was found under the floorboards of the first floor, thought to have been put there when the house was built in the late 17th century, when the custom was to preserve an animal's body by immersing it in hot sand and then building it into the fabric of the dwelling to ward off evil spirits. Nobody knows what happened to this mysterious object, which was put on display for a while in the darkroom of the drawing office at Alderney, next-door to the company's first computer system installed that same year for preparing the half-yearly bills. The year after, a contract was agreed with West Hampshire Water Company to use this system for producing their billing as well, a co-operation that emerged from yet another abortive set of negotiations on

Reservoir-clearing 1960s

amalgamation, which had started in October 1973 and, this time, continued through to the following June. The trigger for these had been the impending introduction of the 1973 Water Act.

This had evolved over the years following the return of a Conservative government in 1970. A 1971 report from the Water Resources Board had advised that effective conservation and treatment of water supplies required the intervention of central government. This opinion was based upon a perception that the majority of water undertakings, being in the hands of local authorities, were reluctant to spend money, or use compulsion, to achieve the required standards. The conclusion was that the remedy lay in a much greater re-use of water and that depended on the existence of a single comprehensive water management plan for every river basin which, in turn, meant a sweeping reduction in the number of separate suppliers.

The Government promised action, and its plan was to replace the twenty-seven River Authorities, well over a hundred water undertakings and over a thousand sewerage authorities in England with ten Regional Water Authorities. In moving the second reading of the water bill in February 1973, Secretary of State for the Environment, Geoffrey Rippon, said the proposed structure avoided heavy centralisation and was radically different from that set up by the Water Resources Act of ten years earlier. He continued: *"The private statutory companies do a good job and are ready to be agents of a water authority. There is no good reason to abolish them and transfer their assets."* The bill was passed by a majority of just ten, bringing a reprieve for the twenty-nine statutory water companies, including West Hampshire and Bournemouth. But there was no space for complacency, as the Labour opposition had reserved the right to bring them into public ownership at a later date, and with the miners once again on the rampage, bringing the misery of the three-day week during the winter of 1973, that opportunity may have been not too long in coming.

Following implementation of the Act in April 1974, the Water Resources Board was abolished and replaced by a statutory National Water Council consisting of the ten Regional Water Authority Chairmen plus independent Government appointees. As well as being a consultative and advisory body, it held statutory responsibilities for national pay, training and pensions. This left each water authority responsible for the whole of the water cycle in its region including pollution control, management of river and groundwater resources, sewage treatment and disposal, water supply, drainage, recreation, navigation and fisheries.

Area number eight, named Wessex Water Authority, contained the District Council Water Boards of West Somerset, East Devon, Dorset, Wessex, North Wilts, South Wilts, and West Wilts plus the Corporation water undertakings in Bath and Swindon. It also included three statutory licensees - Bristol Water Company, Bournemouth & District Water Company and West Hampshire Water Company.

West Hampshire's area had increased slightly in 1972 following the acquisition of Lymington Council's undertaking after several years of negotiation, which brought with it the Ampress works, but essentially the areas of both companies were now fixed by the legislation.

Although both companies may have viewed an uncertain future with some trepidation, not only regulated but literally surrounded by huge nationalised authorities, this would actually prove to be to their advantage, as it caused them to focus on obligations that were, essentially, both set in stone and ringfenced.

People *Bournemouth Water Staff, at Wimborne works, 1959*

People *BFA Senior League Challenge Cup Team, 1960-61*

In-house Magazines

One of the most helpful aspects in the production of this history of the company is the existence of a large number of in-house magazines that were issued by the Bournemouth companies, produced for distribution to the staff over a period of more than ninety years.

The first of these was a quarterly magazine called Co-Partner. The first issue appeared in 1920 and publication continued uninterrupted for nearly thirty years, including right through the war years, until the nationalisation of the gas part of the company in 1949. Right from the outset it was produced to a high quality, and normally contained between thirty and forty-eight bound pages. It was edited for most of its life by the Chief Engineer, Philip Moon, ably assisted by a Mr F Cook who not only produced the cover artwork showing Bourne Valley works, but also the intricately designed initial letter for each article. Those articles covered a wide range of subjects, from company and industry news, through detailed technical descriptions of the latest equipment being installed in the works, to travelogues and, most importantly, staff news. Two aspects of the latter were extensive coverage of sporting events and features on retiring staff, often including the staff member's own recollections of his time with the company. It is from those accounts that a number of the early quotes featured in this book have been drawn.

Unsurprisingly, there was a gap after nationalisation while the water company found its feet, and the in-house magazine did not reappear until November 1971. Entitled 'Tic Tac', this was also produced quarterly, edited by Chief Engineer, Peter Campbell. The first issues were just two sides of an A4 sheet, but over the years it grew in size and content, the latter being much along similar lines to Co-Partner. The staff provided able assistance with

Arfer Mangle Worzle and chum

that content, including Maurice Richmond whose contributions included the musings of the infamously non-politically-correct (by today's standards) Arfer Mangle Worzle, whose light-hearted pieces were delivered in a broad Darzet accent. They ended when Maurice retired in 1979 with a piece entitled "Cheerio me dears" which concluded with the words *"Zo, to all of 'ee, thank 'ee ver your vriendship and kindness and may good vortune be with 'ee all. I can take a bit o' me own advice now and lean on this old gate and ponder 'bout things and I'll be a bit zurprised if I don't think back along to me workin' days and to me vriends. Thank 'ee and God bless 'ee all."* The final issue of Tic Tac was published in 1989, just prior to the acquisition of the company by Biwater. For the next couple of years, this channel of communication was covered by an existing group publication, Biwater News, but in the summer of 1991, the next generation of Bournemouth's own magazine appeared in the form of 'Water Connections'. Initially this was just four pages published quarterly. By the end of the century, it had grown in size, although periodicity had reduced to twice-annually, and since 2002 it has appeared annually containing up to sixteen pages, with a standard of production equivalent to those early days.

Raindancing on the filter beds at Alderney

Drought

For the second time, a change in the legislative framework that the water companies worked within was quickly accompanied by a challenge from mother nature herself, although this one could not have been a greater contrast to that encountered thirteen years earlier.

The summer of 1976 produced the hottest average temperatures in the UK since records began. From 23rd June to 7th July, temperatures reached 32.2°C (90°F), and on five of those days they rose above 35°C (95°F). The hottest of all was 3rd July, when the thermometer hit 35.9°C (96.6°F), one of the hottest July days on record. Temperatures remained above 26.7°C (80°F) for much longer, and many areas went forty-five days without any rain at all during July and August. As a result, the country suffered a severe drought, which was at its worst in August, when devastating heath and forest fires broke out in parts of Southern England. Fifty thousand trees were destroyed in Hurn Forest alone, and crops were badly hit, forcing food prices to increase by 12%.

The seeds of this problem, however, were sown a year earlier. The summer and autumn of 1975 were both dryer than average, and were followed by an exceptionally dry winter and spring; indeed some months during that period produced no rain at all. According to the Meteorological Office, an absolute drought is a period of fifteen consecutive days when less than one quarter of a millimetre of rain falls. In 1975, there was a spell of twenty-one days between 15th June and 7th July when no rain fell at all. Although this was well short of the all-time record, set in 1947 when there were thirty-seven consecutive rainless days in August and September, it was the start of what, at that time, was the driest sixteen-month period in over 250 years.

Toting buckets filled from water tanker

Records of Bournemouth & District Water Company show that during June 1975, the record for total daily output was broken on three occasions with the greatest amount of 17,881,260 gallons supplied on Thursday 12th. In the early part of the hot spell, weed growing on the River Stour rapidly proliferated to cover the surface so densely that moorhens were walking on the water. The August edition of the company's magazine, Tic Tac, noted that *'the weather this year has been exceptional. Seldom have we had such continuous sunshine, such sustained heat'"* There were three further occasions when a record of output was established and then broken again and the whole distribution system had been operating at high output. The record was finally set on 3rd August at 18,369,055 gallons. The following day, the first real break in the weather occurred when a thunderstorm lashed the area with heavy rain.

Despite the high rainfall that September, in October 1975, there was barely any, and it is interesting that this had been the sixth October running of extreme dryness. Because of this, groundwater levels continued to fall, and nine of the ten water authorities applied for drought orders. Record levels of consumption, combined with the exceptionally dry summer, substantially reduced the amount of storage remaining in the major reservoirs. The Bournemouth company obtained some publicity in national newspapers when it brought in an Iroquois Indian to perform a rain dance on the filter beds, but in fact this was a bit of a spoof put on for the local television station's 'South Today' programme.

One of the consequences of this early part of the drought was the proliferation of Dutch Elm disease, which resulted in a major clearance on the company's land at Longham where over 200

People *Bournemouth Water Staff, 1974*

People *Central District Staff, 1970s*

Avon barrage being deployed

Barrage in position

diseased trees had to be felled and removed. This completely transformed the look of the site, but over the years it has recovered due to planting programmes of Willow, Alder and Oak started soon after the land had been cleared.

Although dry winters are not that unusual in the Bournemouth area due to the local climate, 1975 was still an exceptional year. The rainfall for the six months between October 1975 and March 1976 was the lowest recorded since detailed records began in 1917. There were two very long periods without rain, one of fourteen days in December and another of twenty-one in January, the latter officially classed as a drought - during winter! It wasn't until 10th March 1976 that the first real rain began to fall again but even that was short-lived. April followed completely devoid of the traditional showers and set up another all-time record for lack of rain.

There were other consequences of such weather for the local water companies. The low flows in the River Avon caused water temperature fluctuations to increase markedly, and even the big freeze of 1963 did not cause river temperatures to fall as quickly as they did in 1976 when a drop of 10°F was recorded between the 23rd and 26th January. The low flows also caused vorticing, or swirling, at river intakes, a similar phenomenon to that which occurs in a bath drain, but when it happens in large pumps that draw water from a river it can cause them to fail. When this began happening at the River Avon intake at Matchams, a portable fabric barrage was fixed across the river downstream to maintain the river level and thus eliminate pump suction difficulties.

Another light-hearted article in the May 1976 edition of Tic Tac, prompted by the previous lack of success of the Red Indian Rainmaker, considered the approaches of other cultures when faced with such a dilemma: *'In Russia, it was not unusual for local women to suddenly seize a passing stranger and throw him in the River; if that didn't work they would select the local priest for equal treatment. Similar religious intolerance was also demonstrated in Sicily where the locals resorted to stripping the robes from images of saints before clamping them in irons. In China a huge dragon representing the rain was made out of paper or wood and carried in procession; if no rain followed the dragon was torn to pieces. Zulu women would bury their children up to their necks in the ground then retire to a distance and howl dismally; the theory was that, after several hours, the Gods would cry through pity, allowing the child to be dug up.'* Unfortunately, the writer didn't relate what happened if the Gods were unmoved by the howling!

Throughout the summer, there was widespread water rationing, householders in Wales and the West of England being left without tap water for much of the day whenever temperatures exceeded 80°F. Water restrictions on industry brought shortened working weeks and reservoirs reached extremely low levels, as did some rivers; ponds that ran completely dry did not recover for many years, whilst the air filled with plagues of ladybirds and aphids. Gardeners were forbidden to use hosepipes with strict penalties imposed on those who flouted the ban, and driving around in a filthy car was seen as an act of patriotism. Standpipes were erected in some areas of Yorkshire and East Anglia, where they remained for weeks. Consumers were encouraged to put bricks in their toilet cisterns or use washing-up water to pour down the toilet instead of flushing, and everyone was told to bath in less than five inches of water, or with someone else. There was also the only occasion on record when rain stopping play at Lords for a quarter of an hour caused the crowds to start cheering.

The solution, however, turned out to be typically English. The Government became so worried about the national shortage of water that it rushed through legislation at the end of August, created a Cabinet Committee and appointed Denis Howell as Minister in Charge of Drought Co-ordination. Within days he warned that unless consumption was cut by half, the entire country would face rationing until at least the end of the year. The next day it started raining and continued for weeks until Howell was dubbed 'Minister for Floods'. In Bournemouth, it was estimated that the amount of rain that fell during September, had it been conserved and stored for future use, would have kept the area going for two whole years.

As well as widespread flooding, this natural restoration increased the incidence of burst mains in parts of the distribution network, because the long period of dry weather had resulted in abnormal shrinkage of clay subsoils. When this was followed by the sudden and

People *West Hampshire Water Staff, 1975*

People

West Hampshire Water Staff, 1975

Drought sign

continuous heavy deluge, those subsoils began to move in the opposite direction and, as asbestos cement mains did not like movement of any kind, fractures were commonplace. Similarly, the old spun-iron mains had suffered for many years due to the aggressive acidity of the soils attacking the metal, weakening it by causing severe pitting, and the ground movement soon overcame the inherent weaknesses. As the old saying goes - it never rains but it pours.

The district gangs were kept busy for some time dealing with these bursts, but it wasn't the only task they found themselves being called-upon to perform. Norman Bowring was working with another service layer, Peter Clark, outside of the police station in Madeira Road, when a car pulled-up and two plain-clothes policemen got out. He recalls: *"As these two chaps walked over, I said to Peter 'they're on to you mate'*

joking around like you do, then they said to us 'would you mind taking part in a line-up?' Well we didn't look anything like each other, but we went round the back for this line-up, I think we got ten-bob each for doing it. Thankfully neither of us got picked-out, so we went back and finished the job."

Of course the problems experienced by the public during that long hot summer of 1976 were not entirely due to nature, but also to man's inability to plan for such rare occurrences. It is interesting to note that, in the government enquiries and reports that followed these experiences, only two water companies in the whole of the south of the country were able to continue to supply their consumers with no restrictions of any kind. They were the Bournemouth & District Water Company and West Hampshire Water Company.

Construction of Reservoir 7

Privatisation

Within two years of the creation of the Water Authorities, the Labour government issued a green paper, once again reviewing the water industry and specifically proposing the integration of the statutory companies. This was the most direct threat to their existence yet seen.

A public campaign was launched against the proposals, spearheaded by Bournemouth & District Water Company, who published a booklet entitled "Where's the Sense?" featuring a cartoon character called Walter, who also appeared in the local press, and on all of the company's vehicles. The booklet was widely circulated to customers, bringing an unexpected response when, as well as offering help and organising petitions, many paid their next bills by return as a gesture of support. The booklet was adapted by other companies to back their own case, and appeared regularly on desks and tables in the Houses of Parliament. The concerted opposition the Government received in Parliament eventually resulted in the proposals being dropped altogether.

After this, the water industry was left alone by successive governments and, during the next ten years up to the middle of the eighties, both West Hampshire and Bournemouth were able to concentrate more on consolidation and modernisation of their assets, financially assisted by new nationwide charging structures that improved their profitability to enable the necessary investments to be made.

There were three major infrastructure projects at Bournemouth & District Water Company during this period, the first being to extend its ownership of land at Longham to 175 acres. Although the company's presence at Longham dated from 1883, the land was initially leased from Viscount Wimborne and it wasn't until 1909 that the first purchase was made, consisting of five acres, together with the original mill and dwelling house with its yard stable and orchard. A further five acres south of the river on which the filter house now stands was purchased in 1925, followed in 1926 by the addition of the meadow and the land occupied by the balancing tanks, taking the site to twenty-two acres.

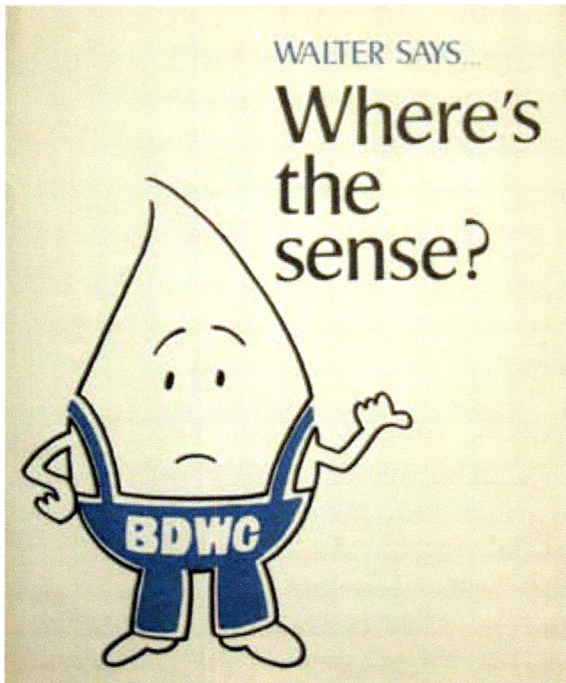

Walter on the cover of the campaign booklet

That was how it stayed until 1978, when five acres south of the river, called the 'skull land', was purchased in connection with investigations into reviving the underground sources at the site. The land acquired the epithet when what is now known as 'The Bournemouth Skull', that of a neolithic male of between twenty-five and thirty years of age, was discovered there in 1932. As there were no burials on the site, the peat strata within which it was found indicated that it had been washed down the river between four and five thousand years earlier, after which it became gradually buried by alluvial deposits. The artefact is on display in the Bournemouth Natural Science Museum.

Within a year of that purchase, and completely out of the blue, the Canford Estate decided to dispose of some portions of land, one of which lay on the northern border of the company's site. This was in an area that had been considered to have good potential for extending the underground source, so 148 acres were purchased in 1981. These contained the main portion of the gravel deposits that held the water to be sourced, subsequent test boring and pumping proving this to be an extremely viable proposition.

The next investment involved the building of a new workshop and stores complex on land at the end of the Alderney site closest to the Ringwood Road. Known as The Quadrant, it comprised two modern industrial units and large external storage compounds, and brought these aspects of the company together in one location, releasing space in the main administration building to relocate and expand the computer and customer support sections. The original IBM computer was replaced by Honeywell equipment, which also involved the conversion and transfer of over a thousand programmes and data files. Many months of concentrated effort by the computer section staff was brought to a successful conclusion in one weekend, this big-bang approach being necessary due to the integrated nature of the company systems, even at that early stage in their development.

The third was the addition of a new seven million gallon service reservoir at Alderney, the seventh and largest on the site and the first to be constructed there for over thirty years. The design of the reservoirs already on the site were a two-storey arrangement with the storage tank underneath the filters on the roof above. The new reservoir was of a more radical

The Quadrant, Alderney

design, primarily because a greater quantity of water was being derived from underground sources, such as Stanbridge Mill, and the expanded Longham site. As this water needed no filtration, a layer of filter beds on the roof was unnecessary; the need was for storage capacity, a fact that had been demonstrated the year before when exceptional demand depleted existing storage to dangerous levels.

The design of number seven reservoir took the form of a circular tank projecting about nine metres out of the ground. The construction followed an American technique utilising precast concrete panels bound together with prestressed wire, which had been discovered by the company's engineers during a fact-finding tour of the USA in early 1980. In the tradition of innovation followed by the company since its inception, this was an entirely unique structure in the UK at that time. The first turf was cut on spare land at the rear of the recreation ground in April 1980, and the new reservoir was inaugurated in a special ceremony on 1st October 1981, in conjunction with a company open day.

These open days had evolved from a special event organised by Peter Campbell for the Queen's Silver Jubilee in 1977, and essentially combined the traditional annual directors' official visit with the sports day, the latter beginning to unfortunately wane in support by that time.

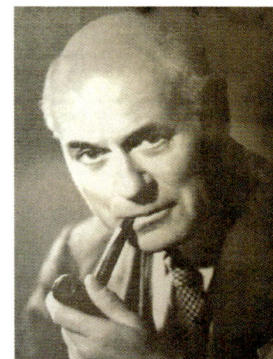

Sir George Jessel

They proved very popular events, particularly with families and pensioners, and the following year was marked by a number of ceremonies, which included the renaming of the administration building to 'George Jessel House' in honour of Sir George Jessel, who had served as a director for forty-eight years, twenty-eight as Chairman, until shortly before his death the previous year. A plaque was unveiled in the entrance foyer by the new Chairman, Brian Turner, marking the event alongside another recording the involvement of the three generations of the Cash family in the development of the company.

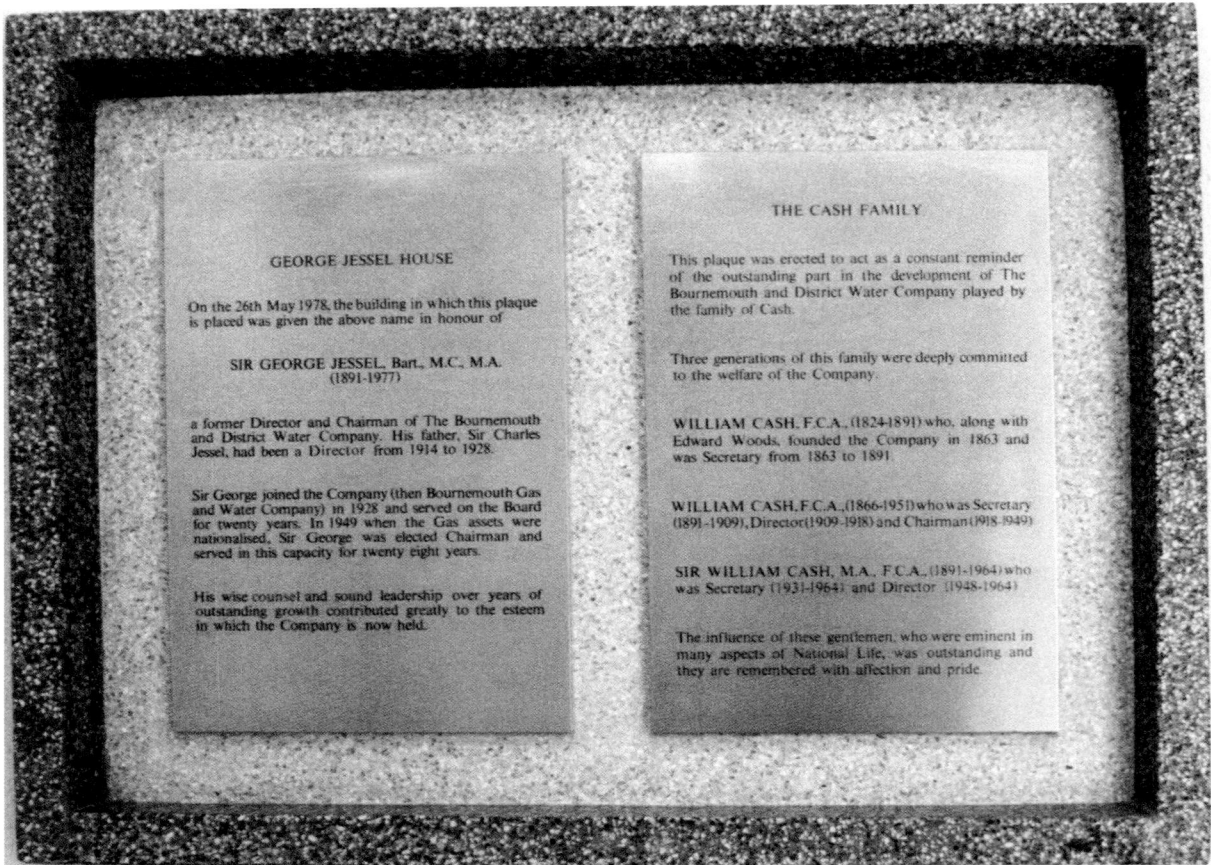

The plaque unveiled at the building renaming ceremony in 1978

The company's 120th anniversary was celebrated at another open day in 1983. The programme extended over two days, and included displays by majorettes, highland dancers and the band of the Gurkha Rifles. Another ceremony involved the unveiling of a memorial window to the Rt. Hon. Sir Geoffrey Shakespeare Bt, who served as a director of the company for more than thirty years until his death in 1980.

Over at West Hampshire Water Company, there were also major changes in both the Board of directors and senior positions, following the retirements of Hubert Kemp-Welch, Norman Chaplin and Philip Ogden. Sir George Meyrick, a director since 1956, took over the Chair and the chief engineer and secretary posts were dropped in favour of a flatter management structure

Lady Shakespeare unveils the memorial window in honour of her husband

under a number of specialist departmental heads. A fountain was unveiled in the entrance hall of the company's headquarters to commemorate Hubert Kemp-Welch's forty-one years as a director. Major investment during this period included the construction of

Jubilee celebrations, Alderney

second reservoirs at Ringwood and Sway, followed by new reservoirs and towers at New Milton, Fordingbridge, St Leonards and Woodgreen.

A more scientific approach to water treatment was adopted as water standards became more rigorous. The company's new Chief Chemist, Robin Walls, worked to World Health Organisation and EC standards to introduce sophisticated analytical techniques, including colorimetry, UV-VIS spectrophotometry, atomic absorption spectroscopy and gas liquid chromatography, all necessary for the detection of low level metals and organics as they became specified for removal. An analytical quality control system and database were introduced for the laboratory staff to handle the vast amount of data produced, from which they provided the Board and management with regular reports.

In 1983, politics again raised the spectre of upheaval in the industry, this time by the first ever strike by workers in the water industry. The dispute was primarily over pay which, since the 1973 Water Act, had been negotiated centrally with the unions by the National Water Council, the rates agreed being also applied to the statutory water companies. When protracted negotiations finally broke down in early January 1983, the industry's unions

Mains-laying, 1970s

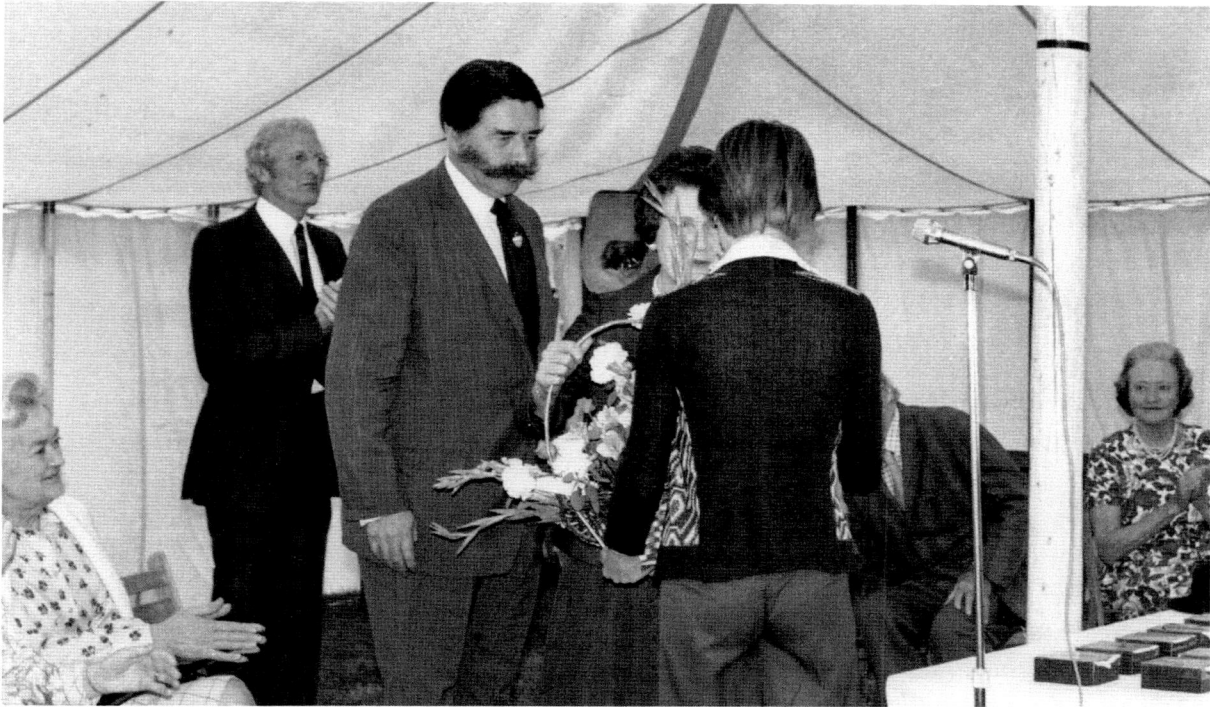

Jubilee celebration presentations

called a national strike of all manual workers from 23rd January, which was immediately supported by white-collar unions as well.

At West Hampshire, workers were not directly part of the dispute but were instructed not to cross picket lines and accordingly withdrew their labour. However, what could have been a disastrous situation was averted by common sense and good labour relations, as the strike committee agreed that the control room should be manned and a duty inspector and mains gang should be on call to deal with emergencies judged to endanger public health and safety. Despite there being only one major burst during the period of the strike, which was speedily repaired, consumers were still inconvenienced by the skeleton nature of the service provided, although they were never cut-off as happened in many other parts of the country.

Over at Bournemouth, the situation was entirely different. Because most workers still belonged to the Co-Partnership scheme, retained after nationalisation of the gas part of the company, they continued to work normally in all areas. When the strike was finally called-off after more than a month, the Board again paid tribute to their staff: *'We note with great satisfaction that many of the company's consumers have expressed their appreciation and thanks for the uninterrupted supply of water which they had enjoyed. The episode clearly revealed the loyalty which exists within the undertaking and demonstrated the operation of the special relationship which exists between the company and its employees.'*

One of those letters from a customer read: *'The last time I wrote to you was in September 1976 after you and your staff had supplied water without any rationing during the worst drought on record. My wife and I were most grateful to you and your staff for the super service during the summer of 1976, and in fact during every summer and winter. My wife has used*

Alderney offices

Bournemouth Water since 1923 and never once in that time have we ever found your company at fault - which must surely be a record for any company. Once again, after the trauma some unfortunate folk have had to suffer during the recent strike, it is our delight and pleasure to write and thank you and your staff for supplying water throughout the strike and for organising themselves into such a company whereby it is in everybody's interest to keep the water flowing. Well done everyone and again many, many thanks.'

Following the end of the strike, the Government abolished the National Water Council and, in the run-up to the election in June that year, passed legislation to end the built-in majority of local government officials on most of the Water Authority Boards, some of which had become unmanageably large. This had evolved because a lot of the assets acquired by the Water Authorities had been transferred from local government ownership without financial compensation, the compromise being that, however small, they were each allowed representation on the new body.

Once re-elected, the Government began to cast an eye over the best way to avert any further problems in the industry, highlighted during 1984 by continual bad press about the Water

Authorities caused by, in quick succession, a major pollution incident in the River Dee, the death of fifteen people in an explosion at a works, a major landslip in a dam embankment, and another drought. Then, in November that year, the Chancellor of the Exchequer altered the rules completely as far as Water Authority budgeting was concerned - in effect it was to be regarded as a nationalised industry with the Government deciding when tariffs should be increased and by how much. This was not a major problem for the Water Authorities, who were already in public ownership, but the statutory companies were put in the precarious position of being small private sprats in a pond full of big public mackerel.

This spurred Bournemouth to make another approach to West Hampshire regarding amalgamation, but it was rejected as the West Hampshire Board thought that, as Bournemouth's charges were so much higher than West Hampshire's, there was little likelihood of customers benefiting from such an arrangement. They also cited Bournemouth's Co-Partnership scheme as another stumbling block. Soon afterwards the privatisation of the Water Authorities was proposed with conversion to public limited company status, although action was to be postponed until after the next general election. This immediately caused anxiety at West Hampshire, who felt that if the Wessex

People *Bournemouth Water Staff, 1970s*

People

Boscombe Water Tower Crew, 1979

Bournemouth & District Water Company – Under Pressure Tapping demonstration

Water Authority became a plc, their size *'rendered it very easy for a predator to gain control.'*

In 1986, the Association of Water Companies recognised that such a move could eventually signal the death of the statutory companies. As well as recommending that they seriously consider amalgamations to give the smaller ones the financial strength to resist any moves against them, they also engaged consultants to ensure that consumers and Parliament were aware of the water companies, their service over a long period of time and their unique 'private' status. Shortly afterwards, the West Hampshire Board was shown the proposed campaign logo which

gave the message 'Local Water - Purely Yours' but considered it to be slightly tawdry and declined to use it.

In June 1987, the Conservative election manifesto stated: *"We will continue the successful programme of privatisation. In particular, after privatisation of the British Airports Authority, we will return to the public the Water Authorities, leaving certain functions to a new National Rivers Authority."* In the view of the West Hampshire Board this meant that the privatised Water Authorities would be relegated to carrying out just the utility functions of water supply and sewage treatment, leaving water conservation, pollution control, fisheries, land

The completed Reservoir 7 at Alderney

drainage and flood protection to the newly-established, and publically-owned, National Rivers Authority. This reduced role would cause the new plcs to rapidly consider the profitability improvements that would be achieved by *'taking over a Company such as ours.'* Regardless, when Bournemouth requested yet another meeting in December that year to discuss amalgamation, West Hampshire said it was not ready.

Bournemouth & District Water's involvement with politicians at the time was not entirely restricted to the corridors of Westminster. During one evening whilst the Conservative Party were holding their annual conference at the town's Highcliffe Hotel, problems arose with the water supply in the building. On standby that night was Les Smith, who recalls receiving the emergency call from the control room to report to the security checkpoint:

"I assumed I would be expected, but when I showed my company ID, I was told, 'you won't even get in this portakabin with that, let alone the Highcliffe.' I had to wait for a plain clothes officer to arrive, who escorted me into the portakabin where I had to walk through a metal detector of the type used at airports. It registered a signal, so I removed all my loose change, keys, etc which were put in a polythene bag. Then I was frisked by hand, after which an electronic sniffer was run up and down my clothing before I could be escorted to the basement plant room, where the hotel's maintenance man told me there was plenty of hot air in the hotel, but no hot water!*

I discovered that the hot water apparatus was gravity-fed from roof cisterns, the mains supply to which was pumped-up from a break tank in the basement. But only one of the two pumps was working, and there were also problems with the ball valves on the three cisterns which were all housed in a small tank room on the roof. It was all very restricted for space, but we eventually got the job done. Being rather hot and stuffy in the tank room, once things were under control the maintenance man and myself opened the door onto the roof and stepped out to get a breath of fresh air, not realising that there were police marksmen stationed out there. The officer in charge came over and told us that his men were rather nervous of people coming up behind them, and not to go out there again!"

When the 1989 Water Act finally appeared, it stripped the newly-created plcs of the responsibility for management of river basins, but allowed them to privately finance all the

Bournemouth & District Water Company carnival float

other requirements placed upon them. They would be regulated by a new Office of Water Services (OFWAT) who had the duty to ensure the companies could finance their requirements whilst maintaining price regulation. Two additional regulators, Her Majesty's Inspectorate of Pollution and the Drinking Water Inspectorate, oversaw the general quality of the water supply. The necessary government debt write-off to enable the flotation was balanced by the income received from the sale of the ten companies, in excess of £5 billion. Although this was probably the most controversial privatisation among the many carried out in the 1980s and 90s, the bullet that the Government dodged in this case was the estimated £28 billion of investment required by the industry over the following ten years, which became the responsibility of the plcs.

Whilst all of this was happening, the twenty-nine statutory companies, which included the still independent Bournemouth & District Water Company and West Hampshire

Water Company, had remained in private ownership. However, these twenty-nine companies together still provided a quarter of the water supplied in England and Wales, and were now subject to the same regulatory requirements as the plcs. The new Act allowed them to individually convert themselves to plc status, if they so wished, and several did so recognising that it would make it easier to obtain the necessary financing on the open markets.

Whether converted or not, these small, but very profitable, companies immediately became attractive bid targets.

Bournemouth & District Water Company logo introduced in the mid-1970s

Burma Star Memorial

A more solemn ceremony at the 1978 Open Day marked the unveiling of a War Memorial in the grounds at Alderney to those who died in the Burma Campaign of 1941 to 1945. The ceremony was intended to be conducted by Earl Mountbatten of Burma, then patron of the Burma Star Association, but he was unfortunately indisposed on the day, so his place was taken by their Chairman, Air Vice Marshall Sir Bernard Chacksfield. A few months later, the Earl was able to make the trip to Alderney to see the memorial, when he was also given a tour of the site.

Air Vice Marshall Sir Bernard Chacksfield takes the salute at the dedication ceremony in 1978

The Burma Star Association was formed in 1951 and its first President was Field Marshal The Viscount Slim, commander of the British Fourteenth Army, known as the 'forgotten army', throughout what was one of the longest and bloodiest campaigns of World War 2. To be a full member, an individual must have been awarded the Burma Campaign Star for service in Burma or the Pacific Campaign Star with Burma Clasp. The Badge of the Association incorporates a replica of the Burma Campaign Star, and was accepted by The College of Heralds after permission was granted by HM King George VI; it is worn in the lapel or regulation green beret. The Association promotes continued comradeship among those who served in the jungles of Burma, and also provides welfare assistance to members and their widows in times of ill-health or other difficult circumstances.

The connection to the Burma Campaign comes through one of the Fourteenth Army units, the 2nd Battalion of the Dorset Regiment, which contained a number of employees from the Bournemouth Gas & Water Co, including Maurice Richmond who became secretary of the Dorset branch of the Association. The original memorial, as dedicated in 1978, was in the form of a mosaic laid in the grounds at Alderney near

The new memorial dedicated in 1995

the front entrance of George Jessel House. When the building was refurbished in 1995, a new memorial stone was erected and rededicated in a specially-constructed memorial garden in a quieter part of the site, which incorporates seating dedicated to some of those past employees.

The ceremony takes place every year on 11th November, and although the number of veterans attending naturally dwindles year on year, the attendance numbers are always bolstered by current members of staff. The veterans recognised this continued support in 2010, when they presented a plaque recording their appreciation, which now hangs in the reception area of George Jessel House.

Alderney new water treatment pumping station 1994

Biwater

Once the details of the new Water Act were published, it became clear that it would create a fundamental change in the structure of the water industry in England and Wales. The timetable that emerged in early 1988 scheduled for it to pass into law in the summer of 1989, followed by flotation of the ten Water Authorities by the end of that year.

At the top end, there was keen international interest in purchasing the Water Authorities, particularly as they were to be offered debt-free and with what was termed a 'green dowry', additional Government cash to kick-start the necessary investment post-privatisation. Large multi-nationals began to assess the profit potential of each authority in order to be in position to bid for their choices in what would, essentially, be an open share placement on the London Stock Exchange.

At a lower level, water service companies around the world assessed the potential of contracting for the large capital projects that would become available once the privatised companies commenced their investment programmes. One of those companies was Biwater, a large British water service contractor with operations in numerous countries worldwide. With specialist subsidiaries in water treatment, infrastructure management and civil engineering, Biwater was well-placed to react to the forthcoming expansion of the British water industry. However, it also had an eye on moving into the area of water supply as well.

Biwater was established in 1968 by Adrian White CBE. The name Biwater, or two waters, was adopted because of the company's involvement in the provision of clean water and the treatment of wastewater. With headquarters in Dorking, the company expanded its own range of skills and expertise by acquiring established companies within the water industry and by forming joint ventures with organisations that provided complementary services. It extended its business activities into world markets with successful contracts in Indonesia, Hong Kong, Iraq, Kenya and Malawi, and in 1975 won the Queen's Award to Industry for Exports, an achievement it repeated on four further occasions.

Early in 1988, the directors of West Hampshire Water Company learned that 15% of their voting stock had been acquired by Biwater, who then advised that they would be interested in making a full bid if the directors supported the move. At the same time, Biwater was also negotiating with the East Worcestershire Water Company, another statutory company of similar size. The West Hampshire Board was unanimous that the company should remain independent if at all possible, but recognised that their shares would become actively traded with a consequent increase in value; indeed there were already other French and British companies that were actively courting shareholders.

If a takeover was to become inevitable, their early preference was to go with Wessex Water, once privatised, but recognised that their first duty was to obtain the best price for the shareholders. The Chairman, Sir George Meyrick, suggested that Esso might be interested in acquiring the company in order to safeguard its bulk supply against unwarranted price increases once the existing contract expired in 1995. The Board authorised merchant bankers Hill Samuel to make contact with Esso, Biwater, Wessex Water and other possible buyers, among whom were Merivale Moore, who were interested in acquiring the land holdings, fishing and mooring facilities controlled by the company. Overseas water businesses such as Lyonnaise des Eaux were buying shares in other statutory water companies, as was General Utilities Ltd, a subsidiary of Compagnie Générale des Eaux.

Major Mills

By June 1988, the Board had decided that the interests of the company would be best served within the Biwater Group, and the shareholders approved a resolution to open formal negotiations. Sir George Meyrick resigned as Chairman in October due to ill health, and was replaced by Major John Mills, the longest serving director having joined the Board nearly forty years earlier. Sir George had been on the Board for thirty-two years, seventeen as Chairman, and continued to serve as a director until his death a few months afterwards. Further negotiations brought a final higher Biwater offer, valuing the company at £10 million.

By March 1989, Biwater Supply Holdings Ltd, a new group subsidiary formed for the purpose, had received acceptances for 75% of the voting shares in West Hampshire Water Company, making the bid unconditional. Having already acquired the East Worcestershire Water Company, Biwater announced that the two companies would continue to operate independently, but co-operate in areas of mutual interest and share experience particularly on network systems. It then emerged that Biwater had not finished with their foray into water supply, as they were also negotiating with the Bournemouth & District Water Company.

Biwater logo

Pressure standpipe test

In June, just weeks before the 1989 Water Act passed into law, Biwater confirmed that it had received acceptances for 97.3% of the voting shares in Bournemouth and that the deal had been cleared of any competition issues by the Office of Fair Trading. The Biwater

Brian Turner

bid valued the company at £17.6 million, and the Board had recommended acceptance of this in line with the wishes expressed by their former Chairman, Brian Turner, that if losing independence was as inevitable as it appeared, he was determined that the company's future should be secure within a British consortium. Mr Turner did not see the conclusion of the deal, as he unfortunately died suddenly at the

end of 1988, just months after the company had celebrated its 125th anniversary with another successful open day event.

The editorial in the final edition of Tic Tac reflected the apprehension within the Bournemouth company: *'However you look at it we are without doubt in for a culture shock - the corporate culture. At best, corporate culture is a Saville-row suit in which the company moves to the rhythm of change; at worst it is a rusty suit of armour in which the company is restrained. A company is born naked and then grows up acquiring a set of attitudes and a suit of values becoming enshrined in an unchallenged company-way of doing things. This company, having existed for 126 years, has survived one major culture shock - the loss of the gas undertaking in 1949, and a number of minor shocks as well. How well we survive depends very much on how we, that is all of us, set out to move with the times. We have to make*

People *Biwater Golf Team*

People *The Bournemouth & District Water Company team who played a special challenge match against a Bourne Valley Southern Gas Board team in 1981*

Bournemouth & West Hampshire Water reception

certain that we adjust to change, accept new cultures and, above all, meet new challenges with wisdom and understanding, not head-on in an arresting suit of armour. From young to old, from labourer to director, we have the needs to adopt a new culture, for if we cannot do that, then we are also signing our own death warrant. We must look forward to the challenge and change; change in mentality and change in the way we operate in the organisation to take on the challenge in the worldwide opportunities which now exist.'

The Biwater press release announced: *'The acquisition of Bournemouth will further enhance the operational capabilities that Biwater is currently able to offer to its customers. Biwater already owns a majority shareholding in East Worcestershire Water Company and West Hampshire Water Company. The area of supply*

in Bournemouth is adjacent to that of West Hampshire and there will be increased scope for joint initiatives to improve the water supply and expanding areas of cooperation between them.' After nearly a hundred years of prevarication, the amalgamation of the two companies had finally become inevitable.

The first move towards this was the appointment of Dr Robin Turrell, Biwater Group Commercial Director, in a non-executive capacity as the Biwater representative on both Boards. In February 1990, the Boards of both companies were harmonised, still meeting separately, but on the same day each month. At that meeting Martin Copp from Bournemouth & District Water Company was elected Chairman of both companies with Major John Mills from West Hampshire Water Company as his deputy. Alan Booker, the widely-respected Chief Executive of East Worcestershire Water Company, was appointed as Managing Director for both companies.

The favourable terms afforded to the former Water Authorities upon privatisation were not available to the statutory companies, but all became subject to the regulatory controls imposed on their newly-privatised counterparts. A new 'price cap' regime demanded tight cost control and efficiency and a review of operations and manning was implemented to evaluate the scope for cost reductions by closer working between West Hampshire and Bournemouth. A joint resource strategy was then developed to optimise resources and thus maximise capital efficiency.

One of the first results was the amalgamation of the laboratories of both companies at Alderney. The new Water Supply (Water Quality) Regulations 1989 were implemented at the beginning of 1990, requiring water suppliers to ensure the wholesomeness of water supplies, to monitor the quality of drinking water and report results. The Drinking Water Inspectorate was set up with the responsibility to ensure compliance, which resulted in annual visits to water suppliers to carry out a meticulous audit over a number of days. With the regulations centred on the role of laboratory and water quality monitoring, that was where the audit was concentrated, the first taking place within months of implementation. Despite the many changes and the way the new regulations affected laboratory operations, the Inspectorate's first annual report showed that Bournemouth & District Water Company and West Hampshire Water Company were first and second nationally on water quality, achieving 99.9% and 99.3% compliance respectively.

Planning the primary treatment plant at Longham

In November 1990, the Government appointed Alan Booker to the post of Deputy Director General of OFWAT, leaving all three water companies in the Biwater group without a chief executive. In the interim, Company Secretary, Barrie Gray, took the reins and, after East Worcester made an individual appointment, Tony Cooke was recruited in May 1991 to be General Manager of both West Hampshire Water Company and Bournemouth & District Water Company, charged with maximising efficiency by integrating operational aspects of the two south-coast companies.

Bringing two companies together is never an easy task, but two neighbouring companies with a common product and service should have provided some common ground to start with. Yet regardless of their close proximity, Bournemouth and West Hampshire had evolved in completely different manners, on top of which there had been numerous occasions over nearly a hundred years when, despite the apparent advantages, they had found a way not to come together voluntarily. Having come from a broad industrial background, with experience in running niche subsidiaries within large multi-national conglomerates, Tony Cooke had the necessary experience to steer two already highly-successful and independent companies into their new corporate fold.

Even so, he found that it wasn't just the ethos of each company that varied: *"You wouldn't believe the differences that could evolve between two companies working side-by-side in the same business. Even the manual shut-off valves of the two companies turned-off in opposite directions."* Nevertheless, not for the first time in the company's history, the right man for the task had arrived in post at the right time, and over the next nineteen years he would guide the organisation to the top of its industry and, more importantly, keep it there whilst maintaining that customer-first ethos that was so deeply embodied in both constituents.

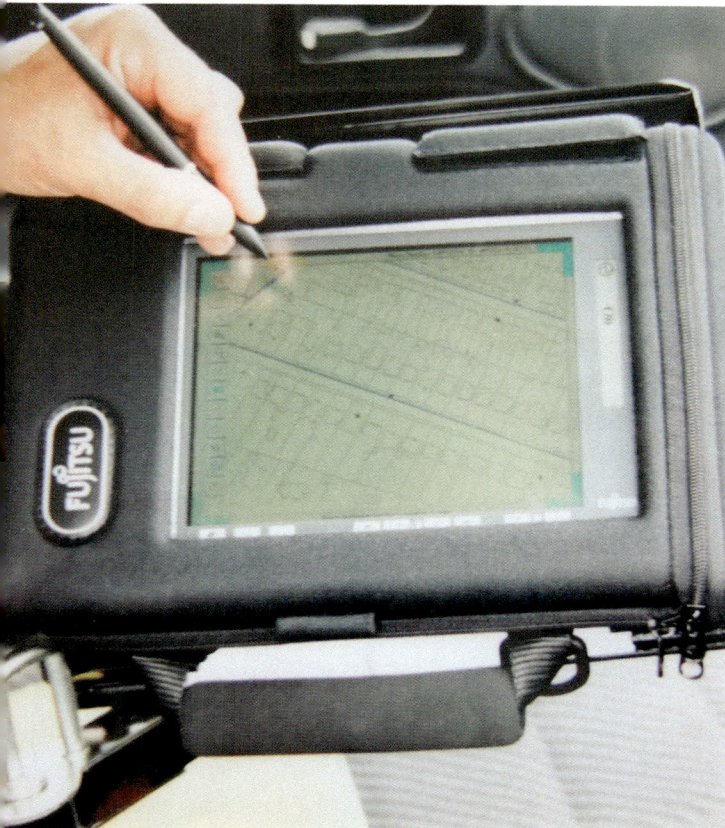

One of the first hand-held computers used in conjunction with GIS

One of the common aspects of both company's operations was the immense knowledge base of mains installations - some that date as far back as the 1880s are still in use 130 years later. This was held as physical paper or linen plans, supplemented, where not available, by the individual knowledge of long-serving district staff. As the plans were gradually digitised, they were physically checked against the actual installations by surveyors equipped with pipe detection equipment. The initial project, utilising software called Smallworld, took around two years to complete, and was introduced as a desktop system for a small number of key users who were authorised to revise plans as the installations evolved. Once this basic system was up and running, further development work added zoning to the plans to create work areas that could be used as the basis for a new work-planning system, named DOJM. Once that stage was completed, an intranet version was rolled-out as a view-only system for a wider group of desk-based users, with job-based local maps downloadable to handheld pen-based computers mounted in all company vehicles.

As part of the joint resource strategy, West Hampshire purchased the disused Ibsley Aerodrome, for the development of raw water 'bankside' storage. Bournemouth, who had a similar scheme under consideration at Longham, added a new seven and a half million gallon circular treated water reservoir at Alderney, number eight, which was of a similar modular construction to number seven. Alongside this work, a new pump house, fitted with high and low-lift pump sets, was created to replace the previous installation that had been in service since the 1930s. Work also commenced on the introduction of a combined computer-based Geographic Information System, a new digital database that would utilise background Ordnance Survey maps with additional layers marking the locations of underground piping, valves and hydrants.

Further results of early co-operation were demonstrated by the development of a modular treatment plant at Matchams to overcome an anticipated resource deficiency at Knapp Mill at times of peak demand. The plant was funded by West Hampshire, constructed on the Bournemouth pumping station site on the River Avon and was designed and built by Biwater Treatment Limited. Water from it was supplied to West Hampshire's customers via the Blashford Trunk Main at a rate of two million gallons per day.

Early in 1992, it was announced that agreement had been reached with OFWAT to merge both of the companies not later than the end of 1994. As an interim stage, both would be converted from statutory companies, governed by Acts and Orders of Parliament, to individual public

Ibsley Water, created on the old aerodrome site and completed in 1996

limited companies governed by the requirements of the Companies Acts. This would remove the individual legislation governing each of them, giving the freedom to run their affairs without having to refer to Parliament for permission as they had, since their inception, for such matters as financing. Kenneth Gardener, who had been non-executive Vice Chairman of Biwater since 1986, was also appointed to both Boards of directors with particular responsibility for financial matters. Later that year, following successful conversion, he took over the Chairmanship of both public limited companies, with Tony Cooke moving to the corresponding Managing Director roles.

In March 1993, Biwater sold East Worcester Water plc to Severn Trent Water plc for £28 million. Making the announcement Peter Robinson, Biwater's Chief Executive, added: *"At the same time the two southern water companies within the Group remain flagship demonstrations of the skills we possess and part of our well-rounded capability that enables us to serve the water industry worldwide."* These comments referred to the latest report from OFWAT which, as well as confirming maintenance of their previous water quality standards, showed both companies had among the lowest levels of loss due to leakage within their distribution systems. The national average reported by the industry watchdog was 22% whereas the two Biwater-owned companies reported just 8%. Later that year Roger Harrington, who previously worked for Wessex Water and the East Surrey Water Company, was recruited to take up the post of Chief Engineer in both companies.

Adrian White CBE

A self-confessed 'serial entrepreneur', Adrian White started Biwater Treatment in 1968 with just £1,000, raised by cashing-in an insurance policy and selling his flat. Initial operations were conducted from his parents' home in Beckenham, but in 1971, he was able to move the fledgling company to Dorking, where the headquarters of the group still remain.

The basis of the company's success was the Biwater Tower, his own design for a compact plant to provide conventional water treatment to World Health Organisation standards. Combining a reliable process with straightforward installation, small footprint and low maintenance, it was ideal for water-stressed locations in more remote areas. Over the next twenty years, through natural growth and judicious acquisitions, he turned Biwater into a multinational group with an annual turnover of £274 million and around three-thousand employees, exporting water products and services to fifty-three countries around the globe. In 1993, Adrian was awarded the CBE for his contribution to the water industry worldwide.

But water is not the only liquid for which Adrian has a passion. In the early 1980s, he purchased a 630-acre farm in Surrey, originally founded in 1754. Over the next ten years he turned just under half of it into the largest vineyard in Britain, Denbies Wine Estate, which now produces around 400,000 bottles every year under the management of his son, Christopher. Some have won prestigious awards, including an IWC Gold for 'Best Rosé in the World' in 2011 and, more recently, the IWC Gold for Dessert Wines, the first time that a British vineyard has won an award in that category.

Yet, despite having turned seventy recently, Adrian shows little sign of taking a back seat, being still a director of Biwater Holdings, and spending much of his spare time working for various charities. He has been a governor of the BBC and, until 2012, was Executive Chairman of the Children's Trust, a national charity for children with multiple disabilities. His advice for budding entrepreneurs is simple: *"Think big and spend small, but more than anything, enjoy what you are doing."*

West Hampshire Water Company centenary celebration, 1993

Amalgamation

On Wednesday 22nd September 1993, West Hampshire Water Company celebrated its centenary. The occasion was marked by a luncheon in a specially-erected marquee at Knapp Mill, attended by special guests and most of the staff of both companies, who tucked into salmon supplied from the company's own fisheries.

The guest of honour was the Sixth Earl of Malmesbury, whose grandfather had opened the Knapp Mill site on 13th August 1895, an occasion marked by a commemorative plaque. As part of the day's ceremony, the current Earl unveiled an almost identical plaque commemorating the centenary, a fitting tribute prior to its merger with Bournemouth & District Water Company which officially took place on 1st July 1994 creating Bournemouth & West Hampshire Water plc.

The newly-amalgamated company committed to achieving various certifications and accreditations, including ISO 9001 Total Quality Management, one of the first companies in the industry to achieve this when obtained in 1995, ISO 14001 for Environmental Management Systems obtained in 2001 and OHSAS 18001 for Health & Safety in 2004, as well as Investors in People in 1994.

OFWAT had requested all water companies during 1992 to compile their own twenty-year strategic business plan in advance of a redetermination of water prices to be carried out in 1995. This would include a programme of new investment over ten years to enable each company to meet growth in demand, water quality improvements and increased standards of service. The Department of the Environment established that, in addition to meeting the cost of inflation, price increases should cover the cost of these capital investment programmes, those additional charges being referred to as the

The Earl of Malmesbury unveils the centenary plaque alongside that unveiled by his grandfather nearly a hundred years previously

'K factor'. Each water company would have its own K factor - the annual percentage rise permissible over and above the retail prices index.

Members of the Customer Services Bureau review information available in reception

As part of this exercise the company undertook a customer consultation exercise to determine their willingness and ability to pay for further improvements in water quality standards, and as a result, a new Customer Services Bureau was created. This was not necessary due to any specific problems; once again, the company had spotted a developing trend and were determined to stay ahead of it, as the current Director of Retail and Corporate Services, Richard Stanbrook, explained:

"Customer Service has always been there, it's in the DNA of the company. A lot of our staff are long-serving, friends who have worked together for a long time, and could make it difficult for some young whipper-snapper who comes along to teach them how to speak to a customer. But they know it instinctively, it's not a new fad to them. They volunteer whenever we have an issue - they will always go that extra yard. Of course, we can improve and because of that we're always willing to learn. That's what keeps us top of the pile."

The new Customer Services Bureau

People *Customer Services Bureau Staff*

People

Chaingang cycle competitors, 1980s

The new department was initially an expansion of the small unit, run by just two ladies, who handled most of the customer telephone calls into the company, which were primarily billing enquiries. Over the years this has developed into a multi-disciplined call centre that handles around 80% of all initial customer interaction without the need for their being passed on to any other department. Where there is a need for the contact to be passed on, Customer Services maintains oversight of the interaction and records all results. Whether the initial enquiry is regarding a simple meter reading, or a major leakage incident, this pro-active approach, along with specific training of staff in other departments, has kept the company at or near the top of national ratings for customer service every year since their creation.

The department's resources are occasionally stretched by unusual events, and one of these occurred in February 2001 when one of the district crews found a parked car in the way of a trench they needed to dig for mains work. Apparently, although the location in Winton had been marked-out with cones, some had been removed by children and Neil Hall parked his car outside of his house as usual during the weekend. When the crew arrived on the Monday morning, his car was still there, but there was no sign of Mr Hall. The Police were advised, but were unable to contact the owner, so when the car had still not been moved by the following morning, the crew dug the trench around it.

When Mr Hall arrived home from work that evening, he found his car marooned alongside the kerb on a small island of tarmac, and covered in dust. The company's Networks Manager, Richard Barton, apologised and arranged for the car to be cleaned and checked-over: *"When the car was still there on Tuesday, an on-site decision was made to go around it. In hindsight, it probably doesn't look the best decision to have been made."* The story even made some national papers, but Mr Hall managed to see the lighter side: *"When I first saw it, I thought 'they can't do this.' I had to laugh, because if I didn't I would have cried. Now they're going to get the car cleaned - that's the best news I've had."*

Workmen dug a trench around Mr Hall's Volvo

A ten-year capital investment programme totalling £65 million was adopted in 1994, the first stage of which merged the company headquarters in the newly-refurbished George Jessel House at Alderney. This allowed the vacated West Hampshire offices at Knapp Mill to be sold, together with an area of spare land, for housing development. As well as the planned bankside storage facilities at Longham Lakes and Ibsley, the programme would include major alterations to the Quadrant buildings at Alderney to provide office accommodation for operations and major changes to the Alderney treatment works. These would be followed

The new £10m Primary Treatment Plant at Longham was opened on 4th November 1996 by Mrs Karen Morgan of the Environment Agency.

Inspection checks at the Primary Treatment Plant

by the replacement of the seventy-year-old primary treatment plant at Longham with a new works with a capacity of ninety megalitres per day, at £10.2 million the costliest single works project ever undertaken by the company. Designs were also well advanced for a new treated water storage and pumping station at Knapp Mill worth £5.1 million and the refurbishment of the Hale works costing £1.5 million. Finally, an 800 millimetre bulk water transfer main 11 kilometres long would be built between Knapp Mill and Alderney to further enhance security of supply. To help finance this, in 1996 the company converted 25 million £1 ordinary voting shares into 8.5% cumulative irredeemable preference shares which were admitted to the official list of the London Stock Exchange and placed with institutional investors.

New reservoir added at Knapp Mill

With the ever-increasing standards of water quality being applied, the company had commenced trials in 1994 to assess the effectiveness of Granular Activated Carbon, a form of carbon capable of adsorbing unwanted pesticides and other trace organics sometimes present in raw water. Those trials proved successful, and it was decided to install a layer of it in all slow sand filters at Alderney and Knapp Mill. This was no small-scale operation, as the two sites together utilised 60,000 cubic metres of sand weighing 100,000 tonnes, which all had to be removed and relaid. This was achieved by the end of 1996 at an initial cost of £2.5 million, with ongoing running costs of more than £1 million a year thereafter.

Despite the summer drought in 1996, and with the co-operation of their customers who responded positively to requests for restraint, in particular to only water gardens on alternate days, the company maintained their enviable record of never having imposed restrictions on their customers' use of water. The decision was also taken to install meters at no charge for all users of garden sprinklers, properties with swimming pools and unmetered commercial properties including guesthouses and bed-and-breakfast accommodation. Trials elsewhere had indicated that metering reduced peak demand by as much as 30%, and if this proved to be the case across the area, investment in new resources could be deferred in the longer term, thus financing the short-term investment in additional meters. As another forward investment, encoded meters were installed to take advantage, initially, of touchpad meter reading to minimise costs, but the meters chosen also enabled the move to remote automatic reading when the technology became available.

When the contract to supply the Esso refinery at Fawley expired in 1996, after forty years, a renewal was secured on a more cost-reflective basis, allowing the company to continue their

Metering programme well underway, 1997

long association with Esso. Gravel extraction commenced to create the voids which would ultimately form the raw water storage lakes at Longham, and the new primary treatment plant there, supplied by Biwater International, was officially opened at the end of the year, on time and below budget. Compliance with the drinking water standards for 1996 was 99.8%, a further improvement of 0.1% over the 1995 level for the merged company.

During 1997, the programme for pesticide removal at Alderney and Knapp Mill works was completed, and the construction of a new twenty-seven megalitre treated water reservoir at Knapp Mill commenced. The company also won a competition organised by the Dorset Training and Enterprise Council in conjunction

Tony Cooke (centre), Hazel Taylor and Barry Short accept the award as Dorset's Friendliest Company in 1997

with the Bournemouth Echo to find Dorset's friendliest company. The Chairman of the TEC, Rex Symons, presented the company with a specially-commissioned commemorative plate made by Poole Pottery and, to celebrate, a cake iced with the similar motif was shared among employees.

The annual OFWAT report showed that, nationally, Bournemouth & West Hampshire Water plc had the lowest unit costs, one of the lowest average charges to customers, best customer service, highest water quality and lowest leakage rates. Year-end accounts showed that overall turnover had increased by 3% to £25 million and profit before tax rose by 4% to £9 million. Ten years after becoming part of Biwater plc, and despite the heavy capital investment costs being dictated by regulatory requirements, the positive impact that the company was making was shown when the

overall group announced a profit before tax of just £5.5 million on a total turnover of £243 million.

During the last decade of the 20th century, the company made numerous investments in technology. Some of those were prompted by the 'Millennium Bug', a perceived major computing timebomb due to the many computer programmes that had been compiled over the years utilising stored year coding with only two decimal digits. Consequently, it was thought they would not be able to recognise the year 2000 when it occurred, so companies and organisations around the world spent billions upgrading their systems to remove the old coding.

Even then, there were doubts as to whether some control systems for vital plant may have incorporated hard-coded microchips that still contained this hidden potential. So all the

Staff and vehicle fleet, 1990s

major utilities had teams on duty at midnight on 31st December 1999, just in case any systems failed. Kevin Hand recalls what happened at Bournemouth & West Hampshire Water on the actual night:

'It was quite an operation to fend off the "bug" with several people positioned at key sites awaiting the anticipated crash of all things IT. If memory serves me right I was at Stanbridge, Andy Shorey at Knapp Mill, Ray Boyt at Hale Site One and Nick Trevett and others, including Roger Harrington, were in the central control room at Alderney. Thankfully nothing happened on the night other than for the unknown bright spark at Knapp Mill who put a box over the camera in the control room there at the stroke of midnight, sending those in Alderney control into a bit of a spin thinking that the security system had crashed!'

Other than that, everything ticked-over into the new century without a hitch and, as almost everywhere, the intensely media-hyped disaster failed to happen, although one of the SCADA systems unexpectedly stopped twelve hours later at midday on 1st January. A quick reset was conducted and it was back in operation, as it has been ever since without missing a beat.

Bournemouth & West Hampshire
WATER

New Bournemouth & West Hampshire Water logo

Institute of Water

Delegates joining-in the spirit of the final evening of the 1998 conference, which had the theme of Beside the Seaside

Founded as the Association of Water Distribution Officers, just four days after VE Day in May 1945, the Institute of Water is the professional body that exclusively supports people working at all levels across the UK water industry. By the time the first annual general meeting was convened a year later on 11th May 1946, over a hundred Founder members were listed, including their first Secretary and Treasurer, Allen Bolton, then Chief Inspector of the Sutton and District Water Company. Mr Bolton, who died in 2011 at the age of a hundred, was for many years the mainstay of what became, in 1990, The Institution of Water Officers, attending every annual conference up until 2008. The organisation adopted its current name in 2010.

In 1949, the Association's annual meeting evolved into an annual conference and exhibition, which moved around the country to be hosted by a different area each year, with Bournemouth as the venue in 1959, 1971 and 1980. Eventually the exhibition became so large that, in 1989, it moved to the National Exhibition Centre in Birmingham to become the International Water & Effluent Exhibition (IWEX). The now separate Annual Conference continues its peripatetic style, and includes in its programme a formal dinner and entertainment known as the President's Evening. Bournemouth & West Hampshire Water hosted this event in 1998 at the Moat House Hotel, where over 300 delegates attended.

Staff from both water companies have been to the fore in the organisation since its very early days, including the Institute's National Chairman for 2013/14 Richard Barton, who is the company's Customer Services Manager. There have been two previous national chairmen from Bournemouth the first of whom was Sydney Bowring, an Inspector with Bournemouth & District Water Company, who served two years from 1964 to 1966. The other was John Clement, who was the company's Distribution Manager during his year in the Chair in 1988/9, and was instrumental in creating the annual drilling and tapping competitions that are a highlight of IWEX. For 2003/4, Bournemouth & West Hampshire Water's Managing Director, Tony Cooke, was made President of the Institute, the only time a representative of the company has held that position.

Institute of Water

Upgrading at Knapp Mill, 2000

Cascal

In March 2000, Bournemouth & West Hampshire Water plc became a component in a joint venture partnership between Biwater and the Dutch utility company, NV Nuon Energy. The company thus formed by this joint venture was named Cascal.

Nuon had substantial holdings in Gas and Electric companies in Belgium, Holland and the UK, and was looking to add water to its portfolio, whilst Biwater, through its various subsidiaries, had acquired water and wastewater facilities serving approximately two million people in six countries worldwide, including Bournemouth. Cascal was created by Biwater bringing together their water and sewage company investments and Nuon adding the finance to enable the joint venture to exploit the growing market for private expertise and investment in the global water sector.

At Bournemouth Board level, John Green OBE took over as Chairman replacing David White, twin brother of Biwater CEO Adrian White, who had taken the role when Kenneth Gardener had retired the previous year. The following year Cascal's Chairman, David Lloyd, also joined the Bournemouth Board. Operationally, a new management structure was introduced with four operating units, under two new director posts. Roger Harrington became Technical Director and headed-up Water Supply and Customer Operations, whilst Finance Director Anthony Ferrar was responsible for Central Services and Enterprise Business.

Enterprise Business was created in 2000 to cover the operational aspects of the Royalty Fishery under the name of Recreational Services, along with several subsidiaries that the company had acquired or created during the latter part of the previous decade, which together in 1999 accounted for 15% of the company's turnover.

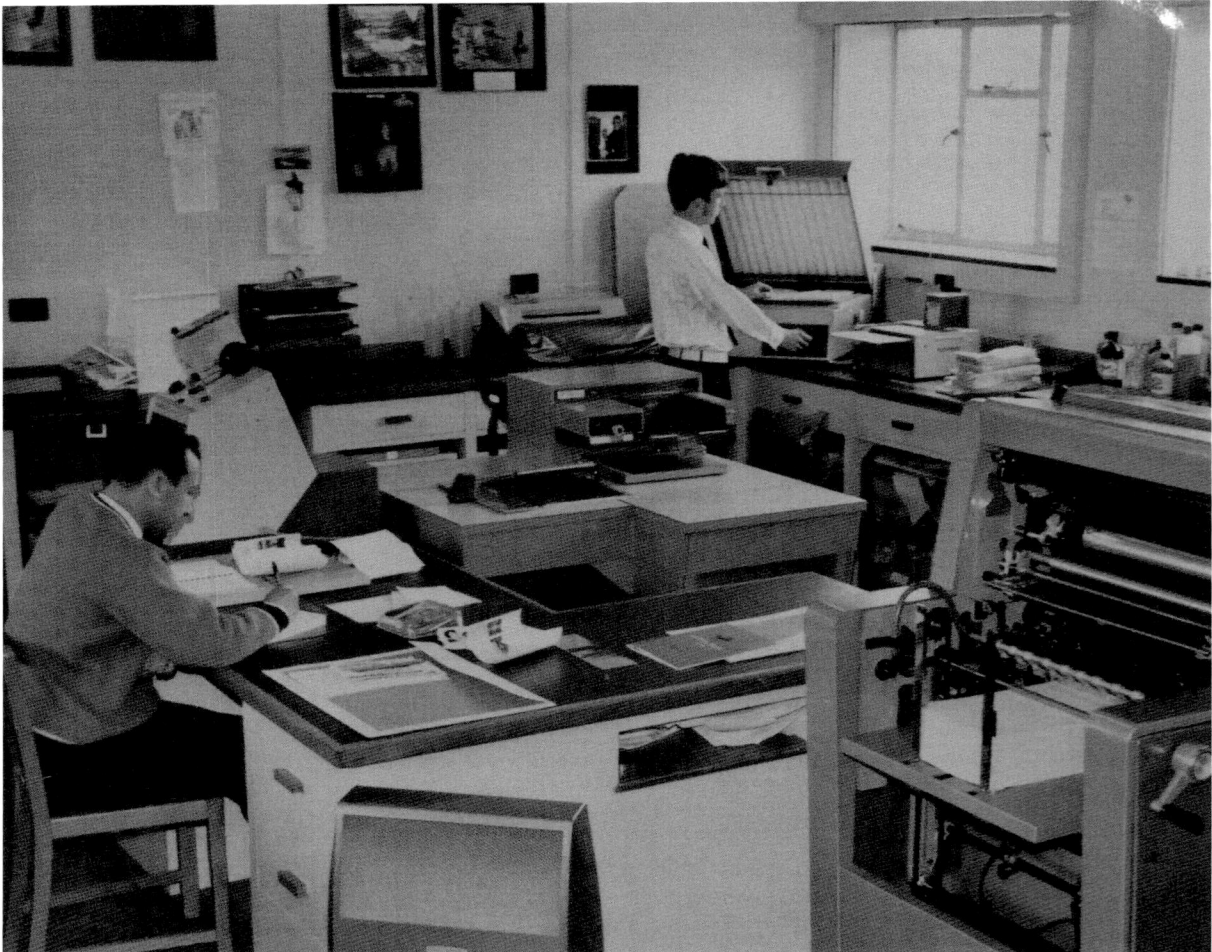

Print Department

These included AquaCare, a supplier of Emergency Insurance and Maintenance Plans to private consumers, and Airmec, which had formerly been called Aquazur before acquisition and provided outsourced specialist services to industrial customers in the areas of water treatment and air hygiene. Airmec was the subject of a successful management buyout in 2002.

Two others, media company Graphis UK and compositors GetSet, were combined with Aquaprint to provide graphic design, typesetting and printing services to commercial customers, all under the combined name of GetSet Graphics. AquaPrint was formerly the company's print department, which had started when Bournemouth & District Water Company installed a small letterpress machine at Old Christchurch Road in 1950, primarily to handle the printing of water bills. That was moved to Alderney in 1952 and evolved into a department which was managed by Ray Cherrett for almost forty years. Ray was a third generation employee, joining as a trainee accountant just as the split of gas and water services occurred. His grandfather, Saul, had been a mains foreman on the district for nearly thirty years, and his father, Albert, served more than forty years as a stoker, and later shift-foreman at Pitwines. Albert was also the shop-steward for the works in 1949, and was

Print Department at Alderney, 1990s

heavily-involved in the negotiations surrounding the maintenance of the Co-Partnership scheme within the nationalised gas company.

Under Ray's management, the print department grew with the installation of in-house offset printing, platemaking and collation equipment, as well as encompassing the creation and printing of maps and plans. He instituted the company's first IBM computer system in 1973 which was eventually superceded by the Honeywell mainframe installed in the early 1980s that would handle all of the company's business systems for over twenty years. The department also provided its expertise and specialist services to other companies, including West Hampshire Water. Printing of company publications and bill distribution for both companies had, in fact, been amalgamated for more than twenty years before the two companies were actually merged in 1994, when the department was created a subsidiary under the name of Aquaprint.

Ray Cherrett

In February 2000, the company was presented with the Government's Charter Mark for providing an exceptionally high quality of service to its users. This is not an award that is easily achieved, and winning it is a tribute to the entire organisation. The company has won the annual award, and its successor the Customer Service Excellence Standard, every year since. When the company received the latest award in January 2013, the assessor remarked that it was among only a small number of organisations to meet all fifty-seven requirements of the standard. Capital projects during 2000 included a £2.8 million upgrading of the

Leak Busters

Presentation of the first Charter Mark

rapid-gravity filters at Knapp Mill, originally installed during the 1950s, and the introduction of a five-year metering project, the target being to fit 28,000 new meters by March 2005, all of which would be a new TouchRead model adopted in preparation for the introduction of a new automated reading system. Half of the new meters would be in selected households to be mandatorily installed on a change of occupation, the other half, optional installations conducted at the customer's request because they had decided they would be financially better off with a metered supply. All remaining unmetered commercial customers in the area would also be converted.

As with the previous scheme introduced in 1996, the entire cost of this project was met by the company to encourage water conservation and to help identify leakage on private properties, in line with Government initiatives to protect the environment and reduce energy consumption. It was calculated that the future savings would more than compensate the investment because, by reducing water consumption, less water has to be treated and pumped, thereby saving chemicals and electricity, lessening impact on the local environment and deferring the need to develop expensive new sources of water.

A sports and social club has always been a strong aspect within the company, and 2000 witnessed the 50th anniversary of the Bournemouth company's evolution of that tradition. It was started in 1950 by the then

Alison Ramsey skipping with the children of a Nepalese village during a WaterAid visit in 1994

General Manager, Norman Martin, to keep the social connections between the smaller number of staff spread around the town after the loss of the original club premises to the gas board following nationalisation. As the water company centred its operations at Alderney, and a sports ground and pavilion were built there, the club blossomed, with even the reintroduction of the annual sports day during the late 1950s.

Peter Campbell kept the momentum going after he became general manager, introducing the very popular company open days in the late 1970s, whilst the social committee kept the sporting teams going and arranged various outings and social events. Not all of these went to plan. For a visit to the Thames Barrier and Greenwich one year, two coachloads left Alderney at 8am taking the party of ninety-nine to the Embankment in London, where a boat conveyed them to Greenwich. Other than the boat turning up late, the day went very well, but in the evening it proved difficult to find the next destination. An article in Water Connections magazine takes up the story:

"Our next and last port of call was the Berni Inn at Epsom's Tattenham corner, and the instructions were to look out for the small clock tower in the High Street near the Castle. Dizzy from going round Epsom so many times and asking for directions twice at the same police station, we turned around then found ourselves in a waste recycling yard. We extracted the two coaches from the pile of rubbish and headed for the restaurant. To our astonishment we were greeted with, 'I'm sorry but we haven't any large party booked in this evening and we certainly can't accommodate 99.' It transpired that we were booked in, not at Epsom, but at Windsor. Ah, so that's where the Castle is, just another hour's drive away! We eventually arrived back at Knapp Mill at midnight to be met by Ginger to say the other coach had broken down at Rownhams. After

unloading, our coach driver turned round and set off to rescue the stranded passengers. It was 1.10am when the final coach returned to Alderney. We have since received many calls from people who said it was the best outing they had ever had!"

After the merger, both company social clubs were also amalgamated and the first social secretary of the combined organisation was Josie Sibley, one of the mainstays of the Bournemouth social scene for many years. Bournemouth's events tended to be outings and social gatherings off site, apart from the occasional open days which had evolved more into family fun days by the end of the 'nineties. West Hampshire, on the other hand, focussed on a clubhouse and bar on the Knapp Mill site that had been opened in 1953, so the two organisations together provided a wider spread of opportunities for social gatherings, an important factor in pulling the two sets of staff together. After she retired at the beginning of 2001, Josie was awarded the MBE for services to the water industry and the local community. She summed-up her thirty-one years at the company:

"I liked the water company so much, every day was a pleasure to work there, it's a very family company that looks after its staff. There were some hard times, on weather issues and that sort of thing, but the staff were always there with you. My heart went out to the men who had broken mains to mend in freezing cold weather, you would get them out of bed and they would be out in a hole at two o'clock in the morning, but their manager would still be there, even though he didn't have to be, he would be running up the road to get them fish and chips or burgers, they were all very much in it together."

Josie remains involved, helping to organise the company's annual pensioners' Christmas lunch, and the social club committee is still going strong, arranging around half-a-dozen outings every year, plus a Christmas party for the children and their main event, the annual dinner dance, which is funded by the company. It also fields teams in sports sections for football, cricket and angling.

The combined factors of the company's standing as a flagship organisation within the UK water industry and it being part of a multi-national group engaged in water projects across the globe, brought a constant stream of overseas visitors to Bournemouth, at least one every month. In one short period there were visits from local government officers from Turkey, the management of a water company in the Philippines, a government Minister from Mauritius and the Mayor of Piura, a city in Peru of a similar size to Bournemouth, with its own municipal water company. They were given presentations on the technical and control software used in the company, and demonstrations of leakage control equipment. The full list of visitors since 1992 includes the names of more than thirty countries outside of the EU, and continues to grow.

Staff were also regularly seconded for overseas projects where their expertise was of benefit, and the experience exposed them to very different conditions. Pipeline Services Manager, Barrie Moore, was seconded to a mains-laying project in Chile, which was completed successfully despite his leak detector being seized by Customs officials, and the excavation in the boulder-strewn hard ground being conducted primarily by hand. Tony Cooke gave a presentation, that focussed upon efficiency, leakage and management systems, to the Ministry of Power, Energy and Water in Bahrain, a country where most of the water supply was provided by desalination plants blended with ground water supplies, and bottled water was the norm for drinking. Mike Rhodes and Eddie Hawkins visited Venezuela to assist with the administration problems encountered in the day-to-day running of one water organisation

that had a serious issue with illegal connections, because it was second nature for farmers to connect into air valves on the distribution system to water their cattle, despite all pipelines being for domestic use only.

When Tony Read visited Angola's capital Luanda in 2003, the year after the civil war there had ended, he was greeted by a man wearing a surgeon's mask, whose job was to check that all visitors had a vaccination against yellow fever before entering the country. Despite the dry climate, his taxi from the airport navigated its way along the main highway, dodging potholes full of water from the leaking water mains, and at the end of the journey he reached a capital city where the infux of refugees had swollen the population by seven times over the twenty-five years of hostilities, during which time the infrastructure had been decimated. *"We spent two days touring water treatment works, all looking very similar to those found in other countries I had visited: ample staff, locked tidy buildings but, as always, multitudes of pumps in pieces - there are never any spare parts. The afternoon trip to Kikuxi twenty miles east of the capital was tortuous, and it is a credit to Toyota that their 4x4s continue to run in those conditions. After two hours and at the end of an unmade track we came across a completely new treatment works, the sort that any company in any city on the globe would want."*

Overseas working was not restricted to commercial projects however. On Boxing Day in 2004, an earthquake in the Indian Ocean created a tsunami that devastated the western coastal areas of Aceh in Indonesia. As well as the huge loss of life, over half a million were left homeless, a tragedy compounded several months later by a second, more powerful, off-shore earthquake in the sea bed between Aceh and North Sumatra. Bournemouth and West Hampshire Water sent three portable

People

Social Club
It's a Knockout Team
2004

People *Social Club Fishing Team, 2012*

Indonesia tsunami trip

emergency water treatment plants, storage tankers and other equipment to provide safe drinking water for 66,000 people living in three refugee camps south of Banda Aceh. This relief was co-ordinated with the Indonesian authorities through another Cascal subsidiary, PT Adhya Tirta Batam, and three members of staff volunteered to travel with the equipment which was airlifted to Batam in Indonesia, then taken by the Indonesian navy to Lhokseumawe - a two-day journey by sea. The team from Bournemouth, Mark Burton, Andy Shorey and Rob Hyler, then set up the plants and trained local staff in their use.

At Board level, John Green OBE retired and was succeeded by Jim McGown, previously the Chief Executive of Three Valleys Water, who is the current Chairman at the time of writing. He was immediately faced by the introduction of new water quality regulations and an OFWAT price review, the results of which would be instituted in 2005 and last for five years.

Jim McGown

Bourne Stream Partnership

Despite a very public personality at its lower reaches, where it continues to babble through Bournemouth's world-famous Pleasure Gardens to reach the sea by the pier, the original source for the town's drinking water, the Bourne Stream, had become somewhat forgotten and neglected in the 120 years since it was superceded by the River Stour at Longham. So neglected, in fact, that its outfall had become responsible for some of the pollution that had caused the failure of the main beach to achieve blue flag status in eleven out of thirteen consecutive years.

This, then, was the background to the formation of the Bourne Stream Partnership in 2000, comprising Bournemouth & West Hampshire Water, The Environment Agency, English Nature, Poole and Bournemouth Councils, Wessex Water, Bournemouth University, Dorset Wildlife Trust, Greenlink, Bournemouth Oceanarium and Dorset Coast Forum. Chaired by the company's Technical Director, Roger Harrington, the partnership embarked on a number of diverse projects over the following seven years. These resulted not only in the improvement of the water quality in the stream, to the extent that in 2013, the main beach received the new Seaside Award for cleanliness, but also in the creation of the Bourne Valley Greenway, a 6.5 kilometre walkway/cycleway formed entirely in natural habitat, that follows the path of the stream as it passes through some of the most built-up areas in Poole and Bournemouth.

Among the projects that were undertaken, there was the occasional echo from the company's history, such as Operation Streamclean, sponsored by Wessex Water, to identify and reduce the incidences of pollution of the stream, although the remedies were not as drastic as mentioned in George Allen's recollections of 1886, related in an earlier chapter.

The Bourne Stream flowing through the Lower Gardens

But it was the creation of Bourne Valley Park, a 15-hectare urban open space less than half a mile northeast of the company's original Bourne Valley works that touched that history most closely, as it involved removing culverts to allow the stream to flow once again on the surface - some of which were the very culverts installed in 1864 by Edward Woods to direct the water to those original waterworks.

Aerial view of Alderney today

To the Top

Bournemouth & West Hampshire Water had consistently figured at the top of national listings on water quality, and in other areas of service performance it was ahead of targets set at the previous review in 1999. In 2005, it reached the position of fourth in OFWAT's National Overall Performance Assessment, the compound measure that included all eight of the regulator's indices, the company scoring 284 out of a possible 288 points.

One aspect where particular progress had been made was with regard to a legacy issue of supply pressures, where some areas operated at lower pressure at times of peak demand. Through the major investments made in the ten years to 1999, the company had reduced the number of properties affected by such fluctuations from 12,000 to 2,650, and had then set a target to reduce that to 750 by the end of 2004. In 2002, the number of those properties at risk had been reduced to 481, all at the extreme limits of the company's supply area; by fitting new booster pumps at Lymington Tower and laying new mains at Minstead and Harbridge, that figure was down to just nineteen by the end of 2004. Those properties were also eliminated the following year by the laying of a new trunk main through to Woodlands, which also provided improved supply to the entire north-eastern sector, and since 2005 there have been no properties at risk of low pressure scenarios.

A major plank of the company's strategy for overcoming these low pressures was identifying and rectifying leakage, but with what was essentially an open system comprising nearly 3,000 kilometres of pipework, this could be almost like looking for a needle in a haystack. In 1995, the decision was taken

New link main between Matchams and Knapp Mill

to divide the network into district metered areas, known as DMAs, smaller zones that can be monitored independently of the remainder of the network. This work, conducted over the following seven years, involved installing valve systems that could be used to isolate a DMA, plus permanent roadside kiosks housing a data logger, meter controller and telephone connection at single feed-point locations. Mobile monitoring equipment for pressure, flow and metering, can be attached at other chosen locations to provide data for a specific part of any DMA. With a defined number of properties

contained within the monitored zone, it became possible to use the obtained telemetry to quickly identify likely leakage, and rectify it.

With the first phase of the new bankside storage facility at Longham Lakes on-line, work commenced during 2003 on a new strategic link main between the company's two main abstraction works on the River Avon, at Matchams and Knapp Mill. Water from Longham Lakes would be used in an emergency situation, such as a river pollution incident, and in the event of an incident on the River Stour it could be pumped to the treatment works at Alderney utilising the existing infrastructure. However, it was not possible to pump it directly to the treatment works at Knapp Mill, which meant that a similar incident on the River Avon was not so easily covered. By temporarily reversing the normal flow in the existing main, water could be pumped from Longham to Matchams, so the new link main was needed to pump that emergency supply onward to Knapp Mill. It was completed in 2005.

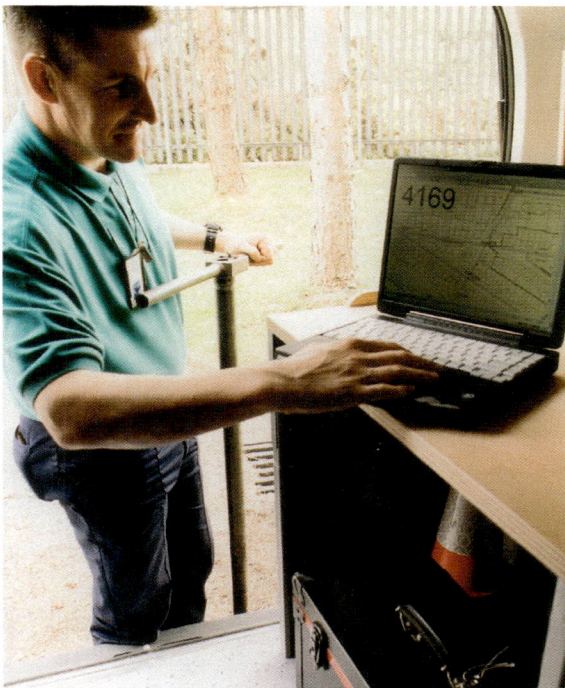

Mobile working

Also in 2003, a mobile field working system was introduced, which allows job and customer information to be uploaded to a vehicle-mounted ruggedised laptop and interact with GIS and mapping information already stored on the computer. It also allows the field crew to submit sketches to enable the GIS to be updated if they find discrepancies whilst in the field. The data is updated either by docking the laptop during a visit to headquarters or via a mobile telephone link. With almost two-thirds of the company's staff working out in the field, instant access to this information greatly improves productivity and efficiency, including less travelling time, less time spent in the office and dramatically reduced printing costs. The system, called NOMAD, was originally based on the Smallworld GIS system that had been introduced in the early 1990s. Smallworld was replaced in 2010 by a new GIS system called ESRI, allowing greater integration with other company systems, including billing and job management.

Automation of the smaller outlying pumping stations had commenced during the 1980s, together with remote control of critical assets. This had been extended during the 1990s, and since the early part of the new century, all of the company's production plant has been monitored and operated from a central control room at Alderney. Gone forever are the days when each waterworks site had at least one operator permanently stationed there to not only deal with emergency situations, but also actually to monitor conditions and manually operate the valves and pumps when required. This was necessary because most of the sites supplied a specific geographical area, but now the entire system is interlinked enabling water to be transferred from a reservoir on one side of the company's area of operation to a village on the opposite side, at the flick of a switch.

This has been made possible by a computerised system known as SCADA, which stands for Supervisory Control and Data Acquisition. Most control functions are performed automatically at the remote sites by Programmable Logic Controllers, which control the flow of water through the system, feeding back alarm conditions, such as equipment failures, that are displayed and recorded on the central panel. The SCADA system monitors the overall performance, and provides analytical readings and equipment status reports, as well as facilities for the central operators to override the processes manually if necessary. The integrated communications systems also provide CCTV feeds from every site that are used for security, and also to enable critical operational periods to be monitored in real time.

One of the last sites to be automated was the Ampress works, which had served the Lymington area since before the Second World War. It was completely refurbished in 2005, including the fitment of new pumps, filters and treatment equipment. Such advances also enabled previously-uneconomic sites to be reassessed. In 2007, work began on bringing the Wimborne works back into operation. Initially developed in 1895, a lot of the machinery had been automated in the early 1970s, but due to the nature of the filtering treatment process, being both chemical and labour-intensive, the works were abandoned in 1989. The buildings and equipment were in a poor condition, and in need of extensive development simply to prevent their becoming dilapidated, so it was decided to refurbish and rebuild the works, including adding modern treatment processes, so that it could be run as an unmanned operational source pumping into the low pressure distribution network at Wimborne.

In essence, those last two projects sum-up the previous twenty years, during which the company made substantial internal investment running into tens of millions of pounds, most of which is invisible to the casual eye. The water still flows from the tap just as it always has, it even looks the same, although it is now cleaner and safer than it has ever been; the only time a consumer may notice anything untoward is if it doesn't appear at all. Similarly, drive over Longham Bridge and the waterworks buildings

look essentially the same as they did more than a hundred years ago, but inside they are full of state-of-the-art equipment, running 24/7 and controlled remotely. The only external clue today is you will rarely see a human being on the site, whereas back in Victorian times it would have been teeming with activity, as the stokers, blacksmiths and engineers manually kept the pumps working.

In 2006, Cascal became a wholly-owned subsidiary within the Biwater Group following Nuon's sale of its 50% interest to Biwater plc. The original strategy for the joint venture had been to bulk-up Cascal with acquisitions and then sell a majority stake to stock exchange investors who would then share the heavy capital requirements of an asset-owning water business. But in 2002, Nuon's own strategy moved away from water in favour of concentrating on energy activities in their core markets, and sought to withdraw from Cascal. Up to that point no additional investments had been made by Cascal, and that became the status quo whilst approval was obtained from the relevant authorities for the withdrawal of Nuon. Following the completion of the deal, Cascal purchased China Water from Thames Water, and then added further interests in South Africa and the Caribbean the following year. In January 2008, Cascal undertook an Initial Public Offering of 42% of its common stock and became listed on the New York Stock Exchange with an enterprise value of $600 million.

In July 2007, devastating flooding hit some areas of the UK when, after one of the wettest Junes on record, more than a month's rainfall was recorded in just one day. Gloucestershire was the worst affected county, with the Gloucestershire Fire and Rescue Service attending 1,800 calls in a single forty-eight-hour period, when normally they attend 8,000 in an entire year. On 22nd July,

Gloucester rescue crew

road access to Tewkesbury was completely cut-off with parts of the town under a metre of water. The Mythe Water Treatment Works was flooded and by 24th July, 420,000 people were without drinking water, including most of the population of Gloucester, Cheltenham, and Tewkesbury. Severn Trent Water estimated that water supplies would not be restored for at least fourteen days.

As part of a 'mutual aid' agreement between all water suppliers, bowsers were brought in from all over the country to distribute drinking water to the stricken area. Bournemouth & West Hampshire Water also sent four emergency road tankers to the city, together with drivers and managers. The tankers operated round-the-clock, filling roadside tanks and delivering 200,000 litres of fresh water a day to the local community. It was not until August that supplies returned to any semblance of normality. In a media interview afterwards, Managing Director, Tony Cooke, described staff efforts as nothing short of

magnificent: *"We had a call to our Control Room for help at two o'clock in the morning and within six hours our staff were at work in Gloucester. We've had letters and emails from people in Gloucester who saw our tankers on the streets and wrote to say 'thank you' and we want to express our own gratitude to our crews as well."* Technical Director Roger Harrington added: *"This was a quite unprecedented event in the water industry and everyone rallied round to help the local water supplier. Our crews spent ten days in Gloucester, playing a vital role at a time when crucial infrastructure was severely disrupted during what was a national emergency."*

In 2007, the Bournemouth company's overall performance saw them rise to second in the OFWAT overall national ratings. In the same year, the Poole-based company Pre-Heat, which provided a gas installation and maintenance service to local authorities and housing associations, became a subsidiary. During 2008,

New Fawley Pumping Station at Knapp Mill

the separate pumping station at Knapp Mill that had serviced the Fawley Refinery supply uninterrupted for over fifty years was replaced. Due to the requirement for continuous running, the old station could not be modernised without an extended shutdown, so the new station was erected alongside and gradually brought on line until the old units could be stopped. The other main capital projects that year were the addition of a second Chase Farm service reservoir plus a new reservoir at Woodgreen, both to overcome local demand issues.

In 2009, Bournemouth & West Hampshire Water reached the top spot in the OFWAT annual overall performance ratings, a position they retained in 2010 as well. That same year, Biwater sold its majority stake in Cascal, the company's ultimate owner, to Singapore-based Sembcorp Utilities, who then launched a full

bid for Cascal on the New York Stock Exchange. Sembcorp Utilities is a subsidiary of Sembcorp Industries, which was formed in 1998 by the merger of two major conglomerates, Sembawang Corp and Singapore Technologies Industrial Corp. The resultant group has a focus on marine engineering, utilities, waste management and industrial parks, the acquisition of Cascal adding municipal water suppliers in Europe and South America to their existing utilities portfolio of water treatment and power generation plants in the Far and Middle East.

In August 2010, Sembcorp announced it had acquired 97.6% of the issued Cascal shares, heralding the beginning of another era in Bournemouth & West Hampshire Water's history.

Drilling & Tapping

Teams from Bournemouth & West Hampshire Water have regularly competed in the Institute of Water Officers National Drilling and Tapping Championships. These involve teams of two, completing the task of a simulated house connection in the highway, competitors having to drill and tap a pressurised 150 millimetre diameter ductile iron main and install the service connection, including a meter, in the shortest possible time. Quality of the work and compliance with safety procedures is paramount, with time penalties being added for any infringements.

The event was instigated in 1989 by John Clement, the company's Distribution Manager at the time, initially as a demonstration within the Watertec exhibition held at the Bournemouth International Centre. The following year, it was turned into an annual contest held during the IWEX show in Birmingham, attracting teams from all over the country and, eventually, international entrants as well. In 2002, a team including Duncan Sharples from Bournemouth and Doug White from the company's main contractors, A H Ball, became national champions, going on to represent the UK in the World Championships in Anaheim in 2003, where they finished a creditable tenth.

In 2005, for the first time teams from the company became UK Champions in their own right in both mens and ladies competitions, Peter Haslock and Danny Hunt achieving a time of just two minutes seven seconds in the mens, just a second outside of the world record. The winning ladies team were Sallyann Vermaak and Kelly Bolt. The following year, Peter and Danny broke the world record, but as it was during a demonstration, it did not enter the record books. The same team took the title again in 2007 and the following year, travelled together with

Drilling and Tapping Team, 2005

James Craig and coach Barrie Light to Atlanta to represent the UK in the World Water Cup, which they also won. Barrie has worked for the company since 1978, and is a third-generation employee, his father having worked on the district and his grandfather in the control room.

In 2008, both teams repeated these successes, this time with Richard Barton replacing Barrie Light as the coach of the 2009 World Water Cup-winning team. Peter Haslock and Danny Hunt won the National Championships for the fourth time in 2011, before going on to be runners-up in the equivalent competition in Holland, and then to representing the UK, together with Barrie Light and Richard Barton in the World Water Cup in Dallas, where they were also runners-up. Further success followed in 2012 with a second win in an International competition between teams from the home nations.

Longham Lakes today

Longham Lakes

What appear at first glance to be two natural lakes alongside the main A348 Ringwood Road in the village of Longham are, in fact, the result of the largest capital investment project ever undertaken by the company - two man-made reservoirs that, from concept to being put into service, took nearly twenty years to complete.

That initial impression is no accident as, right from square one, the intention was to create a large bankside reservoir storage facility in a natural habitat. Bankside storage is a relatively new term in the water industry, and represents the statutory requirement to have sufficient emergency supplies of good quality source water available to provide physical insurance against unexpected interruption to water sources. Such events may be natural, caused by extreme weather conditions, or man-made through pollution incidents. In either case, there must be sufficient stored water available for treatment that can be pumped into the supply system to allow the company to remove the affected source from service for sufficient time, numbered in days rather than hours, to take the necessary rectification action.

In 1991, West Hampshire Water Company purchased the disused Ibsley Aerodrome for raw water storage use. By the time of purchase, the 300-acre aerodrome site had been quarried extensively over nearly twenty years and was earmarked as part of the second phase of the Blashford Lakes project on the River Avon north of Ringwood, developed in conjunction with New Forest District Council and Wessex Water plc. The West Hampshire part of the project was commenced in 1992 to convert two disused quarries on the site to storage lakes, called Ibsley Water and Mockbeggar Lake, which were completed in 1996.

Also in 1991, Bournemouth & District Water Co had a similar scheme under consideration, and

Chairman Kenneth Gardener cuts the first turf at Longham Lakes in 1995

it soon became apparent that the location of that scheme, at Longham, was far more suitable for creating the large-scale bunded reservoirs required to be linked into the existing distribution network. As part of the joint resource strategy introduced after Biwater had acquired both companies, Longham was selected as the primary site for this development, and Ibsley was designated as a back-up facility to reduce direct abstraction during dry summers when rivers could be under ecological stress. Whereas the lakes at Longham would be rapidly refilled from existing pumping stations, those at Ibsley are allowed to refill naturally from ground water sources and winter flood waters.

Because of the longer-term aspect of the use of Ibsley, it is now primarily a nature reserve, managed by Hampshire & Isle of Wight Wildlife Trust. The site is an important bird sanctuary, with widgeon and shoveler the most numerous residents, plus other water fowl such as teal, gadwall, goosander, goldeneye, pochard and pintail also regular visitors, along with the occasional woodpecker or egret. A study centre was opened there in 1996 which is regularly visited by school groups who also use the various nature trails created on the site.

Following two years of assessment and consultation, in 1993 Bournemouth & District Water Co was granted planning consent by Dorset County Council to construct water

Aerial view of Longham Lakes construction

storage reservoirs on the Longham site. It was estimated that the scheme, called Longham Lakes, would take around fifteen years to complete, with the first of three lakes being available for use by the end of the century. The site was on part of the 148 acres of land purchased in 1981, which was fairly low-grade farming land that had not been used for many years. It did, however, contain substantial gravel deposits, and the permissions included the extraction of those deposits to help finance the construction of the lakes, which were to be part of an ecologically-designed scheme.

The essential plan was to take off the topsoil, extract the gravel reserves beneath, then use the displaced topsoil and other sub-soil to construct embankments around the void created by the extraction, after which water would be pumped in to create a lake. Southern Science, part of Southern Water plc, were appointed as consultants due to their recent experience on a similar scheme at Testwood in Hampshire. A local civil engineering company, Warings of Portsmouth, was contracted to remove the gravel within the constraints applied by the planning, which also prevented any other material from leaving the site, then construct the necessary embankments and landscape the surrounding areas.

They, in turn, sub-contracted the mineral extraction to Hall Aggregates, part of the RMC Group, while the design and installation of all of

Pipe-laying at Longham Lakes, 2007

Bank construction on the southern lake in 2008

the water services infrastructure was retained by Bournemouth & West Hampshire Water. The first turf was cut by the company's Chairman, Kenneth Gardener, during a special ceremony on the site in September 1995.

Of course, reality is never as simple as the original plan, and there were many twists and turns in the project as it progressed. The gravel deposits proved to be shallower than originally anticipated and contained a higher percentage of silt and fines. Although this was a potential problem financially, it was managed in a way that did not compromise the overall project budget. It did, however, mean that the completed lakes are shallower than anticipated in some areas, plus a larger number of silt

ponds were required for washing and storage during construction.

After the mineral extraction for the first lake, located at the northern end of the site, was completed in 2000, the decision was taken to combine the other two into one larger southern lake. There were two factors that influenced this decision: firstly, there was a need to reduce infrastructure construction costs to meet efficiency savings under regulatory parameters and, secondly, the amount of engineering soil proved to be far less than required to construct the banks for three lakes. Some of the material shortfall was, however, made up by utilising clay base material, and the extra silt and fines residues were used in the landscaping.

Construction of layers, 2008

This entailed a greater amount of material movement within the site, as only the extracted gravel was allowed to leave the boundaries, and one of the resultant silt ponds could not be fully emptied resulting in an even more shallow area at the south-western corner of this second lake.

The statistics for the lakes are quite impressive: 1.75 million tonnes of gravel was extracted and 750,000 tonnes of material used to build the embankments. The volume of the lakes is around a million cubic metres at depths varying from 2.5 to 6 metres, enough water to cover the company's entire supply for approximately fifteen days, pumped to and from the lakes through 1.5 kilometres of 1-metre diameter pipe. Water is primarily pumped in from the abstraction points at Matchams or Longham, and out to the treatment plant at Alderney.

The material in the bed of each lake is London Clay, but once the gravel was extracted this was shown to be more inconsistent than expected. In some areas there were pockets of sand running through the strata providing potential water flow paths, causing considerable construction problems on the eastern and southern sides, where it proved difficult to lower the water table for sufficient time to create dry-enough working conditions. This was solved by digging cut-off trenches and sealing them with a material called Bentonite, a naturally-occurring clay which is liquid when agitated and, when mixed with cement and water, can be pumped. Once allowed to settle and dry for sufficient time it solidifies to the consistency of custard to form a watertight seal. The delays caused by this factor alone added a quarter of a million pounds to the project cost.

The engineered embankments around each lake had to be constructed in layers approximately 200 millimetres thick, and the biggest problem with this was bringing the material to the correct moisture content of 5% - too wet and it was not strong enough; too dry and it could not be compacted to the correct consistency. Ideal weather conditions for this work are warm with a drying breeze which, in Britain, normally occur between June and September. However, a run of wet summers between 1998 and 2002 played havoc with that part of the programme.

In 1998, the neighbouring property of Longham House was acquired, primarily to provide access to the north lake which, once it was put into use, would otherwise be restricted during construction of the southern lake. It was a rambling, somewhat run-down, 18th century Queen Anne brick house, and was purchased from the executors of Miss Selina Bush. This enabled the company to use the land at the border to create vehicular access to the north lake, and there was sufficient additional area to accommodate a car park and study centre, the latter completed in 2009. Longham House, and Miss Bush, are mentioned in the autobiography of Dame Jane Goodall, the world-famous primatologist, who attended Uplands School in Poole. She regularly visited the house for riding lessons as a teenager just after the war, when it was a riding school run by Miss Bush and her assistant, Sheila McNaughton, whom Goodall nicknamed Bushel and Poosh respectively. The house and the remaining land were sold in 2004 to a property developer, who subsequently restored the house and converted it to two residences.

Environmentally, the original plan essentially focussed around the creation of an artificial badger set to accommodate a local colony that would be displaced. Other indigenous wildlife in the area, such as deer, brown hares, lizards and snakes, were expected to naturally adapt to the change of environment. However, as construction proceeded it created transitory conditions that attracted non-indigenous red-book species. For example, as the fields became gravel pits, they created ideal breeding conditions for ringed plovers moving inland from their normal coastal areas. Once the gravel had gone, the exposed sand and clay beds attracted a rare type of sand wasp. In each case, work had to stop in the affected areas until the temporary residents moved on.

Once the north lake was filled, the area became of interest to all manner of water fowl. However, as Longham is situated below the flightpath for Bournemouth Airport, there was considerable concern regarding potential for birdstrikes. A bird management plan was proposed by the local authority to prevent large flocks of starlings or seagulls from roosting, which contained some strange concepts, such as netting the entire lake surface. When this was rejected as impractical, as it would have prevented all birds from landing, the next suggestion was to set off numerous bird scarers and flares an hour before dawn and an hour after dusk each day. This was also rejected as it would not have been popular with local residents. Some bird scarers were eventually installed, but these simply broadcast distress calls. In addition, low maintenance anti-bird grass was sown which grows only to a certain length, long enough for predators, but not high enough for the birds to hide. This makes them uneasy and reluctant to roost.

Man-made reservoirs can tend to look like a box, with steep earthen banks to contain the water, so it was decided to landscape the embankments at Longham to be as natural as possible. As any large body of water is subject to surface waves driven by prevailing winds, natural curves were incorporated to dissipate the waves and, to counteract the resulting natural erosion process in some areas,

Longham Lakes Study Centre

a planting scheme was added incorporating natural reed beds that would diffuse the wave energy.

Project manager at Longham Lakes was Peter Ferenczy, who recognised the challenges presented: *"Most of our projects are fairly small and on tightly-confined sites that have always been waterworks and do not have significant environmental-impact issues. Longham Lakes was very different. Here we created entire natural habitats with their own eco-systems, and have used some of our other land to the west and south of the lakes to add contrasting environmental landscapes incorporating tree-planting, creating meadows, and so on, to end-up with both dry and wetlands."*

Fundamentally the lakes are there for water storage, but the northern lake was also stocked initially by the company with carp, roach, bream, tench and pike, enabling fishing to take place there in conjunction with the Ringwood and District Anglers Association. However, the lake population is not artificially increased or the fish intensively fed to create large specimens, which makes it quite a hard fishery. There are two islands in the southern lake that predators cannot get to, allowing birds to breed there. One of them was created by natural intervention, as Peter explained: *"I had a heap of topsoil stored on the quarry floor when one of those circumstances occurred when our environmentalist found a rare visitor and had to order us to stop work in the area. We couldn't get to the soil to move it, although we could have done so eventually, but the delay and cost of doing this was prohibitive, so I decided we would work around it. Which is how it became an island."*

It was also necessary to have an archaeologist on site whenever topsoil was stripped, to assess any important discoveries. Between 1998 and 2001, sporadic evidence emerged of a well-established Bronze Age settlement, and then in 2004 a burial site was unearthed in the south west corner, comprising ring ditches and cremation urns, which were all removed to the Dorset County Museum. A mammoth tusk was also discovered preserved within the gravel deposits, which had been washed down the river tens of thousands of years earlier. It was sent away to be treated and preserved, and is now on display in the study centre.

The mammoth tusk on display in the study centre

A project of this nature, with such a long timescale, can cause considerable disruption to the surrounding area, and right from the start a liaison panel was formed, comprising representatives from the company and local interested parties, to manage the various concerns that were emerging, particularly around the potential disruption caused by increased noise, dust and traffic involved with the quarrying activity. The group, which met regularly over the entire period of the project, included Longham Residents' Association, Ferndown Council, Dorset County Council and other local environmental groups. Through this forum, it was possible to mitigate potential problems. Some of these involved specific long-term solutions, such as concerns over the movement of lorries to and from the site, which were overcome by contributions to improvements in the local road network that continue to provide a benefit to the local community long after the lorries have gone. But in a lot of cases, simple common-sense processes were sufficient, such as storing the

removed topsoil in mounds strategically located to attenuate site noise and keep dust down. By and large these measures worked well, apart from one major incident that occurred in 2002.

When quarrying commenced on the southern lake, the first part to be worked edged onto the River Stour floodplain, although the lake itself was outside of that. The water levels in the Stour can rise and fall very rapidly under extreme conditions and, over the years, the River Authority's floodplain engineering had developed to direct flash-floodwaters onto areas of open farmland and away from areas of habitation such as Longham village, where parts of Ringwood Road itself are below the natural level of the riverbank.

In 2001, the quarry operator had removed topsoil in preparation for extraction, including from the river bank, not realising that this had lowered a natural flood barrier. Even so, the lowered bank was only inches below the maximum flood levels and, under average conditions, the river flowed quite normally for many months. However, when a period of severely heavy rain put the river into flood, it overflowed the bank and flooded the quarry. Although this was a major setback in the work programme, the effects should have been contained within the quarry as the outer bank had been raised by the deposit of topsoil but, unfortunately, work was not sufficiently advanced for sealed embankment construction to have started.

Water always finds leakage paths, so the water in the quarry seeped out through an exposed gravel face and onto Ringwood Road, which became flooded to a depth of several inches along with the land surrounding some of the houses on the stretch between Longham Bridge and the church; this was exacerbated by blockages in some of the drainage ditches in the area which prevented the water from

Filling the lakes

draining away more rapidly. The road, a major link between Ringwood and Poole, was closed for several days while the water was pumped away. This was not a simple task as, although the riverbank was quickly reinstated, all of the water already in the quarry also had to be pumped away due to the low level of the leakage path under the outer bank.

Although no water entered the ground floors of any properties, at its peak the level rose to within an inch of the floorboards in properties with basements, taking-out electrical systems. In addition, cess pits, which serve most of the properties in that area, were flooded. Although it was the responsibility of the contractor, the company sent in an emergency response team who quickly organised alternative accommodation for the duration of the incident, pumped-out flooded basements, carried out works around the affected properties to stop any water from potentially re-entering and carried out reinstatement work. This was a very public mishap and did not endear the

company to the residents who, understandably, became very nervous of the potential for future problems, undermining the trust that had been built up over the previous ten years. As a consequence, a liaison team stayed in touch for many months afterwards to rebuild confidence, and there was no subsequent repeat of the problem.

A fair-sized carp

Hoopoe

It did not take long for the lakes and their associated habitats to attract feathered visitors, with over 150 species having been logged since the north lake was filled. On the water these include black-necked grebe, garganey, ruddy duck, and yellow-legged gulls. The tall bushes that surround the northern and western sides of the lake attract reed buntings, while the reed beds that are dotted around the banks have breeding reed warblers, bearded tits and water rails. The islands are home to green sandpipers and ringed plovers, who still return every spring, while the causeway between the two lakes has proved to be the area where the more rare species have been found, ortolan bunting and blue-headed wagtail being spotted there during 2011. Very rare birds can, of course, attract large numbers of birdwatchers, and 2010 produced a flurry of activity as word spread via the internet of the arrival of a hoopoe. This extremely unusual visitor to these shores, with a distinctive crest, hails from Africa and normally migrates to the Mediterranean, but can occasionally overshoot due to unusual changes in prevailing wind patterns.

There were initial concerns from the local community about potential usage as a water park, but the company has ensured that any regular usage is restricted to quiet recreational activities. With the limited parking space and maintenance of a policy of restricting access to authorised users, the quieter nature of the site together with the wide, flat paths around both lakes makes it ideal for school and educational visits in conjunction with the study centre, which incorporates displays of the company's water awareness and education schemes. More recently, the Poole Runners staged a 5 kilometre fun run utilising the lakeside pathways.

As well as the licensed anglers and some official bird-ringing activity, authorised users include the Poole Radio Yacht Club, who started sailing their larger wind-powered models there in 2011. They were soon joined by the Christchurch and District Model Flying Club, who have a small group flying on the south lake with battery-powered model flying boats and floatplanes. The third club using the water is Dorset's Ultimate Canoe Kayak Squad who run twice-weekly club and race training sessions. The club provides teaching, training and playing about in canoes and kayaks for more than sixty members aged from seven to seventy years.

District Model Flying Club

An idyllic spot near the lakes

With the opening of the south lake in 2010 by Milo Purcell, Deputy Chief Inspector of the Drinking Water Inspectorate, the main project reached completion, although ongoing maintenance and impact assessment will continue for many years. The total cost of just over £15 million was within the parameters of the original budget set more than fifteen years previously, a creditable outcome bearing in mind the unexpected nature of some of the developments, including environmental requirements that completely changed during that period. The results provide a significant environmental improvement from the previous underutilised farmland, with a final water storage capacity of around 1,000 megalitres and a recreational area that affords access to the local community to enjoy and walk around.

The final word must go to Peter Ferenczy, who ran this project from shortly after quarrying commenced in 1995, to completion: *"I'm really proud to have been involved managing the project. It gives me a lot of pleasure going down and walking around the lakes on a summer's day - the birds are singing and the ducks are out, all the reeds are growing and you think 'that's lovely'. It's there for a function, it's there for a purpose, but there is added value to peoples' lives over and above the function and purpose it was designed for. It's probably the best project I've ever done, and it's really nice to have left something that people will still be enjoying in perpetuity, long after I'm gone."*

Green-Winged Orchids

The lakes at Longham and Blashford are not the only company sites where rare wildlife flourishes. Originally built over one hundred years ago, and still in service today, No.3 Reservoir at Alderney was roofed during the 1950s and subsequently turfed. Soon afterwards, staff began to notice that, for a few weeks during late spring each year, the roof began to shimmer with a purple haze of colour. Closer inspection showed that a rare wild orchid, Anacamptis Morio, had colonised the area.

Language scholars may observe that Moros is Latin for 'Fool', which comes from the appearance of the flowers that resemble a jester's hat. So why has the plant acquired the title of green-winged? Well, if you look closely at the blossoms, you will see that the side petals, or 'wings', have fine green stripes. This orchid is one of a group of threatened plants dependent on infertile or nutrient-poor grasslands, primarily in the southern half of England. Once widespread, it has declined steadily since the war due to loss of natural habitat through agricultural improvement of native grassland. Despite lacking nectar, the sweet flowers are attractive to insects, particularly queen bumblebees that have just emerged from hibernation.

The reservoir is in an area of land designated a Site of Nature Conservation Interest (SNCI) by the Borough of Poole. Because of this, and the results of studies carried out elsewhere, it was known that the number of orchids would decline should engineering work be required to the reservoir. So when repair work to the reservoir roof became necessary in 2002, the company drew up a management plan to minimise disturbance while the deep turfs were stripped from the roof and stored nearby.

Part of this included a monitoring scheme in conjunction with students from Bournemouth University, who conducted regular counts of the plant population leading up to the work, and afterwards.

The turfs were put back in early 2004, and that year there was a marked decline in the numbers of plants. The following year, the numbers declined even further, but in 2006 they recovered significantly, and by the spring of 2007, the count showed that the colony had returned to its pre-maintenance numbers. In recent years, the flowers have also started to colonise the area surrounding the reservoir, and the project has been hailed as "a great success" by the University's senior lecturer in Ecology, Dr Anita Diaz.

Sembcorp Bournemouth Water sign goes up on George Jessel House

Sembcorp

With Sembcorp as their ultimate shareholder, Bournemouth & West Hampshire Water plc changed their registered name to Sembcorp Bournemouth Water Ltd on 21st January 2011.

The company logo and branding was upgraded to reflect the new ownership and Mr Tang Kin Fei, Group President and CEO of Sembcorp, joined the Board of directors. Throughout 2011 there were other changes at Board level when long-standing Biwater and Cascal representatives reached retirement and stepped down in favour of Sembcorp directors and appointees, including Mr Tan Cheng Guan, Sembcorp's Executive Vice President for Group Business and Strategic Development, who had led the acquisition process.

Operationally there were some major changes, with Tony Cooke retiring after nineteen years at the helm, during which time he had overseen a seachange in the company's operations driven, primarily, by the radical changes in industry regulation. In a feature published shortly before his retirement, a leading industry journal commented: *"Tony is one of the longest serving CEOs in the UK water industry and has done an outstanding job in creating the culture of efficiency and customer service which has been so vital in contributing to the company's success as one of the best performing water companies in the UK."*

He was succeeded as Managing Director by Roger Harrington, who had been the company's Chief Engineer, then Technical Director, since 1993 and was instrumental in overseeing all of the major technical innovations and improvements introduced during that time. A new Finance Director, Peter Bridgewater, also arrived. He had spent 16 years with the E.ON Group during which time he had been Finance Director of their regulated power distribution company and Managing Director of their energy commodity trading business.

New Finance Director Peter Bridgewater (left) is welcomed by Managing Director Roger Harrington

Of course, change is always unsettling, so it is good to know the level of backing a subsidiary company has at group Board level. In an interview shortly after the acquisition, Tan Cheng Guan said: "The UK regulated business is a very good business in our view. It's very well regulated and very stable, and has a lot of competencies, a lot of knowledge and a lot of experienced people, which may be helpful for Sembcorp to grow its business further."

The company's investment programme, running at around £9 million annually through the current five-year pricing period, was focussed during 2011 on leakage and treatment, with the installation of a new ultraviolet treatment system at Woodgreen and the sealing of over 120 metres of a very large diameter concrete pipe at Knapp Mill using polyethylene internal lining. The steel water tower at Beaulieu Hilltop was replaced after more than sixty years of service in two locations, having been dismantled and moved there from Redlynch in the 1950s. A new link main was completed from Ringwood to Verwood at a cost of £1 million to provide the town with an alternative source

of supply and significantly reduce the risk of a water supply failure. A large amount of the 5.7 kilometres of pipe was laid in the New Forest, working closely with the Forestry Commission and Natural England in order to reduce traffic disruption as far as possible.

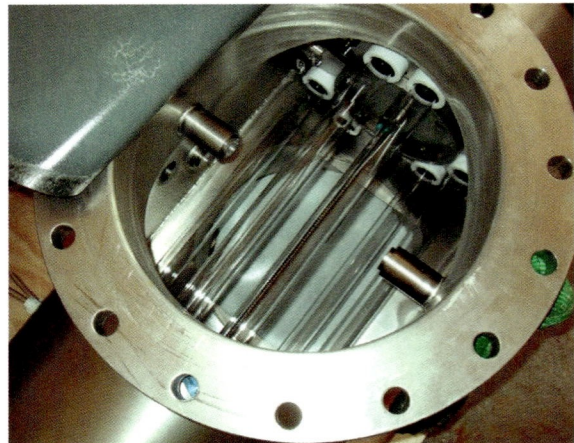

Woodgreen Ultraviolet Plant

The Ringwood to Verwood Link Main being laid across Forestry Commission land

Pupils taking part in a Waterwise Presentation

The company's Waterwise Presentation programme to primary schools was seen by over 4,000 children during 2011. Commenced the previous year, the presentation integrates with the National Curriculum, emphasising the importance of using water wisely and enabling the schools to include the presentations as part of their School Eco Award. Feedback is very favourable, even from parents whose children begin policing their home water usage! At secondary level the company attends school careers fairs and provides tours of the Alderney Treatment Works. It also sponsored a Youth Conference on Sustainability and the Earth Charter attended by pupils from local schools, one from Yorkshire and web-linked with another in South Africa.

The company has been an integral part of the community it serves throughout its history and, together with its staff, supports a wide range of local, national and international charities. It provides long-term support for local charities including Julia's House, Life Education Wessex, Cherry Tree Nursery, BSVI, LV=Streetwise and the Sparkle Appeal amongst many others. Staff fundraising has long been a part of the organisation's ethos, the annual sports days of the 1920s and 1930s benefiting the Cornelia Hospital, now Poole General, which like all hospitals was privately-funded prior to the formation of the NHS in 1947. Today members of staff regularly take part in walks, distance runs, cycle rides, swims, abseils, skydives and some very 'extreme' challenges such as Ironman triathlons and the Kalahari Augrabies Marathon. For the less-athletic there are events such as raffles, dress down days, quizzes and cake sales, whilst others travel overseas to work on projects in orphanages, schools and hospitals.

People *Service Awards 2010, 785 years' combined service*

People

Customer Service
Excellence 2011

WaterAid Speakers

One of the main beneficiaries of this energy is WaterAid, which was originally formed in 1981 by people within the UK water industry, and works to provide safe water, adequate sanitation and hygiene education in the poorest countries of the world. Initially working in just eight countries in Africa and Asia, but now active in twenty-seven, it has provided help to over seventeen million people. The company's staff have been involved with the charity since its inception, organising regular fundraisers, individually taking part in sponsored sporting events and volunteering to take part in the charity's projects overseas. In 1993, the company began sending out appeal leaflets with its bills, and over the ensuing twenty years voluntary donations totalling over half a million pounds have been made to the charity by its customers. In 2002, the 21st anniversary of the charity was celebrated at a Birthday Party Barbecue hosted by the company at Alderney, and in 2011, WaterAid marked its 30th anniversary by presenting the company with the charity's highest honour, the President's Award, for the long-term support it has provided.

One of the 'mane' events in the local community during 2011 was the 'Pride in Bournemouth' public art event which saw fifty life-sized lion sculptures on display throughout the town, each decorated in a unique, specially-commissioned colour scheme. Bournemouth Water sponsored one of these figures, named 'Singha'. The name, the Sanskrit word for lion, was chosen because parent company Sembcorp is based in Singapore - literally 'Lion City' - named as such because of the strange beast spotted by the city's founder, Sang Nila Utama, while hunting in the area during the 14th century, and seen by him as a good omen for building a new city there. Singha's colour scheme, incorporating varying shades of blue, together with glass tiles and beads, was designed and painted by Sallyann Smith and Andrea Todd of GetSet Graphics to illustrate how water would flow over him.

Singha was located in Bournemouth's Lower Gardens where he attracted a great deal of attention, although it was the worst possible place to be during the freak storm that flooded the gardens in August that year, following which Sallyann and Andrea had to give him a thorough bath and tidy-up. At the end of the summer, the company won the bidding for Singha when all fifty sculptures were auctioned at a special charity event hosted by Martin Clunes and Virginia McKenna representing the two charities, Julia's House and The Born Free Foundation, which jointly benefited from the money raised. After being put on display in the reception area of George Jessel House, Singha was donated to Cranborne First School in July 2012, where he took up permanent residence among the flowers in their secret garden.

Singha in the lower gardens, Bournemouth

During 2012, work commenced on a number of refurbishments of company buildings. The workshops and offices at the Quadrant built in the 1970s were showing their age, the roof of the workshop having been repaired a number of times. An external refurbishment was carried out to improve the thermal efficiency and extend the life of the buildings by at least another thirty years, and an internal refurbishment is following during 2013. The offices on the riverside at Knapp Mill that had stood unused for some years were also completely refurbished to house the staff of Sembcorp Utility Services, whose offices in Leatherhead had to be vacated. One of the major projects under consideration for the near future is a replacement for the headquarters building at George Jessel House, which is more than sixty years old and, having been refurbished twice during that period, no longer offers the levels of practicality and energy-efficiency necessary in today's business environment.

People

Drilling & Tapping winning team 2011

People *Staff Briefing 2012*

Solar Panels at Stanbridge

Another priority is on substantially reducing energy bills and lowering carbon footprint. Water is a heavy product, Sembcorp Bournemouth Water produces nearly 150,000 tonnes of it every day, so by far the major cause of the company's greenhouse gas emissions is the electricity used to move it around, pumping it from rivers and boreholes through the treatment works and distribution network to the customer. Savings can be achieved by having to pump less water around, and the company's continued focus on helping its consumers to reduce their usage, and hence their bills, is spearheaded by the ongoing metering project. The results of this are demonstrated by the annual amount of water supplied having fallen by 12% since meters were introduced in 1995, with a direct and equivalent effect on the use of electricity. Meter penetration passed 62% in 2012, and the company is well on track to achieve its target of having every customer metered by 2027.

For some years the company has calculated the amount of carbon created as a result of its activities and, in 2009, gained the Carbon Trust Standard – only the third water company to gain the accreditation at that time. It is currently demonstrating a year on year reduction of 2.5% on carbon emissions, and has ongoing projects to replace electric motors with more efficient types, revisit a wind turbine project at Alderney that was first investigated in 2006, and investigate the possibility of a return to hydropower operation at Knapp Mill and Longham. During 2012, seven trial installations were made in the use of panels for powering pumping equipment and, if the results prove as anticipated, similar installations will be rolled-out across other company sites during the next two years.

Having held the Investors in People accreditation for nearly twenty years, for the latest assessment the company decided to test itself against the highest level of that standard, the Gold Level, an award only attained by 3% of

Investors in People Gold

the companies in the scheme. This was achieved at the first attempt, with this citation received in early 2013 from the independent assessor:

"The leadership and Management at SBW is impressive, blending achievement of business targets with very good people, policies and practices. Staff believe they are well led and managed, they enjoy their work, are proud to work for the company and are committed to its success. The company's core values are alive and kicking throughout the enterprise - customer service is particularly important and it's a pleasure to witness how individuals and teams combine to deliver a quality service to the customer. It was a pleasure to get an 'inside look' into such a good organisation and I look forward to a return visit in a couple of years."

All of this work, and more besides, continues to maintain the company at the forefront of the water industry, and as it approaches yet another milestone anniversary, the headlines from its latest annual report speak for themselves. The company supplies an average of around 145 million litres of safe drinking water every day of the year to an area of 1,041 square kilometres with a population of over 430,000 in more than 203,000 separate properties via a mains network 2,806 kilometres long. To do this it maintains an estate of fifteen reservoir sites, supplied from six separate sources, purified at eight treatment works and powered by numerous pumping stations; and it does all of this with under 200 staff.

In addition, the company maintains positions at or near the top of every league table for criteria set by its regulator, whether they be in water quality, reliability of service and delivery, reduction in leakage, customer service or environmental impact.

Sembcorp Bournemouth Water Headquaters, George Jessel House

So if William Cash and Edward Woods were able to return in September 2013 to inspect the company that has evolved from the small provincial gasworks that they first proposed to the Bournemouth Commissioners 150 years earlier, what would be their reaction? They would doubtless be surprised that it had no involvement in the gas industry, and that the smaller aspect that they also agreed to take on had become such a major undertaking. They would probably marvel at the technological advances, but not at their adoption by a company that, from the outset, sought to be at the leading edge of its industry. Neither would they be taken aback by the environmental priorities of the day, as despite the old heavy industrial manner of Victorian gas production, their works were always made to run as efficiently, and therefore cleanly and safely, as the technology of the times allowed.

But what would probably make them, as well as their many successors as directors and engineers, most satisfied would be the continued outstanding reputation of the company, not only locally with its hundreds of thousands of satisfied customers, but also worldwide in its industry making it an integral part of a major global group based on the other side of the world, a reputation enhanced by the pride exhibited by the employees in being part of what they still see as *their* company. I think they would nod approvingly at what the company has become:

An English jewel in an oriental crown.

celebrating

150 years

Sembcorp Bournemouth Water

To my parents, who taught me to taste the world, and to Craig and Bessie, my favourite people to taste it with. – G.L.

To Edy Tavares, who showed me love through Cape Verdean food. – T.G.

Phaidon Press Limited
2 Cooperage Yard
London E15 2QR

phaidon.com

First published 2024
© 2024 Phaidon Press Limited
Text © Gabrielle Langholtz 2024
Illustrations © Tânia García 2024

Artwork created digitally

ISBN 978 1 83866 770 2 (UK edition)
004-0724

A CIP catalogue record for this book is available from the British Library.

Printed in China

Edited by: Alice-May Bermingham
Production by: Rebecca Price
Designed by: Laura Hambleton

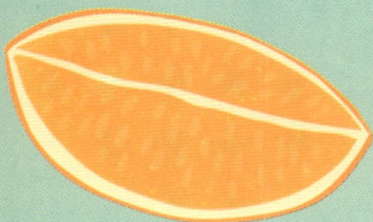

A WORLD OF FLAVOUR

A CELEBRATION OF FOOD AND RECIPES FROM AROUND THE GLOBE

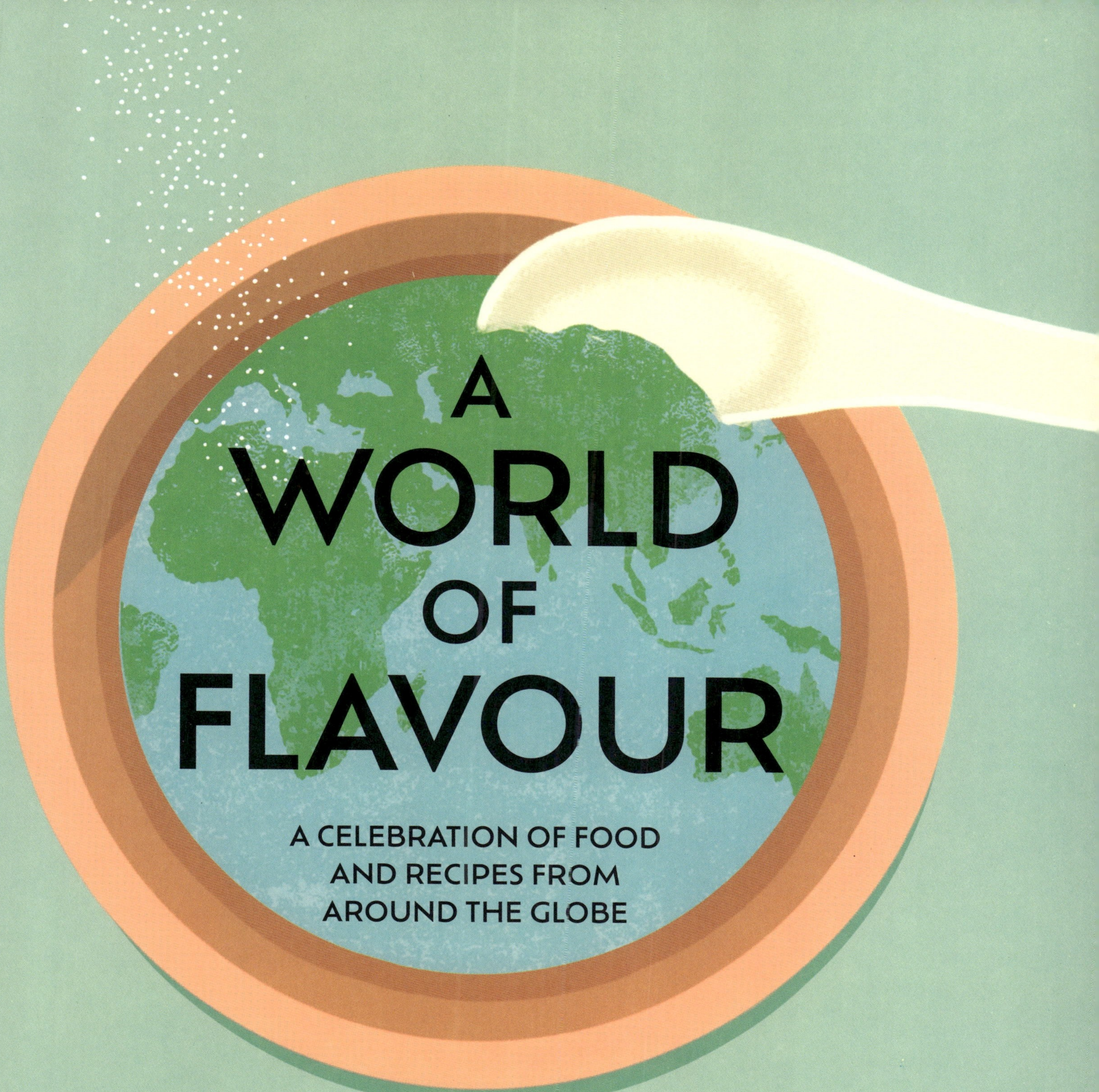

Gabrielle Langholtz

Illustrated by **Tània García**

Φ

TABLE OF CONTENTS

TASTE THE WORLD

Working on this book reminded me that two opposite ideas are both true: one is that all around the world, we're different. The other is that all around the world, we're the same! I'll explain.

These pages celebrate the many wonderful ways that cultures and cuisines are unique. Depending on where you live, you might catch fish or milk goats, cook over coals or in well-seasoned woks, prefer potatoes, pasta or plantains, breakfast on rice congee or mandazi doughnuts, snack on empanadas or injera, shop from street-side carts or floating riverboat markets, eat with forks or fingers, from skewers or chopsticks, smoke salmon or salt cod, pick papayas or pomegranates, offer guests yerba mate or lemonade, feast on camel or go vegetarian, keep jars of togarashi or za'atar, sip sharbat or soursop smoothies, slather toast with Marmite™ or marmalade, ferment cream into yoghurt or cabbage into kraut, crown ice cream with dulce de leche or corn kernels, warm up with hot chai or cool down with the juice of a machete-whacked coconut, or top your dinner with shaved parmesan, spicy mayo, crushed peanuts, fresh lime, smoky salt or fermented fish sauce.

But the more I learn about the different foods we eat, the more I see how much we all have in common. We savour fresh fruit and preserve summer's bounty. We welcome guests with sweet treats, refreshing drinks and handmade hospitality. We celebrate births, weddings, holy days and holidays with feasts rich in memory and meaning. We boil grains, slurp noodles, bake flatbreads, stuff dumplings, simmer soups and sop up the juices. From little villages to big cities, we gather to give thanks for bountiful harvests.

While some cultures make traditional foods that go back millennia – so you might have to travel to Tibet to taste yak-butter tea – many immigrants have now brought beloved recipes to new lands. Today, you can enjoy Indian chapati in Kenya, Brazilian black beans in Canada, Japanese ramen in Peru, Nigerian jollof rice in England, pad thai in Australia and Taiwanese boba in the United States. And as people mix and mingle, our foods do too. Parisians savour North African merguez sausage in baguettes, while Californians top their tacos with Korean kimchi. You might say the world gets a little more delicious every day.

I was lucky to work on this book with super-smart people from around the globe. Of course, we couldn't fit all the world's foods into one book, so we focused on the most populous countries on each continent, with shout-outs to many more cultures along the way.

Some people say kids are picky eaters but I hope this book will help you prove them wrong. Children everywhere love all kinds of foods, including fishy fish, black pudding, spicy broth, stinky cheese and all sorts of fresh vegetables and help in the kitchen from the time they're little. Maybe you already like pita, baba ganoush, fresh ceviche, steaming pho, minty tabbouleh and steak with chimichurri sauce – these pages include recipes to make them all yourself, along with many other world favourites from Afghan plov and Australian pavlova to Moroccan harira and mohinga from Myanmar. And the truth is, you don't need to cook to enjoy this book. I hope just reading it will open your mind and your mouth, inspiring you to seek out global flavours, wherever you are. Food is a wonderful way to learn about how we're different and how much we have in common, no matter what we like for lunch.

Gabrielle Langholtz

With every recipe, you'll see a series of circles indicating how challenging it is to cook. Many have only one circle, indicating they are easier than average; most have two circles and are of average difficulty; and a handful of recipes have three circles, meaning that they are harder than average (and the most challenging in this book). Consider these ratings alongside your own experience level when deciding what to cook.

LEVEL OF DIFFICULTY
●

LEVEL OF DIFFICULTY
● ●

LEVEL OF DIFFICULTY
● ● ●

COOKING TIPS

Check in with a grown-up before you start cooking.
Make sure that there's someone close by who can help with any cooking or chopping, or in case you have questions.

Pay attention to the times given with each recipe to make sure you have enough time to see it through.
In most cases, there is no real way to speed things up and if you're new to cooking, it may take longer than noted.

Always read a recipe all the way through before you begin.
This way, you'll know which ingredients and equipment you need and there won't be any surprises once you've already started cooking.

Measure carefully and accurately.
This makes a big difference, especially when you are learning to cook.

Clean your work surface as you go.
Wash your hands and tools well, especially after touching raw fish or meat; move dirty things to the sink or dishwasher and wipe down the work surface as you move from one step to the next to avoid one big mess at the end.

Avoid throwing away good food.
You can often save bits of unused ingredients for other recipes.

Mind the heat!
Use heatproof gloves when handling food in and around the oven and follow what the recipe says about heat levels.

Learn to use your senses.
Sometimes you may be able tell that something is finished cooking by the way it looks, smells, sounds, feels and, of course, tastes. Recipes give you things to watch out for but if you think that something is ready before the time in the recipe, trust your instincts. Just make sure your meat, fish and eggs are fully cooked.

Have fun!
The goal is not to make something that looks picture-perfect but to be proud of your process and, hopefully, to cook something delicious! Like most skills worth learning, cooking is all about practice. The more you cook, the more you will improve and the more good things you will have to eat and share!

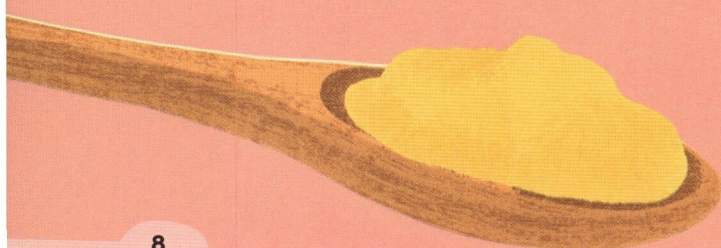

COOKING TERMS

BOILING

You'll know a liquid is boiling when you see large bubbles bursting rapidly on its surface.

SIMMERING

This happens just before boiling, when small bubbles just start to rise up to the surface of the cooking liquid. Often a recipe will ask you to bring something to the boil and then turn it down to a simmer. In that case, lower the heat until you just see bubbles breaking on the surface.

STEAMING

This is one way to cook vegetables with moist, gentle heat. Usually it involves using a steamer basket over simmering water in a pot with a tight-fitting lid.

BARBECUING

Cooking over a live fire. This is almost always over metal grates, with charcoal or gas flames.

ROASTING

This uses dry heat in the oven to make tender meats and vegetables.

BRAISING

This can happen on the hob top or in the oven. When foods are braised, they are partially submerged in liquid and slowly cooked over a low heat until deliciously tender.

GRILLING

Cooking directly under high heat in the oven. It's one way to get meats and vegetables to taste almost as good as those cooked outside on a barbecue.

BAKING

When something bakes, the dry heat of the oven is cooking it. This is usually how breads, cakes, pies and biscuits are made.

PAN-FRYING

Foods such as chicken, meat or fish are cooked in a large frying pan in a small amount of oil or butter until they are cooked through but still crisp.

STOCKING AN INTERNATIONAL PANTRY

Getting to know global cuisines will be easier – and more fun! – if you stock your pantry with global ingredients. Fill your kitchen with staples like these and you'll always be ready to cook your way around the world.

Grains. Get to know basmati rice from India, jasmine rice from Thailand, quinoa from Bolivia, farro from Italy, wild rice from North America and buckwheat groats from Russia.

Noodles. Stock up on soba from Japan, ramen from China, rice noodles from Thailand, little bitty couscous from North Africa and pasta from Italy.

Vinegars. Add acid to everything from salads to soups, with balsamic, apple cider vinegar, rice wine vinegar, coconut vinegar and red wine vinegar. Some are sweeter; some are sharper.

Oils. Try olive oil from the Mediterranean, palm oil from Africa, groundnut oil from Asia, sunflower oil from Europe, avocado oil from Central America and coconut oil from Southeast Asia. Plus ghee from India!

Peanut butter. This savoury peanut paste is a base for everything from Indonesian gado gado to Sudanese salata tomatim bel daqua. (Find recipes for each in this book!)

Spices. Whole or ground, individual or blended, you'll find that a well-stocked cabinet of these treasures is the spice of life. Try saffron from Iran, garam masala from India, berbere from Ethiopia, nutmeg from Indonesia and five-spice powder from China.

Dried beans. These protein-packed powerhouses could keep for years but you'll want to cook them long before then. With dried beans on hand you'll be ready to make chickpeas into hummus from the Middle East, black beans into feijoada soup from Brazil, lentils into dal from India, kidney beans into frijoles from Mexico and broad beans into ful from North Africa.

Hot stuff. Cultures across continents capture chilli heat in spice pastes and bold bottles. Try sriracha from Thailand, sambal from Indonesia, Tabasco™ from the United States, piri piri from Mozambique, harissa from Tunisia and tongue-numbing Sichuan peppercorns from China.

Sweet stuff. Experiment with cane sugar, date sugar, palm sugar, panela, muscovado and jaggery – plus honey, molasses, agave and maple syrup.

Condiments. Whether Dijon mustard from France or ponzu from Japan or gochujang from Korea, everything is better with flavour-packed sauces.

KITCHEN TOOLS

Great cooks around the world may have kitchens full of gadgets or just a knife, a pot and an open fire. You don't need a fully equipped kitchen to start cooking but here are a few of our favourite tools:

Knives and chopping boards. One good, sharp 20-cm knife may be the most important tool in your kitchen. Ask an adult to help you learn to hold it correctly and to use it safely for mincing, dicing, chopping and slicing.

Frying pan. Look for a heavy 20- or 25-cm frying pan with a sturdy, metal handle that's safe to put into a hot oven (cast iron is a good choice). You'll use frying pans for everything from scrambled eggs to stir-fries to shakshuka.

Saucepan. Essential for everything from boiling potatoes to simmering soup. A tight-fitting lid is useful for steaming, or anytime you want to keep in the heat.

Baking tin or baking tray. You'll use it for everything from roasting vegetables to baking biscuits. Don't forget to use oven gloves when handling them hot!

Graters. You'll use them for parmesan, ginger and many other hard ingredients. Graters are great! Watch your fingers.

Peeler. Handy for peeling skins off vegetables like potatoes and parsnips, also for shaving hard cheese and making curls of chocolate.

Tongs. For tossing, transferring, grabbing and serving.

Wooden spoons. For mixing, stirring, spooning and serving.

Instant-read thermometer. Experienced cooks can tell when meat is done just by the look, smell or even sound. For the rest of us, instant-read thermometers are a huge help.

Skewers. For skewering everything from kebabs from Israel and chicken satay from Indonesia to s'mores from the United States. Who doesn't love food cooked on sticks over flames?

Mortar and pestle. An essential since the Stone Age, this tool is used for pounding pesto from Italy, curry paste from Thailand, salsas from Mexico, fufu from Ghana and so much more. These days, many cooks whir things in a food processor instead but there's nothing like hand-pounding your food to smooth perfection with a piece of rock!

Wok. Originally from China, this deep pan with sloping sides isn't just for stir-frying, though it's world-famous for that technique. Woks can also be used for deep-frying, steaming and even boiling. Some chefs say not to wash woks with soap, which would strip the metal of its seasoning.

Rice cooker. OK, you don't really need this plug-in appliance. After all, people have made perfect rice in plain pots for ages. But...these electric tools do make perfect rice every time, keep it warm and even turn themselves off. Millions of families use theirs daily!

Bamboo steamer basket. These pretty, round baskets stack right into your wok or wide frying pan. Simply set them over boiling liquid to steam vegetables, fish, chicken or dumplings.

Tagine. Every kitchen in North Africa is home to these clay pots with domed lids. From Morocco to Algeria, they're used for slow-cooking stews and tagines and they're often hand-painted with gorgeous designs.

Mandolin. Beloved from Japan to France, these slicing tools allow for perfectly precise, paper-thin slices of anything from potatoes to pears. Be careful not to slice your fingers!

Pasta roller. Yes, you could just roll out dough and slice it into ribbons – or buy dried pasta from a shop – but few things are as much fun as feeding dough into one end and seeing noodle shapes come out the other. Manual pasta-makers require turning a crank by hand, while tabletop-mixer attachments are as fast as magic. Both make delicious fresh pasta for everything from lasagne to fettuccini.

Sushi rolling mats. Have you ever tried making your own sushi? These bamboo tools, known as makisu, are essential for shaping each delicate roll. Pro tip: don't overstuff them!

CONTRIBUTORS

TÀNIA GARCÍA

Born in Barcelona, Spain, Tània has always been inspired by travel for her illustrations. This time her passion for learning new cultures, gastronomy and art come together. She loves her native Mediterranean cuisine but she also really enjoys Moroccan or Thai food. When she is not drawing, you can find her preparing some delicious pancakes for breakfast, her favourite meal of the day.

GABRIELLE LANGHOLTZ

Writer Gabrielle loves learning about the world through food. She's worked at *Fortune* magazine, on organic farms and at Princeton University and has been fortunate to visit such places as Argentina, Austria, Belgium, Brazil, Canada, Italy, Jamaica, Paraguay, Scotland, Spain and every state in the US. After working on this book, she really wants to go to Morocco next.

MAYA GARTNER

Born in the U.S. to a Japanese mother and a British father, Associate Publisher Maya grew up in the U.S., Japan, France and the United Kingdom and has been eating food from around the world since she was a baby. She can't live without eating Japanese rice, American cookies, French cheese or drinking British tea at least once a week!

ALICE-MAY BERMINGHAM

Originally from Staffordshire, United Kingdom and now living in London, editor Alice-May's favourite food is anything comforting. Her top food experiences include a bike tour of the taco stands of Mexico City and ordering every pierogi on the menu while sheltering from the snow in Krakow, Poland.

LAURA HAMBLETON

The designer of this book, Laura, is an art director, illustrator and author who has been working in children's books for many years. Laura loves pasta and anything chocolatey and enjoys cooking tasty meals (like those in this book!) with her two children.

LOUISA SHAFIA

Louisa is a chef and author of the cookbook *The New Persian Kitchen*. She has lectured and written widely about the foods of Iran.

MARY ROSE MADDEN

Journalist Mary Rose writes about the intersection of health and sociology, ethics and culture for podcasts, radio and print. Some of her favourite worldwide eating experiences have included a reporting fellowship in East Africa and an anchovy-catching visit to the Basque region of Spain. She loves to cook with her children and share meals and stories with family and friends.

RACHEL NUWER

Rachel is an award-winning writer who has written for the *New York Times*, *National Geographic* and many other publications and has eaten in seventy-nine countries. Her favourite foods from around the world are Vietnamese pho, French butter, El Salvadoran pupusas and Japanese takoyaki. If she had to eat only one thing for the rest of her life, it would probably be cheese.

AHMED KHATER

Growing up in Egypt, Ahmed visited diverse landscapes, from Alexandria's beaches to the vibrant Nile Delta and the historic deserts of Sinai. Now a Fulbright scholar, his favourite foods include Egypt's national dish, koshary. He says nothing compares to the simple joy of a ful and falafel breakfast with fresh pita and olive oil.

MŌNICA VALLIN

Born to a Bolivian mother and Mexican father, Mōnica spent her formative years in Colombia and Bolivia. Her father instilled in her a love of tacos and spicy food and encouraged gastronomic adventuring. Growing up with her maternal grandmother, who hailed from Peru, Mōnica developed a fondness for desserts, particularly suspiro limeño. She holds a PhD in Spanish and Cultural Studies from Georgetown University. Her literature, history and food interests inspired her dissertation, which explores identity in Colonial Latin America.

RACHEL WHARTON

Rachel is an award-winning journalist and cookbook author with a master's degree in food studies from New York University. She remains forever fascinated by the history and the ingredients that connect cuisines across the continents.

MARIE VILJOEN

South African-born food writer and forager Marie grew up in Bloemfontein and in Cape Town, where she learned to grow and gather edible plants and to cook over coals under the Milky Way. She writes books, leads wild-food walks, grows yuzu and transforms persimmons into hoshigaki.

NORTH
AMERICA

SOUTH
AMERICA

SIX INHABITED CONTINENTS
EIGHT BILLION PEOPLE
NEARLY 200 NATIONS
ONE PLANET
ONE HUMANITY
ONE WORLD OF
INNUMERABLE TASTES

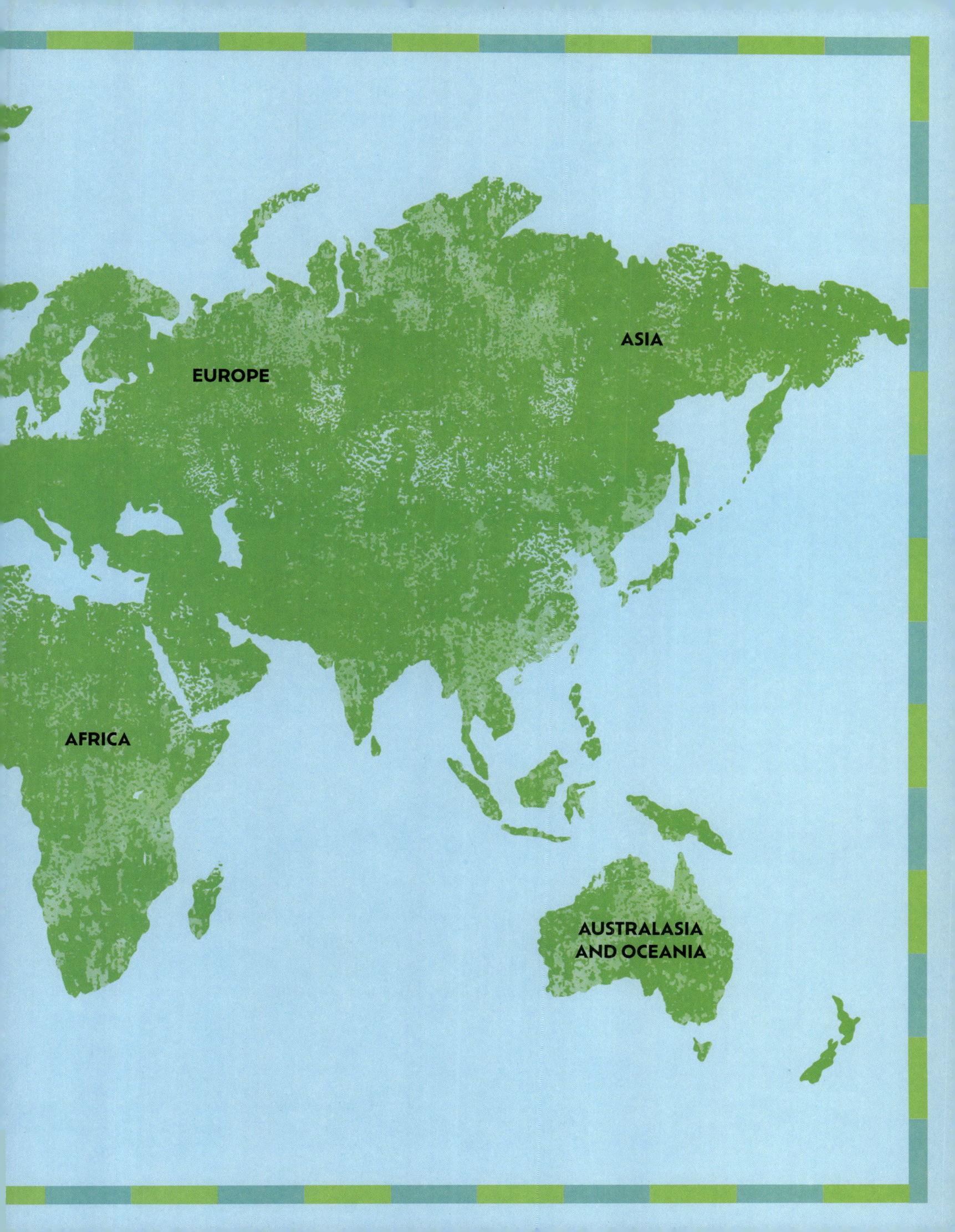

EUROPE

ASIA

AFRICA

AUSTRALASIA
AND OCEANIA

AFRICA

This massive continent is home to fifty-four countries and stunningly rich landscapes: lush rainforests, vast deserts, dramatic waterfalls, towering jungles, deep rivers, majestic mountains, iconic grasslands and beautiful beaches. Africa is famous for lions, elephants and giraffes, and as the birthplace of another species: humans! Ancient civilizations here developed advanced farming, intricate trade networks, iconic architecture and elaborate foods. Today, you'll find a modern mosaic of cultures, languages and traditions. Despite the devastating legacies of colonization and enslavement, this diverse continent is now home to forward-thinking, indigenous-led farming practices focusing on sustainability as well as vibrant and world-leading film, technology and design industries.

From Algeria to Zimbabwe, the flavours are unforgettable. People feast on white yams, great greens and black-eyed beans. They prepare peanut sauces and slippery okra soups, and snack on plantain chips and fried egusi-seed patties. Palm nut oil – made for millennia from trees in the Congo River Valley – gives its signature flavour and pretty red colour to West African recipes. People mash yams, taro, plantains or cassava into fufu – also known as ugali, sadza, nsima or posho – a smooth paste rolled into bite-sized balls to dip in savoury sauces.

ALGERIA

Algeria is big – the size of western Europe – but almost everyone lives in the north, along the coast of the beautiful Mediterranean Sea. If you go south, across the Atlas Mountains, you'll reach the vast Sahara Desert. France occupied Algeria for over one hundred years and cafés still serve French-inspired mussels and steak frites but local food highlights delicious North African ingredients such as couscous, olives, lamb, citrus, dates, aubergine, artichokes and spices – all sold in lively, colourful outdoor markets called souks.

COUSCOUS

Algerians enjoy this tiny semolina pasta so much that it is called ta'am, or 'food', in Arabic. Couscous is served at family dinners, weddings, funerals – and just about every other meal too. Every Algerian kitchen includes a couscoussier, a big pot with an insert for steaming the pearl-shaped pasta over stew.

LAMB

Algerians love lamb, from kebabs and sausages to stew, and mechoui may be their single favourite dish. To make it, a whole lamb is slow roasted on a spit and basted with clarified butter or olive oil for moist meat and crispy skin.

HARISSA

This legendary red paste of hot and sweet peppers – pounded with garlic, salt, olive oil and spices like cumin, coriander and caraway – is found in kitchens across North Africa and has become beloved throughout the world, on everything from cauliflower to kebabs.

SHAKSHUKA

This Ottoman-influenced breakfast features eggs poached in a frying pan over a spicy stew of tomatoes, peppers and onions, often served with pita bread for sopping up the savoury sauce. The origin of this North African dish is much debated between neighbouring Algeria and Morocco and Tunisia!

DEMOCRATIC REPUBLIC OF THE CONGO

Known as the DRC for short, this country is named after the Congo, one of Earth's mightiest rivers, which snakes through the country. The DRC contains Africa's biggest tropical rainforest, home to gorillas, chimpanzees and forest elephants. At different times Portugal, France and Belgium colonized the DRC; today its cuisine combines Central African traditions with European and New World flavours.

MIKATE DOUGHNUTS

While the most popular desserts here are fresh tropical fruits, doughnuts are the second-favourite sweet. Similar fluffy, fried-dough treats are called togbei or bofrot in Ghana or puff-puff in Nigeria. Here in the DRC they're called mikate, which means 'fried dough bread' in the local Lingala language. You'll find vendors frying them up fresh on the street corners of Kinshasa, where people buy them for breakfast with coffee.

CASSAVA

Cassava is a root vegetable from Mesoamerica that has been a staple in the DRC – and much of Africa – for almost 500 years. Congolese cooks fry, mash, ferment, purée, boil and ground cassava but there's one way they never eat it: raw. Raw cassava contains a poison called cyanide but the tuber becomes harmless (and delicious) when cooked.

PILI PILI

Pili Pili means 'pepper pepper' in one of the Swahili languages and refers to a type of super spicy chilli about twenty-two times hotter than a jalapeño called the African bird pepper – it also refers to the sauce made when you combine it with garlic and vinegar or lemon. For delicious heat and creamy relief, people slather a combination of pili pili sauce and mayonnaise onto meat, fish and fried plantains.

FUFU

To make fufu, cassava, plantain or maize is peeled, soaked for days, dried, pounded into a fine flour and shaped into balls to be served with dishes like fish stew or bean soup. Fufu can take time to make, so families and friends gather to prepare and enjoy it together.

KWANGA

A popular accompaniment to daily dishes like meats and stews, kwanga is a traditional cassava flour cake. A bit like Mexican tamales, the dough is wrapped in leaves and then steamed. Since some foods here can be very spicy with pili pili sauce, bites of neutral kwanga can give your tongue a contrast to the hot-pepper heat.

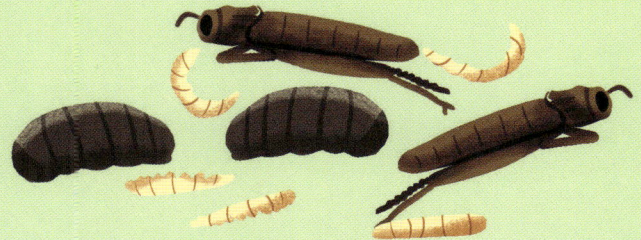

INSECTS

Insects like grasshoppers and caterpillars are popular in the DRC. Their flavour can vary depending on what they themselves ate but some have a deliciously nutty flavour! They are also a great source of protein and rich in amino acids, with a long history in local diets and culture in the DRC.

FRESH FISH

As the DRC only has a tiny ocean coastline, much of the country's delicious seafood is caught wild here in the beautiful Congo River. While in markets, you can buy fresh fish to take home and cook yourself. The local catch is also widely available — alive or fried, steamed, smoked or cooked whole, wrapped in banana leaves, and ready to eat.

SAFOU

The DRC's climate is perfect for growing tropical fruits. One favourite is safou, also called the African butter pear, which is a nutritious tree fruit that is cultivated but also grows wild in the DRC's tropical forests. Safou look like little aubergines and have a buttery texture. Its taste? It may be a fruit but it's not sweet! More like a savoury avocado, with a little sourness like green olives. Safou is great as a jam, and is even used to make ice cream.

GAME

Hunting wild game is still one of the main ways of acquiring meat, from the crocodiles in the Congo River to the antelopes in the forests. One popular way to eat crocodile is to cure it with sugar and salt for a few hours, then smoke the meat in wood chips.

POULET MOAMBE

CHICKEN WITH ONIONS, TOMATOES, PEANUT BUTTER AND PALM OIL

PREPARATION TIME	COOKING TIME	LEVEL OF DIFFICULTY	SERVES
20 mins	1 hr 15 mins	● ●	6

This traditional stewed chicken dish gets its distinctive taste from its rich, flavourful sauce. Palm oil, made from the African palm fruit, gives the dish a red colour. Often served with sides like fufu, plantains or rice, Moambe chicken is widely popular in Central and West Africa. It is considered the national dish of both the Republic of Congo and the Democratic Republic of the Congo, as well as Angola and Gabon, and has become a dinner staple in Belgium too.

INGREDIENTS

1.4 kg bone-in chicken thighs
    or drumsticks
salt
6 tablespoons red palm oil,
    groundnut oil or ghee
2 medium yellow onions, diced
3 cloves garlic, chopped
2.5-cm piece of root ginger,
    peeled and grated
170 g tomato purée
1 400-g tin chopped tomatoes
3 spring onions, thinly sliced
½ teaspoon cayenne pepper
¼ teaspoon ground nutmeg
230 g creamy unsalted peanut
    butter
steamed rice, for serving
fried plantains, for serving

1. Pat the chicken dry with kitchen paper and season with salt.

2. In a large, heavy casserole dish, heat 2 tablespoons of the oil over a medium-high heat until shimmering. Working in batches, add the chicken, skin side down in a single layer and cook until golden brown: 5 to 8 minutes. Flip and cook the chicken on the other side until golden brown: about 5 minutes longer. Transfer to a plate and repeat with the remaining chicken.

3. Add the remaining 4 tablespoons of oil, the onions and a large pinch of salt, and cook over a medium-low heat until softened: about 10 minutes. Add the garlic and ginger and cook until fragrant: about 2 minutes. Add the tomato purée and cook, stirring occasionally, until the purée darkens: 3 to 5 minutes.

4. Add the chopped tomatoes, spring onions, cayenne, nutmeg and 250 ml water and bring to a boil over a high heat. Reduce the heat to medium-low, cover and simmer for 20 minutes.

5. Scoop out about 250 ml of the sauce and transfer to a heatproof bowl. Add the peanut butter and whisk until smooth. Scrape the peanut sauce into the pot, stir in the chicken, and simmer everything together uncovered until the chicken is cooked through and the sauce is thick and coats the chicken: about 10 minutes. Taste the sauce and season with salt, if desired.

6. Serve with rice or fried plantains.

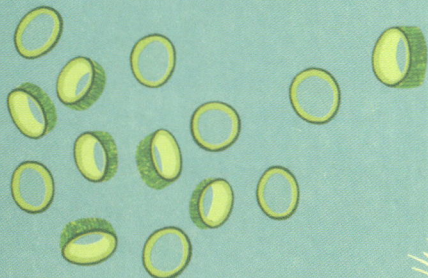

EGYPT

Egypt is mostly covered in vast deserts but people have built thriving civilizations here for thousands of years, thanks to the Nile River and its famously fertile floodplain. This watery lifeline nourished one of the most sophisticated societies in history, a series of kingdoms that we refer to today as ancient Egypt. Ancient Egyptians grew leeks, cucumbers, lettuce, rocket, watercress, carrots, herbs, peas, okra and green beans. Pigeon and quail have been grilled and stuffed since the pharaoh days. Tourists who come from around the world to feast their eyes on ancient Egypt's famous pyramids can afterwards feast on falafel, kebabs, rotisserie-style roasted meat called shawarma and filled puff pastry known as fateer.

COFFEE

Egypt has had a thriving coffee culture since the sixteenth century, long before it was widespread in Europe. Today, Egyptians make espresso with cardamom in stove-top pots called *kanaka*, or hang out in coffee shops called *ahwa* – the Egypt-dialect Arab word for coffee.

DESERT FRUIT

Egyptians long ago mastered the skill of growing fruit in the desert – including dates, figs and melons, all of which are still popular here today. Grape, tamarind, pomegranate and strawberry juices are simmered into sweet syrups to make drinks and flavour fruity pastries.

KHAN EL KAHLILI

Khan El Kahlili is one of Egypt's oldest surviving bazaars, held in the heart of Cairo, the capital city. Locals still frequent the market for daily needs, while visitors come to soak up the bustling atmosphere and friendly bargaining. There are also countless cafés to stop at for a refreshing cup of Egyptian mint tea.

FOOD FOR ETERNITY

Ancient Egyptians were famous for mummifying leaders and placing them in elaborate tombs with items to use in the afterlife – King Tut's tomb held seventeen boxes of food, including grapes, figs, pomegranates, jujubes, a jar of honey and meat preserved in resin from pistachio trees.

KAHK

This sweet, crumbly biscuit dates back to the times of pharaohs. Sometimes stuffed with gold coins and given to the poor, today they're often sprinkled with icing sugar and stuffed with nuts or dates and decorated with elaborate swirls of icing. They are also given as gifts at Egyptian weddings and during religious holidays such as Eid al-Fitr and Easter.

KOSHARY

Lentils have been popular here for thousands of years and today Egyptians still simmer red, brown and black lentils, into savoury stews. Koshary – a street food staple and Egypt's national dish – features lentils, rice, chickpeas and small pasta, with cumin-scented tomato sauce and crispy fried onions.

MOLOKHIA

This thick, green soup is named after the type of leaf that gives it its bright colour. Molokhia leaves may be chopped then boiled with garlic and coriander. Some cooks throw in shredded chicken too. Served over rice, or sometimes with bread, a warming bowl of molokhia turns into a full meal.

LATE EATERS

No wonder Egyptians love a nutritious, filling breakfast like ful medames – lunchtime is between 1:00 p.m. and 4:00 p.m. Dinner typically starts from 8:00 p.m. and can last until midnight! Some people skip dinner and instead have a light late meal of leftovers from lunch.

NUTS FOR NUTS!

At late-night movie-watching parties and sporting events, Egyptians snack on peanuts, cashews, walnuts and pistachios, while watermelon seeds, sunflower seeds and spiced, roasted chickpeas are favourite street-vendor snacks.

FUL MEDAMES

This native variety of broad bean was one of the first crops ever cultivated in human history. The name also refers to a breakfast favourite, a savoury stew made from the softly cooked ful, simmered with olive oil, cumin, chopped parsley, garlic, onion, lemon juice and chilli peppers.

EGGS

AROUND THE WORLD

People have been eating eggs throughout history, since long before we domesticated poultry. Eggs are a cheap protein source with endless uses in cooking. While duck, goose and chicken eggs are the most common eggs to eat, local specialities from other bird species are important in some cultures. And chicken eggs alone are cooked into thousands of recipes around the world, from scrambled eggs at breakfast to custardy desserts.

PRESERVED EGGS

Fresh eggs can spoil quickly, so before refrigeration, people around the world found ways to preserve them. Throughout Southeast Asia, eggs have long been preserved with salt. A traditional Chinese recipe called 'century eggs' uses ash, clay, salt and quicklime. The process doesn't really take a hundred years; after a few months, the eggs are black, salty and creamy – a delicacy!

EGG HOPPERS

Sri Lankan egg hoppers are a popular breakfast street food. A crispy rice and coconut milk pancake is baked into a deep, lacy cup shape to nest the cooked egg. Egg hoppers might be served with spicy sambal sauce and soft lentil dal.

SCRAMBLED EGGS

This quick breakfast starts the day around the globe. In Mexico, migas are eggs scrambled with fried tortilla chips and crumbs. In Malta, balbuljata includes onions, tomatoes and parsley.

FRIED EGGS

Fried eggs are a staple in cuisines worldwide. In Egypt, egg aagwa is a dish of eggs fried with dates. Often served with a fried egg, nasi goreng is a smoky, chilli-infused fried rice known throughout Indonesia and Malaysia, also popular in South America's Suriname and in the Netherlands in Europe.

KHACHAPURI

This beautiful boat-shaped cheese bread is a centuries-old national dish from the country of Georgia. An egg is cracked onto the bread's cheesy centre, then it's popped into the oven to bake. Tear off the crust to dip into the hot runny centre!

MERINGUE

Meringues are like magic, created with sugar and egg whites beaten with a whisk until fluffy with air, then baked into sweet pillows of cloud-like dessert. Costa Rican suspiros cookies ('tiny sighs') are miniature meringues flavoured with lime juice.

EGG SOUP

In many cuisines, eggs make soups richer. Colombian changua is an eggy breakfast soup with spring onions and fresh coriander. In Azerbaijan, dovga is a chilled yoghurt soup with chickpeas, eggs and fresh herbs like mint, parsley and coriander. In Greece, avgolemono is a smooth, golden, thick soup made with eggs and lemons that often includes chicken and rice.

EGG BRICK

If you see brik à l'oeuf or 'egg brick' on the menu in Tunisia, the name is actually referring to the 'brick' dough, a light, flaky, paper-thin semolina dough fried so quickly that when you cut into this treat, the barely cooked egg yolk within will drip right out!

LEITE DE CREME

This sweet, rich, eggy custard, popular in Portugal, is flavoured with lemon peel and cinnamon. Chefs sprinkle sugar on top and brown it with a torch, giving it a crisp caramelized top over the smooth, warm confection within.

TOPPED WITH AN EGG

Many Asian soups bob with poached or boiled eggs. South Korean jang-jorim is a savoury side of soy-sauce-braised beef, often studded with spicy peppers and jammy, golden-yolked hard-boiled eggs.

SHAKSHUKA

POACHED EGGS IN TOMATO AND PEPPER SAUCE

PREPARATION TIME
15 mins

COOKING TIME
40 mins

LEVEL OF DIFFICULTY
● ●

SERVES
4 to 6

This dish of eggs poached in a sweet-spicy pepper-tomato sauce is now beloved around the world. Named after the Arabic word for 'mixture', it's all simmered in a single frying pan. First you make a simple savoury sauce of tomatoes, onion, garlic and red peppers, spiced with cumin, coriander and sweet or smoked paprika, then you gently crack the eggs into the sauce, where they cook to a jammy perfection in just a few minutes. This version calls for sweet peppers but some cooks also add fiery hot chillies – other variations include cured olives, salty white cheese, artichoke hearts or spicy sausage.

INGREDIENTS

3 tablespoons olive oil
1 medium yellow onion, finely chopped
3 to 4 fat garlic cloves, thinly sliced
1 red or green pepper, de-seeded and diced
salt and pepper
1 tablespoon sweet paprika
2 teaspoons ground cumin
2 teaspoons ground coriander
1 800-g tin chopped tomatoes
4 to 6 large eggs
chopped parsley or mint, and crusty bread, for serving (optional)

1. In a large, deep frying pan with a lid, heat the olive oil over a medium heat. Add the onion, garlic and pepper, and season with ½ teaspoon salt and a few grinds of pepper. Cook, stirring, until softened: 5 to 6 minutes. Add the paprika, cumin and coriander and cook until fragrant: about 30 seconds. Add the tomatoes and bring to a simmer. Reduce the heat to medium-low, cover and simmer the sauce for 15 minutes. Uncover and cook until the sauce is thickened: about 5 more minutes.

2. Using your spoon, make 4 to 6 indentations in the sauce, depending on the number of eggs you're using. Carefully crack the eggs into the wells, then cover the frying pan, and cook until the egg whites are set but the yolks are bright and jammy: about 6 minutes. (If you prefer hard-boiled eggs, leave them to cook to desired doneness.)

3. Spoon the shakshuka into bowls, scatter the parsley or mint on top and serve with crusty bread.

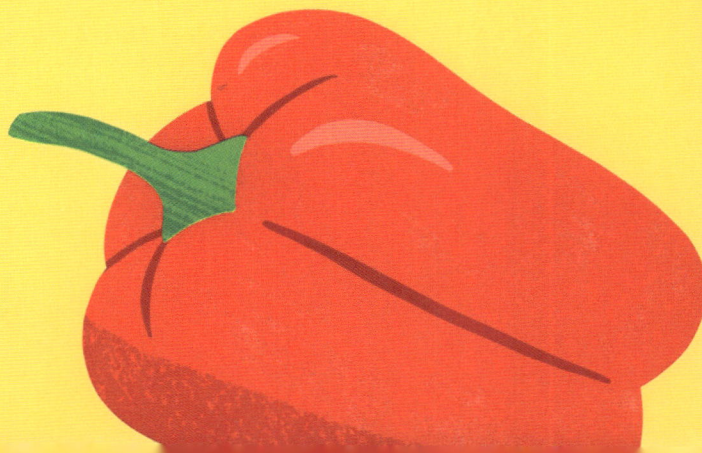

Bread makes the perfect 'scoop' for the delicious sauce!

Shakshuka is traditional to have at breakfast, brunch or lunch but it's just as delicious at dinner.

ETHIOPIA

One of the oldest countries in the world, Ethiopia is called 'the cradle of humanity' because archaeologists have found so many early human fossils here. It's also one of only two countries in Africa never to have been colonized. Maybe that's why the food in this rugged country on the Horn of Africa – the continent's easternmost peninsula – is unique in all the world. Here you'll find the wonderfully spongy injera bread, flavourful butters, succulent meats spiced with berbere, and the world's first coffee.

COFFEE'S BIRTHPLACE

Legend has it that a ninth-century Ethiopian goatherd discovered coffee when he noticed certain berries gave the goats more energy. Today, most Ethiopians enjoy a daily coffee ceremony: raw beans are roasted, then pounded in a mortar (*mukecha*) with a pestle (*zenesena*), and boiled in a pot called a *jebana*. Even young kids drink coffee here!

INJERA

This national dish of Ethiopia also serves as plate and utensil! Injera is a spongy, slightly sour flatbread made from teff – a tiny supergrain native to Ethiopia. Stews, meats and vegetables are each placed in mounds on a big circle of injera, which may be up to 50 centimetres across. To eat, you tear off a small piece of injera and use it as a scoop to pick up each delicious bite.

BERBERE

This key Ethiopian spice blend usually includes chilli peppers, garlic, ginger, black pepper, fenugreek, allspice and cloves. It can be used dry or mixed with oil to form a paste. Berbere packs a spicy punch, so have some soothing injera on hand!

ENSET

The enset looks so much like a banana tree, people call it the 'false banana'. Ethiopians mash parts of the plant with yeast, bury it underground for as long as two years, then make the fermented paste into a dense, bread-like staple called kocho.

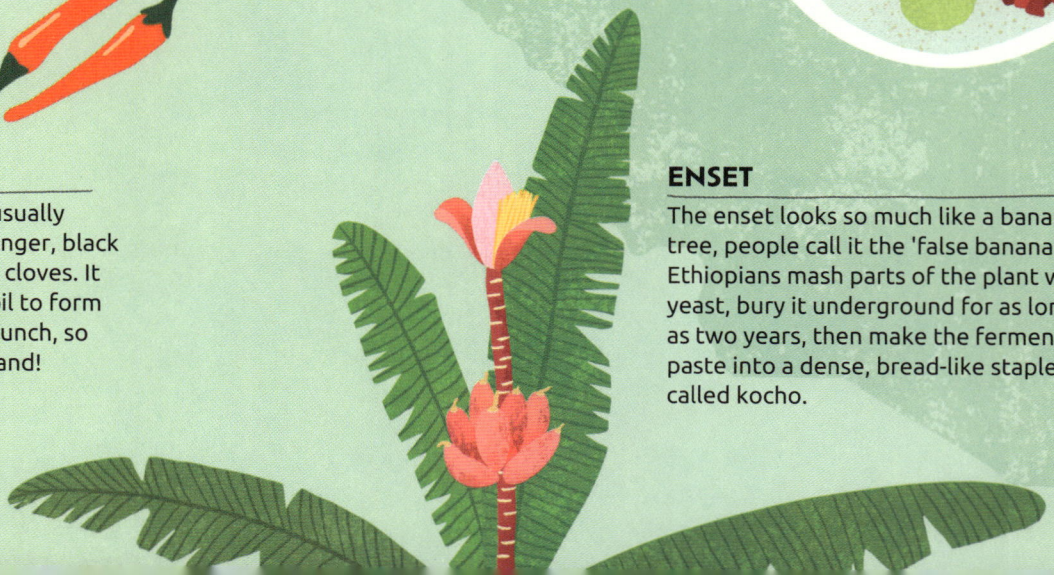

DORO WAT

This chicken stew is often served at celebrations, especially weddings, and can take days to make. First you simmer onion in water with berbere; then you add nit'ir qibe (a spiced, clarified butter), aromatics, marinated chicken and hard-boiled eggs. It's served with a ricotta-like cheese called alibi and, of course, injera.

SPICES

Spices are extremely important to Ethiopian cuisine. These include cayenne peppers, pointed peppers, amharic cabbage seeds, black mustard, cardamom, coriander, basil, black pepper, ginger, black cumin, fenugreek and garlic.

VEGETARIAN FOOD

Members of the Ethiopian Orthodox Christian Church are vegetarian for much of the year. They feast on meals like yetsom beyaynetu: injera topped with heaps of veggie-based curries and stews in a kaleidoscope of colours.

GURSHA

Ethiopians are widely known for their hospitality. One way guests are shown respect is through the very old tradition called *gursha*, the Amharic word for 'mouthful'. When people perform *gursha*, they each pick up a portion of food with a piece of injera by hand and graciously feed each other.

KITFO AND OTHER MEATS

Many Ethiopians love meat... especially when it's raw! Kitfo is minced raw beef marinated in a spice blend and nit'ir qibe; gored consists of raw beef cubes with chilli sauce and lemon; and tere siga (literally 'raw meat') is a long strip of meat cut straight from the hanging carcass.

TIBS

A cross between a stir fry and a stew, tibs is often the first dish prepared on holidays. The meat – cubes of beef, lamb or goat – is usually pan-fried in a rich sauce of nit'ir qibe, vegetables, aromatics and berbere.

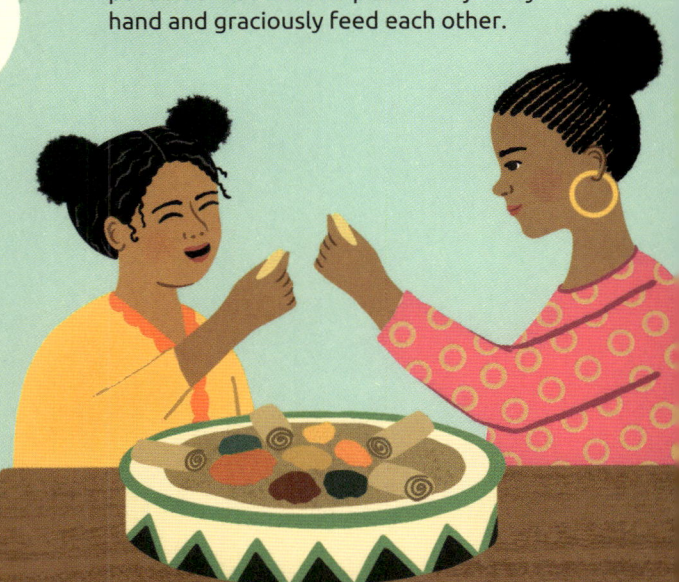

NIT'IR QIBE

CLARIFIED BUTTER WITH GARLIC, GINGER AND SPICES

PREPARATION TIME
15 mins

COOKING TIME
1 hr 15 mins

LEVEL OF DIFFICULTY
● ●

MAKES
About 225g

This clarified butter, infused with onion, garlic, ginger and spices, is essential in many Ethiopian recipes – and is delicious on its own. Clarifying the butter is when you slowly heat it and remove the solids, like making the world-famous ghee of India! The result is a butter that keeps longer and can cook at higher temperatures. Ethiopian cooks use nit'ir qibe in a raw beef dish called kitfo and when cooking doro wat, their beloved, slow-cooked, deeply spiced chicken dish.

INGREDIENTS

450 g unsalted butter, cut into small cubes
1 teaspoon ground turmeric
⅛ teaspoon nutmeg, freshly grated
½ teaspoon ground cardamom
1 whole clove
1 cinnamon stick
½ an onion, coarsely chopped
3 cloves garlic, chopped
2.5 cm piece of root ginger, peeled and grated
1 teaspoon fenugreek seeds
½ teaspoon cumin seeds

1. In a medium saucepan over a medium-low heat, slowly melt the butter but do not let it brown.

2. Meanwhile, in a dry, heavy frying pan over a medium-low heat, toast the turmeric, nutmeg, cardamom, clove and cinnamon for 4 to 5 minutes, until fragrant. Be careful not to let them burn.

3. Once the butter is fully melted, add the toasted spices, onion, garlic and ginger. Raise the heat and bring to a boil. Lower to a simmer and cook gently for 1 hour. Leave to cool slightly.

4. Strain the nit'ir qibe through two layers of muslin cloth draped over a sieve or use a coffee filter. Stir in the fenugreek and cumin. Store in a glass jar in the fridge for up to three months.

Drizzle over meats and stews, add a tasty spoonful to beans or lentils, or use when cooking eggs or for seasoning boiled vegetables.

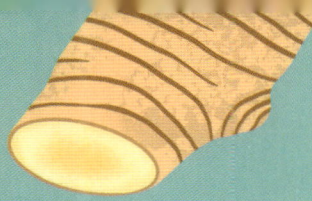

It's also pretty
great on popcorn!

KENYA

Kenya is famous for its wildlife, its stunning Indian Ocean coastline and its vibrant mix of traditional and modern cultures, foods and architecture. Lions, leopards, elephants, rhinos and Cape buffalo roam Kenya's fifty national parks and reserves. The East African nation's capital city of Nairobi is home to skyscrapers, international corporations and a hip music scene, along with amazing street food. Its more rural areas feature a rich history and variety of traditional cultures and tribes, each with their own distinct foods and recipes.

CHAI

Visit a Kenyan family and you'll likely receive a hot cup of chai, made by boiling tea leaves in a large pot with milk, lots of sugar, and spices like cardamom, cinnamon and black pepper. In rural areas, chai is made over a wood fire, with milk carried fresh from the cow – or goat – to the pot!

INDIAN INFLUENCE

Kenya, like India, is a former British colony. In the late 1800s, the British brought more than 30,000 Indian labourers to Africa to build the Kenya–Uganda railway. It was a brutal job: some workers were even eaten by lions. But many survived and stayed, and today Indian recipes for samosas, chapatis, curry and biryani are beloved across Kenya.

STREET FOOD

Kenyan cities are bursting with street food. Try makai – grilled corn seasoned with chilli powder, lime and salt. Or sink your teeth into mshikaki, a marinated, grilled kebab. Don't forget mandazi doughnuts – for a local experience, grab another for tomorrow's breakfast!

UGALI

This East African staple is made by boiling cornmeal until it is almost like an edible spoon. At mealtime, Kenyans roll a lump of ugali into a little ball, press a dimple with one thumb, and scoop up other foods – sauce, cooked greens or meat – so each delicious bite includes the corny ugali base. To be polite, only use your fingertips!

NYAMA CHOMA

In Swahili, nyama choma – often simply roasted goat meat with salt and pepper – means 'burned meat'. Originating from the nomadic Maasai people, it may be Kenya's most popular dish, served everywhere from roadside shacks to Nairobi's finest restaurants, often with ugali.

GITHERI

A traditional food of the Kikuyu tribe of central Kenya, githeri is a nutritious stew of corn and beans that often includes greens, onions, potatoes, meat and curry powder. It's popular across Kenya – in fact, many locals eat it in school cafeterias as children!

MURSIK

Kenya's world-champion marathoners are perhaps helped by training at high altitudes and eating nutritious foods like this fermented milk. To make mursik, the cook brushes the inside of a dried gourd, or calabash, with soot from a particular type of tree. Cow or goat's milk is poured in and sealed for up to a month. The soot blocks harmful bacteria and gives the milk a smoky flavour.

SUKUMA WIKI

Sukuma wiki is a green vegetable (a cousin of kale), chopped and braised with tomatoes and onions. Its name means 'stretch the week' because its energy can help fuel you for days! Most Kenyans eat it nearly every day of the year.

FRUIT

Kenya's warm climate is perfect for growing tropical fruits. Mangoes, guava, pineapples, papaya, bananas, limes, watermelon, coconut and paw paws are often sliced and served for breakfast. Coconut is cooked with a variety of fresh fruits to make a mousse-like dessert. People enjoy amazing fresh juices, from passion fruit to sugar cane.

TEA

AROUND THE WORLD

The practice of drinking tea originated in southwestern China during the Bronze Age, when the leaves were mixed with herbs in a medicinal drink. A tea tree in the region's Yunnan province is said to be the oldest in the world – 3,200 years old! Portuguese traders wrote about tea-drinking during their travels in the 1500s but it was not until the early seventeenth century that tea arrived in Europe, on a Dutch East India Company ship. By the mid-1600s, people everywhere in Europe were drinking tea, and it quickly spread to European colonies in Africa, India and the Americas.

THAI ICED TEA

Thailand's sweet drink is caffeinated and cold, so it cools you down and wakes you up! It features strong brewed black tea, and its creamy orange colour comes from tamarind and creamy sweetened condensed milk. Sometimes steeped with aniseed or cardamom, Thai iced tea will cool down your tongue between bites of spicy Thai dishes like kua kling and pad prik king.

BUBBLE TEA

In Taiwan bubble tea can now be found in flavours from brown sugar to strawberry but it's often made with just brewed tea, milk, sugar and big, black, chewy tapioca balls called boba or pearls. People drink the tea and suck up the boba through special giant straws.

AMERICAN ICED TEA

In the U.S.'s southern states, tea is served ice cold and enjoyed on sweltering summer days. Hosts will ask if you like 'sweet or unsweet', and you'll find it everywhere: poured from crystal jugs on grand porches and sipped from red plastic cups next to paper plates of barbecue. Sometimes it's even steeped in the sun!

YERBA MATE

Made from the leaves of a plant in the holly family, yerba mate is served hot or cold in traditional cups made to resemble gourds. This herbal drink is served with special metal straws that strain as you sip and originated with the indigenous people of present-day Paraguay. It is now drunk in many South American countries.

ROOIBOS TEA

South African rooibos 'tea' is named after the Afrikaans word for 'red bush', after the local native plants used for the tea. Its leaves are steeped for their naturally earthy, slightly sweet flavour. Rooibos is enjoyed hot or iced, and people may add milk, lemon, sugar or honey.

TEA CEREMONIES

Many East Asian countries have elaborate tea ceremonies, with special objects and rituals for brewing and serving tea, many of which reflect the influence of Buddhism. The Japanese tea ceremony *sado/chado* ('the way of tea') is a preparation and presentation of matcha (powdered green tea) using a special procedure called *otemae*, which can be a formal (*chaji*) or informal (*chakai*) tea gathering.

MINT TEA

In North African countries like Morocco, many people sip tea made with fresh mint leaves and lots of sugar all day. Often poured from ornate silver teapots and served in clear glasses, this Maghrebi mint drink is sometimes brewed with green tea, too, for a caffeine kick.

CHAI

Born in India and beloved across South Asia, chai is made by boiling black tea in milk. Masala chai is spiced with ginger, cardamom, cinnamon, cloves and black pepper, and served sweet. Immigrants from India brought chai to East Africa, where it's still popular today.

BISSAP

ICED HIBISCUS TEA

PREPARATION TIME	**COOKING TIME**	**LEVEL OF DIFFICULTY**	**SERVES**
5 mins, plus 2 hrs cooling	15 mins	●	4

This beautiful ruby-coloured tea, the national drink of Senegal, is an iced tea brewed from a species of hibiscus flower native to West Africa. People have brought the flower – and the drink – around the world, and it now goes by many names: sorrel in the Caribbean, sobolo in Ghana, agua de Jamaica in Central and South America, zobo in Nigeria, and karkade in Egypt and northern Sudan, where glasses of it are raised in wedding toasts. In Senegal, it's known as bissap.

Tart when first brewed, bissap is sweetened with sugar and sometimes also spiced with ginger, cloves, allspice or cinnamon.

INGREDIENTS

20 g dried hibiscus flowers
1 small bunch fresh mint
   (optional)
2 cinnamon sticks (optional)
4 tablespoons sugar, plus more
   to taste

1. In a small pot, bring 950 ml of water to a boil. Add the hibiscus flowers, reduce the heat to medium and simmer for 2 minutes.

2. Add the mint and cinnamon sticks and remove the pot from the heat. Leave the tea to steep for 10 minutes. Stir in the sugar and taste. Add more sugar, if you prefer.

3. Refrigerate for at least 2 hours, then serve over ice.

MOROCCO

Mountainous Morocco is the only country in Africa that borders both the Mediterranean Sea and the Atlantic Ocean. Foods here reflect the influences of its neighbours: France, Portugal and Spain, as well as the other North African nations of the Maghreb and the indigenous Amazigh cultures. In Morocco's famous maze-like marketplaces, people sell everything from spices to silk scarves to citrus. As you might expect in a country with so much coastline, lots of people here make their living catching and selling fish – which also features in the gorgeous cuisine here – served with couscous, fresh olives, pickled lemons and warm bread.

FISH

In Morocco, which boasts more than 2,400 kilometres of coastline, fish virtually leap onto your plate. Sea bream, sardines, anchovies and tuna are all major catches, and Moroccans feast on them poached, marinated, braised, grilled, simmered and fried. Fish also play a starring role in couscous dishes or tagines, and fresh fish is often served alongside a selection of Moroccan salads.

COUSCOUS

This tiny traditional pasta has been eaten daily in North Africa and many other parts of the world for centuries, and while it's now easy to buy in stores, many cooks still make it from scratch. First, they will sprinkle salted water into a bowl of semolina flour, then move their fingers in a circle so small granules form. They then sort each granule by size for drying. After steaming, it's time to eat.

TAGINE

This stew is one of the best-known dishes in Morocco and much of North Africa. It is named after the vessel in which it's made: a clay pot with a cone-shaped lid. Tagines vary but a chicken tagine might be made with onions, garlic, parsley, olive oil, cooked until the meat is tender, then served with paprika, almonds, ginger and more olive oil!

LAMB

Lamb has been a favourite meat here for centuries, and some preparations date back to the Middle Ages. Steamed sheep's head, often served with couscous, is traditional at *Eid al-Adha*, a major Muslim holiday commemorating Abraham's willingness to sacrifice his son (fortunately he sacrificed a lamb instead!).

DAIRY

Moroccans make magic with milk. Sheep, goat or cow's milk may be made into jben (cheese), or into rayeb, a sweetened custard-like preparation, made by curdling milk with wild artichoke.

PASTILLA

This giant pie – also a speciality in neighbouring Algeria – may be the grandest of Moroccan dishes. Pastilla is traditionally filled with stewed pigeons (although now chicken is often used), with toasted almonds, eggs, saffron and cinnamon. The layers of flaky pastry are so thin they're called warqa, a word that means 'leaf' in Arabic, as in leaf of paper.

LEMONS

In Morocco, round, sweet lemon varieties called doqq and boussera are pickled in salty brine and then used as a condiment in salads or stews. Moroccans call preserved lemons lim mraqqed, which translates to 'lemons put to sleep'!

ARGAN OIL

The tree argan oil comes from is famously thorny and bears fruit just once a year. Each nut's oily kernels are toasted, ground and pressed by hand. But all this work is worth it for the rich oil. You can dip bread in the nutty-flavoured oil or drizzle it over pasta.

SMEN

Known as smen, preserved butter makes many Moroccan dishes even more delicious. Made from clarified butter, salt and sometimes herbs, smen is fermented for months or even years. The flavour is intense, something like aged cheese. Smen is used as a spread, added to stews and even sometimes enjoyed in coffee.

KSRA

Many Moroccans knead and shape this semolina flatbread at home, then bring the dough to a local bakery to pop in the oven. The round dense loaves are flavoured with aniseed, nigella, fennel or sesame seeds and are often served with tagine.

HARIRA

SPICED VEGETABLE SOUP

PREPARATION TIME	COOKING TIME	LEVEL OF DIFFICULTY	SERVES
20 mins	1 hr 10 mins	● ●	6

This flavourful savoury Moroccan soup is lush with vegetables and perfumed with spices. During Ramadan, a holy month for Muslims, so many Muslims break their daily fast with this soup that you can smell it cooking every afternoon. There are many regional variations, including some with vermicelli or rice and meat versions.

INGREDIENTS

4 tablespoons olive oil
2 onions, diced
2 cloves garlic, chopped
5 sticks celery, including leaves, chopped
3 to 4 carrots, sliced into moons or half-moons
½ teaspoon ground turmeric
½ teaspoon ground ginger
½ teaspoon ground cumin
½ teaspoon harissa
1 cinnamon stick
1 800-g tin tomatoes, crushed or chopped
1 teaspoon salt
1 bunch fresh coriander, chopped
1.6 litres vegetable stock or water
230 g dried green lentils
1 400-g tin chickpeas
salt and black pepper
juice of 1 lemon

1. In a large, heavy-bottomed pot over a medium heat, warm the olive oil and pan-fry the onion, garlic, celery and carrots for 10 minutes, stirring occasionally.

2. Add the spices, tomatoes, salt, half of the fresh coriander and the stock or water, and bring to a boil.

3. Reduce the heat to medium-low and simmer for 20 minutes, then add the lentils and chickpeas and simmer for 30 minutes. Test a lentil to be sure it's cooked through.

4. Season with salt and pepper to taste, and finish with the remaining fresh coriander and the lemon juice.

Lamb is also delicious in harira. If you'd like to include 450 g of cubed lamb-stew meat, first lightly brown it in oil for a few minutes on all sides, then add to the pot in the first step.

NIGERIA

Nigeria is home to plains and plateaus, tall mountains, a long coastline on the Gulf of Guinea and the Niger River, for which the country is named. This varied tropical landscape is rich in natural resources, including excellent farmland that produces deliciously diverse flavours. The city of Lagos is one of the biggest metropolitan areas in the world, home to over 20 million people, including many millionaires and billionaires. Nigerian culinary traditions have influenced food as far away as Brazil, Cuba and the United States.

YAMS

Yams are an edible tuber grown in enormous quantities in Nigeria. Yams here are a daily staple, prepared in many ways: they are boiled, fried and pounded into a paste; made into flour; sliced into chips; and cooked into porridge. To quote a Nigerian saying, 'Yam is food and food is yam'.

EGUSI SOUP

Egusi soup gets its rich umami flavour from a special ingredient: the edible seeds of an inedible watermelon-like gourd. The seeds are ground to a fine powder and mixed into a silky soup with spices, onions, tomatoes, leafy greens and sometimes chicken, or dried crawfish.

GARRI

Garri, a staple across Nigeria, is made from freshly harvested cassava. The roots – poisonous raw – are carefully peeled and cooked, grated into granules and dried. Once reconstituted, garri can be eaten hot or cold, sweet or savoury, and as eba, a 'swallow'. The Yoruba, one of Nigeria's largest ethnic groups, often enjoy garri as a doughy accompaniment to okra stew or egusi soup.

SWALLOWS

Several Nigerian meals consist of a soup and 'a swallow', the term for any starchy paste that you don't need to chew – simply swallow! Nigeria is a land of many swallows. Examples include eba (made from garri), pounded yam, amala (a paste made from the yam's skin) and fufu (made from fermented and ground cassava).

RED PALM OIL

Extracted from the pulp of the oil palm fruit, unrefined palm oil is a deep orange-red with a nutty flavour. It has been a staple of the West African diet for a long, long time. Archaeological evidence found that people in the region were cultivating and eating it 5,000 years ago!

KOLA NUTS

Kola created that world-famous 'cola' flavour but in Nigeria, the nuts, which grow in West Africa's tropical rain forests, are also known as a typical snack and sometimes form part of sacred Igbo ceremonies, where they can symbolize hospitality, respect and ancestors. Kola nuts contain caffeine and some believe they can taste bitter at first but they become sweeter as you chew.

MOIN MOIN

This savoury bean pudding is made by grinding black-eyed beans into a paste, adding palm oil and seasonings and, once they are wrapped in banana leaves or a heat-proof container, placed in a pot to cook. Some cooks add meat, prawns and hard-boiled eggs. If you add enough extra ingredients, you end up with moin-moin elemi meje, meaning 'seven lives'.

KULI KULI

These salty, spicy, crunchy snacks are often sold at roadside stands in Nigeria, Cameroon, Benin and Ghana. Vendors roast groundnuts (peanuts), grind them into a paste, and mix in spices and sometimes sugar. The paste is then shaped into balls, skinny squiggles, flat squares or rings and deep-fried until crisp.

MEMORIES OF OKPA

The world-famous Nigerian writer, Chimamanda Ngozi Adichie, reminisced in the *New Yorker* about her childhood memories of 'warm okpa, which remains my favourite food: a simple, orange-coloured, steamed pie of white beans and palm oil that tastes best cooked in banana leaves'.

JOLLOF RICE

RICE WITH TOMATO PURÉE AND SPICES

PREPARATION TIME
20 mins

COOKING TIME
45 mins

LEVEL OF DIFFICULTY
● ●

SERVES
6 to 8

This wonderfully flavourful and often a little spicy rice recipe is beloved across West Africa and south of the Sahara. While every family has their own recipe – some add curry powder, cloves or mint – most include puréed tomatoes, making the finished dish a beautiful red. You might taste versions with chicken, ham, seafood, pumpkin or peas, and in some French-speaking parts of West Africa, cooks might add carrots, aubergine or cabbage. While most cooks make their own tomato purée, this recipe simply asks for tinned tomato purée. The whole chilli gives the dish a lovely citrusy flavour and heat.

INGREDIENTS

400 g long-grain white rice, such as basmati
4 tablespoons olive oil
1 medium red onion, thinly sliced
3 garlic cloves, thinly sliced
2.5-cm piece of root ginger, peeled and finely chopped
140 g tomato purée
1 teaspoon smoked paprika
1 Scotch bonnet or Habanero chilli, stemmed but kept whole
1 teaspoon garlic powder
1 tablespoon onion powder
1½ teaspoons salt
530 ml chicken stock, vegetable stock or water

1. Preheat the oven to 180°C.

2. In a bowl, cover the rice with water and stir a bit to rinse it. Drain. Cover the rice again and leave to soak for 30 minutes. Drain and shake dry.

3. In a large, heavy saucepan or casserole dish, heat the olive oil over a medium heat. Add the onion, season generously with salt and cook, stirring, until softened: about 8 minutes. Add the garlic and ginger and cook until softened: about 3 minutes. Add the tomato purée, smoked paprika and whole chilli. Reduce the heat to low, and cook, stirring frequently, until the tomato purée loses some of its acidic bite: about 10 minutes.

4. Add the garlic powder, onion powder and 1½ teaspoons of salt.

5. Add the rice and stir to coat with the seasonings. Add the stock or water.

6. Increase the heat to high to bring to a simmer, then turn off the heat and put the lid on. Transfer the dish to the oven and cook for 20 minutes, or until all the liquid is absorbed and the rice is tender. Remove the pot from the oven and leave to stand for 10 minutes, then fluff the rice. Remove the whole chilli and taste the rice. Season with more salt, if desired, then serve.

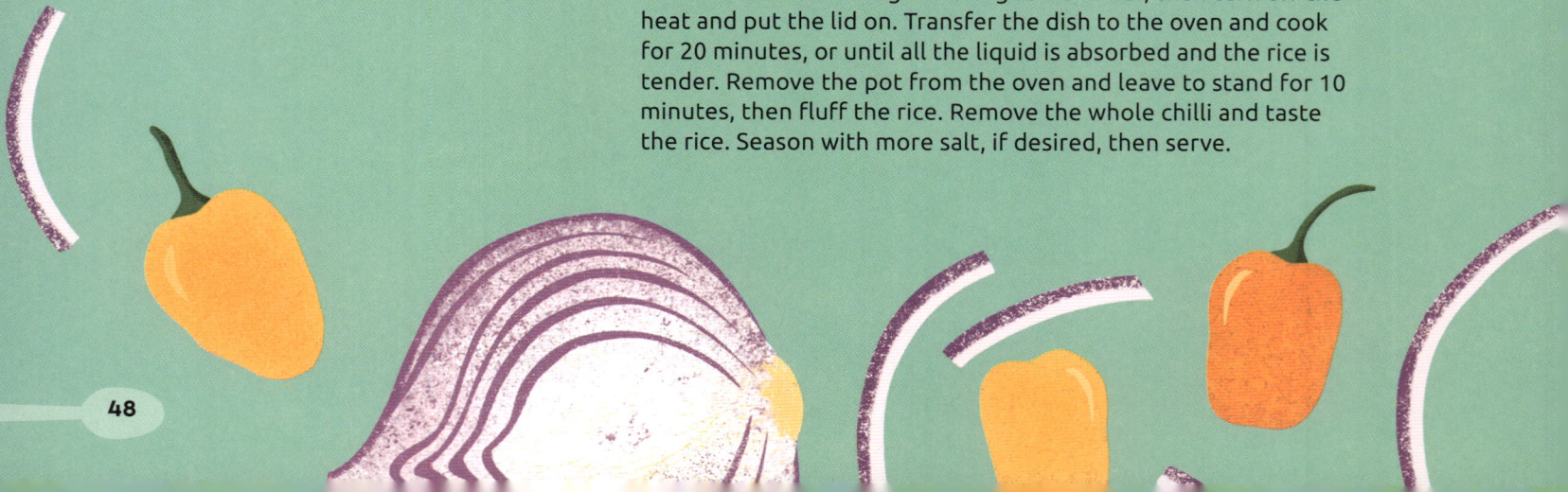

The African diaspora brought versions of this rice recipe around the world, where it evolved into dishes like the flavourful jumbalaya in the American city of New Orleans.

A popular main dish at festivals and special occasions, it's often made in giant batches to serve a crowd and served with braised goat and fried plantains.

SOUTH AFRICA

At the southern tip of Africa between the Indian and Atlantic Oceans sits sunny South Africa. The foods here are influenced by diverse cultures and by native plants and animals. With deserts and grasslands, forests and fynbos, magnificent mountains and coastline, South Africa's regions are extremely varied. In 1652, the Dutch East India Company created a settlement at the Cape of Good Hope (now Cape Town) to provide fresh food to their ships travelling between Europe and Indonesia on the spice trade route. Enslaved people and political prisoners exiled to Cape Town from Southeast Asia brought with them local culinary traditions and spices that still influence recipes here today.

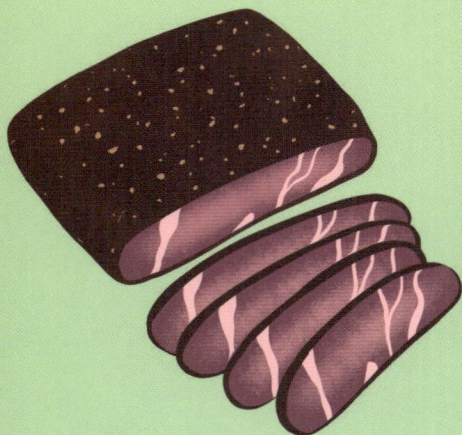

BILTONG

These strips of air-dried beef, venison or ostrich are flavoured with dried coriander. Biltong is salty, nutritious and – according to South Africans – much, much better than beef jerky!

BRAAI

This beloved, communal tradition of open-fire cooking uses charcoal or wood to traditionally braai meat, from lamb chops to sheep's intestines. Boerewors – lamb sausage spiced with coriander seeds and malt vinegar and coiled like a snake – are beloved at a braai. The sausages even hiss while braaing.

LAMB AND MUTTON

South Africans love to eat lamb! The arid Karoo region grows the best-tasting sheep because of the aromatic wild plants they graze on. An affordable alternative to lamb chops is a smiley: a sheep's head, boiled and braaied, or barbecued. Another beloved lamb dish, bobotie, features curried lamb baked with savoury custard and lemon leaves.

BREDIE

This one-pot family meal is a lamb or chicken stew, with vegetables like spinach or tomatoes, all spiced with ginger, cinnamon or chillies. Waterblommetjie bredie is made with the flowers and tender seed pods of a juicy, crunchy, fragrant aquatic plant, gathered from ponds in winter and spring. The sour stems of cape sorrel are added instead of lemon juice.

RUSKS

Rusks are slightly sweet biscuits that start off soft but are sliced open while hot and allowed to air dry. They become wonderfully crunchy and can be dunked into hot tea or coffee for breakfast or a snack.

AMAGWINYA

These deep-fried, yeasted dough balls – a bit like doughnuts without the hole – are eaten as a snack, as breakfast with syrup, or lunch with a curried or saucy topping.

AMASI

Creamy and tangy, amasi (or suurmelk – 'sour milk') is a cultured drink similar to buttermilk. It probably evolved as a way of using milk that had turned sour before fridges were invented. Amasi is sold in supermarkets alongside milk and is also easy to make at home.

BUNNY CHOW

This traditional dish is a hollowed-out white bread stuffed with steaming-hot meat or vegetable curry, made with a local curry powder blend. It evolved in Durban, a city in KwaZulu-Natal province that's home to a large Indian community, many of whom are descendants of indentured labourers brought here in the late nineteenth century.

NELSON MANDELA

Nelson Mandela was an activist who fought the white-supremacist system of apartheid and was imprisoned for twenty-seven years before becoming South Africa's first Black president in 1994. Supporters smuggled chicken curry to him in prison. The day he was released, he celebrated with a curry and rum-raisin ice cream with Archbishop Desmond Tutu, his days of hunger strikes long behind him.

SEAFOOD

The coast here is nearly endless, so people feast on seafood like mussels, oysters, abalone and kreef (spiny rock lobster). Barracuda-like snoek is braaied. Bokkoms (a herring) are salted and dried. Fish and chips are eaten everywhere, served with slapchips (floppy chips), soused with malt vinegar.

51

POTELE

SIMMERED CORNMEAL WITH WILD GREENS, BROTH AND BUTTER

PREPARATION TIME	COOKING TIME	LEVEL OF DIFFICULTY	SERVES
5 mins	20 mins	●●	4

Potele is the Sotho name for a dish of mealie meal – mealie is the South African word for corn or maize – cooked with edible wild greens. It is an inexpensive and nourishing meal and a beloved traditional comfort food for many Black South Africans. Potele is often made with umsobo (black nightshade leaves) but any wild edible green – or so-called weed – can be used, such as amaranth (also known as pigweed), lamb's quarters, nettles, quickweed or sowthistle.

INGREDIENTS

FOR THE GREENS
340 g washed cooking greens, such as kale, Swiss chard, spring greens or spinach
85 g spring onions, chopped

FOR THE MEALIE MEAL
55 g mealie meal (cornmeal)
¼ teaspoon salt
2 tablespoons butter

TO MAKE THE GREENS

1. In a pot, bring 350 ml water or broth to a boil and add the greens and the spring onions. Cook, stirring, for a few minutes until the greens are tender but still bright green. Turn off the heat and transfer the greens and their broth to a bowl. Return the pot to the hob.

TO MAKE THE MEALIE MEAL

2. In a bowl, mix the mealie meal with 250 ml of water to form a loose slurry and stir until no lumps remain.

3. Pour this into your (now empty) pot, add the salt and cook over a medium heat, stirring continuously. Add the rest of the water gradually as the mixture stiffens. Cook until the mealie meal is done: about 8 to 10 minutes.

4. Stir in the blanched greens and their broth and the butter. Cook for another 3 minutes to gently heat the greens, then serve warm, with a spoon.

Fresh corn cobs are delicious roasted on the braai or boiled and munched hot. The kernels are often added to steamed mealie bread, eaten hot with butter and golden syrup.

CORN

AROUND THE WORLD

Corn, now a global crop, was first grown in what is now southern Mexico over 9,000 years ago, when the people of ancient Mesoamerica cultivated and cherished a wild grassy plant called teosinte until it bore delicious kernels. Over time, people developed diverse varieties, from the sweet tender kernels eaten right off the cob to the broad, starchy dent corn eaten in the Andes paired with salty fresh cheese or cooked into a tortilla.

POPCORN

Some types of corn, once dried, can be heated until the moisture within causes the kernel to POP. This was likely discovered by accident when kernels fell too close to a fire. Today, it's topped with everything from melted butter to lime and Salsa Valentina™.

CORN TORTILLAS AND TORTILLA CHIPS

Tortillas – made from corn masa dough, cooked on a hot griddle – become tacos when wrapped around delicious fillings or quesadillas when layered with cheese. Fry left-over tortillas into crispy tortilla chips to dip into guacamole and salsas, or make chilaquiles for breakfast!

TAMALES

This traditional Mexican dish isn't just made of delicious corn dough. Since pre-Hispanic times, they've also been cooked in yellow corn husks. The ribbed husks naturally leave tiny beautiful stripes imprinted in the cooked tamale.

SUB-SAHARAN AFRICAN CORN PORRIDGE

Corn was brought to Africa by Portuguese merchants in the sixteenth century. From there, it quickly became a favourite ingredient for porridge – for example, used in the stiff, thick ugali served in Kenya or for the softer pap served in South African stews.

CHICHA AND TEJUINO

Special corn drinks date back to pre-Hispanic times. Chicha is originally from the Andes, where sprouted corn kernels are mashed and fermented until sour and bubbly. In Mexico, people make tejuino by mixing corn masa with boiling water. Once cooled, it's served over shaved ice with lime and a dash of chilli powder.

CORNBREAD

Originating from Native American recipes, people in the United States today bake cornmeal into golden cornbread, often cooked and served in a cast-iron frying pan. People like to argue about whether to add sugar – only in the north, never in the south! – but many people add buttermilk, bacon, chilli peppers or fresh corn kernels.

ITALIAN POLENTA

Corn was sailed back to Europe and is enjoyed in Italy as a ground grain simmered into a golden yellow porridge called polenta. Often cooked with flavourful stock or parmesan, polenta can be served in place of pasta or cooled until firm, cut into slices and fried or grilled.

SUCCOTASH

A traditional Native American dish of North America, succotash combines sweet yellow corn and lima beans. Meaning 'broken corn' in the Narragansett language, the recipe was adopted by English colonists and is still enjoyed from coast to coast today.

ESQUITES

In Mexico, boiled corn kernels are served warm in a cup, topped with your choice of lime juice, mayonnaise, chilli powder or butter and salt! The sweet-salty-spicy snack can be served as a side or bought on the go.

BABY CORN

A favourite in Chinese cuisine, baby corn is exactly what its name describes. Harvested very young, tiny, 2.5-cm-long immature corn is treasured for its sweetness, soft cob and complete munchability. It's tossed into stir-fries and eaten whole.

SUDAN

Sudan is a vast country in northeastern Africa, bordered by seven other countries and the Red Sea. Two strands of the Nile River converge in Sudan's capital, Khartoum, and while Sudan is famous for its deserts, it is also home to mountains, savannas and woodlands. At the crossroads of Africa and the Middle East, it's a cultural melting pot of Arab, Nubian, Egyptian, Turkish and Levantine influences. More than one hundred tribes live here, speaking one hundred languages, and many of the foods enjoyed by the Sudan's 45 million citizens have roots going back for centuries!

GUHWAH COFFEE

Coffee first grew wild in East Africa, and people here in Sudan and in neighbouring Ethiopia have been enjoying it for centuries. The traditional Sudanese coffee ritual starts with grinding roasted beans in a mortar and pestle, and simmering the grounds in a clay pot or jar, often with spices like cardamom, ginger and black pepper.

KAJAIK

Sudan is country rich with rivers, lakes and swamps, and people who live near these waters feast on lots of freshwater fish. Kajaik is a classic fish stew that originated in South Sudan. It's made with dried fish, tomatoes and vegetables like onions, carrots, peppers and potatoes. The ingredients are cooked together in coconut water, and some cooks add curry powder for extra flavour.

MEAT LOVERS

In much of Sudan, meat makes the meal. Lamb, mutton, goat, beef, chicken, fish and camel are popular. Some chefs like to flavour their meat with ground-up roasted peanuts, cumin and salt before threading it onto skewers and grilling.

ESSENTIAL MANGOES

Mangoes have thrived in Sudan for generations and are highly prized. Today, dozens of different varieties of the juicy-sweet fruits grow all across the country.

SWEET TREATS

Desserts here showcase the influence of Arabic flavours. Many people enjoy dried dates or apricots, as well as treats like assidatal-boubar (a pumpkin-based dessert), basbousa (a semolina cake soaked in sugar syrup) and mukhbaza (a pudding made of breadcrumbs blended with mashed banana and honey).

STREET FOOD CITY

Some of the capital city Khartoum's most delicious food can be found at street stalls. Some vendors specialize in grilled meats cooked with a technique called salat, which uses a bed of hot rocks for searing. Kisra, a type of super thin pancake made of fermented sorghum flour, is a popular street snack often served alongside savoury stew.

FUL MEDAMES

The single most beloved dish here might be ful medames – a delicious blend of broad beans mixed with garlic, lemon juice, tomatoes, chilli pepper and spices, which is enjoyed across North Africa and the Middle East. Ful medames can be eaten for any meal but it's beloved at breakfast – when it's served with eggs and bread.

MOULLAH (OR MULLAH)

This classic, savoury Sudanese stew is often studded with lamb or fish, and can also contain robe – the Arabic word for 'yoghurt'. Garlic, onions, red peppers and aromatic spices give the stew big flavours, while okra or peanut butter can make it nice and thick.

ASEEDA (OR ASIDA)

This staple Sudanese starch is made by stirring wheat flour, sorghum or millet into boiling water. The resulting oatmeal-like porridge can be topped with salt and melted butter or honey and is a favourite for breakfast. In the afternoon or evening, it often accompanies moullah or other savoury stews.

DATES

Behhah, or Sudanese dates, are prized for their large size and great flavour. Farmers cultivate date palms along the banks of the Nile and anywhere else that groundwater can support the tall trees. Sudanese farmers pollinate the fruits by hand, which can require expertly climbing quite high up the narrow trunks!

57

SALATA TOMATIM BEL DAQUA

PEANUT-PASTE SALAD

PREPARATION TIME	COOKING TIME	LEVEL OF DIFFICULTY	SERVES
30 mins	0 mins	●	2 to 4

Peanuts, also known as groundnuts, are a Sudanese favourite. Farmers grow them for both eating and to export, and people across the region enjoy them in their daily diet. Street vendors offer roasted peanuts everywhere, and Sudanese cooks add peanut-paste to meat dishes, stews and more. Peanut-paste is also the base of the sweet-tart dressing in this refreshing salad, which is commonly served alongside Sudanese favourites like spiced goat and the cracker-thin bread called kissra.

INGREDIENTS

40 g peanuts, freshly ground (or
   3 tablespoons peanut butter)
2 tablespoons sesame oil
   (or peanut or olive oil)
1 lime, juiced
1 teaspoon salt
1 teaspoon sugar
pinch ground cloves
pinch ground curry leaves
¼ teaspoon ground coriander
1 clove garlic, chopped
4 to 5 medium tomatoes, diced
1 medium cucumber, diced
1 small red onion, diced, or
   4 spring onions, finely sliced
1 sweet pepper, de-seeded and
   diced
small handful fresh coriander,
   chopped

1. In a medium bowl, combine the ground peanuts or peanut butter, oil, lime juice, salt, sugar, spices and garlic. Add 60 ml of water and whisk gently into a smooth paste. If the paste is too thick to dress a salad, add more water, 1 tablespoon at a time, until thin enough. Taste and adjust seasonings.

2. Add the chopped vegetables to the bowl and toss gently to dress. Serve the salad garnished with the fresh coriander.

If you enjoy a little heat, try adding a chopped chilli pepper to the dressing.

TANZANIA

This East African country is home to Africa's tallest mountain (Kilimanjaro), the world's second-largest freshwater lake (Lake Victoria) as well as the world's second-deepest freshwater lake (Lake Tanganyika). Tanzania is also home to the fertile island of Zanzibar, where the tropical climate and rich soil are perfect for growing prized spices! Combining African, Arab, Indian and European traditions, and drawing upon a spectacular selection of fresh seafood, Tanzanian menus offer a tantalizing range of seafood–coconut stews, grilled goat, flavourful chutneys, healthful greens, sweet doughnuts and dizzyingly diverse bananas.

MEAT OF THE MATTER

Meat here is highly prized. Beef, chicken and pork (except in Muslim areas) are on the menu but goat is the favourite. Meats may be cooked over charcoal fires and served with chapati (Indian flatbread). Barbecued nyama choma, typically made with goat, is roasted slowly over hot coals and served in restaurants or sold on the street.

THE SPICE TRADE

The Island of Zanzibar grows nearly every spice you can think of, like nutmeg, cinnamon, cardamom, turmeric, fresh ginger, vanilla pods, liquorice, ylang-ylang, lemongrass and a rainbow of brilliantly coloured (and flavoured) peppers. Many people from India settled in East Africa, and today Tanzanian recipes incorporate Indian spices too – few home kitchens here are without mchuzi (curry powder).

THE MAASAI

The Maasai people raise cattle and goats, roaming where the flock can find good grazing land. Maasai enjoy a diet of goat meat, milk and the blood of the cattle they raise.

FLUSH WITH FISH

With its amazing coastline and huge lakes, Tanzania sparkles with fresh fish. Open-air stalls sell prawns, squid, tilapia, catfish and octopus that has been grilled whole or skewered into kebabs. Many fish dishes here are rich with coconut milk – thanks both to the Asian influence and to the many coconut trees!

BANANAS

Tanzanian farmers grow over twenty varieties of bananas. The little ndizi kisukari is so sweet, it's named after the Swahili word for 'sugar'. The nkonjwa variety with its thick peel and bigger fruits is often roasted over a low flame. And the mbire banana is used to make banana beer! Bananas also feature in many traditional dishes, including supu viazi.

CAMEL HUMP

Ever wonder why camels have humps? Mostly fat, a camel hump is sort of a fuel tank that helps the animal sustain itself for up to two weeks by using up this stored fat as energy. Young camel hump meat is also considered a delicacy in Tanzania, especially on the island of Zanzibar.

CLOVES

Tanzania clove – karafuu in Swahili – comes from the plant's flowers. The spice isn't just an ingredient – Tanzanians also have a tradition of offering cloves to dinner guests and chewing cloves before a meal to aid digestion.

BAOBAB

The beautiful, fat-trunked baobab tree, which is found in Tarangire National Park, is known as the tree of life. Tanzanians enjoy the tree's papaya-shaped, coconut-sized fruits, which are called monkey bread, as well as the leaves, which can taste similar to spinach.

SUPU VIAZI

This traditional Tanzanian coconut–potato soup starts with a base of peppers, onions and tomatoes, an essential flavour trio across the region. Next, cooks add potatoes, coconuts and green banana, yielding a lusciously thick and velvety soup. And to make it even creamier, locals top it with sliced avocado.

NDIZI KANGA

FRIED PLANTAINS

PREPARATION TIME	COOKING TIME	LEVEL OF DIFFICULTY	SERVES
10 mins	15 mins	●	4

People across Africa have been growing and eating bananas for many centuries. Some varieties, like plantain, are best cooked. Eating it raw would be similar to trying to eat a raw potato! In Tanzania, plantains are so popular that people enjoy millions of tons of them each year. They're simmered into stews, cooked in coconut, braised with beef, fried into crisp cakes or even brewed into beer. But perhaps they're most famous as this simple snack. If you haven't cooked plantains before, here's a great way to try them. Use plantains that are yellow but firm.

INGREDIENTS

2 yellow plantains
4 tablespoons unsalted butter
salt

1. Peel the plantains and cut them into slices that are about 15 mm thick.

2. Line a plate with kitchen paper.

3. In a large non-stick frying pan, melt the butter over a medium heat. Add the plantains in a single layer (you might need to do this in batches) and cook until nicely golden on the bottom: about 3 minutes. Flip each slice over and cook until golden on the bottom: 2 to 3 minutes longer.

4. Transfer the cooked plantains to the kitchen-paper-lined plate to drain, and season with salt to taste. Enjoy warm.

In the Caribbean, some people of African ancestry fry sliced salted plantain to make tostones – crunchy on the outside and pillowy soft inside – and maduros – pan-fried green plantains that caramelize into super sweet treats.

FRUIT

AROUND THE WORLD

Fruit has beckoned us since our days as hunter-gatherers. Ancient civilizations in such places as Egypt and India tended orchards of luscious fruits like dates, figs and pomegranates, celebrated by sacred ceremonies and heartfelt poems. Even today, when we can choose from endless processed and packaged sweets, there's still nothing as magical as spring's first strawberries, a perfectly juicy summer mango or the ripe crunch of apples in autumn.

COCONUT

Native to Oceania, coconuts have ridden waves to distant shores, planting themselves as palm trees on tropical beaches worldwide, from the Philippines to Tanzania, Mozambique and the Caribbean. Hack one open and you can drink its sweet juice, eat its gelatinous flesh with a spoon or make coconut cream, oil, sugar or vinegar. People even serve food in the shells!

PAPAYA

The fruit of a giant herb native to Central America, papaya has soft, sweet, orange flesh when ripe, with glistening black seeds at its centre. Eat it fresh with a spoon or pick it green and shred it into Thailand's famous som tum salad, dressed with chillies, peanuts, fish sauce and lime juice!

PASSION FRUIT

The passion fruit plant bears beautiful purple flowers and egg-sized fruit that wrinkle when ripe. The soft orange pulp is delicious straight or when made into jelly, juice or ice cream. Brazilians make passion fruit mousse and cocktails, while Australians put passion fruit icing on cakes.

BANANA

Growing wild in Southeast Asia for a million years, bananas are now farmed in warm climates worldwide and beloved everywhere. There are countless varieties of sweet bananas, eaten raw or added to smoothies and muffins, while plantains are pounded into African fufu and fried into Caribbean tostones. In India, giant banana leaves are used as beautiful green platters.

PINEAPPLE

The pineapple is native to Brazil, where many types grow wild. Christopher Columbus was wowed by pineapple in Guadalupe so brought cuttings with him to Spain, and soon the fruit was growing in Asia, Africa and beyond. Today, it's farmed from Hawaii to Malaysia, and while much ends up in cans, some people grill it, put it on pizza or bake it into pineapple upside-down cake.

MANGO

Mangoes first grew wild in India and have been cultivated there for over 4,000 years. The 'king of fruits' is now farmed as far away as Mexico, but India still grows the most mangoes in the world. Try mango in spicy mango chutney, sour mango pickles, sweet yoghurt drinks called lassis or simply enjoy its sweet flesh raw, sprinkled with lime and chilli pepper.

POMEGRANATE

Native to Iran and Afghanistan, where they still grow wild, pomegranates were so beloved by ancient Egyptians and Greeks that they appear in their classic mythology. Pomegranates are eaten fresh, sprinkled over salads, pressed into juice, made into jam and simmered into a sweet grenadine syrup that's stirred into pink drinks.

FIGS

Each little fig is actually over a thousand tiny fruits, historically pollinated by a tiny insect called the fig wasp. First farmed in Egypt 6,000 years ago, figs were beloved by ancient Romans and today Italians still enjoy them in salads and on cheese plates. Fig skins may be yellow-green or blue-black with soft, sweet, pink-purple flesh.

LYCHEE

Native to China, lychees were so prized by imperial courts that they were transported from the south by special fast horses. During the Ming Dynasty, people met in temples and gardens to eat hundreds at a time; once you taste its aromatic white flesh, you'll see why. Now many markets carry them tinned in sweet syrup, no fast horses needed.

GRAPES

Grapes have been celebrated since ancient times, appearing in Egyptian tomb paintings and the Bible. They are eaten fresh, dried into raisins, turned into wine and made into what many in the U.S. would consider peanut butter's best friend, grape jam!

SOURSOP

Native to the West Indies and South America, this tropical fruit with spiny, prickly skin grows on flowering evergreen trees. The soft, sweet pineapple-y pulp is refreshing in juice, ice cream, custards and sweets.

UGANDA

Uganda is a lush, land-locked East African country stretching from the shores of Lake Victoria, which is home to crocodiles and hippos, to the slopes of the Rwenzori Mountains, where gorillas famously roam. It is also home to over 47 million people. The land is extremely fertile and more than 70% of Ugandans work in farming. The most important crops are coffee, tea and sugar cane.

MATOOKE

Matooke, a popular starch in Uganda, is made from green bananas that are peeled, tied into packages made of banana leaves and steamed. The whole bundle is then squeezed and mashed until the contents are smooth. Matooke, sometimes cooked over a charcoal fire, is often served with a peanut sauce and may be paired with smoked fish or mushrooms.

FOOT STEW

Kigere, also known as mulokoni, is a stew made of cows' or pigs' hooves. When slow cooked, the hooves become gelatinous and release their marrow into the thickening broth. Recipes vary but kigere commonly includes onions, garlic, peppers, carrots, tomatoes, potatoes and coriander.

MEAT LOVERS

Ugandans enjoy a meaty diet with lots of beef, chicken, goat and pork. Arguably the country's most famous dish is luwombo, said to have been created in 1887 by the personal chef of King Kabaka Mwanga. It's made with diced meat that's pan-fried with onions, tomatoes, peanuts and mushrooms, then wrapped in a banana leaf and steamed.

BANANA BONANZA

Ugandans have literally hundreds of ways to prepare bananas, including frying, stewing, roasting, grilling and steaming. Green bananas are usually served as an accompaniment or ingredient in savoury main dishes, whereas sweeter, ripe yellow ones are reserved for desserts. Gonja, or sweet plantains, are also very popular and are eaten ripe or unripe.

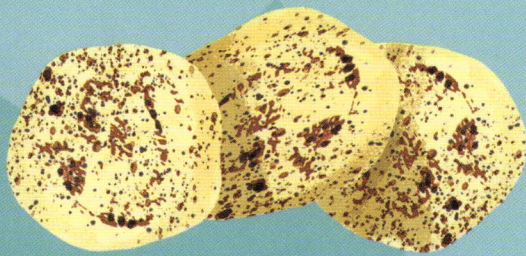

CHAPATI

Chapati – pan-fried, unleavened flatbreads – were introduced to the region by Indian labourers who came to East Africa to build a railway from Kenya into Uganda. Although many Indian Ugandans were forced to leave during the 1970s, their influences on the country's food culture remain today.

ROLEX

If someone in Uganda says they want a rolex they probably aren't referring to a watch but to a favourite food sold by roadside vendors around the country. Rolex is slang for 'rolled egg', and these savoury treats consist of a vegetable omelette rolled up in a chapati – creating a perfect on-the-go street breakfast, lunch or snack.

SALT MINING

Uganda's salt mining industry stems from its many lakes. Formed by ancient volcanoes, these lakes evaporate during the dry season, allowing people access to the delicious, crusty salt left behind. Salt has a rich cultural significance in Uganda and is added to rice, used for preserving fish or sprinkled over fried plantains.

FRIED GRASSHOPPERS

Nsenene, or fried grasshoppers, are a popular rainy season snack. To prepare the grasshoppers, their feet and wings are pulled off before they're fried. According to some Ugandans, they taste like crispy chicken skin. Some cooks add them to rolexes for extra crunch and flavour, or make them into burgers.

COFFEE VERSUS TEA

Uganda produces millions of bags of coffee for export each year, representing up to 19% of the country's foreign exchange. Yet Ugandans usually prefer tea – a legacy of British colonialism. Commercial tea cultivation began in the 1920s, and Uganda is now the second-largest tea producer in Africa, after Kenya. Ugandans take their tea 'cooked and spiced', short for adding milk, sugar and ginger.

MANDAZI

BAKED DOUGHNUTS WITH CARDAMOM AND ICING SUGAR

PREPARATION TIME
45 mins

COOKING TIME
20 mins

LEVEL OF DIFFICULTY
● ●

MAKES
About 16
doughnuts

These not-too-sweet doughnuts are beloved across East Africa, especially in Uganda, Tanzania and Kenya. They can be enjoyed with a cup of spicy-sweet chai at breakfast, as a snack at teatime, or served with dinner to sop up the savoury sauce of pigeon peas simmered in coconut milk. While mandazi dough is often yeasted and deep-fried, in this super simple version it's leavened with baking powder and then simply baked in the oven, rather than boiled in oil. For extra sweetness, dust the finished mandazi with icing sugar.

INGREDIENTS

450 g plain flour
100 g caster sugar
1 teaspoon baking powder
1 teaspoon ground cardamom
½ teaspoon salt
120 ml full-fat milk or coconut
    milk
4 tablespoons unsalted butter,
    melted and cooled
2 large eggs
30 g icing sugar, for dusting
    (optional)

1. In a large mixing bowl, whisk together the flour, sugar, baking powder, cardamom and salt.

2. In a separate bowl, whisk together the milk, melted butter and eggs.

3. Gradually pour the wet ingredients into the dry ingredients, stirring until a sticky dough forms. Turn the dough out onto a floured surface and knead until it becomes smooth and elastic: about 5 minutes. Cover with a tea towel and leave to rest for 30 minutes.

4. Preheat your oven to 180°C and line two baking trays with greaseproof paper.

5. Roll out the dough into a rectangle so it's about 5mm thick and, using a sharp knife or pizza cutter, slice it into eight rectangles, then cut each rectangle in half on the diagonal to form triangles.

6. Transfer the triangles to the prepared baking trays and bake for 18 to 20 minutes, or until the mandazi are lightly golden and cooked through.

7. Leave the mandazi to cool for a few minutes, then dust them with icing sugar, if using.

Don't skip the cardamom,
which perfumes mandazi with
its unmistakable aroma.

ASIA

Asia is the largest, most populous continent, stretching from the Mediterranean Sea to the Pacific Ocean and from snowy Siberia to Indonesia's tropical islands. Asia boasts the world's largest freshwater lake (the Caspian Sea) and the world's highest mountain (Mount Everest). Forests shelter Siberian tigers, Indian elephants and Sumatran orangutans, while sea turtles swim in Malaysian coral reefs. Asia includes the two most populous countries – India and China. Here you'll find past and future; cities like Tokyo and Beijing are home to both ancient temples and modern skyscrapers.

While Asia's 4.5 billion residents enjoy diverse cuisines, some ingredients cross cultures. Tea goes back thousands of years, and today you can sip Thai iced tea or Indian spiced chai, attend a Japanese tea ceremony and eat a tea-leaf salad from Myanmar. Noodles were invented here, and now include ramen, udon, soba, jap chae, laska and lo mein just to name a few. Asian chefs have perfected dumplings, like Chinese wontons, Nepalese momo, Japanese gyoza, Korean mandu and Filipino siomai. And rice is a nearly universal staple, often paired with soy that's been transformed into tofu, soy sauce, miso or simply steamed into edamame.

AFGHANISTAN

This ancient land includes high mountains, vast deserts, great fertile green valleys and plains, and lots of winter snow. This diverse terrain grows diverse ingredients, from grapes and mulberries to sour oranges. Along a major crossroads on the ancient Silk Road (a network of trade routes that linked countries across Europe and Asia), Afghanistan was a place for the exchange of ideas, ingredients and recipes. Despite conflicts that have led to hardship, many families here still prepare traditional elaborate nightly dinners, with home-baked bread, rich cheese, unctuous lamb, steaming tea and sweet cakes.

LAMB

Afghans love to eat lamb, often from special sheep with extra-fat tails! The flavourful tail fat is made into roghan-e-dumbah, used for traditional Afghan cooking.

RICE

This essential daily staple is often cooked with meat and stock into a delicious dish called pulao. For weddings and other special feasts, Afghans make special kabuli pulao – rice studded with lamb, carrots, raisins and almonds.

NAAN

This flatbread is often used to scoop up food or soak up yummy juices. Many Afghans bake theirs in a clay tandoor built into the ground at home – or you can take your home-made dough to be baked in a tandoor at a local bakery. For breakfast, naan is often topped with butter, yoghurt, honey or jam.

KORMAS

These traditional Afghan curries are made of braised meats or vegetables in a flavourful base of fried onions, tomatoes and turmeric. Kormas are served with rice and bread, and with mast – a homemade yoghurt sauce with lemon, salt and mint, or salata – a refreshing salad of diced tomatoes, cucumbers, onions, lemon juice and mint.

TEA

Friends and family love to visit for teatime, when hosts steep loose green or black tea with flavourful cardamom pods. Afghans also love to meet for tea at cafés called samovar or chikhana, some of which serve a dish called teapot soup, made of lamb, onions, split peas and fresh coriander, simmered in a teapot!

MANTU

These traditional dumplings require lots of handwork – cooking the onions and beef, sealing the filling into little pieces of dough, and then steaming – so they are best made by groups of people to share the work. The results are an Afghan favourite.

DAIRY

Afghanistan is home to diverse dairy, especially in the mountains, where herders enjoy milk from cows, water buffalo, sheep and goats, and make it into maska (butter), panir (cheese) and mast (yoghurt). Afghans rarely drink milk but do enjoy dogh, a refreshing drink of yoghurt with water and mint.

SAMANAK

Nowruz, the annual Persian new year, celebrates the start of spring, with festivals, picnics and a special treat called samanak. To make it, people carefully sprout wheat, grind the young green shoots with water and walnuts, and cook it over an outdoor fire into a sweet pudding!

ROSE WATER

Roses grow all over Afghanistan, and many people make the fragrant flowers into aromatic rose water, used to perfume Afghan desserts.

SWEETS

Favourite desserts, especially to end Ramadan fasting, include jalebi, a sweet-syrupy-crunchy cake served in swirls; faluda, thin noodles, with ice, custard, rose water and pistachios; roht, a cardamom-kissed yeasted cake; and gosh-e-feel, crisp pastries whose name means 'elephant ears' – which they resemble!

PLOV

SAVOURY RICE PULAO WITH LAMB AND SPICES

PREPARATION TIME
20 mins

COOKING TIME
45 mins

LEVEL OF DIFFICULTY
● ●

SERVES
4 to 6

Descriptions of this delicious dish go back to tenth-century Arabic cookbooks written in Baghdad and Syria. Today, plov – and its cousins pilaf and pulao – are enjoyed in endless combinations of rice simmered in aromatic liquid with meats, spices, vegetables and often fruits and nuts. Persian pilafs may include sour cherries or pomegranate, while Turkish cooks may add almonds and currants. In Central Asia, plov is cooked in a cauldron-like pot called a qazan, and slow-simmered until fluffy and flavourful. In Afghanistan, where plov is the beloved national dish, it's often served outside in summer with gherkins and platters of cabbage, carrot, aubergine and beetroot salads.

INGREDIENTS

280 g basmati or other long-grain white rice

4 tablespoons rapeseed or vegetable oil

2½ teaspoons salt

680 g boneless leg of lamb meat (or substitute an equal weight of goat or chicken meat), cut into bite-sized pieces

1 small or ½ large onion, chopped

3 medium carrots, grated

1 tablespoon ground cumin

2 teaspoons ground coriander

pepper, to season

475 ml chicken stock or water

1 head garlic, halved through the middle crosswise

3 bay leaves

1. Put the rice in a fine-meshed sieve and rinse it well while moving it around with your hands until the water goes from chalky–looking to a bit more clear. Tip the rice into a bowl, cover with water, and leave to soak for 30 minutes.

2. When you're ready to start cooking, drain the rice in the sieve and shake it dry.

3. In a large casserole dish or other heavy saucepan with a tight-fitting lid, heat 2 tablespoons of the oil over a medium-high heat. Season the lamb with 1 teaspoon salt. Add the lamb pieces in a single layer, taking care not to crowd the pan (you might need to do this in batches) and cook until nicely browned on the bottom: 3 to 4 minutes. Flip the meat and cook until browned on the other side: 3 to 4 minutes longer. Transfer the lamb to a plate.

4. Add the remaining 2 tablespoons of oil to the empty saucepan, then add the onion and carrots, and cook over a medium heat until very soft and starting to brown: about 12 minutes. Add the cumin, coriander, ½ teaspoon salt and a few grinds of pepper, and cook until fragrant: about 1 minute. Add the rice and stir to combine. Add the stock or water and the two halves of the head of garlic and the bay leaves and bring to a boil over a medium-high heat.

5. Reduce the heat to medium-low, stir in the lamb with the rice, and cover with the lid. Cook until the rice is tender and absorbs the liquid: about 20 minutes. Turn off the heat and leave to stand for 5 minutes.

6. Uncover and fluff the rice. Season with more salt and pepper if necessary and serve hot.

People say that when U.S. President Nixon visited Uzbekistan in 1966, where this dish is also popular, he loved plov so much that he requested the recipe.

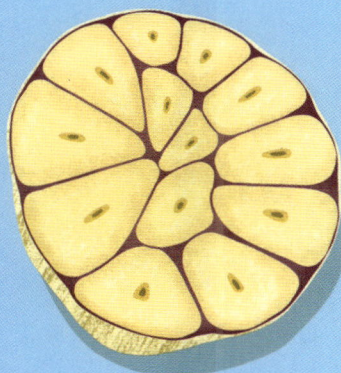

BANGLADESH

This lush country of mangroves and rivers is often described as a food-lover's paradise. It's also the eighth most populous nation in the world. The cuisine here stars abundant rice, luscious fruit, tangy dairy, rich nuts, and fresh fish from the rivers, canals, floodplains, ponds and lakes, as well as the Bay of Bengal. Aromatic spices are essential, and some recipes still show a centuries-old love of cream, cardamom, cloves and cinnamon.

DAILY DAIRY

Bangladesh diets are rich with dairy. Many rural women raise goats, whose milk is made into ever-popular goat yoghurt and churned into goat butter. Cow's milk, on the other hand, is usually reserved for making sweets.

RICE AND FISH

The rivers here produce abundant fish and rice, two foundations of the daily diet. Rice is served alongside all sorts of fish and meat curries, dahl (soupy lentils), bhorta (mashed veggies) and bhaji (pan-fried vegetables). Bangladesh's favourite fish is a deliciously oily, bony type called hilsa.

FANTASTIC FRUIT

The Bangladeshi climate is perfect for farming tropical fruits like mangoes, jackfruit, pineapple, lychees, guava, papaya, coconuts, tamarind and palmyras, a coconut cousin whose fruits are harvested when they're young and gelatinous. Many other delicious fruits grow wild in the jungle, including latkan, durian, rattan and the wild date palm.

BREAKFAST

Bangladeshi breakfast is often a bowl of cheera: flattened rice, sweetened with sugar and served with fruits and yoghurt. Rural people often start the day with panta bhat, boiled rice soaked overnight so it starts to ferment, which is then mixed with salt and chillies.

GRILLED CHICKEN

As sunset approaches in Bangladesh, across the country the street vendors come out, selling savoury pastries, kebabs and salty snacks. But don't miss the chicken, which is marinated in spices and then grilled, creating a tasty evening snack that has a spicy crunch on the outside and is super moist on the inside.

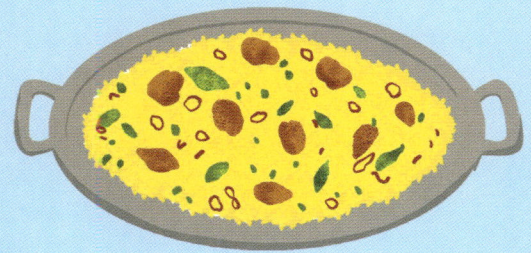

BIRYANI

Biryani is a popular dish usually consisting of rice mixed with meat, vegetables and spices. One type, kachchi biryani, is strongly connected to Bangladeshi festive occasions and family gatherings. A version of this dish sees raw meat and vegetables layered with the rice, then the dish is sealed with dough, forming an edible lid that traps steam, tenderizing the meat and vegetables inside while cooking.

THE NATIONAL COMFORT DISH

Patla khichuri is a soupy mix of rice, lentils, vegetables and potatoes flavoured with green and red chilli, ginger, garlic paste, turmeric, cumin, garam masala, mustard oil and sugar. It's a cozy comfort food during the rainy monsoon season.

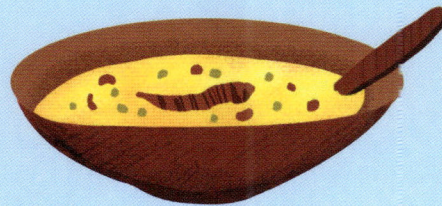

FUCHKA

These crunchy-yet-soupy snacks are the most popular street food in Bangladesh. Mashed potatoes are mixed with spices and lime juice, then the mixture is spooned into thin, hollowed-out shells of puffed rice. Fuchka is finished with a tangy tamarind sauce and a sprinkle of grated eggs.

BANGLADESHI DESSERTS

Sweets are one of the glories of Bangladeshi cuisine, and they're often given as gifts. A thick, sugary yoghurt called mishti doi is a treat after lunch or dinner, sometimes mixed with rice, bananas and other fruit to create doi chira. A richer after-dinner option is rasmalai: soft cheese balls simmered in cardamom-flavoured milk.

POTATOES

Here potatoes may be mashed with mustard oil and fried chillies or roasted with spices like cumin, turmeric, mustard seed and ginger. Spiced mashed potatoes are wrapped around a hard-boiled egg and deep-fried into aloo chops, potato croquettes served at teatime.

SHONDESH

SWEET PRESSED CURD WITH ROSE WATER AND CARDAMOM

PREPARATION TIME
1 hr 30 mins

COOKING TIME
20 mins

LEVEL OF DIFFICULTY
● ● ●

MAKES
About 12

This confection – sweetened, pressed curd cooked into a wonderfully plush, fudge-like consistency – is one of the finest sweets in India and Bangladesh. There are countless types, flavoured with everything from almond extract and saffron to mango, topped with pistachios (as here), almonds or dried fruit. This version calls for rose water, which was first made by the ancient Egyptians, Greeks and Romans. The aromatic elixir is still beloved across the Indian subcontinent and Middle East, perfuming recipes from halva and baklava to lassi and Turkish delight.

INGREDIENTS

950 ml full-fat milk
2 tablespoons lemon juice or
   white vinegar
35 g icing sugar
½ teaspoon cardamom
½ teaspoon rose water
shelled pistachios, for topping

You can also make this dish with premade paneer but it's fun to make your own from scratch. If you prefer to use premade paneers, start at step 4.

1. Line a large bowl with muslin cloth, allowing it to overhang on all sides.

2. In a medium pot over a medium-high heat, bring the milk just to a simmer. Reduce the heat to medium-low and add the lemon juice or white vinegar and stir. After a few minutes, when the milk looks curdled, carefully pour it into the bowl with the muslin cloth. Leave to cool.

3. When it's cool enough to handle, gather the muslin cloth and twist it from the top so you can strain out the whey (liquid) from the curds (called the chenna). Squeeze to release as much liquid as you can. While holding the curds in the cloth, run them under cold water to remove any flavour from the lemon or vinegar, then squeeze out any excess moisture again. Set the wrapped chenna in a colander in the sink and place an unopened can of beans or something similarly heavy on top to weigh it down. Leave to drain for 30 minutes.

4. Unwrap and transfer the chenna to a clean bowl and lightly knead it for several minutes until it becomes smooth, like dough. Add the sugar, cardamom and rose water, and knead them in until evenly incorporated. (If you have a tabletop mixer, you can knead in its bowl, fitted with a dough hook.)

5. Heat a non-stick cast-iron frying pan over a medium-low heat. Add the chenna and cook, stirring occasionally, until it looks soft and cohesive but no longer liquid: 8 to 10 minutes. Remove from the heat, and leave the mixture to cool to room temperature.

6. Form the mixture into slightly flattened balls that are about the size of your palm and transfer to a plate. Press a pistachio in the centre of each shondesh. Serve right away or cover and refrigerate for up to 3 days.

Shondesh can also be made in a tray and cut into squares. Some confectioners press it into wooden moulds to create pretty shapes.

CHINA

China's civilization formed over 4,000 years ago, making it one of the oldest cultures in the world. The world's oldest known cookbook, *The Yinshan Zhengyao*, was written there in the tenth century. Today, China is home to more than 1.4 billion people, more than 90% of whom identify as Han – the world's largest ethnic group – while the rest are divided among about fifty-five other ethnic groups. China's landscapes include mountain ranges, rivers, deserts, forests and seas. China's size has resulted in cultural diversity, with at least eight unique culinary styles, including Sichuan, Cantonese and Hunan cuisine.

TEA

Around 2737 BCE, Shen Nong, the first emperor of China, discovered that he preferred the taste of water when herbs or leaves were added. Today, it is a daily drink for just about everyone, day and night.

RICE

People have been farming rice here for more than 10,000 years. Today, China is both the world's largest consumer and producer of the grain – a daily staple for two-thirds of the population – which is used to make everything from rice noodles to rice wine. Rice is so fundamental that when greeting someone, instead of asking how they're doing, you ask, 'Have you eaten your rice today?'

CHOPSTICKS

Invented in China over 2,000 years ago, chopsticks are still used for everything from dipping dumplings to slurping noodles. (Just please don't point your chopsticks at anyone – that is considered rude!)

PEKING DUCK

This elegant dish originated in Beijing's Imperial court over 500 years ago and has changed little since then. The duck is roasted for hours and served tableside, along with the crackly-crispy glazed skin.

YUM CHA AND DIM SUM

The Cantonese brunch tradition of *yum cha* – 'drink tea' – is closely linked to *dim sum*, or 'touch the heart' foods. Dim sum includes delicious bite-sized snacks that number in the thousands. Diners order from servers who wheel carts laden with stacks of bamboo baskets from table to table.

HOT POT

This tradition is just what it sounds like! A flavourful stock simmers at the table in a large metal pot, and diners add helpings of meat, fish, shellfish, vegetables, noodles, sauces, herbs and other aromatics to the bubbling broth. The hot pot is now popular in Japan, South Korea and Vietnam.

SNACKS GALORE

Chinese cuisine includes a famous snacking culture and lots of nibbling between meals. Street-food stalls called *xiaochi*, sometimes also known as *xiaoye*, or 'midnight snack', are open day and night and usually specialize in just a few or even one food.

LUNAR NEW YEAR

An important holiday in many parts of Asia and in China especially, Lunar New Year is a springtime celebration that marks the beginning of a new year on the lunar–solar calendar. Throughout the sixteen-day festival, people feast on traditional foods with symbolic importance. Fish represents prosperity; dumplings and spring rolls signify wealth; sweet rice is thought to bring family harmony; and longevity noodles embody a wish for long life.

SICHUAN PEPPER

Have you ever eaten a Chinese dish that made your entire mouth tingle? That sensation was likely thanks to Sichuan pepper, a spice that, despite its name, is more closely related to citrus than it is to chilli peppers or black pepper. Chinese people refer to the special tingly-mouth feeling it produces as *mala*, or 'numb-spiciness'.

DUMPLINGS

PORK AND CHIVE DUMPLINGS

PREPARATION TIME
1 hr

COOKING TIME
10 mins

LEVEL OF DIFFICULTY
● ● ●

MAKES
35 to 50
dumplings

These adorable dumplings are sometimes filled with both prawns and pork but this delicious version is pure pork. To encase the pork, there are two main types of dumpling wrappers: Shanghai style, which are thin and white, and Hong Kong style, which are even thinner and yellow because of the use of eggs. Shanghai wrappers are more common but you can use either style here. This recipe includes two methods – you can either steam the dumplings in batches in a bamboo steamer or boil them in a pot all at once. Try both ways and see which you like best!

INGREDIENTS

225 g fatty minced pork
115 g garlic chives or spring
   onions, thinly sliced
5 cm ginger, peeled and finely
   grated
2 garlic cloves, chopped
1 tablespoon toasted sesame oil
1 tablespoon soy sauce
1 tablespoon Shaoxing wine
2 teaspoons sugar
½ teaspoon salt
½ teaspoon vegetable oil
1 pack dumpling wrappers

1. In a chilled metal bowl, combine the minced pork, chives, ginger, garlic, sesame oil, soy sauce, Shaoxing wine, sugar and salt. Use a sturdy spoon to vigorously mix until it forms a paste.

2. It's best to cook a small amount so that you can test a mouthful of the filling to adjust the flavours as needed. To do this, heat ½ teaspoon of oil in a frying pan over a medium-high heat. Add a small spoonful and cook, turning, until cooked through. Taste the cooked filling and add more salt or seasonings to the raw filling, if necessary.

3. Remove one dumpling wrapper from the pack. Keep the rest covered with a wet kitchen paper until you're ready to use. Have a small bowl of water nearby and line a baking tray with greaseproof paper.

4. Dip your finger in the water and moisten the edges of the wrapper. Put 1 teaspoon filling in the centre of the wrapper. Fold the wrapper in half over the filling to form a rectangle and press the edges to seal. Bring the lower corners of the rectangle (the side with the filling) together and pinch to make the traditional curved dumpling shape. Use a little water if you need to help them stick. Arrange the dumplings on the prepared baking tray.

5. To steam the dumplings: fill a wok or deep frying pan with 2.5 cm or so of water. Line a bamboo steamer with a liner or sheet of greaseproof paper. Bring the water to a boil over a high heat. When you see steam coming from under the basket, use tongs to place the dumplings in a single layer in the basket. (You will need to do this in batches.) Cover and steam until cooked through: about 7 minutes. Use tongs to transfer the cooked dumplings to a plate and cook the remaining dumplings.

6. Alternatively, you can boil the dumplings: bring a large pot of water to a boil. Add the dumplings and stir once or twice to help prevent them from sticking. When the dumplings float to the surface, cook them for 1 minute longer. Use a slotted spoon to transfer them to a plate.

To serve, you can float your dumplings in good-quality chicken broth or toss them with a little chilli oil or chilli crisp.

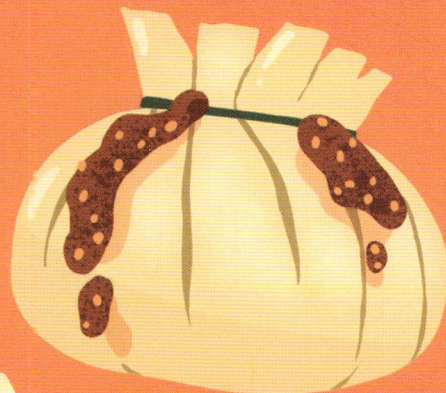

DUMPLINGS

AROUND THE WORLD

What's better than eating pasta or bread with a delicious topping? Eating pasta or bread with a delicious filling! Cooks love to enclose yummy bite-sized morsels inside little pieces of dough. Whatever you call them, these filled dumplings are usually simmered or steamed, sometimes served in soups. People love to bite into them and find a sweet or savoury surprise inside! Some historians say the first dumplings were made in China at least 1,800 years ago, during the Han Dynasty, while Italians have been stuffing ravioli for nearly a millennium. Today, there are hundreds of types of dumplings worldwide but they're especially popular across Asia and Europe, where just about every country has its own favourite dumpling, especially in colder climates.

SOUSKLUITJIES

Meaning 'sauce dumplings' in Afrikaans, these South African sticky dessert dumplings have a light and fluffy texture and are served soaked in custard or sweet cinnamon syrup.

SAMOSAS

These hand-held savoury Indian pastries often have a pyramid shape and a crisp crust. They may be filled with anything from green peas and spiced potatoes to cheese and minced meat. A popular snack, they're often sold from street vendors and served with sweet-tart chutneys.

MANTOU

This diverse family of dumplings are found from Turkey to China. Variations in some parts of Asia are called manti and stuffed with minced lamb, spiced with sumac, red pepper and dried mint, and served slathered with yoghurt, garlic or melted butter. In Central Asia, manti may be stuffed with meat, onions, diced winter squash, mashed potato, mung beans, radish, sugar and sheep fat – served with yoghurt and vinegar.

RAVIOLI

The earliest record of Italy's famous filled pastas is found way back in the fourteenth century, when people wrote letters describing them as stuffed with pork, eggs, cheese, and parsley. Today, they're popular around the world, and may be stuffed with seafood, wild boar, chanterelle mushrooms – or those same great fillings from the 1300s!

MANDU

Korean mandu are little beef-filled dumplings served floating in a soup – this recipe, called mandu-guk, is one of the most popular in all of Korean cuisine.

PIEROGIES

Polish and Ukrainian pierogies are doughy half-moons often filled with potato, cheese or minced meat, served with a pat of butter and fried onions or a dollop of soured cream. These dumplings are so beloved, many Polish families serve them at Christmas Eve dinner.

MOMO

Tibetan momo are meat-filled dumplings, related to mantou and often served at formal meals and celebrations. To tell someone to be quiet, Tibetans say 'Kha momo nangshin dhe', which means 'keep your mouth like a momo' – because momo dumplings are sealed shut!

ONDE ONDE

This Indonesian sweet dumpling (also known as klepon) is a sticky, bite-sized cake made from glutinous rice flour, filled with palm sugar, boiled until the filling melts, then rolled in grated coconut. It's popular in Java and often served on banana leaves!

EMPANADAS

With a name that literally means 'wrapped in bread', empanadas are crisp, folded pastries stuffed with fillings from beef to fruit. Descended from a Spanish recipe for pepper, onion and meat pie, brought west by sailing conquistadors, the dish took root and is now popular across Latin America, from Mexico to Argentina.

KNÖDEL

Knödel are a family of dumplings made across East and Central Europe, including Austria, Hungary, Romania, Bosnia, Croatia, Slovenia and Czechia. Sometimes filled with meat or potatoes, they're also often popular filled with fruit. Some variations, like the German Zwetschgenknödel dumplings, may each contain a whole plum or apricot.

INDIA

India's landscapes include deserts, lush forests, tropical beaches and the soaring Himalaya mountains. The seventh largest country by area, it is also home to a huge population and has recently overtaken China as the world's most populous country. Its more than 1.4 billion people speak over one hundred different major languages and belong to more than 700 ethnic groups. Not surprisingly, all this natural and cultural variety has resulted in some of the world's most famous cuisines.

SPICES

Indian cuisine boasts spectacular spices, including coriander, cumin, pepper, fenugreek, cardamom, cinnamon and turmeric. Traditionally, Indian cooks freshly prepare their spices for cooking by roasting the whole seeds, bark or roots and then grinding them into a powder. Spices add flavour to everything from rice dishes, roast meats and sauces to drinks and desserts.

VEGETARIANISM

India is one of the best places in the world to be vegetarian or vegan. This is thanks in part to the ancient philosophy of ahimsa, or non violence, which means causing no harm to other living beings, including animals. Today, up to 39% of India's population is vegetarian, and the country is home to several distinctive vegetable-based cuisines.

CEREAL STAPLES

Cereals star in most Indian meals. Indians use wheat to make breads such as naan, which is pillowy like a pita, and roti, which is flat like a tortilla. For serving, rice or bread is often placed at the centre of a platter or large banana leaf. This arrangement of small containers is often called a *thali*.

KARI VERSUS CURRY

Kari is a Tamil word that means 'spiced sauce'. When the Portuguese and British colonized India, they misunderstood this word to be 'curry'. They also began wrongly referring to all kinds of Indian dishes – from saucy ones to dry-spiced ones – as curries. Today, the giant, generic label 'curry' is applied to dishes with spiced sauces all over the world.

PANEER

Paneer is India's favourite cheese. It's made from fresh buffalo or cow's milk that's been curdled into a soft block, usually by adding lemon juice. Mild and very versatile, it can be paired with spinach or potatoes in different karis, rubbed with spices and grilled, or just eaten on its own.

CHATNI

Chatni are tangy, spicy, flavourful relishes served as side dishes to brighten up milder foods like rice, dal or crispy papadums (a wafer-like flatbread). These relishes may feature a paste of anything from mango to tomato and be seasoned with lots of ground spices and herbs like ginger, mint and coriander leaves, plus flavour boosters like tamarind, garlic or coconut.

SWEETS

India has dazzlingly distinctive desserts, and people here love to give sweets as a sign of hospitality. Milk often serves as the basis of sweet treats here, including a special type of dense, creamy ice cream called kulfi that is traditionally flavoured with rose, saffron or pistachio. India also has lots of deep-fried desserts, including gulab jamun – little doughy dumplings soaked in sugar syrup.

DAL

In India, dal can refer to two things. It can be an ingredient, specifically a split pulse like beans, peas, lentils or chickpeas, and it can also be one of about sixty different dishes made from those pulses. Dal dishes are a delicious daily staple, ranging in colour from golden yellow or bright orange to deep green or black. Many are simmered to a soupy consistency, while others are thick and hearty.

YOGHURT

India's traditional yoghurt, dahi, is made from cow, buffalo or goat's milk. It is thought people started making yoghurt in India as long ago as 6000 BCE, and for millennia, this was the only way to keep milk from quickly going bad. Lots of Indians continue to make their own yoghurt today, and it's a key ingredient in many dals, karis and smoothie-like lassis that are seasoned with anything from mango or banana to salt.

MASOOR DAL

RED LENTIL STEW

PREPARATION TIME	COOKING TIME	LEVEL OF DIFFICULTY	SERVES
30 mins	25 mins	●	2 to 4

India is wonderfully, wildly diverse with many cultures and cuisines but nearly everyone across the vast subcontinent enjoys this lentil dish – sometimes at every meal. Dal is often served with rice and roti, sometimes alone, and at feasts with dozens of other delicious dishes.

Millions of people in India cook dal daily, so there are countless versions. Some cooks add vegetables, from sweet potatoes to spinach to cauliflower, and spices may vary from kitchen to kitchen, ranging from curry leaves to black onion seeds. This version calls for red lentils, which cook in a snap, and it's aromatic with ginger, turmeric, lemon and fresh coriander.

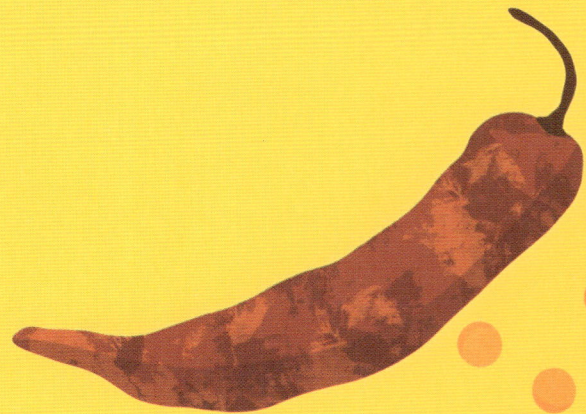

To draw out their full flavour, you can heat spices in oil. This is called 'blooming'.

INGREDIENTS

230 g dried red lentils
1 teaspoon salt
1 small onion, roughly chopped
3 fat cloves garlic, peeled
5 cm ginger, peeled and coarsely chopped
1 chilli pepper, stem removed (optional)
2 tablespoons ghee or canola oil
1 teaspoon cumin seeds
1 tablespoon tomato purée
½ teaspoon turmeric
30 g finely chopped fresh coriander or mint leaves, plus more for garnish
1 tablespoon lemon juice
fresh coriander, for garnish (optional)

1. In a sieve, rinse the lentils very well and run your fingers over them to make sure there are no little stones in the mix.

2. In a pan, combine the lentils with 950 ml water and ½ teaspoon salt and bring to a boil over a high heat. Reduce the heat to medium-low and simmer until the lentils are tender: about 20 minutes.

3. While the lentils simmer, combine the onion, garlic, ginger, and chilli pepper in a food processor and pulse until the ingredients are finely chopped. (If you don't have a food processor, you can also mince these ingredients with a knife or pound them into a paste in a mortar and pestle.)

4. In a small frying pan, melt the ghee. Add the cumin seeds and bloom until they just start to darken – about 10 seconds – then add the onion mixture and ½ teaspoon salt. Cook, stirring frequently, until just starting to brown: about 4 minutes.

5. Add the tomato purée and turmeric to the onion mixture and cook until the tomato purée just starts to darken: about 1 minute. Stir in the fresh coriander.

6. Scrape the onion mixture into the lentils and continue to simmer: about 5 minutes. Stir in the lemon juice.

7. Ladle the dal into bowls and garnish with more fresh coriander, if desired.

INDONESIA

Bridging Southeast Asia and Oceania, Indonesia is the world's largest archipelagic nation (meaning it's made up of islands – over 17,500 in Indonesia's case!). Indonesia's more than 275 million citizens, spread over 6,000 of these islands, speak hundreds of languages and belong to over 1,100 ethnic groups. The wildlife is unique: over a third of local birds and mammals live nowhere else on Earth, and Indonesians enjoy 6,000 different spices! No wonder the country's motto is 'Unity in Diversity'!

SACRED RICE

Indonesians eat rice with practically every meal. More than just a food, it's also a sacred symbol of prosperity and fertility. Special celebrations like weddings are usually held in rice-harvesting season and often include nasi tumpeng – a mountain of rice coloured golden with turmeric. The most important person at the celebration has the honour of cutting off the top of the rice cone.

THE SPICE ISLANDS

Renaissance-era Europeans craved flavour but grew few spices. Around 1520, Portuguese traders began sailing to Indonesia to buy boatloads of prized spices that grew nowhere else on Earth: cloves, nutmeg and mace. Soon the Portuguese, Spanish and Dutch were fighting over control of the flavourful, valuable trade.

SALAK

This golf-ball sized fruit is covered in shiny brown scales that look so reptilian, its nickname is 'snakefruit'. The scales peel off to reveal spongy flesh inside, which tastes a bit like a pineapple blended with lemony soap. The flavour can be surprisingly tart the first time you taste it.

SAMBAL

Indonesian dishes are often served with a side of sambal, a spicy condiment made from crushed chilli peppers mixed with aromatic ingredients like prawn paste, garlic, ginger, lime juice or palm sugar. Other countries have adopted it, too, including Thailand, Sri Lanka, Brunei, Singapore, Suriname, and the Netherlands, creating their own versions.

COFFEE

Indonesia is so famous for its coffee that people around the world nickname the drink 'Java', after one of Indonesia's largest islands. Kopi luwak is a local delicacy: coffee beans that have been eaten and then pooped out by an Asian civet cat. These beans have a smooth, less-bitter taste and sell for hundreds of pounds per kilogram!

RENDANG

One of Indonesia's most beloved national recipes, rendang is a creamy, complex, caramelized curry of beef that's slow-cooked in aromatics like lemongrass, galangal, ginger, coconut and chillies, until the meat is tender. A dried, jerky-like version can keep for months.

DURIAN

Known here as the 'king of fruits', the durian's giant spikes hold famously smelly flesh. The fruit's perfume is sometimes compared to the aroma of sweaty gym clothes. For this reason, some airlines ban people from taking the fruit in carry-on luggage! But many Indonesians love it, and compare the fruit's taste to cheese, caramelized onions or butterscotch pudding.

BANANA TREATS

Banana fritters called pisang goreng are a popular snack across Indonesia. People eat fried bananas for breakfast, sometimes with boiled rice and grated coconut, soursop juice or avocado-chocolate smoothies.

CRISPY KRUPUK

Much of Indonesian cuisine combines salty and sweet with a crispy crunch. The most famous example is krupuk, a wafer that may be nibbled between bites of rice, dipped in gravy or eaten straight. Krupuk's name is likely derived from the crunch when you eat it!

SPECTACULAR SEAFOOD

With so many islands and so much coastline, it's no surprise Indonesians enjoy spectacular seafood. On 17 August, people celebrate Indonesian Independence Day with feasts of spicy salads, salt fish and contests for who can eat the most prawn crackers.

GADO GADO

SAVORY SALAD WITH PEANUT DRESSING

PREPARATION TIME
20 mins

COOKING TIME
45 mins

LEVEL OF DIFFICULTY
● ●

SERVES
4 to 6

Peanuts appear in many Indonesian dishes but the best-loved is gado gado. Literally 'mix-mix', the term is often used to describe situations that are all mixed up – the big city Jakarta, for instance, is a gado-gado city. This dish is an Indonesian favourite and is essentially a vegetable salad bathed in the country's classic peanut sauce, with its sweet, nutty, slightly spicy flavours. Everyone here has their own version. Some stick to raw vegetables like cucumbers, carrots or tomatoes; others add cooked tofu or tempeh, boiled potatoes, hard-boiled eggs or pressed rice cakes.

Some season the sauce with lime leaves, prawn paste, chilli peppers, tamarind paste or the sweet Indonesian soy sauce called kecap manis.

INGREDIENTS

FOR THE SAUCE
1 tablespoon sunflower or
    groundnut oil
3 shallots, peeled and sliced
1 clove garlic, chopped
175 g peanut butter
2 tablespoons Indonesian palm
    sugar (or coconut sugar or
    brown sugar)
3 tablespoons soy sauce
1 teaspoon chilli–garlic sauce or
    sambal oelek (optional)

FOR THE GADO GADO
8 baby potatoes
225 g trimmed green beans
salt and black pepper, to taste
1 400 g pack extra-firm tofu
1 tablespoon sunflower or
    groundnut oil
4 hard-boiled eggs, halved

Many serve gado gado
with crunchy prawn
crackers called krupuk
for extra crunch!

TO MAKE THE SAUCE

1. To make the sauce, heat the oil in a wok or large frying pan over a medium heat. Add the shallots and garlic and cook, stirring occasionally: about 2 minutes. Don't let them brown. Remove from the heat.

2. In a mini food processor or blender, combine the cooked shallot mixture with the peanut butter, sugar, soy sauce, chilli–garlic sauce, and 2 tablespoons water, and purée until smooth. Taste and add more chilli–garlic sauce if you'd like a spicier sauce! Add a little more water, 1 tablespoon at a time, if you like a thinner consistency. Transfer to a bowl.

TO MAKE THE GADO GADO

3. In a medium pot, cover the potatoes with water and bring to a boil over a high heat. Season the water generously with salt. Reduce the heat to medium and simmer the potatoes until tender: 15 to 20 minutes. During the last 3 minutes of boiling, add the green beans. Drain the potatoes and green beans and run them under cold water until cooled.

4. Meanwhile, drain the tofu of any liquid and cut it widthways into eight slabs. Dry it well between layers of kitchen paper and season with salt and pepper. In the same wok or frying pan you used for the shallot mixture, heat the oil over a medium-high heat. Add the tofu slabs in a single layer and cook until well browned on the bottom: 3 to 5 minutes. Flip and cook until the other side is brown: 3 to 5 minutes longer. (If your pan is crowded, you can cook the tofu in two batches.) Transfer the cooked tofu to one part of a serving platter.

5. Arrange the potatoes, green beans and hard-boiled eggs in separate piles on the platter.

6. Drizzle some of the peanut sauce on top and serve.

CHILLI PEPPERS

AROUND THE WORLD

Columbus sailed across the Atlantic looking for a shortcut to pick up the spice called black pepper. Instead, he ran into Hispaniola and pocketed something spicy he thought might substitute for pepper: chilli peppers. Spaniards started growing the hot little fruits and soon bred their own varieties like pimento and padron. Portuguese ships then brought chillies to West Africa, the Middle East, India and Southeast Asia, where they became essential and changed global food flavours forever.

CHILLIES IN CHINA

Chillies arrived in China port cities in the late sixteenth century. Today, Chinese cuisine is unimaginable without their heat. In China, where red is a good-luck colour, many people string up peppers for Lunar New Year, like little firecrackers. Chinese chilli-infused oil is a superspicy condiment that can act like a firecracker in your mouth!

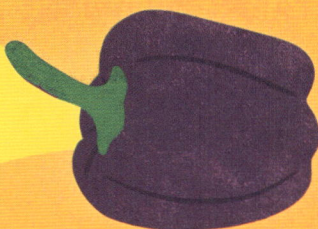

JALAPEÑOS AND CHIPOTLES

Fresh, green jalapeño peppers have an alter ego. They can be dried and smoked, emerging as wrinkled, browned chipotles, which are simmered into everything from chilli con carne to barbecue sauce.

PEPPERS

Northern European cuisines don't have much heat. Italians instead bred sweet peppers, which range from yellow to dark purple. Sweet peppers can be snacked on crisp and raw, and are especially beloved roasted.

AJI AMARILLO

Literally meaning 'yellow pepper', aji amarillo is the most important ingredient in Peruvian cuisine. This pepper is hot but fruity. It adds its sweet heat to everything from papa a la huancaina (potatoes in spicy cheese) to fried yuca to ceviche (citrus-pickled fish).

HABANERO PEPPER

Habanero literally means 'from Havana'. They are essential to Caribbean cuisine. These little, lantern-shaped peppers are a cheerful bright orange and smell like tropical fruit but don't be fooled – they are very, very hot! Habaneros used to be regarded as the hottest chillies around. Then 'chilliheads' made breeding and eating ever-spicier peppers a competitive sport. Today, India's crazy-hot ghost pepper, and the Carolina reaper, are the world's hottest peppers – for now.

HARISSA PASTE

This sweet, smoky paste made of ground chillies spiced with cumin and coriander is the most popular condiment in northern Africa. The iconic flavour is eaten on eggs, whisked into yoghurt, and slathered on grilled lamb.

SHISHITO PEPPER

Quickly blistered in a smoking-hot frying pan until their green skins blacken, shishitos are sprinkled with salt and served whole as an appetizer or snack from Japan to Spain and beyond. People eat piles of them, seeds, skins and all, using the stems as handles. About nine out of ten shishitos are mild but when you eat them by the plateful, you never know which ones will be hot!

WIRI WIRI

Iconic in Guyana, wiri wiri peppers look like little berries – which they are! Bright red, super spicy and smaller than a marble, wiri wiri are enjoyed morning to night, in everything from eggs to stews, and are essential in Guyana's national dish, pepperpot, a meat soup seasoned with cinnamon and clove.

POBLANO PEPPER

The mild, dark-green, heart-shaped poblano pepper is named after its origins in the valley of Puebla, Mexico. They're often served as chiles rellenos (stuffed chillies) – filled with meat and cheese, then fried in a thin batter and simmered in succulent tomato salsa.

PAPRIKA

Hungary's national spice is one of the most popular spices in the world. Bright red – its name is literally Hungarian for 'pepper' – this mild pepper powder is used to flavour Hungary's favourite recipes like chicken paprikash and beef goulash, and sprinkled by the pretty pinch over everything from hummus to devilled eggs. Spanish paprika is similar but smoked.

TABBOULEH

BULGUR WHEAT, HERB AND TOMATO SALAD

PREPARATION TIME	COOKING TIME	LEVEL OF DIFFICULTY	SERVES
1 hr 30 mins	0 mins	●	4

Whether it's spelled tabbouleh, tabouli or tabouleh, this traditional summer salad is fragrant, healthful and refreshing! Common throughout the Middle East, it's made with bulgur – a nutritious, nutty cracked wheat that's been partially cooked and then dried – plus tomatoes, lemon juice, olive oil and enough fresh parsley to turn the finished dish bright green. The parsley is traditionally chopped by hand but a food processor will do it in a snap. If you have extra parsley to use up, this is the dish for you.

INGREDIENTS

45 g fine bulgur wheat
140 g curly parsley leaves and
    tender stems (from about
    4 bunches)
1 small bunch fresh mint, leaves
    picked from the stem and
    finely chopped
2 spring onions, thinly sliced
225 g tomatoes, finely chopped
2 large lemons, juiced (about ⅓
    cup juice)
salt, to taste
60 ml extra-virgin olive oil

1. In a bowl, soak the bulgur with water to cover by 13 mm and leave to stand until softened: about 20 minutes. Drain in a fine sieve, shaking well. Transfer to a bowl.

2. In a food processor, pulse the parsley until finely chopped. (You might need to do this in batches.) Add the parsley to the bowl.

3. Add the mint, spring onions and tomatoes to the bowl and toss. Add the lemon juice and a large pinch of salt and toss.

4. Refrigerate the salad for 1 hour, then add the olive oil and toss. Taste and season with more salt and lemon juice, if desired. Serve.

Some people soak the bulgur not in water but in the juice of the chopped tomatoes, with more lemon juice, for extra flavour!

IRAN

Iranian cuisine is full of bright, beautiful ingredients like red pomegranates, golden saffron, sour cherries, pink rose petals and bunches of fresh green herbs. The ancient Persians used the melted snow from nearby mountains to create an irrigation system for their large deserts. So, despite the climate – and the landscape – they were able to grow all kinds of fruits and vegetables in glorious gardens. A classic Persian meal consists of fluffy saffron rice, vegetables like cucumbers or beetroot in spiced yoghurt sauce, a meat stew or grilled kababs, and a platter of flatbread with fresh herbs and salty white cheese. Don't forget the gherkins, and definitely not the raw onions.

FRUIT LEATHER

Children here love to eat lavashak, a traditional fruit leather. It's made each summer from harvests of ripe fruits like sour cherries, plums or tiny red berries called barberries, that are puréed, poured out into thin layers and dried to last all year. No sugar is added; in fact, a little salt is thrown in the pot. It can be deliciously sour.

BEETROOT TO GO!

Bright-red boiled beetroot is the most popular street food in Iran. Called laboo, they're sold piping hot all autumn and winter by vendors with wheeled carts who display them in tall stacks according to size.

RHUBARB

According to Persian lore, the very first man and woman sprang from a rhubarb plant in paradise. Today, Iranians use rhubarb in dishes like khoresh riva – a stew made with the sour stalks, plus onions, spices, a meat like lamb, and fresh mint on top.

TAHDIG

The most famous treat here is the fried, crunchy layer that forms at the bottom of the rice pot that can be flipped out of the pot whole. It's called tahdig. Iranian cooks make different kinds of tahdig by adding ingredients like noodles, flatbread, potatoes – even a whole fish! – at the bottom of the pot, so that when the tahdig is flipped over, it has a crown of fried food on top.

SWEETENED YEASTED BUNS

The city of Fuman is famous for a sweet treat called koloocheh. These are yeasted buns filled with a sticky mixture of walnuts and dates, seasoned with cinnamon and cardamom, and made in a special press that stamps the buns with a beautiful geometric pattern.

SAFFRON

Saffron is the signature flavour of Iranian food. It's the world's most expensive spice, worth more than gold by weight but you only need a tiny amount to perfume a dish. Each tiny thread comes from the stigma of a crocus flower and must be carefully picked from the centre of each bloom by hand!

POMEGRANATES

Pomegranates with their jewel-like seeds have been central to Iranian cuisine for centuries. They are native to Iran, and today you can find fresh pomegranates, dried pomegranate seeds, freshly squeezed pomegranate juice and all manner of pomegranate pastes that range from sweet to sour. More than half the world's pomegranates are grown here today.

PERSIAN NEW YEAR PICNICS

For the Persian New Year, known as *Nowruz*, just about everyone goes on a picnic. They feast on meat-and-potato patties called kotlet, savour spring foods like herbs and eggs in a kuku sabzi frittata, and dip spring lettuce into a vinegar–honey mixture called sekanjabin.

ROSE PETALS AND ROSE WATER

Roses have been part of Persian cuisine for thousands of years since wild roses were first cultivated and brought into gardens. People here eat fresh and dried rose petals, add them to teas and spice mixtures, and use rose water to flavour drinks or desserts, like ferni – a rose water rice pudding.

BORANI CHOGONDAR

YOGHURT WITH BEETROOT AND MINT

PREPARATION TIME	COOKING TIME	LEVEL OF DIFFICULTY	SERVES
1 hr 10 mins	0 mins	●	6

In Iranian cuisine there are many yoghurt–vegetable 'salads', and they're often served with rice and stew, or grilled kebabs. This one also makes a delicious dip, served with flatbread or even crisps. Bright-pink beetroot yoghurt is a showstopper and is simple to make. For the best flavour, leave it to sit in the fridge for a day or two before serving.

Note: to roast the beetroot, preheat the oven to 232°C. Place the beetroot, unpeeled, in a pan with an ovenproof lid. Add a few tablespoons of water and a dash of salt and close the lid. (Alternatively, you can also cook the beetroot wrapped in foil.) Roast the beetroot until a knife slips in very easily – about an hour. Wait until it's cool enough to touch and then rub off the skin with your fingers.

INGREDIENTS

1 red beetroot, roasted, cooled, and peeled
1 clove garlic
2 tablespoons dried mint, plus extra for garnish
3 tablespoons extra-virgin olive oil
455 g thick, Greek-style yoghurt
salt and black pepper

1. Coarsely chop the beetroot, then pulse together with the garlic in a food processor to form a smooth purée.

2. Transfer the purée to a bowl and mix in the mint and 2 tablespoons of the olive oil. Stir in the yoghurt. Season to taste with salt and pepper.

3. Cover and chill in the fridge for at least 1 hour, or up to 48 hours.

4. To serve, spoon the remaining 1 tablespoon olive oil over the yoghurt and garnish with a pinch of dried mint.

CONDIMENTS

AROUND THE WORLD

Sometimes a little drizzle or dollop can transform a whole dish – making it sweet, tart, tangy, rich, pungent, spicy, salty – or all of the above! Throughout history and around the world, people have cherished little bottles and jars of sauces with strong flavours, from ancient Egypt, China, India and Rome to modern-day Mexico, Malawi and Malaysia. Eaters add soy sauce, fish sauce, tzatziki, mayo, tahini ketchup, mustard, relishes and hot sauces, each with magical abilities to make food sing.

ACHAR

These Indian pickles are made from a variety of vegetables and under-ripe fruits, packed with spices in oil or brine or both. Nearly always on the table throughout the Indian subcontinent, achar is now also made in parts of South Asia, Africa and the Caribbean.

WORCESTERSHIRE SAUCE

This sauce was born in the 1830s in Worcester, UK, when a barrel of soy sauce and spiced vinegar was accidentally left in the cellar for years. People have been making it on purpose ever since. Cooks use a drop of the tangy–sweet liquid in marinades, seafood dishes, steaks, stews, soups, sauces and even cocktails.

KETCHUP

Slathered on American burgers, hot dogs, onions rings, chips and even breakfast eggs, ketchup is thick, sweet and tart, thanks to tomatoes, sugar and vinegar. Although it's an American icon, ketchup is the culinary descendent of an Asian fermented fish sauce called ketsiap that traders brought to Europe centuries ago.

TKEMALI

A sweet–sour sauce made of tiny tart, purple and green plums. It's used like ketchup in the Caucasus country of Georgia. Locals dab it on cheese-filled breads, roast pork and sausages.

SRIRACHA

This spicy sauce of chilli peppers, garlic, vinegar, salt and sugar originated in Thailand but is now beloved across continents, drizzled onto Thai noodles, Vietnamese summer rolls and even Mexican tacos.

PIKLIZ

This spicy Caribbean coleslaw is made of finely shredded cabbage, carrot, onion and hot chillies submerged in sour orange juice or vinegar. You'll find a glass jar of it in every Haitian kitchen, where the flavours bring a spicy, tangy zip to dishes like roast chicken or beans and rice.

YASSA

In Senegal and the Gambia, locals slow cook piles and piles of onions until they're sweet and soft to use as both a condiment and a sauce. It's a signature dish from the Wolof people who live across the region.

PEBRE

You could say that this Chilean salsa is a blend of the Andes and Spain, just like Chile itself. The salsa is sometimes green (fresh coriander, garlic and chillies), sometimes red (add a few tomatoes), and usually made tangy and rich with vinegar and olive oil.

PYLSUSINNEP

Iceland's famous hot dogs are made with lamb and topped with a dark, sweet, creamy brown mustard, whose secret thickener is powdered potatoes. Tourists often buy a tube to take home.

IRAQ

Iraq is a Middle Eastern country with huge cultural diversity. Most people in Iraq are Muslim but there are five other recognized religions, reflecting the many ethnic groups that call this country home. Iraq has a varied landscape, from vast deserts to rolling green hills and craggy mountains. Its two main rivers, the Tigris and the Euphrates, create a moon-shaped region of rich soil called the Fertile Crescent that is often referred to as the 'cradle of civilization', where people first developed farming and writing – both essential to this book!

ANCIENT CUISINE

Iraq's culinary history dates back at least 10,000 years. Ancient 3,700-year-old tablets, which some people call the world's first cookbooks, include recipes for stews with cumin, coriander, mint, dill and sheep's tail. A version of this ancient stew is still enjoyed here today.

MASGOUF

Many Iraqis consider masgouf to be their national dish. It's a whole carp, spread open, marinated in olive oil, salt, tamarind and turmeric, and then impaled on sticks and grilled around a fire. Today, restaurants along the Tigris river serve the freshly grilled fish late into the night.

LAMB LOVERS

Iraqis have loved lamb for millennia. Traditionally, all parts of the animal are used, so nothing goes to waste. A special breed of Iraqi fat-tailed sheep called liyya are prized for their tasty tails! Sheep heads, stomachs, tails and feet are key ingredients in a traditional broth called pacha.

YOGHURT

Milk from sheep and goats is made into rich yoghurt, especially in spring when the animals are grazing lush green pastures and giving the best milk of the year. In summer, Iraqis pour thinned, salted yoghurt over ice for a refreshing drink called shineena.

SKIP THE POPCORN

Baghdadis enjoy beef tongue, which can be served by the slice with lemon or stuffed into sandwiches with pickled cucumbers. Some Iraqis even bring this snack to the cinema!

WARM UP OR COOL DOWN

In winter, many Iraqis wake up to cured sausage with eggs, clotted cream and date syrup. In summer, they might choose cheese sandwiches with refreshing watermelon or cucumber. For an elaborate weekend brunch, families might cook broad beans topped with river mint and hot oil.

TURNIPS FOR THE WIN(TER)

Turnips store well all winter, and some Iraqis believe they help relieve colds. The roots are a key ingredient in a warming white stew of ground almonds, milk, rice, chickpeas and meatballs. Street vendors even sell turnips with a drizzle of date syrup.

GREAT STUFF(ED)!

Iraqi cooking includes many stuffed dishes. The most famous is kubba, rice and potato balls filled with minced meat. Iraqis also love stuffed vegetables, like squash or leaves of swiss chard, carefully filled with a savoury mixture of seasoned rice and minced meat.

HOLY DATE PALMS

Super-sweet date palms are prized here, and even mentioned in religious texts. In ancient Mesopotamia, Ishtar, the goddess of love and fertility, lived in a date palm, earning her the nickname 'lady of the date clusters'. Now, dates are eaten on their own, in desserts like stuffed sweet bread, and drunk as date wine!

FRIED FOODS

Up until the 1950s, most people did not have an oven, and frying was the preferred option for cooking. These days, some Iraqis tweak traditional recipes. For example, pueta chap – deep-fried potato discs stuffed with meat – are often assembled in layers and baked like a casserole instead.

BABA GANOUSH

AUBERGINE DIP

PREPARATION TIME
15 mins

COOKING TIME
30 mins

LEVEL OF DIFFICULTY
●

MAKES
4 to 6 appetizer
servings

This creamy, smoky aubergine dip is a close cousin to hummus – and the two are often served together across the Middle East. Both dips are made with the sesame paste called tahini, and the two recipes are almost interchangeable – to make hummus instead, simply swap out the cooked aubergine for a can of drained chickpeas.

INGREDIENTS

1 large aubergine
juice of 1 lemon
4 tablespoons sesame tahini,
   stirred if separated
2 garlic cloves, peeled and
   smashed
salt, to taste
1 to 2 tablespoons natural
   yoghurt, to thin (optional)
extra-virgin olive oil, to drizzle

1. Preheat oven to 150°C.

2. Pierce the aubergine a few times with the tip of a knife. Place on a baking tray and bake until soft: 30 to 40 minutes.

3. Once the aubergine is cool enough to handle, cut it open and scoop the cooked flesh into a blender or food processor, discarding the skin. Add the lemon juice, tahini, garlic and salt to taste. Blend until smooth, or leave a chunkier texture if you like.

4. If the baba ganoush is thicker than you'd prefer, add 1 to 2 tablespoons of natural yoghurt or cold water and purée again, to thin.

5. Serve in a bowl, drizzled with a glug of your best olive oil. Baba ganoush keeps several days in the fridge and will thicken as it cools.

The amounts here are just a guide – add as much garlic, lemon juice, tahini and salt as you like.

Garnish with sesame seeds, parsley, pine nuts or pink pomegranate seeds.

JAPAN

Japan is made up of nearly 15,000 islands! Inland, much of the country is covered in steep, mountainous terrain. This is why Japanese people describe their food as 'umi no sachi, yama no sachi' – 'the delights of the sea and the mountains'. With borders that were long closed, today the population is nearly 100% ethnically Japanese, and the traditional cuisine still celebrates indigenous ingredients. While essential seasonings include soy sauce, rice vinegar, dashi broth and sweet rice wine called mirin, Japanese kitchens use very few spices, instead emphasizing the freshest ingredients and a refined presentation, letting the flavours shine for themselves.

SOYA BEANS

These little beans are big in Japan. They're made into shoyu (soy sauce), tofu and miso – a deliciously complex fermented paste that gives a distinctive, nutty flavour to hundreds of Japanese dishes. Young soya beans, called edamame, are delicious steamed, salted and eaten as a snack; you pop the beans from their pods into your mouth and pile the empty shells up.

SEAWEED

Japanese people harvest many delicious wild seaweeds! These include nori, dried, greenish-black and paper thin, used for wrapping sushi, and kombu (kelp), which is simmered into the famous soup stock, dashi. Other delicious sea vegetables include wakame and hijiki.

EELS

Eels have been eaten in Japan since ancient times. Traditionally caught wild, today eels are raised in ponds or tanks. The most popular preparation is kabayaki – fillets of eel skewered, dipped in a sweet soy sauce and grilled.

SUSHI

This island nation has such spectacular sea-food that many people eat it at every meal. For sushi, raw fish is paired with vinegared rice, often wrapped in paper-thin pieces of nori (dried seaweed). Sashimi – exquisitely fresh raw seafood – is carefully sliced and traditionally served with soy sauce, wasabi (special horseradish) and pickled ginger.

SYMBOLIC PRAWNS

Many foods here have special meanings. Prawns can convey longevity, as their rounded backs and long whiskers make them look a bit like old men!

WASABI

One of the most famous flavours in Japanese cuisine, this special horseradish was originally picked wild and is now grown along mountain streams or in flooded mountain terraces. The prized root is peeled and grated into a pale-green paste that brings a hot, spicy punch to everything from soups to sushi.

OODLES OF NOODLES

Noodles were introduced from China to Japan in the 700s, and today they're an edible art form. The two main types are soba (thin buckwheat noodles) and udon (thick, soft wheat noodles). Both are beloved hot or cold, piled high on plates or in ramen broth.

SUMO STEW

Many sumo wrestlers swear by huge bowls of a stew called chanko-nabe. Recipes vary but often include meat, vegetables, fish, soft-boiled mushrooms and noodles, all cooked together in a rich, flavourful broth. This packed stew helps body-building athletes keep up their impressive weight before a match!

WAGYU BEEF

Literally meaning 'Japanese cow', wagyu is a prized Japanese breed of beef whose meat is so supremely tender, marbled, rich, buttery and luxurious, it's widely considered the finest steak in the world. One animal can go for over 20,000 pounds, and a single steak can cost hundreds of pounds!

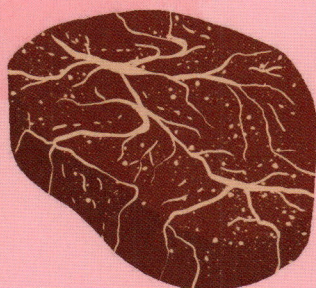

BENTO BOXES

People of all ages love these special lunch boxes. Each bento box includes lots of little compartments, brimming with treats like onigiri (rice balls), boiled eggs, seafood, salads and pickles. Some people design ingredients elaborately into kyaraben, or 'character bento' – shaping them into popular anime or manga characters, or adorable animals.

ONIGIRI

RICE BALLS WITH TUNA, MAYONNAISE AND SEAWEED

PREPARATION TIME	COOKING TIME	LEVEL OF DIFFICULTY	MAKES
1 hr 15 mins	20 mins	● ● ●	8

These traditional balls of rice are tucked into toasted seaweed and filled with salty salmon, mayo-kissed tuna, pickled plums, cod roe or even fried chicken! People in Japan have been making onigiri for more than a thousand years. Whether sold in stores or made at home and tucked into bento boxes, they're a beloved snack on the go or on picnics. Most often shaped into triangles, onigiri can be made into rounds, logs or even into cute animal shapes such as pandas.

INGREDIENTS

320 g Japanese short-grain white
  rice (sometimes sold as sushi
  rice)
fine sea salt, for sprinkling
145 g tin tuna in water
2 tablespoons Kewpie
  mayonnaise or other
  mayonnaise
1 teaspoon soy sauce
8 (3 x 2.5-cm) sheets nori

Don't forget to wash and
drain the rice well before
cooking. This removes
starch, helping create the
perfect texture of rice that
sticks together with grains
that feel separate.

1. Place the rice in a large bowl and add water to cover the rice.
    Using your hands, stir the rice until the water becomes cloudy,
    then drain. Cover again with fresh water and repeat the washing
    process until the water runs almost clear. Pour the cleaned rice
    through a sieve set over a bowl and leave to drain for 30 minutes.

2. In a medium, heavy-bottomed saucepan, cover the rice with
    415 ml of water and bring to a boil. Cover the pot with a lid,
    reduce the heat to low, and cook until the rice absorbs all the
    water: about 10 minutes.

3. While the rice cooks, drain the tinned tuna and transfer to a bowl.
    Add the mayonnaise and soy sauce and use a fork to mix.

4. When the rice is cooked, turn off the heat and leave the rice to
    stand, covered, until fluffy: about 5 minutes. Using a rice paddle
    or flat spoon, stir the rice to fluff and separate the grains.

5. Arrange a sheet of clingfilm on a work surface. Lightly sprinkle
    the clingfilm with salt. Scoop 45 g of the rice onto the clingfilm.

6. Use a spoon to make an indentation in the rice and add about
    1 heaped teaspoon of the tuna-mayo mixture into the indentation.
    Lift up the sides of the clingfilm to help you press the rice so you
    can enclose the filling, then fully wrap the rice in the clingfilm
    and lightly press it to form a triangle or square shape.

7. Turn on one burner of the hob to medium. Holding a sheet of nori
    with tongs, wave the seaweed over the flame for about 5 seconds
    until fragrant and pliable. Unwrap the onigiri from the clingfilm
    and press the seaweed so it wraps one side of the onigiri.

8. Repeat with the remaining rice, tuna and seaweed, remembering
    to sprinkle the wrap with salt each time. (You can reuse the same
    clingfilm each time, if it's not too messy.)

RICE
AROUND THE WORLD

Some people call rice the most important ingredient in the world, with billions of people relying on it as a daily staple. People began cultivating this water-loving grass 10,000 years ago, along China's Yangtze River and India's Ganges River. Today, you can try many varieties, from jasmine to basmati, short grain to long. You'll find rice steamed, fried, rolled into sushi, slowly simmered into congee, and transformed into rice noodles, edible rice, paper and even rice wine. Used in cuisines around the globe, there seem to be as many prized rice recipes as there are grains of rice. Favourites include Indian biryani with saffron and cardamom, Iranian tahdig with its crunchy golden crust, and sweet Nordic rice pudding, crowned with plenty of butter.

RICE FESTIVAL FOODS

Chuseok is a Korean harvest festival, when people honour their ancestors and express thanks for the rice harvest during a three-day celebration. Families play games, sing traditional songs and eat special foods made from rice. Rice flour is made into traditional half-moon shaped songpyeon rice cakes, which are steamed over a layer of pine needles.

RISOTTO

One of the most famous recipes in Italian cuisine features Italian arborio rice. To make risotto, you don't just put a pot of rice on to boil and leave it to cook. Instead, you add flavourful broth or wine, just a little at a time, stirring the whole time, for a creamy, luxurious, fragrant dish that may be studded with anything from porcini mushrooms to peas to pumpkin.

ARROZ CON GANDULES

Every family in Puerto Rico has their own recipe for arroz con gandules. A classic combination of rice and pigeon peas is seasoned with sofrito – a combination of peppers, onions, garlic and fresh coriander is the essential base for Puerto Rican cuisine.

SUSHI

When someone says sushi, do you think of fish? Seaweed? Don't forget the rice! Sushi chefs have perfected cooking sticky short-grained sushi rice and seasoning it just so with vinegar. Japanese cuisine also stars rice in everything from kids' adorable onigiri to adults' sake, which is wine made of rice.

BLACK WILD RICE

On the U.S.–Canada border, along the shores of Lake Superior, native Anishinaabe people have been harvesting deliciously nutty-tasting black wild rice for thousands of years. After harvesting the crop by canoe and drying over a fire, people traditionally jumped up and down on the rice to husk it. Today, people still enjoy wild rice in salads with nuts and berries.

ROPAIN FESTIVAL

This festival in Nepal takes place during the monsoon season to celebrate planting rice. Everyone enjoys special dishes like deep-fried ring-shaped rice-flour roti or beaten rice served with curd. Young people traditionally play in the mud and get covered head to toe!

LA BANDERA DOMINICANA

Beans and rice are common around the Caribbean but one national rice dish is super symbolic. La Bandera Dominicana is the national lunch of the Dominican Republic. That's because the three colours on the plate – rice, beans and braised meat – remind residents of the colours of the Dominican flag.

MANDI

Have you ever eaten something from an underground oven? Mandi is a saffron-seasoned Yemeni rice dish popular throughout the Arabian Gulf. Rice is placed in a clay pit dug into the ground and meat, like goat, chicken, or even camel, is suspended above. The pit is sealed with more clay, and the smoky oven slow roasts the meat while the rice is infused with the drippings.

CAROLINA GOLD

Enslaved West Africans brought their rice cultivation expertise and harvesting technologies to North America. One variety they developed, Carolina Gold rice, is now proudly served in expensive restaurants. On New Year's Day, many American southerners still eat Hoppin' John, a dish of cow peas, bacon and Carolina Gold rice served with cooked greens, for good luck.

CHAMPORADO

What happens when a Spanish ship takes an Aztec corn-and-chocolate breakfast-drink recipe around the world? Filipinos developed a porridge called champorado made with chocolate discs and glutinous rice. Now it's a popular breakfast with sweetened condensed milk, sometimes served alongside salted fish.

MYANMAR

Myanmar – formerly known as Burma, for the country's largest ethnic group – has suffered invasions and conflict for 150 years but through the people's resilience and resourcefulness, their culture, community and culinary heritage have endured. The largest country in mainland Southeast Asia, Myanmar is extremely diverse, with 135 distinct ethnic groups and more than one hundred different languages spoken. Its food is considered some of the most delicious in the world, containing distinct flavour combinations that blend elements of neighbouring Chinese, Indian and Thai cuisine.

TEA SHOPS

You'll find tea shops on nearly every street corner in Myanmar. Each morning, people rush in for a cup before work. By afternoon, tea shops fill up with friends at low tables, chatting, snacking and sipping teas such as thick, creamy cho seint made with sweetened condensed milk.

LUNCH LOVE

Lunch – the biggest meal of the day – usually includes rice, at least one meat-based curry, and sides like steamed vegetables, clear soup, fresh salads and spicy chilli paste. Lunch comes with condiments, like Kachin salsa (a mix of chillies, tomatoes, shallots and dried prawn powder), sour-plum chutney or tomato chutney. Dessert is usually fresh fruit and a bowl of palm sugar for dipping, and the meal is usually washed down with a pale, clear warm tea.

TEA SALAD

Myanmar is famous for its thoke, or 'salads', which may contain a dozen or more ingredients. A salad might include tea leaves, poached fish, roasted seeds or nuts, grapefruit, tofu, banana flowers or roasted aubergine.

TURMERIC

Brilliant yellow-orange turmeric is a favourite spice in Myanmar. People usually add a pinch of it to their cooking oil as it heats up. This is as much for health as it is for flavour: turmeric is believed to have anti-bacterial and anti-inflammatory properties. It's also an anti-flatulent – a polite way of saying it prevents farts!

NOODLES FOR BREAKFAST

Many people here start their day with a big bowl of mohinga – Myanmar's national dish. This flavour-packed breakfast soup features fresh fish and thin noodles, plus rice powder, lemongrass, ginger, turmeric, red onions, lime wedges, fresh coriander and hard-boiled eggs.

FESTIVALS AND CELEBRATIONS

Thadingyut is a festival held on the full moon day of the seventh month of the country's traditional calendar to welcome the Buddha's descent from heaven. After a day of fasting, at night people celebrate by visiting food stalls selling barbecue meat skewers, curries and fried snacks amid firecrackers and beautiful paper lanterns.

GOLDEN TOFU

Tofu in Myanmar is not made from soya beans – it's made from the flour of ground yellow split peas and chickpeas. The result is wonderfully light and creamy, with a gorgeous golden colour from turmeric. It is eaten fresh in salads or deep-fried into fritters.

ELDERS

When enjoying a meal in Myanmar, elders at the table are always served first. Even if no grandparents are present, it's customary for a family to set aside a small bowl of rice in honour of their older relatives.

ALMS

Myanmar is a predominately Buddhist country, and in the morning, you'll see scarlet-robed monks walking barefoot and carrying bowls. This is an ancient ritual called the alms round. People in the community drop offerings of food into the bowls. Before eating, the monks mix everything together so as not to favour any one food over the other. Sometimes this leads to unusual blends, such as cake mixed with curry.

MOHINGA

FISH NOODLE SOUP

PREPARATION TIME	COOKING TIME	LEVEL OF DIFFICULTY	SERVES
45 mins	45 mins	●●	4 to 6

This wonderfully aromatic fish noodle soup is considered the quintessential dish of Myanmar, where it's most often enjoyed at breakfast. While there are endless variations across the country, whether simmered at home or slurped on the street, you'll almost always find flavourful lemongrass, ginger and fish sauce perfuming the broth, and gorgeous garnishes of hard-boiled eggs, lime wedges and fresh coriander. Catfish is common in Myanmar, and this dish often calls for whole fish but you can swap in any mild white fish.

INGREDIENTS

FOR THE BROTH

1 stalk fresh lemongrass, cut into 5-cm pieces
1 small piece ginger, thinly sliced
4 garlic cloves, smashed
½ teaspoon whole black peppercorns
1 teaspoon ground turmeric
¾ teaspoon salt
900 g to 1.1 kg fillets catfish or other mild fish, cut into bite-sized pieces

FOR THE SOUP

1 stalk lemongrass, papery layers and tops removed
8 cloves garlic, roughly chopped
2 large shallots, roughly chopped
5 cm root ginger, peeled and chopped
salt
60 ml vegetable oil
1½ teaspoons paprika or cayenne pepper (if you like it spicier)
½ teaspoon ground turmeric
45 g toasted rice powder (see Note)
1 tablespoon fish sauce
340 g thin rice noodles (sometimes labelled as vermicelli)

GARNISHES FOR SERVING

6 hard-boiled eggs, sliced
55 g fresh coriander, chopped
2 limes, cut into wedges
thinly sliced red onions

TO MAKE THE BROTH

1. For the broth, combine the lemongrass, ginger, garlic, peppercorns, turmeric, salt and fish with 950 ml water in a deep frying pan. Bring to a boil, reduce heat and simmer, covered, until the fish is just cooked: about 15 minutes. Transfer the fish to a plate and strain the broth into a saucepan.

TO MAKE THE SOUP

2. For the soup, combine the lemongrass, garlic, shallots, ginger and pinch of salt in a food processor and grind to a paste. In a wok or large, deep frying pan, heat the oil. Add the paprika, turmeric and shallot paste and cook, stirring, for 2 to 3 minutes. Stir in the cooked fish.

3. Bring the saucepan of broth to a boil, whisk in the rice powder until smooth and cook until thickened. Add the fish mixture to the broth, then add the fish sauce.

4. Bring a pot of water to a boil, add the noodles and cook for 3 minutes or according to the package instructions. Serve the noodles in bowls, ladle the soup into the bowls and serve with the garnishes.

Note: to make toasted rice powder, toast 85 g uncooked jasmine rice in a dry frying pan over a medium-high heat, stirring, until fragrant: about 5 minutes. Transfer to a food processor and grind to a powder. Keep any extra to sprinkle over salads.

PAKISTAN

Pakistan is bordered by India, Afghanistan, Iran and China, and its diverse geography ranges from the towering Hindu Kush mountains to barren deserts, green, fertile plains and a coastline along the Arabian Sea. People settled in this region at least 8,500 years ago, and the country's cuisine has been shaped by many influences over the centuries. Middle Eastern scholars brought rose water, saffron, almonds, pistachios, dried fruits and other delicacies between the twelfth and fifteenth centuries, and the Mughal Empire's influence from the fifteenth to nineteenth centuries introduced cloves, cardamom, nutmeg, mace and other spices, plus yoghurt, cream and butter.

CURRY FAVOUR

There are a seemingly endless variety of curries to choose from in Pakistan but the one that perhaps reigns supreme is haleem. This stew-like dish features a mix of meat and legumes flavoured with lemon, ginger and coriander, and cooked for several hours at least. Pakistanis call haleem the 'king of curry'.

MANY INFLUENCES

While Pakistan shares many ingredients and recipes with neighbouring India – they were one country until 1947 – Pakistani food also reflects many Middle Eastern traditions, such as its use of pomegranate seeds and saffron.

TANDOOR

Pakistan has a long history of using the tandoor, a type of super-hot oven now popular throughout the Middle East and South and Central Asia. Tandoors are traditionally made of clay and used over fire (although there are modern, electric versions now too). Shaped like a cylinder that tapers in at the top and then opens up to let heat escape, they're used for cooking Pakistani breads, kebabs and biryani.

CARDAMOM

A favourite spice in Pakistani cuisine is cardamom, which can take the form of whole, dried seed pods or an aromatic ground blend of several types of cardamom. It's used in many recipes, including thandal, a popular drink made from milk, ground almonds and rose petals.

NIHARI

This classic, slow-cooked dish features beef, or sometimes lamb, goat or mutton shanks, simmered for hours overnight in a rich bone broth with cardamom, cumin, cloves, coriander, ginger and chillies. Originally a filling breakfast for cold mornings, it's now so popular that restaurants across the region serve it all day long.

CHUTNEY

Pakistani dishes are often served with a side of chutney – or several. These sweet–sour condiments come in all types, from fruit chutneys to versions featuring peanuts or chillies. Chutneys are also popular in neighbouring India, but there are special varieties specific to Pakistan. Green chutney, usually made with fresh coriander, is considered the national chutney of Pakistan because it matches the colour of the nation's flag.

RAMADAN FEASTING

As an Islamic republic, Pakistan observes Ramadan, a holy month when people fast from dawn until sunset. After sunset, many Pakistanis traditionally break their fast with fresh dates and homemade lemonade, followed by a meal called *iftar*, which may include an array of delicious foods such as samosas, kebabs and biryani.

FOOD STREET

Pakistan's second-largest city, Lahore, was once at the centre of the Mughal Empire and is now Pakistan's most famous food district. *Gawalmandi*, which means 'food street', is packed with restaurants serving diverse traditional dishes like fried fish, Pakistani barbecue and classic nankhatai.

MALALA

Malala Yousafzai is a Pakistani activist who has long advocated for girls' education. She survived being shot and, at just seventeen, became the world's youngest winner of the Nobel Peace Prize. Her work and story have inspired people around the world. Now living in the UK, she has said that her favourite dish is still her mum's rice and chicken curry.

BREAD CULTURE

Bread is almost always served with Pakistani meals – and may be soft, puffy, flat, spongy, crispy, baked, fried or even pan-fried. One favourite is naan, a pillowy, leavened flatbread that sometimes contains fillings like minced meat or a sweet mixture of dried coconut, almonds and sultanas.

HALWA

RICH, SWEET CARROT PUDDING WITH NUTS AND SPICES

PREPARATION TIME
15 mins

COOKING TIME
1 hr 30 mins

LEVEL OF DIFFICULTY
● ●

SERVES
2 to 4

Carrots for dessert? Yes please! There are many types of halwa, from fruit to beans, usually simmered with sugar, spices and milk, ghee or coconut milk, and eaten for breakfast or dessert, on special occasions or as an everyday treat. In this famous dish, which is especially popular for Diwali and Eid, carrots are coarsely grated, then slowly cooked until completely soft, sweet and aromatic.

INGREDIENTS

450 g carrots, trimmed and
    peeled
175 ml full-fat milk
6 tablespoons sugar
55 g ghee or clarified butter
¼ teaspoon ground cardamom
shelled pistachios, slivered
    almonds and/or crushed
    cashews, for garnish

1. Grate the carrots using the large holes on a box grater or the grating blade of a food processor.

2. In a dry, heavy-bottomed pot, warm the grated carrots over a medium heat for 2 to 3 minutes until they start to dry out a little bit. Stir in the milk and bring to a simmer, then reduce the heat to low. Cook, stirring the carrots every 5 minutes or so, until the carrots are very soft and all the liquid evaporates; this should take 45 minutes to 1 hour.

3. Stir in the sugar and cook over a medium heat, stirring, for 6 to 8 minutes. Add the ghee and cook, stirring, for about 5 minutes. Stir in the cardamom and cook until fragrant: about 1 minute.

4. Serve warm or at room temperature, garnished with the nuts.

PHILIPPINES

There are more than 7,000 islands in the Philippine archipelago, which is one of the most biodiverse places on the planet. Some of these islands don't have any people at all, while the island of Luzon is home to the capital city of Manila, one of the world's biggest cities. The Philippines' vibrant cuisine celebrates rice, fresh fish, roasted pork, all-day snacks, super–sour flavours and lots of sweets!

VINEGAR

In the Philippines, people love sour flavours! Vinegars here may be made from sugar cane, coconut, palm or pineapple. They're used as a condiment – sometimes infused with hot peppers and garlic – and as an ingredient in dishes like the world-famous adobo, a deliciously tart vinegar-spiked stew.

BAGOONG

This pink seasoning paste is almost as important as vinegar here, and the two are often used together. Bagoong is a thick condiment made of salted and fermented seafood, sometimes with a little garlic, oil and tomato added in. Bagoong is salty and a little bit fishy, and it gives Filipino food its own special flavour.

PANDESAL

This big, soft, fluffy roll is topped with toasted breadcrumbs and eaten as a snack, sometimes with jam or ham and cheese. Like many Filipino dishes, it has a Spanish name, because Spain colonized the Philippines for more than 300 years. In Spanish, pan de sal means 'bread of salt' – even though this roll is more sweet than salty!

PURPLE YAMS

They really are purple! These sweet tubers are a deliciously colourful part of Filipino cooking. Known as ube in Tagalog, the Filipino language, they keep their colour when cooked and are made into purple cake, purple ice cream, purple doughnuts and even purple pandesal!

STREET NAMES

Grilled meats are sold from street carts all over the Philippines, usually on a stick. And every piece has its own nickname! If you want grilled pig ears, you order a 'walkman'. If you want chicken feet, you order an 'adidas'. And for chicken tails, ask for the 'pope's nose'.

LUMPIA

These crisp rolls come in many shapes and sizes. Some are skinny, filled with meat and deep-fried. Others are big like burritos and filled with crunchy vegetables. You can even find fried sweet lumpia, stuffed with sugar and bananas and served for dessert.

MERYENDA TIME

In the Philippines, snacks between meals have their own name: *meryenda*. These can include a pre-breakfast snack, breakfast, a post-breakfast snack, lunch, an after-lunch snack, dinner and then snacks before bed. *Meryenda* may include mooncakes, noodles, dumplings or sticky-rice pastries.

HALO-HALO

Halo-halo, which means 'mix-mix', is a wild dessert of many flavours, colours and textures. To make halo-halo, fill a tall glass with shaved ice, evaporated milk, ice cream and a rainbow of treats like coconut strips, jackfruit, purple-yam jam, tapioca pearls and shredded cheese. Then take a tall spoon and – as the name says – mix it all up!

SINIGANG NA ISDA

Another Filipino dish is the sinigang na isda, which means 'sour fish stew'. Locals add ingredients, such as tamarind-tree pod pulp, green tomatoes, tiny limes and unripe pineapple, to make their soup extra sour.

THE POINT-POINT

For lunch, Filipinos often go to what is known as a *turo-turo* spot, meaning 'point-point'. At a *turo-turo*, the food sits on display. You might find trays of rice, lines of stews, big simmering pots of soup or piles of fried fish and vegetables. All you have to do is point at what you want!

123

ADOBO

CHICKEN STEWED IN VINEGAR

PREPARATION TIME
5 mins

COOKING TIME
40 mins

LEVEL OF DIFFICULTY
● ●

SERVES
4

This quintessential Philippine chicken stew uses so much vinegar it's famously tart, though this can be adjusted depending on your taste. Filipino people have been stewing food in vinegar for centuries, and when the Spanish arrived and tasted this dish, they called it after a similar Spanish recipe, adoboado, and the name – or a version of it – stuck. Today, people use the traditional acidic bath of vinegar and soy sauce to cook any kind of meat or vegetable, such as beef, pork, squid, catfish, water spinach or even lizard. This version sticks to chicken.

INGREDIENTS

1.1 kg skin-on chicken thighs and/
    or legs
½ teaspoon salt
1 tablespoon oil
5 cloves of garlic, thinly sliced
2 bay leaves (optional)
205 ml soy sauce
205 ml white or rice vinegar
1 teaspoon brown sugar
white rice, to serve
spring onions, sliced, to garnish

1. Dry the chicken with kitchen paper and season with salt.

2. In a large heavy-bottomed pot, heat the oil and brown the chicken pieces, uncovered: about 5 minutes per side. It's best to do this in batches so the pan is not too crowded. Add more oil if the pan gets dry. Using tongs, transfer the chicken pieces to a plate.

3. Add the garlic to the pot and cook, stirring, for 30 seconds. Add the bay leaves, if using, soy sauce, vinegar, 150 ml water, brown sugar and the browned chicken to the pot. Bring to a boil, then reduce to a simmer and cook, covered, for about 25 minutes, turning the chicken pieces over occasionally for even cooking.

4. Remove the bay leaves.

5. Serve with white rice and spring onions, for garnish.

The vinegar nearly pickles the meat, which helped it to last before fridges were common.

Turn up the acidity by marinating the meat in the fridge for a few hours before cooking.

SOUTH KOREA

South Korea boasts diverse geography – mountains in the north and fertile plains in the south – and a varied climate, with hot and humid summers and very cold winters. Today, the ancient country boasts super modern cities but the culture's long history is alive in its traditional dishes. Essential elements of Korean meals are rice, kimchi and soups made with lots of vegetables, soy, meat and seafood, all seasoned with chillies, onions, ginger, garlic, sesame and vinegar.

RICE

Boiled short-grain rice is eaten at almost every meal – unless you're having noodles (which may also be made of rice!) During the Lunar New Year festival, many people enjoy dumpling and rice cake soup, and during the harvest moon festival, foods eaten include rice wine, and crescent-shaped rice cakes stuffed with pumpkin, chestnut paste, sesame seeds or acorns.

GOCHU

Chilli peppers (gochu), first brought to Korea in the fifteenth or sixteenth century by Portuguese or Dutch traders, transformed the country's cuisine. Ground up, they can be mixed with rice and fermented into gochujang, a sweet, savoury, spicy condiment essential in Korean cooking.

KIMCHI

Long before refrigeration, Korean people developed a way to preserve and ferment vegetables like Chinese leaf, radishes and cucumbers into magically spicy pickled kimchi. It is served at just about every meal, and many people have special fridges, just for kimchi!

BIBIMBAP

This beloved dish is often prepared for special events. A mound of rice, topped with vegetables, an egg, seasonings and gochujang, is served in a dolsot – a hot, heavy bowl of stone or cast iron. The heat from the stone or iron browns the rice at the bottom to form a delicious crust. The name means 'mixed rice' because just before eating, you mix the ingredients together.

SWEETS

While Korean cuisine is famous for salty and spicy flavours, they're also great at sweet treats! Favourite desserts include hotteok pancakes, honey and sesame biscuits called yakgwa, and bingsoo, a centuries-old recipe of shaved ice commonly crowned with sweet toppings like fruit syrup, condensed milk and sweet red beans.

EAT YOUR INSECTS!

A popular snack in the autumn is crickets boiled whole, and seasoned with soy sauce. Another street snack is beondegi (pupa) made with silkworm pupae that are boiled or steamed, and served in little paper cups with cocktail-stick skewers. The snack looks like prawns and is nutty and crunchy on the outside but chewy on the inside!

SEAFOOD

South Korea enjoys a long coastline and spectacularly fresh seafood. All types of fish and shellfish – sea cucumbers, oysters, crabs, cod, cuttlefish, herring, clams, prawns, and even jellyfish – are marinated, fried or enjoyed raw. For centuries, specially trained and experienced women divers on South Korea's largest island, Jeju, have plunged nearly ten metres beneath the ocean – without oxygen tanks – to collect sea urchins, abalone, conch and sea snails.

SOUP ALL DAY

Soup or stew is eaten all day, every day, and there are lots to choose from! This includes seolleongtang, made from simmering ox bone for a white, milky broth, combined with brisket and seasoned at the table, and samgyetang, or chicken ginseng soup, for which a whole young chicken is stuffed with garlic, rice, ginseng and jujube (a kind of date).

TABLE-SIDE COOKING

Some Korean dishes are made right at the table! Korean barbecue is often prepared on gas or charcoal grills built into dining tables or using portable hobs placed table-side. Thinly sliced beef, pork or chicken is seasoned or marinated and then quickly grilled to order – by a chef or by diners themselves!

HAEMUL PAJEON

SPRING ONION AND SEAFOOD PANCAKE

PREPARATION TIME
15 mins

COOKING TIME
15 mins

LEVEL OF DIFFICULTY
● ●

SERVES
1 25-cm
pancake for sharing
as an appetizer

This savoury Korean pancake has a surprisingly simple batter – just flour, egg and water. Pajeon pancakes are usually studded with spring onions and seafood like scallops or squid – but you can customize them endlessly. Some people add oysters, sliced veggies, left-over rice or meat, or that most quintessentially Korean ingredient: kimchi. It all cooks in just a few minutes and is delicious any time or day or night. If you like a little heat, consider adding a few threads of pretty, dried Korean peppers at the end of step 3. It's even more delicious with the simple dipping sauce included here.

INGREDIENTS

FOR THE DIPPING SAUCE

3 tablespoons soy sauce
1½ tablespoons rice vinegar
¼ teaspoon toasted sesame oil

FOR THE PANCAKE

70 g cup plain flour
1 large egg
120 ml cold water
salt
115 g peeled prawns or scallops,
   cut into bite-sized pieces
3 tablespoons canola oil or
   vegetable oil
3 spring onions, cut into 2.5-cm
   lengths

TO MAKE THE DIPPING SAUCE

1. In a small bowl, mix together the soy sauce, rice vinegar and sesame oil.

TO MAKE THE PANCAKE

2. In a separate bowl, for the pancake, stir together the flour, water and ½ teaspoon salt until just combined. Stir in the prawns. In a 25-cm non-stick or cast-iron frying pan, heat 2 tablespoons of the oil over a medium-high heat. Add the spring onions in a single layer, and cook for 1 minute. Pour the batter over the spring onions, using a spatula to spread it into a pancake.

3. In the same bowl used for the batter, lightly beat the egg with a fork. Season with a pinch of salt, then pour over the batter.

4. Let the pancake cook until it's set and golden on the bottom and the prawns are cooked: 3 to 4 minutes.

5. Slide the pancake onto a chopping board or plate, cut it into wedges and serve hot with the dipping sauce.

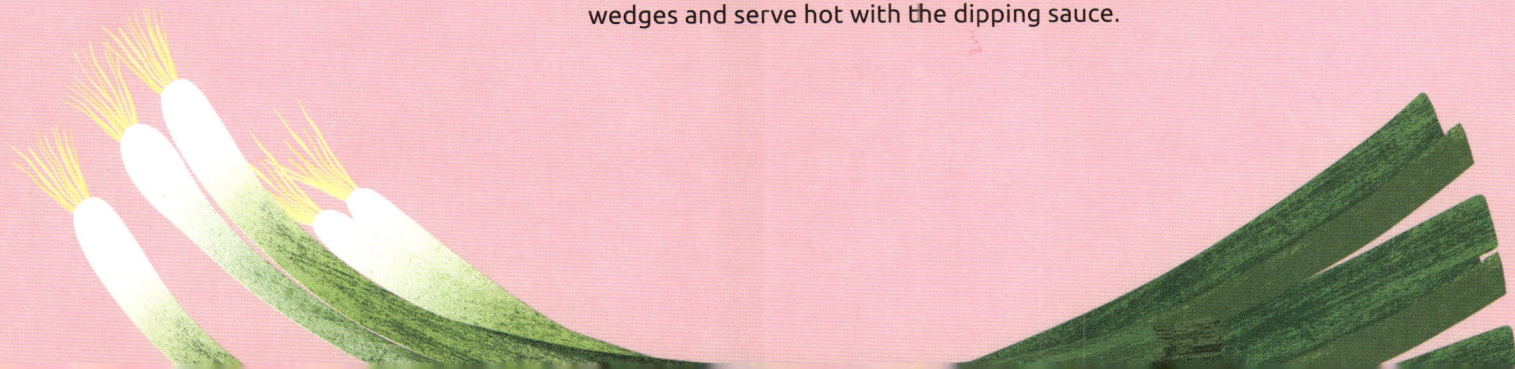

NOODLES

AROUND THE WORLD

Pasta and noodles go back millennia to the Shang Dynasty in China (1700–1100 BCE), when rice or wheat flour was made into the very first noodles. Legend has it that explorer Marco Polo first brought pasta from Asia to Italy but some historians say Greeks were cooking pasta by the first century CE; others say that what we know as pasta was introduced to Sicily by Arabs in the ninth century. Whichever way it arrived in Europe, pasta dishes began to appear in literature during the Renaissance. Dried – and therefore much more portable and long-lasting – noodles also allowed the ingredient to travel in merchant ships, furthering its popularity around the globe!

THAI

Thai people feast on noodles of many shapes, from wide and thick rice noodles (sen yai) to slender glass noodles made from mung-bean flour (woon sen). And don't forget the noodles in the country's national dish, pad thai.

ETHIOPIA

The Ethiopian recipe for pasta saltata traces its roots to the Italians' brief occupation of the country in the 1930s. Today, this Ethiopian dish combines penne with potatoes topped with a sauce of garlic, onions, lemon juice and harissa plus basil and rocket folded in just before serving.

GERMANY

German spätzle are made from a super simple dough of eggs, flour, water and salt, pressed through a colander into little squiggly pastas whose name originally meant 'little sparrows'. Spätzle is often served with butter, cheese, caramelized onions or gravy alongside rich meat dishes like sauerbraten, goulash and schnitzel.

CHINA

In China, skilled chefs make lamian wheat noodles by hand from a single piece of dough that is pulled, stretched and folded over and over until the noodles are verrrrrrry long and very thin!

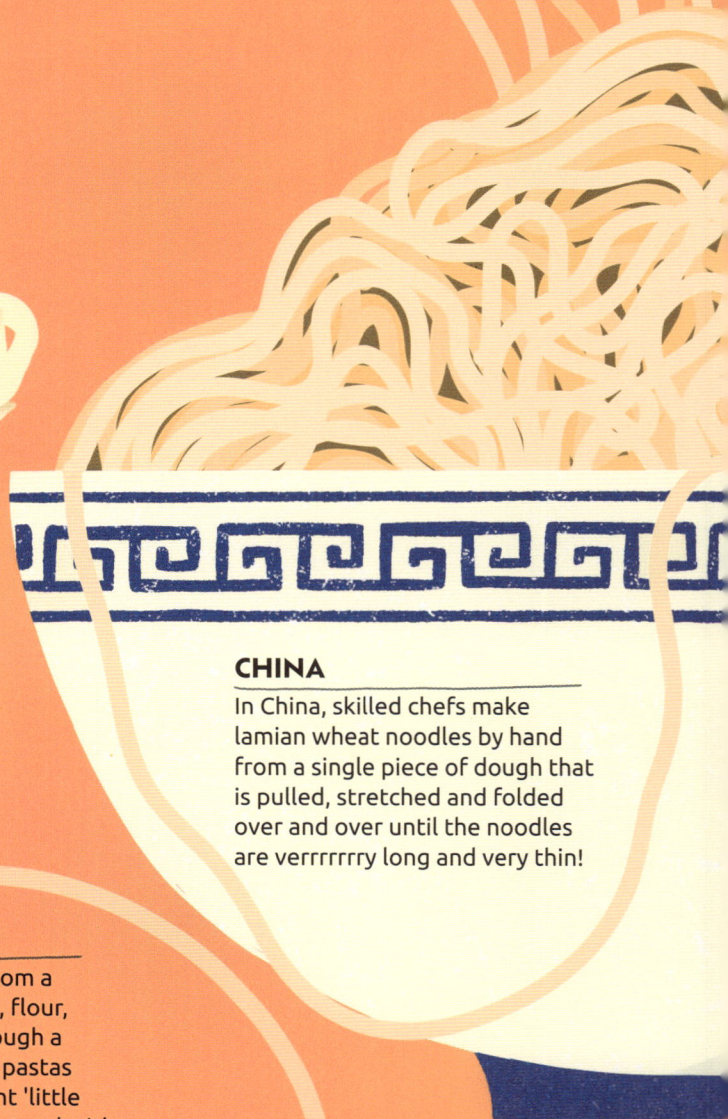

HALUSKI

This dish – noodles with buttery fried cabbage, bacon and onions – is a favourite comfort food in Poland, Hungary, Slovakia and Ukraine. Related to a Viennese specialty called krautfleckerl, it includes caramelized cabbage with square noodles known as fleckerl – it's a delicious way to warm up during Austria's cold winters.

CROATIA

In Croatia, dough is shaped into a roll, stuffed with fillings and cooked to make štrukli – like a dumpling crossed with lasagne! The Slovenians have štruklji, a sheet of pasta filled with apples or cheese, rolled up, poached and sliced. When arranged on a plate for serving, they look like cinnamon buns.

MEXICO

In Mexico, noodles get a spicy treatment with lots of chillies! For fideos seccos (dry noodles), noodles are boiled, fried in oil, mixed with chipotle sauce and then baked in the oven. Another pasta dish in Mexico is espagueti verde (green spaghetti), pasta topped with the spicy green chilli poblano.

DOMINICAN REPUBLIC

Here, locals top spaghetti with garlic, tomato sauce, olives and salami, and like to eat it at the beach, with fried plantains, slices of pan sobao (a sweetened bread) or pan de agua (water bread).

URUGUAY

Many Italians immigrated to South America, bringing with them a rich food heritage. Uruguayans enjoy pasta con salsa caruso, pasta with a rich sauce of cream, nuts, mushrooms, ham and cheese. Further north, Peruvians enjoy tallarines verdes, spaghetti tossed with a green sauce of basil, cheese, spinach and onion.

FINLAND

In Finland, people enjoy suomen makaronilaatikko, baked macaroni with minced beef and a creamy egg sauce topped with cheese. Next door in Sweden, stuvade macaroni or 'milk-stewed macaroni' – is seasoned with nutmeg and served with meatballs. Some Swedes also enjoy a quick meal of pasta topped with ketchup!

THAILAND

Thailand, in Southeast Asia, is known for its royal palaces, tropical beaches and gorgeous national parks, which cover almost 30% of the country. In Bangkok, the capital city, you can find sleek skyscrapers next to ancient temples and buy delicious meals from street vendors. Thai cuisine is centred on the concept of yam – literally! The Thai word yam means 'mix', to get just the right combination of spicy, sour, salty and sweet. Recipes here call for lots of coconut milk, fresh herbs and fiery chillies. Favourite dishes vary by region and foods may be tom (boiled), yam (spicy salads), tam (pounded) and gaeng (curries).

CURRY

Curries (gaeng) are essential to Thai cuisine. Versions of Thai red, green and yellow curry pastes can be found on supermarket shelves worldwide. Each colour has a different flavour and green is considered by many to be the spiciest!

NAM PLA

Fish sauce or paste is essential to many Thai recipes. It's made by taking little fish and shellfish that are salted, dried, pounded into a paste and then fermented in jars for a month or more. Nam pla can be used on seafood, to enhance meat dishes or as a dip for spring rolls.

ESSENTIAL INGREDIENTS

Thai cuisine features lots of flavourful herbs and spices like turmeric, garlic, galangal, chillies, lemongrass, fresh coriander and coriander root, many of which are also prized for medicinal properties. Pastes made from prawns, fish and chillies bring big flavours to many sauces and dishes.

JASMINE RICE

Known as hom mali, jasmine rice is the staple food here, made into noodles, flour, special desserts and even wine. Rice also plays an important role in Thai folklore and culture. Many Thai homes and restaurants have small shrines where special bowls filled with rice are offered to ancestors.

FISH

Thailand has long coastlines and shellfish like lobster, crab and prawns, as well as squid and octopus, star in many Thai recipes. Snapper, catfish and mackerel are among the most popular fish in Thai cuisine. Many rural, inland Thai families raise fish in small ponds, so they can always catch fresh fish for dinner!

KAE SA LUK

This is an ancient art form you can eat! The practice of *kae sa luk* (fruit carving) dates back at least 700 years to the royal court, and is now beloved across the country. Special schools teach the skill, and people also learn from masters how to create amazing displays.

SOM TAM

This sweet-tangy-spicy salad is made from shredded, unripe green papaya, mixed with lime, chillies, fish sauce and sugar. Some cooks also add dried peanuts, prawns, freshwater crabs and asparagus beans. In Bangkok, you can get som tam containing an entire fistful of spicy chillies!

PRESENTATION

In Thai culture, when plating food, every detail is important, from the colour combinations to how the food is arranged. But food isn't always served on plates or bowls – it might be wrapped in banana leaves or presented in coconuts, cucumbers or pineapples!

COCONUTS

Coconuts grow well here and their rich, creamy milk transforms many Thai recipes, from mango sticky rice to spicy curries and seafood stews. Tender young coconuts offer a refreshing drink, while the white flesh of mature coconuts is grated for rich, velvety cream.

PAD THAI

FRIED NOODLES WITH PRAWNS

PREPARATION TIME
25 mins

COOKING TIME
15 mins

LEVEL OF DIFFICULTY
● ●

SERVES
4

The national dish of Thailand was actually created in the 1930s by the country's prime minister, who wanted a unique dish to unite the nation. Pad thai – meaning 'Thai-style fried noodles' – first became popular as a street food in Bangkok. Today, the irresistible combination of stir-fried rice noodles with eggs and aromatics topped with lime slices, peanuts, sliced cucumbers and fresh herbs is popular worldwide. Some cooks also add palm sugar, tamarind paste, chilli–vinegar sauce or Thai fish sauce for maximum flavour.

INGREDIENTS

FOR THE SAUCE AND NOODLES

225 g flat rice noodles (sometimes sold as pad thai noodles)

4 tablespoons chicken broth or water

3 tablespoons fish sauce (nam pla)

50 g palm sugar (or coconut sugar)

1 tablespoon tamarind paste

FOR THE PRAWNS

340 g medium shelled and deveined prawns

salt

2 tablespoons cornflour

2 tablespoons sunflower or groundnut oil

FOR THE PAD THAI

1 tablespoon sunflower or groundnut oil

2 medium shallots, thinly sliced

4 cloves garlic, thinly sliced

2 eggs, lightly beaten

55 g beansprouts, for serving

55 g roasted peanuts, finely chopped or crushed, for serving

1 lime, cut into wedges

fresh coriander or basil leaves, for serving (optional)

TO MAKE THE SAUCE AND NOODLES

1. In a medium bowl, soak the noodles in warm water until just bendable: 10 to 20 minutes. Drain them well in a colander and cut them into 20-cm pieces.

2. In a small bowl, stir together the broth, fish sauce, palm sugar, tamarind paste and noodles.

TO MAKE THE PRAWNS

3. In a bowl, toss the prawns with ½ teaspoon salt and the cornflour.

4. In a wok or large non-stick frying pan, heat 1 tablespoon of the oil over a high heat until shimmering. Add the prawns and stir-fry until pink on the outside and white throughout: 2 to 3 minutes. Transfer to a clean bowl.

TO MAKE THE PAD THAI

5. In the same wok or frying pan, heat another tablespoon of oil. Add the shallots and cook, stirring, until softened: about 2 minutes. Add the garlic and cook until softened: about 2 minutes longer. Add the noodles and your sauce and stir-fry until the sauce is incorporated with the noodles: 1 to 2 minutes. Push the noodles to one side of the pan. Add the lightly beaten eggs and cook, moving them around slightly but keeping them away from the noodles, until set: 1 to 2 minutes.

6. Toss the cooked eggs with the noodles, breaking them up slightly. Return the prawns to the pan and toss to heat through.

7. Serve the pad thai with beansprouts, crushed peanuts, lime wedges, and fresh coriander or basil leaves, if using.

You could substitute chicken or tofu for the prawns. To do so, slice 340 grams boneless, skinless chicken breasts into bite-sized strips or cut one 400 to 450 gram pack extra-firm tofu into cubes. Follow the instructions as written for the prawns.

TURKEY

At the crossroads of Europe, Asia and the Middle East for thousands of years, Turkey is the meeting place of many cultures – and many cuisines. Its high mountainous terrain and rich farmland have made it the world's leading producer of hazelnuts, raisins, dried figs, dried apricots, dried cherries and quince. Turkish rituals and recipes blend with those of Central Asia and the Middle East, reaching to the Mediterranean and the Black Sea and all the way back in time to Mesopotamia, when farming first began in this region.

STRONG COFFEE – NO FILTER!

Istanbul's first-known coffee house opened in the 1600s, and coffee culture has been central here ever since. According to one Turkish saying, coffee should be 'strong as death, sweet as love'. This is due not to the type of beans used but to the method: boil finely ground beans but don't filter them; simply let the solids settle, usually in a copper pot with wooden handles.

POPULAR PASTRIES

Yufka – layered sheets of paper-thin dough – are made in almost every neighbourhood here and baked into borek pastries filled with meat, cheese or spinach. Originally cooked on the *saj* (a flat sheet of iron used by nomadic Turks), these days they may be fried or baked.

TURKISH DELIGHT

Known here as lokum, delicate gummy-like jellies cut into cubes and rolled in sugar are popular throughout the Middle East. Favourite flavours include lemon, rose, orange and orange blossom.

BREAD AND YOGHURT

A Turkish–Arabic dictionary from the eleventh century includes names for breads and yufka, and dairy products like yoghurt and cheeses. Today, Turkey has a wide range of delicious breads and yoghurts that still appear in everything from soups to desserts to drinks.

VERSATILE AUBERGINE

Iconic aubergine recipes in Turkey include musakka (pan-fried with peppers, onions and minced meat but, unlike in Greece, not layered), Sultan's delight (puréed with cheese) and the beloved appetizer imam bayildi (meaning 'the holy man fainted' – because it tastes so good!).

PICK YOUR PROTEIN

Lamb or mutton is one of Turkey's favourite meats – often roasted, grilled, baked, slow-cooked or made into kofte (meatballs). People don't waste any part of the animal, enjoying lamb's head, trotters, liver, tripe, brain and kidneys. Lamb intestines are perfect for making little sausages – which are grilled as a street snack.

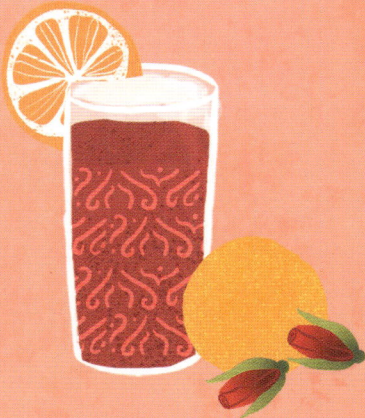

SWEET SIPPING

A cold drink enjoyed here for centuries is sherbet: fruit juice sweetened with honey or sugar, sometimes with spices, served over ice or snow. Turkish sherbet is an ancestor of global frozen treats, including Italian sorbetto, French sorbet and English sherbet. Traditional flavours here include violet juice, rose water, tamarind or mulberry, each a different beautiful colour.

CATCH OF THE DAY

The Black Sea is renowned for fresh anchovies, called hamsi and also sea bass, red mullet, bream, sole, turbot, bonito, swordfish and sardines. Some of the most consumed seafoods include mussels, squid, octopus and prawns.

ANCIENT OVENS

The *tandir* is a traditional oven consisting of a large earthenware pot in the ground. Most Turkish towns continue the tradition of stone-lined, wood-burning communal ovens, called *tas firin*.

BREADS

AROUND THE WORLD

Is there anything better than the smell of freshly baked bread? People have been perfecting combinations of flour, water and leavening since the days of ancient Egypt. Today, cultures around the world cherish their daily bread, like South Asian roti flatbread, Middle Eastern pita pockets, Italian focaccia, Ethiopian injera, French baguettes, Colombian pan de bono and loaves of sliced white bread from the U.S. People start their day with toast and jam, tear off flatbread to sop up curry and pack sandwiches, pitas and rolls for lunch, all slathered with toppings from mustard to Marmite™, hummus to herring. You might say that few things unite humanity as much as breaking bread.

PÃO DE QUEIJO

The name literally means 'cheese bread' but some say the ancestral recipe didn't contain any dairy. Originally made by enslaved Africans who baked the South African manioc into balls of starchy sustenance, the bread was eventually enriched with cheese and milk. Today, pão de queijo is puffy, soft, gooey and cheesy. Sold at bakeries and coffee shops across Brazil and northern Argentina, it is often enjoyed with a mug of hot chocolate.

JAPANESE MILK BREAD

This moist, fluffy bread, known as shokupan, has a pillowy, feather-light texture and subtly sweet flavour. Each loaf has a tender crumb and a crisp golden crust. A staple for many Japanese families, milk bread may be spread with butter and jam at breakfast, made into bento-box sandwiches for lunch or served at Japanese tea ceremonies.

BLACK PUMPERNICKEL

Made from the flour of Russia's famous rye, this dark, dense, chewy, deeply flavourful bread can feature minced onion, caraway and fennel seeds and molasses. Usually baked overnight, it's delicious topped with smoked herring with fresh dill, caviar or just butter!

NAAN

This famous flatbread from the Indian subcontinent and the Middle East is made from a yeasted dough moistened with natural yoghurt. Traditionally, naan isn't cooked on a hob-top frying pan or baked on a tray. Instead, skilled bakers slap the dough against the interior of a clay oven called a tandoor, and it bakes clinging to the hot walls! Once out, the smoke-tinged naans are often brushed with ghee, a golden clarified butter.

GRISSINI

Italy is home to many world-famous breads, from sweet panettone to pizza's cousin, focaccia. One favourite is the looong, pencil-thin, delightfully crunchy breadsticks called grissini. Dip them in olive oil or wrap them in slices of salty prosciutto.

SCANDINAVIAN BREADS

In Sweden, a thin type of flatbread called tunnbröd is often used to wrap food. Nearby Finland is known for its love of rye bread. It's a staple in the Finnish diet and comes in various forms, from dense loaves to crispbreads.

BRIOCHE

France is famous for the croissant and baguette but also its wonderfully rich brioche. This buttery loaf has been baked in Paris since the 1600s. The recipe is probably from Normandy, known for its butter since Medieval times. Often baked in special, fluted tins, brioche is made with almost as much butter as flour! Some French bakers make a sweet brioche filled with fruit, custard or whipped cream.

PAN DE MUERTO

In Mexico, 'bread of the dead', – a sweet loaf decorated with bone shapes and often flavoured with orange blossom water – is traditional for *Día de Muertos*, or Day of the Dead, when many Mexican families gather in cemeteries to clean and decorate gravestones, share favourite memories and enjoy loaves of Pan de Muerto with hot chocolate.

CHALLAH

In Jewish family kitchens in Eastern Europe and around the world, you'll often find bagels for breakfast and matzoh at Passover but don't miss the challah! This rich, eggy, yeasted bread is shaped into braids and baked into golden loaves. Thick slices make excellent French toast.

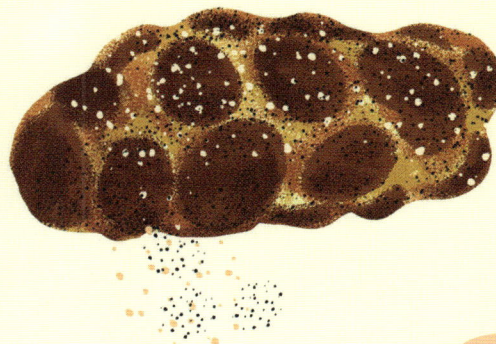

PITA

ROUND FLATBREAD POCKETS

PREPARATION TIME
2 hr 30 mins

COOKING TIME
5 mins

LEVEL OF DIFFICULTY
● ●

MAKES
6 pita breads

This little flatbread shaped in a circle has been a staple in the Middle East for a long time – some say for 4,000 years! It's now daily bread in Syria, Iraq, Turkey, Jordan, Lebanon, Egypt, Iran, Greece, Bulgaria and more, where that little bread pocket is stuffed with delicious fillings like shawarma, kebabs, falafel, baba ganoush and hummus. The pita's pocket forms as if by magic while baking – so long as you roll the dough verrry thinly and bake it in a super-hot oven!

INGREDIENTS

2 teaspoons fast-action yeast
1 tablespoon honey or sugar
1 teaspoon salt
1 tablespoon olive oil, plus more
   for the bowl
35 g wholemeal flour
285 g plain flour

1. In a large mixing bowl, dissolve the yeast in 250ml warm water with 1 teaspoon of honey or sugar. Leave until bubbles form: about 10 minutes.

2. Add the remaining ingredients and stir with a wooden spoon until a shaggy dough forms. With clean hands, knead the dough in the bowl for 5 to 10 minutes, until it's smooth, soft and stretchy. Turn the dough onto a floured board and knead for a few more minutes, until smooth and elastic. Cover with a clean tea towel and leave the dough to rest for 10 minutes, then knead again for 2 more minutes.

3. Rub the mixing bowl with a bit of oil to coat, then return the dough to the bowl, cover with the clean tea towel, and leave it to rise in a warm place until it doubles in size: about 1½ hours.

4. Place an oven rack in the lowest rung and heat the oven to 240° C.

5. Meanwhile, gently punch down the dough to deflate it, divide it into 6 equal pieces, and roll each piece into a ball. Cover with a clean towel and leave to rest for 15 minutes.

6. Once the oven is fully preheated, roll out the dough: working with one ball at a time, roll to 6-mm thickness. Place each onto an ungreased baking tray. They should not touch – bake in batches if needed.

7. Bake in the bottom of the preheated oven for about 5 minutes. Watch through the oven window – as soon as the pita breads puff up, they're done! Take care not to overbake.

8. After baking, wrap the hot pita in a clean tea towel to prevent it from drying out while you wait for it to cool. Some even place the cooling pita in a brown paper bag for 15 minutes, to keep it soft.

Pita bread is often served on a meze plate with hummus or baba ganoush, tabbouleh or falafel.

Wholemeal flour adds a nice nuttiness but you can use all white flour if you prefer.

If your pita didn't form a pocket, try topping it with tomato sauce and cheese to make another flatbread: pizza!

141

VIETNAM

Vietnam is long and narrow – in some places it is only 48 kilometres wide. In addition to over 3,000 kilometres of coastline, this biodiverse Southeast Asian country also has many rivers, jungles, deltas, mountains and islands. Vietnamese cuisine reflects its complicated history with ties to China and France, both of which ruled Vietnam in the past. But while some recipes include stir-fries or freshly baked baguettes, Vietnamese chefs always add their own unique spin.

FISH AND SEAFOOD

Catfish, eel, prawns, crabs and shellfish are all favourites in Vietnamese cuisine. People buy fish caught the same day, so fresh it's frequently still alive. Seafood is often simply steamed and seasoned with lime juice, salt and pepper, plus a side of a tangy dip made from fish sauce, lime, sugar and hot peppers.

RICE

More than half of Vietnam's arable land is used to grow rice – from fragrant, long-grain jasmine rice to white rice to deep purple glutinous rice, which becomes super sticky once cooked. Rice is also turned into noodles, translucent rice 'paper', rice wine and a sweet, nutty powder made from the toasted grains.

BÁNH TRÁNG

Vietnam's famous rice 'paper', or bánh tráng, is super-thin, circular wrappers. To make them, rice-flour batter is spread over fabric, which is dried in the sun. The result looks like translucent paper! People then dip the brittle, dried rice paper into water for a few seconds, making it instantly soft and ready to be stuffed with fresh fillings.

GỎI CUỐN

These fresh summer rolls are one of the most popular treats made from bánh tráng, stuffed with freshly boiled prawns, fresh coriander, cucumbers, pickled carrots and radishes and rice noodles. Gỏi cuốn are served with a deliciously rich, thick peanut dipping sauce.

NƯỚC MẮM

Vietnamese flavours get a big boost from nước mắm, a dipping sauce with a 300-year history! Its sweet and tangy taste is the result of a delicious mix of lime juice, garlic, chillies, sugar and fish sauce, in which tiny fish, prawns and crab are preserved in salt and fermented for months.

VEGGIES AND HERBS

Aromatic herbs are essential to Vietnamese cuisine, with fresh coriander, basil, mint and leafy lettuce starring in almost every dish. Everything must be fresh, and greens are often served raw or only lightly cooked. Vietnamese soups and stir-fries celebrate bitter melon, long beans, taro stems and rau muống, or 'water spinach' – which grows wild along Vietnam's rivers and canals.

BÁNH MÌ

French colonizers brought the baguette to Vietnam, and locals still enjoy their own lighter, pillowy version of the bread. Baguette sandwiches here are called bánh mì and are popularly served by street vendors for breakfast and lunch. Breakfast bánh mì usually features fried eggs, while lunch sandwiches include a mouth-watering array of ingredients like pâté, sliced cucumber, pickled radish and plenty of fresh aromatic herbs.

FRUIT AND FRUIT DRINKS

Popular fruit drinks are varieties of limeade with bubbly water, sometimes flavoured with salty plums. Coconut trees grow everywhere here, and people love to sip nước dừa, the clear, refreshing liquid found inside young coconuts. Another popular drink is the sweet juice of freshly squeezed sugar cane, which is probably as close as you can get to drinking liquid sugar.

VIETNAM'S FAVOURITE HOLIDAY

Celebrations for *Tết*, the Lunar New Year, in Vietnam last for a week and include much feasting, as well as symbolic foods given as gifts. A favourite holiday dish includes glutinous rice cakes stuffed with mung beans and pork, seasoned with fermented prawn paste, chilli peppers, lemongrass and black pepper. The cakes are wrapped in banana leaves and boiled, creating sticky, flavour-infused morsels.

PHO

BROTH WITH BEEF AND RICE NOODLES

PREPARATION TIME
10 mins

COOKING TIME
40 mins

LEVEL OF DIFFICULTY
● ●

SERVES
4

Originally a street food and now Vietnam's national dish, pho is a soup of rich, beefy broth with rice noodles, thinly sliced meat and aromatic herbs. At its heart, great pho is a wonderfully flavourful clear broth, usually made from long-simmered beef bones – the broth is traditionally cooked over a low heat for many, many hours or even overnight for a deep, rich, complex flavour. This version saves time by calling for stock, which you quickly infuse with aromatics like ginger, cloves, cinnamon and star anise, so that it all comes together in less than an hour.

INGREDIENTS

340 g boneless top sirloin
1 5-cm piece of ginger, halved
    lengthways
2 onions, halved
3 cloves
2 star aniseed pods
1 small cinnamon stick
1.9 litres good-quality beef or
    chicken stock (or 950 ml
    of each)
285 g dried flat rice noodles or
    pho noodles
1 tablespoon fish sauce
1 teaspoon brown sugar
salt

GARNISHES, FOR SERVING:

55 g beansprouts
4 spring onions, thinly sliced
2 limes, quartered into wedges
115 g of mixed herbs: mint, fresh
    coriander and Thai basil
1 jalapeño, sliced thinly across
hoisin sauce
sriracha

1. Place the meat in the freezer for 30 minutes to make it easy to slice.

2. In a large pot, toast the ginger, onions, cloves, star anise and cinnamon over a medium-high heat, stirring frequently, until fragrant: 2 to 3 minutes. Add the stock and 475 ml of water and bring to a boil, then reduce the heat to a medium-low and cook for 30 minutes, allowing the aromatics to infuse the broth.

3. While the broth simmers, soak the noodles in a bowl of hot water until they bend and look bright white, then drain in a heat-proof strainer.

4. Remove the beef from the freezer and slice it very, very thinly.

5. Using a slotted spoon, remove the solids from the broth and discard them. Add the fish sauce and sugar, then taste and season with salt and more fish sauce and sugar, if you like. Keep on a low simmer.

6. When you're nearly ready to eat, dunk the noodles in the broth to warm, then transfer them to 4 bowls.

7. Increase the heat of the broth to medium and add the thinly sliced beef. Cook for 2 minutes for medium-rare meat, or longer if you prefer.

8. Ladle the cooked beef and hot broth over the noodles, dividing the beef evenly.

9. Serve the pho with garnishes of beansprouts, spring onions, lime wedges, herbs, jalapeño slices, hoisin sauce and sriracha.

In this recipe, the beef is sliced so thin, it cooks almost instantly in the hot broth. If you prefer, you can replace the beef with cubed tofu or cooked, shredded chicken.

AUSTRALASIA AND OCEANIA

This island-rich region spans a vast expanse of the Southern Hemisphere, including Australia, New Zealand, New Guinea and thousands of islands, from Indonesia and Guam to Fiji and Tahiti.

While Australasia is home to lush rainforests, arid deserts, towering mountain ranges and even glaciers and volcanoes, this part of the globe is dominated by water. Here people swim, surf and sail the Indian Ocean, the Pacific Ocean and the world's third-largest ocean – the Southern Ocean. Even young children in Australasia are often expert swimmers and fishers. Locals feast on the freshest catch, like tuna, barramundi, sea urchins, octopus, squid and prawns, and meet many more sea creatures while snorkelling in the Great Barrier Reef, the world's largest coral reef system. No wonder this watery part of the world is also known as Oceania!

If fish don't float your boat, fear not. Coconut palm trees line many island shores here, and people drink coconut water, bake coconut bread, add coconut cream to curries and sweeten desserts with coconut sugar. Taro root, a centuries-old starchy staple, can be boiled, steamed, fried or baked but is beloved as poi, a thick, sticky dish popular across Polynesia.

FROZEN DESSERTS

AROUND THE WORLD

Whether eaten from a cup on the street or from a bowl after dinner, people around the world enjoy frozen sweets – especially delightful on a hot summer afternoon. Most evidence indicates that the first true ice cream originated in the seventeenth century in Italy. From there, it spread to France, England, India and beyond, becoming an internationally beloved sweet treat on hot days.

FROZEN FRUIT

At least 2,500 years ago, ancient Mesopotamians liked to add crushed ice to bowls of dates or honey. In modern Iraq, specialized parlours sell ice cream flavoured with pistachio and qamar'l deen, or 'apricot fruit leather' – apricots boiled in sugar and then left out in the sun to dry.

GELATO

In summer, Italians line up for scoops of luscious ice cream that goes by the name gelato. It contains 4 to 9% fat compared to American ice cream's 14 to 25% fat, giving it a less creamy but more intense taste.

SORBETEROS

The Philippines are home to amazingly diverse ice cream flavours. Vendors called sorbeteros push brightly coloured carts and tout scoops with flavours like avocado, sweetcorn and purple yam. There's even a salty-sweet Cheddar cheese-flavoured ice cream, sometimes studded with corn kernels for extra crunch.

MOCHI

Mochi is a traditional sweet snack in Japan made by shaping pounded sticky rice into small cakes filled with sweet bean or yam paste. In California in the 1990s, the recipe was tweaked to include a filling of ice cream, a delicious version that quickly spread around the globe.

I-TIM-PAD

Also known as rolled ice cream or stir-fried ice cream, this is a unique innovation pioneered by Thai street vendors. It's made by pouring then swishing sweet, flavoured milk onto a freezing-cold steel surface until it hardens, then rolling the frozen cream into tight cylinders.

IRANIAN DESSERTS

After dinner in Iran, people often eat faloodeh, a frozen sorbet-like dessert made primarily from thin, starchy noodles – similar to vermicelli – covered in a semi-frozen syrup flavoured with saffron, rose water or pistachio. Iranians also enjoy a thick ice cream called bastani sonnati – flavoured with rose water, saffron, vanilla and pistachios, sometimes with pure chunks of frozen clotted cream.

HAWAIIAN ICES

Also known as snowballs in the Southern US, Hawaiian ices are made by grinding off shavings from a huge block of ice and dousing them with brightly coloured sweet syrups. First introduced to Hawaii in the early twentieth century by Japanese immigrants, kakigōri, as the chilly desserts were known in Japan, were invented centuries before as a special extravagance for wealthy people.

KULFI

This ice cream, enjoyed in Bangladesh, Pakistan, Myanmar, Nepal, India and Sri Lanka, is made from reduced milk, giving it a custard-like consistency. It is often shaped like a cone and served on a stick like an ice lolly. Some accounts indicate kulfi originated in the sixteenth century, as a favourite treat of Indian royalty. If true, India is the inventor of ice cream.

FAGYLALT

Hungarians love fagylalt – several scoops are served in a small cone. In summer, one can also buy hókristály (snow crystal) – ground or crushed ice with a shot of brightly coloured fruit syrup.

AUSTRALIA

Australia is a country, a continent *and* the largest island on Earth! It's also home to tropical rainforests, dry deserts, snow-capped mountains, palm-fringed coasts and beautiful beaches. Aboriginal people have lived here for 50,000 years. But in the 1700s, the British arrived, turning parts of Australia into a prison colony. Today, of Australia's 21 million citizens, approximately 3% are indigenous, descended from ancestors who lived here and on nearby islands before the British arrived – but they cherish their cultural and culinary heritage and maintain vibrant food traditions, which now blend with the food cultures of Australia's many citizens of European ancestry.

KANGAROO FOR DINNER

Wild game meat includes kangaroo, wallabies, emus, echidna (porcupine), turtles and tiny little marsupials called bandicoots. Today, you can find kangaroo meat in grocery stores – people cook it over coals or in a stew.

WILD FOODS

Aboriginal Australians developed knowledge of over a thousand wild plants, from the desert to the rainforest. This expertise was largely ignored by white settlers but today people are rediscovering bush tucker (as wild foods are called) like watercress oil, wild mountain pepper, wattleseed (which has a coffee–hazelnut flavour) and bunya nuts, collected from the giant cones of bunya pine trees.

THE BARBIE

Avid outdoors people, many Australians love cooking and eating outside too. They gather around the barbecue – the *barbie* – to grill steak and sausages. Goanna lizard is also often grilled and 'carpetbag steak' – a thick steak split open and stuffed with oysters – is popular, served with anchovy sauce.

WITCHETTY GRUBS

These plump, white moth larvae look like little mushy marshmallows. A traditional wild food, some Australians still enjoy these grubs roasted over the barbie's coals.

VEGEMITE ™

Just about every Australian kitchen has a jar of this thick, salty dark brown yeast paste. It's very high in vitamin B and people here love to spread it on toast.

FRUITS

Fruit salad is popular at the barbie! The Australian climate grows amazing fruits, including passion fruit, pineapples, pawpaws, figs, guava, chokos, tamarillos, kumquats, lychees, kiwi, custard apples and plums.

ANZAC BISCUITS

Anzac Day (25 April) honours people who died in wars for Australia and New Zealand. People commemorate them by baking and eating Anzac biscuits, big oat biscuits that were traditionally sent to soldiers.

MEAT PIES

Australia and neighbouring New Zealand are home to so many shepherds, they are two of the world's leading producers of lamb. Australians love lamb prepared many ways, including baked into little pies with a pastry crust. Some Australians serve meat pies floating in split pea soup!

GLOBAL FLAVOURS

The British brought their favourite foods like tea, biscuits and corned beef. Australia is also home to many immigrants from nearby Indonesia, Vietnam, Malaysia, India and the Philippines, making satay and stir-fries with noodles or rice daily favourites.

DAMPER

This Aboriginal Australian flatbread is made by grinding seeds into flour, making dough and then cooking it over fire. It is still popular today but is now often made with self-raising flour and baked in an oven.

PAVLOVA

MERINGUE WITH WHIPPED CREAM, STRAWBERRIES AND KIWI

PREPARATION TIME	COOKING TIME	LEVEL OF DIFFICULTY	MAKES
1 hr	1 hr 15 mins	●●	1 20-cm pavlova

This meringue cake with a marshmallow-soft centre is as light as air. The national dessert of Australia, it is also beloved in nearby New Zealand. Some say the recipe was created for the ballerina Anna Pavlova, who danced her way through both countries in 1926. After all, pavlova floats on your tongue like a ballerina sailing through the air, and the sides of it look a bit like a tutu.

But while being a ballerina is hard work, making this dessert is not. If you haven't made meringue before, you'll be surprised how easy it is to whip up! Just be sure to start with a perfectly clean, dry bowl, and don't allow even a smidge of yolks in. If you try to beat the whites by hand, you'll get a ballerina-level workout – but use the whisk attachment of a hand mixer or tabletop mixer and you'll have magically fluffy meringue in just a few minutes!

This version is topped with kiwi, the fuzzy-skinned, green-fleshed fruit that was first commercially grown in New Zealand – but you can crown pavlova with berries, peaches, passion fruit or any favourite fruit in peak season.

INGREDIENTS

FOR THE PAVLOVA

4 large egg whites
pinch of salt
200 g caster sugar
1 teaspoon apple cider or
    distilled white vinegar
1½ teaspoons cornflour
1 teaspoon pure vanilla extract

FOR THE TOPPING

250 ml double cream
2 tablespoons caster sugar
140 g strawberries, sliced about
    6 mm thick
2 kiwi, peeled and sliced about
    6 mm thick

TO MAKE THE PAVLOVA

1. Preheat the oven to 180°C. Line a baking tray with greaseproof paper.

2. In a large bowl, combine the egg whites and salt. Using an electric mixer (or a tabletop mixer fitted with a whisk attachment), beat the egg whites at a medium-high speed until they form soft peaks: about 5 minutes. (When you flip over one of the beaters, the peak of the whipped egg white will flop over into soft peaks: like a Santa hat.) With the mixer running, add the sugar, 1 tablespoon at a time, until you have a stiff, shiny meringue. Gently fold in the vinegar, cornflour and vanilla.

3. Spread the meringue on the greaseproof paper in a circle-blob about 20 centimetres across. Use a fish slice or spatula to create fun, artful swoops if you like. These will set as the pavlova bakes.

4. Place the meringue in the oven, lower the temperature to 150°C and bake for 1 hour and 15 minutes or until crisp on the edges. Leave to cool completely. Don't worry if the surface is cracked – you'll soon slather it in whipped cream!

TO MAKE THE TOPPING

5. In a small bowl, whip the double cream and sugar until stiff peaks form.

6. When ready to serve, spoon whipped cream over the cooled pavlova, then top with the sliced fruit. Serve sliced into wedges.

REFRESHING DRINKS

AROUND THE WORLD

When you're heated up, nothing cools you down like a nice cold drink. While minty herbs and citrus slices are popular in glasses worldwide, regional beverages are also made with locally beloved ingredients like ginger, kola nuts, black tea, boba, sugar syrups, corn, rice and even bread. The refreshing results may be sweet or salty, light or thick, flat or bubbly, and topped with anything from cinnamon sticks to pineapple chunks.

SIMA

In Finland, they make a bubbly lemonade with lemon, honey, raisins and a little bit of yeast. The resulting fermentation creates fizzy bubbles!

NIMBU PANI

This thirst-quenching Indian drink is made with a yellow-green citrus called the nimbu, finished with Himalayan salt and sold from street carts all summer.

LIMONANA

This lemonade is green! That's because it's made with mint leaves, which get blended with sugar, lemon juice and water. It's so good it's the national drink in Israel but it's made all over the Middle East.

PAPELÓN CON LIMÓN

In Venezuela, the secret lemonade ingredient is a special brown sugar. It's called papelón, and it comes in a big brick! A bit gets dissolved in hot water for sweetness, then mixed with sour lemon or lime juice and chilled with lots of ice.

ARNOLD PALMER

In the United States, an Arnold Palmer is half lemonade and half iced tea. It's named after a famous golfer who always cooled down with this refreshing combination.

SALTY LEMONADE

In Vietnam, lemons and limes are preserved in salt so they will keep throughout the year. Put half of one in a glass with a little sugar and water – ta-da! You've got salty lemonade.

GINGER BEER

This non-alcoholic fizzy drink has a sweet flavour, a spicy kick and a global history. First brewed in eighteenth-century England using spices from Asia and sugar from the Caribbean, it's now sipped around the world.

SLAVIC KVASS

Drink your bread! This traditional Slavic drink is made from black or rye bread mixed with water, sugar and yeast, then left to ferment until fizzy. Sweet and sour, sometimes kvass is flavoured with fruits like raspberry, cherry or lemon.

HORCHATA

In Mexico, this thick, white drink is made from cooked, puréed rice, seasoned with cinnamon and vanilla, and often served over ice. It's like a rice pudding that you sip through a straw!

CHICHA MORADA

People in Peru make this sweet drink from an ancient type of purple corn still grown in the Andes. It's often seasoned with cinnamon and cloves, and studded with chunks of pineapple.

LAMB CHOPS

LAMB CHOPS IN A ROSEMARY MARINADE

PREPARATION TIME	COOKING TIME	LEVEL OF DIFFICULTY	SERVES
2 hrs 30 mins	10 mins	●●	4

In New Zealand sheep outnumber people and its lamb is famous around the world. Locals, too, love it many ways, from slow-roasted leg of lamb to spicy little lamb sausages. One of the quickest, most delicious preparations is lamb chops, which cook up juicy and tender in just a few minutes. Many people like their lamb medium rare with a dark sear and rosy-pink interior. If you have an instant-read thermometer, these chops are done when they reach 65°C. You can cook them slightly longer if you prefer medium but the meat can quickly go from tender and juicy to tough and dry, so take care not to overcook it.

INGREDIENTS

1 tablespoon of fresh, chopped
    rosemary or ½ teaspoon dried
2 tablespoons olive oil
3 cloves garlic, peeled and
    chopped
salt and black pepper
4 loin lamb chops

1. In a small bowl, combine the dried or fresh rosemary with the olive oil and garlic to make a paste marinade. Season well with salt and pepper.

2. Place the chops on a large plate, pat them dry with kitchen paper, then rub them on all sides with the marinade. Seal the chops in a ziplock bag and marinate in the fridge for 2 hours.

3. Leave the marinated chops to sit for about 20 to 30 minutes, to reach room temperature. Meanwhile, preheat the oven to 200°C.

4. Heat a large, heavy frying pan or cast-iron pan over a high heat. Once it's hot, add the chops and let them sear on one side for 2 to 3 minutes. Using tongs, carefully turn each chop over, then transfer the pan to the hot oven and cook for an additional 6 minutes. Test for desired doneness (you can slice into one to be sure the inside is done to your preference); allow chops to rest for 5 minutes before serving.

Serve with a fresh salad,
steamed asparagus, pan-fried
spinach, glazed parsnips or
buttered peas, plus roasted
potatoes or fresh bread.

EUROPE

Europe is one of the smallest continents – and one of the most densely populated. Ancient Greek and Roman civilizations from thousands of years ago still influence government, philosophy and architecture today. Many food traditions – like harvesting mushrooms, olives, root vegetables and berries; turning milk into butter, yoghurt and cheeses; growing grain for breads, pasta and pastries; and fermenting grapes into wine and apples into hard cider – go back thousands of years.

Europe is now home to over 700 million people, some in rural villages, others inhabiting big cities like London, Paris, Rome, Madrid, Istanbul and Berlin. The continent also draws immigrants from around the world – including from the many global countries once colonized by European powers, from Barbados and Brazil to Botswana and Bangladesh.

FRANCE

As the largest country in western Europe, France enjoys coastlines on both the Atlantic Ocean and Mediterranean Sea and also enjoys the towering French Alps, beautiful beaches, bustling cities and famously fertile farmland. People here have been growing wheat, grapes and olives – and making them into bread, wine and olive oil – for thousands of years. France is so celebrated for great cooks and food culture that people worldwide have adopted the French words 'chef' and 'cuisine'.

FAVOURITE VEGETABLES

The French love in-season and perfectly fresh vegetables. Favourites include artichokes, asparagus, little beans called haricots verts and young fresh peas called petite pois, shimmering in buttery glaze or a French salad dressing called vinaigrette.

BOULANGERIES AND BAGUETTES

French families seldom bake their own bread because every neighbourhood has great *boulangeries*! Here, they bake perhaps France's best-known daily bread: the baguette. These long loaves have a crisp crust and soft centre and the French eat up to 30 million each day. Fresh baguettes are on the table for almost every meal but *s'il vous plaît*, don't ask for butter – baguettes are only buttered at breakfast!

CROISSANTS

Made from yeasted dough, rolled to incorporate lots and lots of butter and baked to flaky perfection, the crescent-shaped croissant is sometimes filled with ham and cheese, almond paste or chocolate, though many consider them perfect just as they are.

CREAM IN EVERYTHING

Milk and cream go into everything from café au lait to cheesy gratins. Many French sauces are golden with eggs, too, like mayonnaise, hollandaise and bearnaise. One pastry favourite, choux a la crème, is filled with plenty of whipped cream!

CHEESE

Charles de Gaulle, France's former prime minister, once asked, 'How can anyone govern a nation that has 246 different kinds of cheese?' Today, there are over 400! From creamy Brie and Camembert to blue Roquefort, a cheese course appears on the menu of just about every restaurant in France.

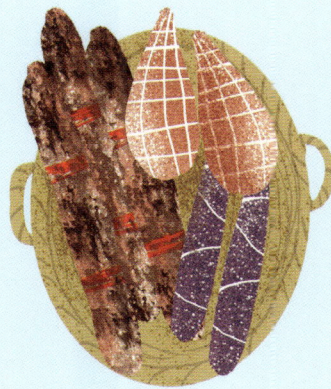

DIJON

France's world-famous mustard is named after a town in Burgundy, where people have been making the smooth, creamy, strong-flavoured spread since the Middle Ages. Made with mustard seeds and white wine, it's stirred into vinaigrette, slathered on sausages or smoothed into a jambon beurre (ham with butter) sandwich.

GLOBAL FLAVOURS

Global trade brought France beans and potatoes from the Americas, coffee and chocolate from Africa, tea from Asia and sugar from the Caribbean. Today, it is Europe's most ethnically diverse nation. These days, you'll find everything here from Egyptian falafel to Vietnamese bánh mì!

BOUCHERIES AND CHARCUTERIES

The French eat lots of meat. *Boucheries* (butchers) sell goose, rabbit, duck, quail, beef, lamb, goat, pork and horsemeat, including cuts like veal, brain, tongue, kidneys and the famously fattened livers called foie gras. The French have made an art of charcuterie and special shops sell these cured, smoked and pickled meats, as well as pâté, the classic spread made of liver cooked in butter and wine.

OYSTERS

In Brittany and Normandy on France's northeast coast, oysters reign supreme. Over the centuries, the French have refined raising and harvesting oysters along the shore but their preparation remains sublimely simple: a spritz of lemon or a dab of a vinegar–shallot dressing. Or simply shuck, slurp and swallow.

CRÊPES

People here have been eating crêpes – France's beloved, super thin pancakes – since the thirteenth century. During the twentieth century, crêperies opened all over but especially in the Paris neighbourhood of Montparnasse. Enjoyed in cafés or at home, crêpes may be savoury or sweet, filled with ham and cheese, mushrooms, strawberry jam or hazelnut chocolate spread, or simply enjoyed with butter.

TRUFFETTES

CHOCOLATE TRUFFLES

PREPARATION TIME	COOKING TIME	LEVEL OF DIFFICULTY	MAKES
3 hrs	10 mins	●	About 35 truffettes

You may have heard of wild truffles, which are underground fungus that people hunt with specially trained sniffing dogs. French farmers forage nearly a third of the world's truffles, which are so intensely flavoured that people pay lots of money to have even a tiny bit shaved over their dinner.

Chocolate truffles, however, have no relation to the wild kind – other than being as round, brown, beloved, luxurious and intensely flavoured as the little dug-up orbs after which they're named. And while they're famously luscious, chocolate truffles are surprisingly simple to make. Just chop up some chocolate, melt it with butter, whisk in some cream and roll spoonfuls into little balls of rich ganache. Once cooled, toss them in cocoa powder. That's it!

INGREDIENTS

340 g plain or dark chocolate, chopped
3 tablespoons cold unsalted butter
pinch of salt
225 g double cream
½ cup unsweetened cocoa powder or ¼ cup cocoa powder mixed with ¼ cup icing sugar

1. In a mixing bowl, combine the chopped chocolate with the butter and salt.

2. In a small saucepan, bring the cream just to a simmer. Pour the hot cream over the chocolate. Leave to stand until the chocolate and butter are melted: about 5 minutes. Whisk until the mixture, called a ganache, is smooth and shiny. (If you're going to add any extracts to flavour, do so now.)

3. Cover and refrigerate the ganache until firm: 1 to 2 hours.

4. Line a baking tray with greaseproof paper. For each truffle, scoop out about 1 tablespoon of the ganache, roll it into a ball and set it on the baking tray. Refrigerate until firm: about 1 hour.

5. Put the cocoa powder in a large bowl and line another baking tray with greaseproof paper. Roll the ganache in the cocoa powder until well coated. That's it!

6. Pack the truffles in a resealable container and refrigerate for up to 5 days.

You can have fun flavouring your truffles. Try stirring in a dash of almond extract, grating some lemon or orange zest over them or adding a pinch of sea salt.

Serve truffles with coffee or after dessert, or give them as a gift. Your friends will say, 'Ooh la la!'

GERMANY

In 100 CE, a Roman described German food as simple and hearty: breads, grains, fruits and berries, milk and cheese and wild game roasted on huge spits. These days, few Germans roast meat on huge spits but in other ways, that description holds true! Modern Germans still savour traditional foods that date back centuries: satisfying stews, squiggly little pasta called spätzle, rich lard known as schmaltz, rye bread spiked with caraway seeds and plenty of pork and sauerkraut.

PASS THE PORK

Until the 1800s, most Germans were peasants who raised their own pigs. Today, most Germans live in cities but pork still reigns supreme. Every part of the pig is used: tongues, brains, ears, tails, trotters – even the blood, in beloved black pudding.

DAILY BREAD

Bread is served with just about every German meal. You'll see dark, whole-grain loaves, chewy rye called pumpernickel and an incredible array of soft and crisp, plain or seeded, yeasted or sourdough loaves, made from wheat, oats, spelt, buckwheat, linseed or millet, in every shape and size.

POTATOES

After potatoes arrived from the Americas, it took Germans almost 200 years to start growing them but by the 1800s, they were on every table. Today, Germans love potatoes in salad, pancakes, dumplings soup and more.

SPEAKING OF SAUSAGE...

Dinner here is the wurst! That's the German word for sausage and there are more than a thousand varieties. Bratwurst are sausages to boil or grill; weisswurst means 'white sausage', traditionally made of veal, while liverwurst is a spreadable pâté.

ASPARAGUS

Prized white asparagus is an annual spring obsession in Germany. Families cook it at home, chefs create special menus highlighting it and it is savoured in all sizes and styles. In fact, April, May and June are known as the *Spargelzeit*, or 'asparagus time'.

BLACK FOREST GATEAU

Germany's most famous cake is this chocolate sponge cake filled with sweetened cream, decorated with cherries and brushed with kirschwasser – a cherry liqueur. Some say the cake looks like the traditional white blouse, black dress and hat with red pom-poms worn by women in the Black Forest region!

KAFFEE UND KUCHEN

Many gather to catch up over coffee and cakes, a *zwischenmahlzeiten,* or 'in-between meal', also enjoyed in neighbouring Austria and Luxembourg.

BEER HERE

Traditionally, beer here was made in winter and stored in underground cellars. In summer, brewers would set up tables at the cellar entrance to give buyers a shady spot. This *biergarten* or 'beer garden' dates back to the seventeenth century. Beer is often served in a large, heavy glass called a stein, especially during the annual *Oktoberfest* – beer festival.

HAMBURG(ERS)!

The German city of Hamburg is the ancestral home of the hamburger, the minced beef sandwich on a bun now popular all over the world. Its sausage friend the frankfurter (rechristened in New York as the hot dog) takes its name from the German city of Frankfurt.

BREZEL

Brezels, called pretzels in English, get their crunchy exterior and brown colour from being dipped in lye (an alkaline liquid). In Bavaria, a popular mid-morning snack is a soft pretzel with weisswurst.

CABBAGE AND BRATWURST

SWEET-AND-SOUR BRAISED CABBAGE WITH PORK SAUSAGES

PREPARATION TIME	COOKING TIME	LEVEL OF DIFFICULTY	SERVES
20 mins	1 hr	●●	4

Germans love both cabbages and sausages – and they're even better together! This sweet-and-sour braised cabbage gets extra flavour from a tart apple and the zing of apple cider vinegar, plus juniper berries or caraway seeds, if you like. You can use red or green cabbage but the purply red gives the dish a pretty colour. Cabbage stores well all winter and traditionally kept peasants fed months after harvest. Today, this dish will warm you from the inside out on a cold, dark night. In this recipe, the pork sausages cook on the hob top but it's also easy to pop them into the oven to bake while the cabbage cooks.

Consider serving this with a pile of mashed potatoes, a slice of hearty German bread and some strong mustard!

INGREDIENTS

3 tablespoons oil
1 medium yellow onion, diced
½ head cabbage, thinly sliced
1 medium-sized tart apple, diced
120 ml chicken or vegetable
    stock, or apple cider or water
1 tablespoon sugar, plus more to
    taste
1 bay leaf
3 whole cloves
3 juniper berries or ½ teaspoon
    caraway seeds (optional)
½ teaspoon salt, plus more to
    taste
4 bratwurst sausages
2 tablespoons apple cider
    vinegar, plus more to taste

1. In a heavy pot or casserole dish, heat 2 tablespoons of the oil. Add the diced onion and cook until it begins to brown: about 8 minutes.

2. Add the cabbage and cook, stirring, until wilted: about 5 minutes. Add the apple, broth, vinegar, sugar, bay leaf, cloves, juniper berries or caraway seeds and salt. Bring the liquid to a boil, reduce the heat to medium-low, cover and simmer, stirring occasionally, until the cabbage is tender and infused with all of the flavours: 20 to 30 minutes. Add more liquid if the pan starts to dry out.

3. While the cabbage cooks, heat 1 tablespoon of oil in a large frying pan over a medium-high heat. Add the sausages in a single layer and cook until browned on the bottom: about 4 minutes. Turn the sausages and cook until browned on the other side: about 3 minutes longer. Add 250 ml water to the frying pan and simmer until the sausages are cooked through: about 10 minutes.

4. Taste the cabbage and season with more salt, sugar and vinegar, to taste. Serve with the sausages.

ITALY

For millennia, the Italian peninsula's location – jutting into the Mediterranean Sea – made its ports busy places for exchanging ideas – and ingredients! In the Middle Ages, Venice was part of the spice route connecting Europe to Asia. Soon, sailors like the Italian-born Christopher Columbus brought ingredients from the Americas, like tomatoes, beans and chocolate, which would become essential to Italian cuisine. Thousands of years ago, ancient Romans were already making breads, salads, olive oil, spiced sausages, wine, cheeses and cakes! Variations on cuisines from ancient Rome are all still enjoyed here today.

PASTA

Some historians say Marco Polo introduced noodles from China to Italy in the 1200s. Whatever the lineage, there are now over 600 shapes of pasta here, many with names that describe how they look. Orecchiette resemble ears, linguine are like long tongues and rotelle are like wagon wheels, while radiatori resemble a car's radiator.

PORK

Italians eat lots of pork and also wild boar, which they make into sausages like salami and mortadella. Some pork legs are salted, hung to dry for months and cured into prosciutto, which is served as a thinly shaved delicacy.

BREAD

Thousands of specialty bakeries across the country bake breads, including grissini, ciabatta, panini, crostini, bruschetta and focaccia, for every occasion. Archaeologists excavating the ancient city of Pompeii discovered a bakery with an oven that still contained round loaves of sourdough bread!

VEGETABLES

Italian gardens are lush with aubergines, artichokes, beans, spinach, fennel, chicory, rapini and aromatic herbs like oregano, basil and rosemary. Global exploration brought tomatoes, which Italians called the pomo d'oro (golden apple). Today, tomatoes are essential to Italian cuisine.

SEAFOOD

Italian cuisine has always boasted amazing fresh seafood. Recipes call for octopus, clams, mussels, eel, shrimp, prawns, squid and more. It may be grilled, fried, simmered in stews, served in cold salads or tossed with pasta.

NUTELLA®

The Italian confection called gianduja – a paste of chocolate, sugar and hazelnuts – can be used as a sweet filling, in ice cream or as thick icing. In 1951, Pietro Ferrero developed his own recipe of spreadable gianduja. In 1964, a variation of this spread became Nutella®. Today, children and adults around the world slather it on toast.

PIZZA

Italians have been covering flatbreads with toppings since long before tomatoes arrived, and many variations have stories behind them. In 1889, after Italy's unification, Queen Margherita of Savoy visited Naples and asked its most celebrated *pizzaiolo* (pizza maker) to make her something new. Her favourite was a new, simple combination: tomato, mozzarella and basil, in the colours of the Italian flag. Today, it is called pizza Margherita.

CHEESES

Italians make hundreds of cheeses from the milk of cows, sheep, goats and even water buffalo. Favourites include nutty, aged parmesan, mild asiago, quick-melting fontina, fresh mozzarella and blue-veined gorgonzola. Parmesan was mentioned in 1398 in one of Italy's most famous books, Boccaccio's *Decameron*, and ricotta gets a mention in Homer's 800 BCE epic poem *The Odyssey*!

PESTO

In Italian, pesto means 'smashed' or 'made into a paste', which you can do with a diverse combination of fresh greens, types of nuts and a fat like olive oil. Look for the tomato-based pesto rosso (red pesto), as well as parsley pesto, kale pesto, broad bean pesto, avocado pesto and pesto trentino (from the city of Trento), which includes egg yolks.

FOCACCIA

OVEN-BAKED FLATBREAD

PREPARATION TIME
2 hr 50 mins

COOKING TIME
20 mins

LEVEL OF DIFFICULTY
● ●

MAKES
1 22 x 33 cm
flatbread

This traditional Italian recipe was known as panis focacius in ancient Rome, and today focaccia remains as popular as ever. A close cousin to pizza, this yeasted flatbread is rich and golden with generous use of Italy's famous olive oil. Topping combinations are endless – experiment by adding fresh rosemary, sliced onions, whole olives, garlic cloves, cherry tomatoes and Parmesan cheese – or just savour the simple perfection of flaky salt. Serve with more olive oil, of course!

INGREDIENTS

1 envelope (7 g) fast-action yeast
350 ml warm water
2 teaspoons honey
500 g plain or bread flour
1¼ teaspoons fine salt
6 tablespoons olive oil, plus more
    for drizzling
flaky salt, for sprinkling

1. In a large bowl, whisk the yeast with the warm water and honey and leave to stand until foamy: about 5 minutes. (If it doesn't foam, discard the mixture and start with a fresh packet of yeast.)

2. Stir in the flour, fine salt and 3 tablespoons of the olive oil, and vigorously mix with a wooden spoon until a dough forms: about 2 minutes.

3. Lightly flour a work surface and turn out the dough onto it. Knead the dough until smooth and elastic: 10 to 15 minutes. (If you have a tabletop mixer, you can mix and knead the dough with the dough hook attachment.) Form the dough into a smooth ball and transfer to an oiled bowl.

4. Cover the dough with clingfilm and leave to rise at room temperature until doubled in size: 60 to 90 minutes.

5. Pour 3 tablespoons olive oil into a 22 x 33 cm pan and use a brush to coat the sides of the pan, allowing the rest to pool at the bottom.

6. Deflate the dough by softly punching it down and turning it out into the prepared pan. Gently stretch the dough to help it fill the pan. Cover again and leave to rise until puffy: about 30 minutes.

7. While the dough is rising, preheat the oven to 220°C.

8. Using your fingers, poke the dough all over to create focaccia's famous dimples.

9. Drizzle the dough with a few more tablespoons of olive oil and use a brush to spread it around. Sprinkle with a few pinches of flaky salt or other toppings, as you wish.

10. Bake until golden brown: about 20 minutes.

11. Leave to cool for 5 minutes, then place upside down onto the rack, releasing it from the pan. Now carefully flip it so it's right-side up. Serve warm or at room temperature.

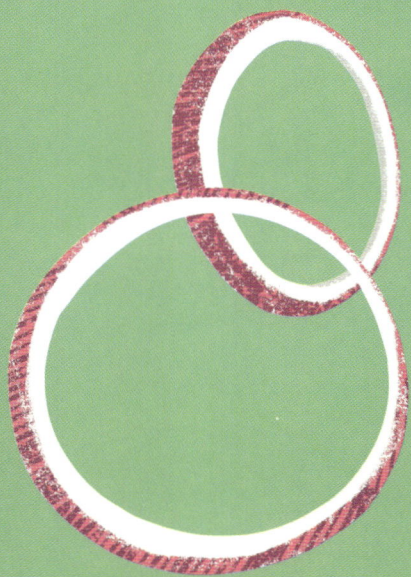

POLAND

Poland is a large country in Eastern Europe that shares borders with Germany and Ukraine – and the Baltic sea. It has beautiful beaches, fertile farmland and thousands of lakes, mountains and rivers. Poland became a unified state in the tenth century, expanded its borders and endured tumultuous times. Throughout it all, Polish cuisine has been a hearty celebration of potatoes, cabbage and beetroot, with beloved dishes of rustic breads, tangy sauerkraut, pillowy pierogi dumplings, mouthwatering kielbasa sausages and roast pork and sweet, jam-filled doughnuts.

BAGELS

In the late Middle Ages, Poland became a haven for European Jews, who shared their baking traditions that led to the development of bagels. In the first written account describing bagels, the city of Krakow required that they be fed to women after giving birth.

HUNTER'S STEW

Bigos, or 'hunter's stew', is a national dish that often features wild game, kielbasa sausage, foraged mushrooms, sweet plums and spicy juniper berries, all cooked with cabbage or sauerkraut. It's often served with rye bread or mashed potatoes.

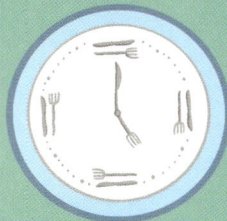

FOUR MEALS A DAY

Most people in Poland eat four meals a day, which goes back to farming times. Early breakfast is *śniadanie*, and it's usually bread with jam, cheese or cold meats. Second breakfast, *drugie śniadanie*, is often fruit and yoghurt. Then comes a hearty dinner or *obiad*, in late afternoon, when famished farmers come in from the field. The fourth meal, or *kolacja*, is when Poles often enjoy cold meats, toast, cheese or tomatoes before bed.

DUMPLINGS

Some dumplings are hearty like kartacze, which is made of mashed potatoes, some are donut-shaped kluski śląskie served with meat sauce, and then there are tiny uszka – 'little ears' – served in beetroot soup on Christmas Eve. The most popular, pierogi, can be stuffed with mushrooms, meat, potatoes or onions, or with sweet cheese for a berry-topped dessert.

PUCKER UP FOR PICKLES

Polish winters are cold, so people here long ago learned to preserve their fresh vegetables. They pickle cabbage, often as sauerkraut but they also pickle cucumbers, beetroot, cauliflower – as well as fish and mushrooms. Poles love pickled cucumbers so much they even make pickled cucumber soup!

DOUGHNUTS

Pączki are soft, rich doughnuts often filled with plum jam or wild rose jam, with a pinch of orange zest. Polish Catholics enjoy them on Fat Tuesday, the seventh week before Easter.

MILK AND DAIRY

Poles savour the sour flavours of fermented dairy, like buttermilk, kefir and yoghurt. There's even a Polish cheese soup called polewka z serwatki. It's hard to think of food that wouldn't receive a kiss of soured cream here, where it is a common garnish for meats, salads, cakes, kasha and soups.

HERBS AND SPICE CABINET

You'll find dill in every Polish kitchen, alongside parsley and caraway seeds. Marjoram and juniper berries often flavour meat dishes. Polish farm fields grow lots of pretty poppy flowers, an essential ingredient in Polish cakes, buns and rolls!

CHEESECAKE

Poles love cheese, including in cheesecake! First, a fresh, firm, creamy cheese, known as twaróg or ser biały ('white cheese') – which also appears in breakfast spreads and pierogi – is stirred into a rich batter with eggs and sugar, for a popular Christmas and Easter dessert.

STUFFED CABBAGE

Stuffed cabbage, or gołąbki, is a favourite Polish dish. Meats, rice, onion and herbs are cooked in butter, then stuffed into a rolled-up cabbage leaf and baked. People say this hearty meal gave Polish troops the strength to beat Teutonic knights in the fifteenth century.

173

ZUPA OGÓRKOWA

PICKLED CUCUMBER SOUP

PREPARATION TIME
20 mins

COOKING TIME
30 mins

LEVEL OF DIFFICULTY
● ●

SERVES
5

Eastern European cuisine includes lots of pickled cucumber – including this traditional pickled cucumber soup! Like many Polish and Ukrainian recipes, this dish also features rich, tart soured cream. Tangy, hearty, creamy and bright with just a little dill-pickle flavour, this simple soup will warm you up on a cold winter's day. Serve with slices of crusty bread.

INGREDIENTS

2 tablespoons butter
1 medium onion, diced
2 carrots, diced
1 celery stick, chopped
2 garlic cloves, chopped
1.4 l vegetable or chicken stock
4 new potatoes, diced
6 pickled cucumbers, roughly
    chopped and grated, plus
    more for garnish
120 ml soured cream, plus more
    for garnish
1 tablespoon flour
150 ml pickled cucumber brine

1. In a large pot, melt the butter over a medium-high heat, add the onion and carrot, and pan-fry until soft: about 5 minutes. Add the celery and garlic, and cook, stirring occasionally, until the vegetables soften and begin to brown: about 8 more minutes. Add the stock, cover and raise the heat to high.

2. Once the stock comes to a boil, add the potatoes and pickled cucumbers, reduce the heat to medium-low and simmer, covered, until the potatoes are cooked through and a fork slips in easily: about 25 to 30 minutes. Remove from heat.

3. Ladle a cup of warm broth into a bowl, add the soured cream and flour, and whisk until smooth. Then stir the mixture into the soup.

4. Use a potato masher to partially mash the cooked vegetables, leaving some of them chunky if you like.

5. Add the pickled cucumber brine and stir to combine. Ladle into bowls and serve warm, garnished with soured cream and extra pickled cucumber slices, if you prefer!

Want more dill flavour?
Garnish each bowl with a
pinch of chopped fresh dill.

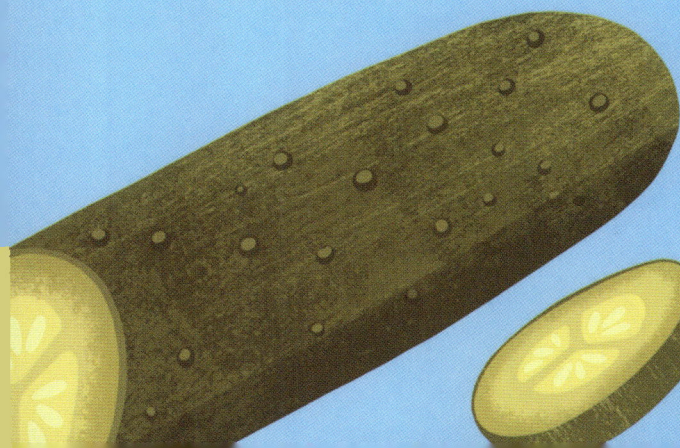

SPICES
AROUND THE WORLD

Since ancient times, people have used the intense tastes of herbs and spices to preserve foods and boost flavours. Egyptians were using fennel seeds, coriander seeds, juniper berries, cumin, garlic and thyme in cooking as far back as 3500 BCE. Today, people around the world use countless varieties of spice blends, and just a pinch can provide essential, iconic flavours that have come to define regional cuisines.

FIVE-SPICE POWDER

Five-spice powder combines five core elements prized in Chinese cuisine: sweet, bitter, sour, salty and spicy. The powder almost always includes ground star aniseed, cloves, cinnamon, Sichuan pepper and fennel seeds but despite its name, sometimes it can include many more. Chinese recipes use it to flavour rich meats like roasted duck or pork, while in Vietnam, the blend more often seasons roast chicken.

MASALA

Masala means 'mixture of spices', and there are dozens of types of masala in India. While each version varies with the region and maker, in north India, a classic garam masala likely includes coriander, cumin, cloves, nutmeg and chillies – all roasted and ground together.

ZA'ATAR

This spice mix, which usually includes dried thyme, oregano, salt, sesame seeds and sumac, has been used throughout the Middle East for thousands of years. Traces of what seems to be za'atar were discovered in the tomb of the Egyptian pharaoh Tutankhamun! In Lebanon, a classic breakfast is manaqish flatbread topped with za'atar, drizzled with olive oil and eaten with olives, cucumbers, tomatoes, fresh mint and a creamy dairy spread called labneh.

BERBERE

Berbere is the fiery red spice blend that gives many Ethiopian and Eritrean dishes a complex, earthy kick. Berbere can include over a dozen different spices, most notably red chilli peppers, fenugreek, ginger, coriander, cardamom, cumin, allspice, peppercorns, cloves and cinnamon. Essential in slow-cooked stews, it can also be made into a dipping sauce for injera, Ethiopia's iconic flatbread.

JERK SPICE

Jamaica's famous jerk spice combines allspice, thyme, nutmeg, onion, garlic and Scotch bonnet peppers. Jerk spice is believed to have been invented by the Maroons, Jamaican descendants of Africans who freed themselves from slavery. The Maroons used jerk spice primarily as a preservative for meat, which they cooked in holes they dug and covered up to prevent smoke from escaping and giving away their location.

TOGARASHI

Togarashi is the Japanese word for a number of chilli-pepper-based spice blends made in Japan since about the seventeenth century. Shichimi is probably the most famous, and includes red chilli pepper, sesame seeds, dried seaweed, orange peel and a Japanese pepper. Today, it's often set out as a condiment at ramen and udon restaurants.

HARISSA

Prepared as a paste or powder, this is a favourite way for North Africans to turn up the heat. Harissa's name derives from the Arabic verb for 'to pound' or 'to break into pieces' because the blend is made by pounding together roasted peppers, garlic, caraway seeds, coriander seeds and cumin.

RAS EL HANOUT

Beloved in Tunisia, Morocco and Algeria, there are infinite varieties but most include cinnamon, cumin, coriander, allspice, black pepper, ginger and salt, toasted and ground together in a mortar. Ras el hanout is a key ingredient in b'stilla, a savoury Moroccan pie traditionally made with pigeon.

HERBS DE PROVENCE

Provence, in southeastern France, is known for picturesque villages, lavender fields and sunshine. Traditionally, home cooks would gather their herbs from the countryside – especially rosemary, thyme, oregano, savoury and even lavender – and create their own blends. Today, you can buy jars of dried, mixed herbs de Provence around the world.

PUMPKIN PIE SPICE

The origins of this spice blend predate the founding of the United States, to the seventeeth century, when Dutch spice traders visited Indonesia and made a blend of cinnamon, ginger, nutmeg and allspice. By 1796, a similar blend of mace, nutmeg and ginger turned up in a recipe for 'pumpkin' pie in the U.S. In 1934, McCormick, the world's largest spice seller, started selling the mix as 'pumpkin pie spice'.

RUSSIA

The world's largest country spans eleven time zones and is home to more than 240 million people! The landscape is diverse with mountains, treeless plains called steppes, coastline, marshes, Arctic tundra and forests. Today, Moscow has one of the highest concentrations of billionaires in the world and is a centre of great chefs and culinary innovation. However Russians still savour traditional hearty fare of black bread, soured yoghurt, cabbage and potatoes, handmade dumplings and big communal soups – seasoned with the bright, sharp flavours of garlic, dill, peppercorns, salty brine and lots of horseradish.

PICKLES

Russians enjoy lots of pickled vegetables year-round, including tart and tangy pickled garlic, cucumbers and peppers. Many families buy abundant fresh produce in summer to pickle and preserve to enjoy all winter.

CABBAGE

Cabbage soup is an iconic national dish. And no Russian can go long without eating kvashenaya kapusta – fermented cabbage similar to sauerkraut. Russians use it in salads, stuffings, sides and stews – in fact, soup made with fresh, rather than fermented, cabbage is called 'lazy soup'.

POTATOES

Peeled, boiled potatoes are often topped with butter, dill and soured cream. Russians also enjoy potatoes mashed, in salads, stuffed into dumplings, fried with bacon and mushrooms, or fermented to make vodka.

BREAD

The average Russian eats nearly 1 kilogram of bread each day. Tables here may offer white bread, dark rye bread, Russia's famous black bread – or all three! Bread is the foundation of the Russian diet and is so important that the Russian term for hospitality, *khlebosol'stvo*, means 'bread and salt'.

FISH

In Russia, fish is often smoked or salt cured. Little salted Baltic herring are enjoyed with onions or in a cold salad. A mixed platter of smoked fish here may include eel, mackerel, sturgeon, whitefish, shad and salmon. Large, bright-orange Siberian salmon caviar and black caviar from sturgeon fish are famous worldwide.

WILD MUSHROOMS

Nearly a thousand years ago, in the 1100s and 1200s, starving people survived on foraged wild foods, including mushrooms. Many wonderful mushrooms still grow in Russian woods and hunting for them is a national obsession.

KASHA

Boiled buckwheat groats called *kasha* are a Russian superfood that has nourished people here for more than 1,000 years. Kasha can be sweet or savoury, boiled with milk or water and served as breakfast or a side dish. Almost anything might be mixed in – including fruit, cheese, eggs, pork, liver, onions or mushrooms.

MEAT MANIA

Russians are the world's leading eaters of meat and some say the manual meat grinder is the most important tool in a Russian kitchen! Beloved dishes include meat pies, pelmeni dumplings and meat rolled in cabbage.

RUSSIAN SALAD

Russian salad is neither green nor raw! Potatoes, carrots, beetroot and turnips are boiled, chilled and dressed in soured cream or mayonnaise.

PIES

Handmade pies are the glory of the Russian kitchen. A savoury slice is served alongside almost every soup, whether it's a little handpie called pieroski, an open-faced pie filled with farmers' cheese or a grand pie stuffed with fish.

BLINI

TINY BUCKWHEAT PANCAKES

PREPARATION TIME
20 mins

COOKING TIME
15 mins

LEVEL OF DIFFICULTY
● ●

MAKES
20 to 25

These tiny pancakes are beloved throughout Russia and Eastern Europe, where they're traditionally made with buckwheat flour that cooks into a soft, spongy treat. An iconic appetizer, you can enjoy blini with sweet or savoury toppings – sometimes butter, jam or honey but often with rich soured cream and salty caviar. Buckwheat is actually a plant from the rhubarb family, and its tiny, triangular fruit seeds are used to make rich, hearty, gluten-free flour. While some blini recipes call for yeasted batter that needs time to rise, this version comes together quickly with just a bit of baking powder.

Old Slavic folklore celebrates the Sun's return in late winter, symbolized by the round blini. The Russian Orthodox Church incorporated the tradition of eating blini into 'Butter Week', or *maslenitsa*. Russians make as many buttery blini as they can eat all week long, as part of a Russian Carnival celebration before fasting for Lent.

You can also enjoy blinis with sweet toppings such as butter, honey or jam.

INGREDIENTS

70 g plain flour
70 g buckwheat flour
½ teaspoon salt
½ teaspoon baking powder
1 large egg, separated
250 ml milk
1 tablespoon melted, unsalted
    butter, plus more melted
    butter for cooking
soured cream and smoked
    salmon and/or caviar, for
    serving

1. In a bowl, whisk together the plain flour with the buckwheat flour, salt and baking powder. Push the flour mixture to the sides of the bowl to form a well in the middle. Add the egg yolk, milk and 1 tablespoon of melted butter to the well and whisk until the wet ingredients are well mixed, and then stir it together with the flour mixture.

2. In another bowl, using a handheld mixer, beat the egg white until it becomes cloud-like. It's ready when you lift a beater out of the egg white and its peaks turn over like a Santa hat (soft peaks).

3. Using a spatula, gently stir the egg white into the batter until no streaks remain.

4. Brush a large non-stick frying pan with melted butter and set over a medium heat. Add 1 tablespoon of batter to the frying pan for each little pancake and cook until you see bubbles form at the edge and the bottom turns golden: about 2 minutes. Flip and cook the blini until golden on the other slide: about 1 minute longer. Transfer to a plate.

5. Cook the remaining blini, brushing the frying pan with more butter as needed.

6. Serve with a small dollop of soured cream and a small piece of smoked salmon or a ½ teaspoon of caviar.

SPAIN

With fertile plains, snow-capped mountains, the Mediterranean Sea and the Atlantic Ocean, Spain is a food-lover's delight, offering deliciously fresh seafood, abundant olives, almonds and pimenton (paprika), a spice made from smoked peppers. People here have long feasted on everything from octopus to wild boar, with food influences from around the world. North African Muslims, known as Moors, introduced chickpeas, rice, citrus, saffron and couscous, while Spanish conquistadors returned from the Americas with potatoes, beans, tomatoes, peppers and chocolate.

GAZPACHO

This red, refreshingly chilled soup originated in southern Spain's sunny Andalusia and is almost like a salad you can slurp with a spoon. Best at the peak of the summer tomato season, gazpacho is a purée of raw tomatoes, cucumbers, onion, sweet peppers, garlic, olive oil, salt and vinegar.

PATATAS BRAVAS

Today, Spanish cuisine is unimaginable without potatoes, tomatoes and peppers – all brought to Spain from Mesoamerica – which star together in this beloved recipe of fried potatoes slathered in a sauce of olive oil or mayonnaise with pimenton.

TAPAS

These little bites with big flavours, widely served at bars, might include steamed mussels, tiny fried fish, chorizo slices, olives, shaved jamón, triangles of manchego cheese or pan con tomate, tasty grilled bread rubbed with tomato, garlic, salt and olive oil.

JAMÓN IBERICO

Spaniards have been curing ham for generations. First, black Iberian pigs eat a rich diet of acorns, which gives their meat a wonderfully nutty flavour. After butchering, the legs are salted and hung up, sometimes for years. This cures, or preserves, the ham, until it is shaved into thin slices. One leg can cost over 3,000 pounds!

PAELLA

This iconic Spanish dish includes rice, saffron, vegetables and seafood or meat, all cooked in a wide paella pan. Every family has their own recipe but Valencians, who likely invented the dish, say a real paella must include rabbit, chicken and white broad beans.

CHURROS CON CHOCOLATE

This may sound like a dessert but in Spain, it is breakfast. A sweet dough is squeezed through a star-shaped nozzle called a *churrera*. The ridged cylinders that emerge – some over a foot long – are deep-fried until crisp. Eat while hot, dipped into a cup of thick hot chocolate.

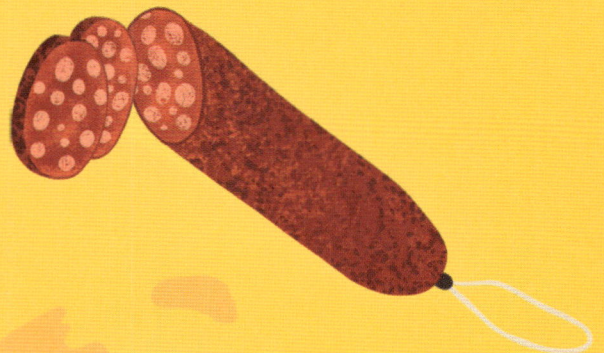

WORLD-FAMOUS

Ferran Adrià never went to culinary school but his restaurant, El Bulli (the bulldog), was named the best in the world. Chef Adrià used chemistry to invent new ways of cooking, making edible paper, food in tubes, and airy foams and sprays.

CHORIZO

Spanish chorizo is ready to eat, unlike Mexican chorizo, which needs to be cooked. Butchers stuff minced pork, garlic and lots of paprika into a sausage casing, then cure it. Different regions add sweeter or spicier paprika, and some smoke the sausage. Slices of spicy chorizo are enjoyed as a snack or lend their deep flavour to stews and paella.

MANCHEGO CHEESE

Spaniards on the central plains have long herded sheep and made their milk into fine cheeses, of which manchego is the most famous. Wheels of the rich, slightly salty cheese have a zigzag pattern from the special basket moulds they're aged in, which are traditionally made of braided grass.

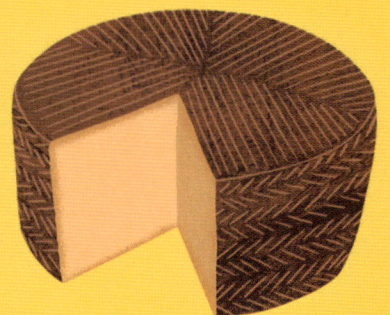

TORTILLA DE PATATAS

POTATO FRITTATA

PREPARATION TIME	COOKING TIME	LEVEL OF DIFFICULTY	MAKES
20 mins	40 mins	●●●	1 25-cm tortilla

Unlike the Mexican flatbread of the same name, a Spanish tortilla is a thick, savoury potato and egg omelet, deliciously rich thanks to lots of Spanish olive oil. One of the most popular dishes in Spain, tortillas are tucked into lunchboxes and eaten as a snack or meal, anytime, day or night! They're quite easy to make – sometimes made with yesterday's potatoes or even left-over chips – though flipping the tortilla in the pan without spilling takes a bit of practice.

INGREDIENTS

120 ml plus 1 tablespoon olive oil
680 g potatoes, peeled and thinly
    sliced
1 small onion, finely chopped
5 eggs
salt and pepper

1. In a 25-centimetre non-stick frying pan, heat 120 ml of the oil over a medium heat, until shimmering. Add the potatoes, onions and a generous pinch of salt and cook, stirring occasionally. They'll seem crowded but will shrink as they cook.

2. Meanwhile, beat the eggs well in a bowl, and season with 1 teaspoon salt and a few grinds of pepper.

3. When the potatoes are tender, after about 25 minutes, reduce the heat to medium-low and add the eggs to the pan, moving the potatoes around to allow them to settle.

4. After the edge of the tortilla looks firm, cook for 5 more minutes, then peek under the edge. When the bottom of the tortilla is set and browned and the top is somewhat set but still soft and maybe a little runny, carefully flip the tortilla. To do so: place a plate over the top then quickly flip the frying pan and plate over so the tortilla is cooked side up on the plate. Return the pan to the heat. Add 1 tablespoon olive oil and swirl it around. Slide the tortilla back into the frying pan, cooked side up, to finish cooking the bottom, until done: about 5 more minutes.

5. Transfer the tortilla onto a plate or chopping board and leave to cool slightly. Slice into wedges and serve.

Bored of your lunchtime sandwich?
Pack this in your lunchbox instead!

You can skip the flip and instead finish cooking the tortilla in a 190°C oven, until the eggs are just done. This will create a bit of a different texture and shape but it's still delicious!

UKRAINE

Ukraine's capital city, Kyiv, has been a centre of Slavic culture since the Middle Ages. Ukraine's cuisine has some dishes and ingredients in common with many of its bordering countries but Ukrainian recipes retain their own distinctive national identity. With its temperate climate and vast fertile steppe lands, Ukraine is one of the largest producers of grains in the world and is often referred to as the 'breadbasket of Europe'. Ukraine's four meals a day are often served family-style, with platters arranged on tables decorated with hand-embroidered cloths.

PREPARATION

Typical Ukrainian dishes involve many ingredients and complex steps, and traditional methods for preserving foods in winter are still employed today. These include storing vegetables like beetroot and potatoes in wooden chests buried in the ground and drying, brining or smoking meat and fish so they are still tasty months later!

ESSENTIALS

Ukrainian food is not spicy but it is very flavourful. Tart, sour and sweet-and-sour flavours shine in popular drinks such as kvass (a fermented cereal-based drink), or in the pickles served with many meals; juice from pickles and sauerkraut are added to soups for flavour. Spices like dill and caraway are beloved in Ukrainian kitchens, as are onion and garlic.

BREAD

There are estimated to be almost 780 varieties of breads baked here! Breads are often braided or formed into gorgeous, elaborate shapes for special occasions. Grains of rye are even scattered across coffins.

PORK

Pork is stuffed into dumplings (varenyky), made into sausages like kyshka and sardelky and even seasoned into salt-cured pork. Bacon ends and rendered salt pork add a smoky kiss to many favourite dishes and cured pork fat (salo) is essential to many Ukrainian recipes – a favourite dessert is doughnuts fried in salo.

FRUITS AND VEGETABLES

Both farmed and foraged fruits appear as preserves, relishes or jams, stewed with sugar into compotes, or stuffed into dumplings. Vegetables are often stuffed, tucked into dumplings, or pickled and brined into condiments like beetroot relish and sauerkraut.

FISH

Herring, perch, pike, sturgeon and carp are among the favourite finned foods, which may be poached, jellied, fried, marinated, pickled or baked. Fish meatballs (kotlety) are popular, as is battered-and-fried fish served with mushrooms and cheese. Pickled herring is a favourite appetizer for Jewish Ukrainians.

SWEETS

Ukraine is home to many beekeepers and beehives and honey is commonly used in baked goods, drinks and dishes made with grains. Favourite desserts are kutia (poppy seeds, wheat, nuts and honey), served at Christmas, syrniki (fried cheese fritters served with smetana, honey or jam) and beautiful jellied fruits called zhele.

DRINKS

Ukrainians love kompot (a sweet beverage made from dried or fresh fruits boiled in water) and baked milk (pryazhene moloko), which has a caramel flavour and is made by simmering milk for at least eight hours. For an extra treat, try ryazhanka, a baked, fermented milk drink!

SUNFLOWERS

Ukrainian farmers grow fields of sunflowers. The seeds are popular as a snack and feature in many recipes. Sunflower oil is a common cooking oil in every kitchen cabinet.

BORSHCH

BEETROOT SOUP

PREPARATION TIME	COOKING TIME	LEVEL OF DIFFICULTY	SERVES
30 mins	35 mins	●●	6 to 8

This vibrant ruby-red soup is a staple from Latvia and Poland to Russia but this root vegetable soup originated in Ukraine and it remains the country's national dish. Borshch is best known for its beetroot – the most beloved vegetable in Ukraine. This hardy, hearty root vegetable gives the soup its earthy flavour and gorgeous garnet hue. Some people like meat in their borshch, such as fresh pork shoulder, beef shin, ham hock, bacon or sausage but this version is deliciously vegetarian.

INGREDIENTS

1.4 kg beetroot
2 onions
2 carrots or parsnips
1 small red cabbage, or half
   a large red cabbage
2 tablespoons oil
1.2 litres of water or broth
1 tablespoon of lemon juice
salt, to taste
soured cream, fresh dill and
   caraway seeds, to garnish

1. Peel the beetroot. Using a knife, a large box grater or the shredding attachment of a food processor, thinly slice or shred the vegetables. Take care not to grate your fingers too!

2. Heat the oil over a medium-high heat in a large pot, then add all the vegetables and cook, stirring occasionally for 5 minutes. Add the water or broth, bring to a boil, and reduce to a simmer. Cook for about 25 minutes, until the vegetables are tender. If they are still crunchy, simmer a few minutes longer and try again.

3. When the vegetables are soft, season the soup with the lemon juice and salt to taste.

4. To serve, ladle hot into bowls and garnish with soured cream, a pinch of fresh dill, and a sprinkle of caraway seeds.

There are over 30 main types of borshch in Ukraine alone, including variations made from turnips and celeriac.

Some cooks add a little sugar at the end, for more sweet–sour contrast.

Serve warm in winter with some crusty bread or serve refreshingly cold on a hot summer's day.

DAIRY

AROUND THE WORLD

Humans have been drinking milk for thousands of years, from ruminants like cows, goats, camels, horses, water buffalo, yak, sheep and reindeer. But milk goes bad quickly, so people developed cultured creamy foods that could last. Cheese has been called milk's leap towards immortality. Today, refrigeration keeps milk fresh for weeks or more but humanity has come to love cheese. It's here to stay.

LABNEH

A bit like a cross between yoghurt and cream cheese, labneh is made by adding salt to full-fat yoghurt, then straining the liquid out of the yoghurt with a muslin cloth and letting the remainder sit out to dry for half a day or so. The longer the labneh sits, the thicker it becomes. People like to eat it as a spread, dip or simply on its own in yummy spoonfuls.

BUTTERMILK

This looks like milk except it's thicker, tangier and sometimes has a few yummy lumps. That's because it has been fermented, typically by adding bacteria that produce lactic acid. In North America, buttermilk is a key ingredient for making fluffy pancakes or as the base of a creamy salad dressing. However, in places like India, Pakistan, Nepal and the Arabian Peninsula, buttermilk is enjoyed as a deliciously refreshing beverage on its own or as a base for smoothies.

YAK-BUTTER TEA

In Tibet and the Himalayan regions of India, Nepal, Bhutan and Pakistan, there's no better way to warm up and fuel up than with a cup of steaming yak-butter tea. This savoury beverage is usually made with black tea that is brewed with salt, with a dollop of yak butter thrown in.

BULGARIAN-STYLE YOGHURT

People in Bulgaria like to claim they are the original inventors of yoghurt. Whether that's true is up for debate but we do know that yoghurt-making in this part of the world dates back thousands of years, to when the Thracians – the region's ancient inhabitants – carried sheep's milk in animal skin bags around their waists. The heat from their bodies and the bacteria in the bags would slowly ferment the milk into yoghurt.

CRÈME FRAÎCHE

This thick, soured cream is made with a bacterial culture. Slightly different versions of the same dairy product exist in most countries in northern Europe and in Central America. In Romania, for example, it's called smântâna, and in Mexico, it's called crema fresca.

AARUUL

These dried curds are pungently sour, extremely hard blocks of dried cheese and a favourite snack for nomadic people in Mongolia. Aaruul is made by first boiling milk from cows, yaks, horses or camels to thicken it up, then putting it into a cloth bag that's left out in the sun to solidify.

FONDUE

The earliest known fondue recipe, which was published in 1699 in Zürich, Switzerland, called for cut-up cheese to be melted with wine and served with dipping bread. Fondue is now considered one of Switzerland's national dishes, a perfect meal for warming up after a cold day on the ski slopes.

CONDENSED MILK

Condensed milk refers to cow milk from which 60% of the water has been removed. Usually, sugar is added too. The thickened final product is typically sold tinned and serves as a popular dessert topping or ingredient around the world, including for snowballs in the Southern U.S., for a type of flan in Brazil and – when boiled to become even thicker – as cake icing in Russia (essentially, this is dulce de leche). In Vietnam and Cambodia, condensed milk is also a favourite sweetener for strong cups of coffee.

AMERICAN CHEESE

Some people say that American cheese – the thin, rubbery, bright-orange squares individually wrapped in plastic – is not actually cheese. Indeed, depending on the other ingredients, legally, these products must be referred to as 'pasteurized process American cheese food' or 'pasteurized prepared cheese product' rather than simply 'cheese'.

UNITED KINGDOM

In England, Scotland, Wales and Northern Ireland – which together make up the United Kingdom – traditional foods include roast pheasant, black pudding, spiced cakes and glacé fruits. For centuries the United Kingdom colonized much of the globe and while the English exported many customs, the cuisines of many former colonies also came to influence British flavours. Today, the United Kingdom has a population of over 60 million, including about 5 million people of Asian, Caribbean, African and other non-British origin, who have contributed to the diverse cuisine now available. Over the centuries, the UK's diet of wheat, meat, potatoes, vegetables and dairy has greatly expanded to include tastes from around the world.

PUBS

Short for public house, pubs are centres of social life, hosting everything from quizzes to live music. Going to the local pub for a roast dinner of meat, potatoes, Yorkshire pudding and vegetables like cabbage and cauliflower is a traditional and much-loved Sunday activity.

TEA

For many in the United Kingdom, drinking tea is an essential daily tradition going back to the 1600s when England's East India Company sailed the world and brought boatloads of tea back to England. Today, the Scots, Irish, Welsh and English together brew more than half the world's tea!

CHEESES

Farmers here have tended herds of cows and sheep for centuries and milk from these dairies is made into many fine English cheeses. Cheddar, the most famous hard cheese in the world, is named after a village in Somerset. The strongly flavoured stilton blue cheese also enjoys international fame – it's the only British cheese to have legal protection!

FULL ENGLISH BREAKFAST

In England, this traditional way to start the day includes bacon, eggs, sausages, black pudding, mushroom, tomatoes, baked beans and toast, plus tea, of course! A full Irish breakfast may also include white pudding; a full Scottish breakfast often includes haggis; and in Wales you may get laverbread as part of your full Welsh breakfast.

BOUNTIFUL BAKING

British bakers are famous for their breads, pies, cakes, tea cakes, scones and biscuits. Crumpets are a flat griddled bread with wonderful bubbles, served buttered for breakfast. Desserts are called puddings and traditional favourites include apple crumble, Eton mess and trifle (a layered, wine-soaked sponge cake with fruit preserves, custard and cream).

FISH AND CHIPS

Battered-and-fried cod has been a favourite street food here since the 1800s. Brits still love fish and chips – chips being thick-cut fried potatoes, sold hot, salted and drenched with malt vinegar before eating.

CLOTTED CREAM

Traditionally from southwest England, thick, rich spreads called Cornish cream and Devonshire cream are slathered on scones with jam at afternoon tea. But which to put on first? The Cornish say jam goes first but in Devon they argue cream should go on first.

MORE THAN TWO VEG

Readers of Beatrix Potter know that English gardens – like Mr McGregor's, which Peter Rabbit raided – grow gorgeous vegetables! Favourites include cabbages, brussels sprouts, beans, peas, asparagus, cucumbers, radishes and watercress, plus carrots, turnips and parsnips in winter.

TASTES OF EMPIRE

In towns and cities across the UK, you can eat your way around the world. Indian tikka masala has been called England's favourite dish, while flavours of many past colonies can be found here in Jamaican jerk chicken, Malaysian laksa, Nigerian jollof rice, South African bobotie, Ghanaian fufu and banku, Barbadian fish cakes and Sri Lankan roti.

SCONES

SWEET LITTLE CAKES WITH SULTANAS

PREPARATION TIME
2 hrs

COOKING TIME
15 mins

LEVEL OF DIFFICULTY
● ●

MAKES
12 to 14 scones

Light, flaky baked scones are a classic teatime snack in the UK. They're just barely sweet – until you slather them with jam and clotted cream! For that wonderfully flaky texture, use cold butter and chill your dough in the fridge after you roll it out – and again before baking. While some use a pastry cutter or tabletop mixer, you could also crumble the butter into the flour mixture using your fingers. For a golden finish, paint your scones with a little egg mixture before popping them in the oven.

Sweet scones are often studded with dried fruit, like currants, sultanas or cherries. Bakers making savoury scones may add cheese or herbs. In Scotland and Northern Ireland, some people add mashed potatoes for potato scones.

INGREDIENTS

95 g sultanas (optional)
500 g plain flour, plus more for
    dusting
2 tablespoons plus 1 teaspoon
    baking powder
100 g sugar
115 g cold, unsalted butter, cut
    into small pieces
2 eggs, lightly beaten for the
    scones, plus 1 egg for the egg
    wash
175 ml buttermilk
butter, jam and clotted cream,
    for serving

1. If you're using the sultanas, place them in a small bowl, cover with hot water, and leave to stand until plump: about 30 minutes.

2. In a large bowl, whisk together the flour, baking powder and sugar. Add the butter pieces and, using your fingers, mix the butter into the dry mixture until it is crumbly and the pieces are the size of small peas. (You can also do this in a food processor.)

3. In a medium bowl, whisk the eggs and the buttermilk together. Add the liquid and the sultanas to the crumb mixture and stir the dry mixture until only just mixed in. Gently knead a few times until the dough just holds together.

4. Arrange a piece of clingfilm on the work surface. Turn out the dough onto the clingfilm, then dust the top of the dough with flour.

5. Gently press or roll out the dough until it's 2.5 centimetres thick. Wrap the dough in the clingfilm and refrigerate for 30 minutes to 1 hour.

6. Using a 5-centimetre round biscuit cutter, stamp out as many rounds as you can and transfer them to plates. Gently press together the dough scraps and stamp out more rounds, putting them onto plates. Cover these plates and refrigerate again for 20 minutes.

7. Meanwhile, preheat the oven to 200°C and line two baking trays with greaseproof paper.

8. Place the rounds on the prepared baking trays, leaving at least 2.5 centimetres between each round. In a small bowl, beat the remaining egg with 1 tablespoon of water and brush this mixture over the rounds.

9. Bake until lightly golden: 12 to 15 minutes. Leave to cool on the baking trays. Serve with butter or jam and clotted cream.

There is a hot debate about how to pronounce scone. Some say it rhymes with 'bone', while others insist it rhymes with 'bon' or 'con'.

NORTH AMERICA

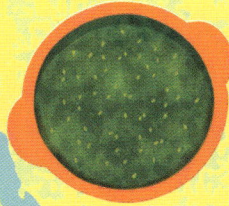

This vast continent spans from the jungle tropics to the icy Arctic, and from the Atlantic to the Pacific, encompassing mountains, deserts, forests and more. It includes the nations of Central America such as Guatemala and Panama, Caribbean islands such as Cuba and Costa Rica, and three of the globe's most populous countries – Canada, Mexico and the United States.

The Rocky Mountains – home to game like wild elk, bighorn sheep and river trout – extend north from New Mexico to British Columbia. Vast grasslands also span the continent once grazed by bison and now by millions of cattle. These Great Plains also grow great grains, yielding harvests baked into flour tortillas, loaves of bread, pie crusts and more. Down south, Mexico's highlands yield abundant corn, beans and squash, plus harvests of avocados, tomatoes and chilli peppers, all at the heart of the culture's traditional cuisine.

While Native peoples still inhabit many parts of these ancient lands, North American cultures and cuisines have been greatly reshaped by immigrants, especially from Europe. Today, nearly everyone here speaks English, French or Spanish, the languages of the people who colonized this continent centuries ago.

CANADA

Running across the top of the North American continent, Canada is one of the largest countries in the world by size – but it still has fewer people than tiny Japan! This vast land is known for its natural resources, from the snow-speckled mountain forests in the north and the central plains filled with wheat and cows to the sparkling cold waters of the east and west coasts. Toronto – Canada's biggest city – was named the most diverse city in the world by the United Nations. You can enjoy the cuisines of Korea, Vietnam, Greece, the Caribbean and more, all without leaving town.

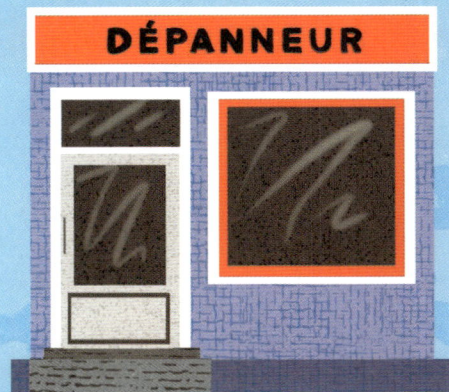

THE DEP

In Canada, you can call a small grocery store a dep, short for the French-Canadian word dépanneur. The word came from the eastern Canadian province of Quebec, once a French colony. Dépanneur originally meant 'someone who fixes things'.

MAPLE SYRUP

For thousands of years, the First Nations people here have collected the late-winter sap of sugar maple trees and boiled it down into sweet, thick (and nutritious!) syrup. Canadians are so proud of their world-famous maple trees, they put its leaf on their flag.

POUTINE

After a long winter's day, nothing will warm you up – and fill you up – like poutine: chips smothered with gravy and crowned with melted cheese curds. First invented in the province of Quebec, poutine is now one of Canada's most famous foods. Restaurants that specialize in making it are called poutineries!

WILD FOODS

Half of Canada is forest, so it is no surprise wild and foraged foods are still a big part of Canadian cooking. You can hunt for moose and caribou, then make a pie with wild Saskatoon berries, which taste like blueberries mixed with almonds. If you prefer seafood, you can roast Chinook salmon from Canada's Pacific coast.

NANAIMO BARS

Nanaimo bars, named after a city in western Canada, is an extra-sweet biscuit bar with three delicious layers: a coconut and Graham cracker base, a custard-icing blend in the middle, and a thick and creamy chocolate top.

COWTOWN

The western city of Calgary is called Cowtown, thanks to the cows still raised in the nearby open plains. It's also home to the annual Calgary Stampede, a giant rodeo famous for foods like pancake breakfasts, mini-doughnuts and beefsteaks, of course!

VICTORIA DAY

This holiday began in honour of a British queen named Victoria, at a time when most of Canada was still a British territory. (They didn't officially become independent until 1982!) Today, this holiday is mainly treated as the unofficial beginning of summer, celebrated with picnics, barbecues, fireworks and the annual planting of backyard gardens.

CORNBREAD AND GRAVY

Across Canada, many First Nations people make a boiled bread of ground white corn. In Kahnawake Mohawk Territory just south of the city of Montreal, everyone eats it with steak and brown gravy on Sundays!

KETCHUP CHIPS

From coast to coast, Canadians love ketchup-flavoured potato crisps, a kind rarely found in other countries. They're sweet and sour and turn your fingers bright red.

BREAKFAST

AROUND THE WORLD

Every hour, the sun rises somewhere and people break their overnight fast, with breakfast! Some start with spicy fish stew, soybean soup or salted cod cakes. Eggs are popular: with refried beans and pico de gallo in Mexican huevos rancheros, with bacon and black pudding in a full English breakfast, or with peppers and tomatoes in North African shakshuka. Or have a sugar-showered fritter, like Spanish churros, Filipino cascarons or Ugandan mandazi doughnuts.

MEZE

In the eastern Mediterranean and Middle East, breakfast is often a meze mix of lots of little plates. You might see labneh, fresh tomatoes, cucumbers, feta, olives, ful and hummus, all served with fresh-baked pita. Another beloved breakfast in the Middle East is shakshuka: eggs poached in a warming tomato-pepper stew.

INDIAN BREADS AND SNACKS

In southern Indian regions, people often start their day with appam, a bowl-shaped pancake made with rice flour and coconut milk. You'll also see idli, puffy savoury cakes, and dosa, thin crepes, both made with a fermented rice and lentil batter. In northern India, people wake up to paratha, buttery, flaky wheat-based flatbreads, or fried savoury pastries, like samosas, poori and kachori.

RICE PORRIDGE

Throughout Asian cuisines, many people cook white rice for hours until the grains become a silky porridge, often called congee, although the name varies by country. At breakfast, this mild porridge is often topped with lots of delicious strong flavours like salted fish, braised meats, salted duck eggs, seaweed and spicy vegetables.

MANGÚ

In the Dominican Republic, just about everyone loves to start their day with a plate of boiled green plantains called mangú. They're mashed with oil or butter topped with fried eggs, pretty, pink pickled onions, slices of fried salami and a slice of salty queso frito (fried cheese).

MUESLI

A Swiss physician in the late 1800s is credited with creating muesli. His original recipe called for raw grated apple, nuts and oats mixed with water, lemon juice, condensed milk and honey. The word muesli comes from the Swiss-German word for 'mush', and when combined with milk or yoghurt, after a few minutes, that's a good description!

NIHARI

For centuries, people in Pakistan have loved to wake up to nihari – a shank of beef, mutton or goat, cooked overnight with ginger, fried onions, green chillies and aromatic spices, served with fresh coriander. Named after an Arabic word that means 'morning', today it's so popular in Pakistan that people enjoy it all day long.

MISO SOUP

A traditional Japanese breakfast balances many types of flavours, textures and nutrients, including white rice, miso soup, pickled vegetables, cooked fish and natto – fermented soybeans that have a strong flavour and sticky texture.

PASTELILLOS DE GUAYABA

GUAVA CHEESE PASTRIES

PREPARATION TIME
30 mins

COOKING TIME
25 mins

LEVEL OF DIFFICULTY
●

MAKES
8 pastelillos

The Caribbean is home to many wonderful tropical fruits, like pineapple, mango, papaya, passion fruit and guava, which are enjoyed in everything from fresh fruit salads to shaved-ice drinks drizzled with sweet syrup. For this recipe, you don't need fresh guava – just pop open a pack of thick, sweet guava paste and stack slices with salty cheese to bake into pastelillos (little pastries). These are delicious for breakfast or as a sweet snack any time of day.

INGREDIENTS

500 g ready-rolled puff pastry, thawed but still cold

200 g guava paste (half a 400-g pack), cut into 8 even slices

170 g queso fresco en hoja, farmer cheese or well-chilled cream cheese, cut into 8 even slices

1 egg, lightly beaten with a pinch of salt

2 to 3 tablespoons turbinado sugar or icing sugar

1. Preheat the oven to 200°C. Line a large baking tray with greaseproof paper.

2. Spread out one layer of puff pastry on the baking tray. Arrange the guava-paste slices on the pastry so there are two across and four down, at least 2.5 centimetres apart. Top each piece of guava paste with a slice of cheese.

3. Arrange the second layer of puff pastry on top. Using a knife, slice the puff pastry between the filling into 8 pastries.

4. Use a fork to crimp the edges and seal in the filling, then arrange each piece evenly on the baking tray, leaving spaces between. Lightly brush the tops and edges with the beaten egg and sprinkle with turbinado sugar, if using. Using a knife, make two slits on the top of each pastry. Refrigerate for 15 minutes before baking.

5. Bake for 20 to 25 minutes or until pastelillos are golden brown. Leave to cool for at least 10 to 15 minutes, then enjoy warm or at room temperature.

Instead of sprinkling crunchy demerara sugar before baking, you could dust with icing sugar after they cool.

Don't worry about making the pastries look perfect — handmade individuality is part of their charm. It's also OK if the filling oozes out of the edges. It caramelizes and tastes delicious.

MEXICO

Mexico's diverse geography varies from warm coasts to inland mountains, from deserts to jungles, from rivers to fertile plains. It is also known for whale-watching and as the destination of one of the world's largest butterfly populations – Monarch butterflies spend the winter in the Michoacán forests. Visitors from around the world also flock here, not just to holiday on the beautiful beaches but to feast on Mexico's world-famous cuisine! Morning and night, markets and public squares fill with taco carts, tamale stands, trays of churros and spectacular hot chillies, fresh fish and tropical fruits.

MOLE

There are over forty varieties within this iconic family of special sauces, which are often served over turkey or beans. To be called a mole, a sauce must contain nuts, chillies and spices. Two of the most beloved are Puebla's mole poblano, complex with chocolate and chillies and Oaxaca's velvety mole negro, made from chillies cooked until they're as black as coals.

SPANISH FLAVOURS

In 1519, Spaniards landed on Mexico's eastern shores. In the following years, Spaniards brought cows, pigs, chickens, sheep, goats, dairy, wheat, citrus and fresh coriander. Today, Mexican cuisine combines these foods with traditional foods, including corn, chilli peppers, avocado, chocolate, turkey, duck, insects and beans.

CACAO AND CHOCOLATE

Ancient Mesoamericans valued cacao so much that cacao beans were currency. Today, most drinking chocolate is hot and sweet – but back then, people drank it cold and spicy – spiked with powdered chilli! The Spanish adapted the mixture by swapping the cold water for milk and the chilli pepper for cinnamon.

SPICY SWEETS

Stroll down the sweets aisle in a Mexican supermarket and you'll find boiled sweets with chilli, chewing gum with chilli, soft mango and tamarind chews with chilli – sometimes with a hint of lime. People say that once you get used to this sweet-spicy combo, the more you eat, the more heat you'll crave!

FISH TACOS

Created in Baja, these tacos feature fresh fish filets cooked in a flour and egg batter. Some say Japanese immigrants adapted the tempura tradition to local catches. Whatever the original source, today fish tacos are topped with shredded lettuce, radish, fresh coriander, onion, tomato, a squeeze of lime and spicy salsa.

WHEAT AND MEAT UP NORTH

Iconic corn tortillas are the daily bread in central and southern Mexico but in the northern states farmers grow beautiful fields of wheat – and make their tortillas of wheat flour instead. This region is also famous for the country's best grilled meats – sometimes tucked into those flour tortillas.

VITAMIN T

A frequent expression among Mexicans, Vitamin T is the nickname for treats that begin with the letter T. Chief among them is tacos but vitamin T can also refer just to tortillas, tlacoyos (oblong corn patties filled with cheese or beans), tlayudas (large flat tortillas, typical of Oaxaca), tamales, totopos (tortilla chips) and tostadas (fried tortillas with toppings).

ALEGRÍAS

Alegrías (Joys) are one of the most common sweet snacks sold by street vendors in Mexico. Made of popped amaranth seeds mixed with dark sugar syrup, the bars are sold at fairs, outside cinemas and museums and beloved for their filling protein and light, sweet flavour!

SWEET TAMALES

You may have heard of bean, chicken and beef tamales but did you know there are sweet tamales too? Often eaten in the late afternoon or evening, sweet tamales can be recognized by their pink colour, which is added to distinguish them from the pale-yellow savoury kind.

QUESADILLAS

In most of Mexico, a quesadilla is a folded tortilla filled with queso (cheese). But in Mexico City, it is a folded, stuffed tortilla cooked in a griddle. That means that when you order a quesadilla in Mexico City, you have to specify whether you want it filled with beans, mushrooms or... cheese!

SALSA VERDE CRUDA

GREEN TOMATILLO SAUCE

PREPARATION TIME
20 mins

COOKING TIME
0 mins

LEVEL OF DIFFICULTY
●

MAKES
About 350 ml

The word salsa simply means 'sauce', and salsa verde means 'green sauce'. In Mexico, it's often made with tomatillos, which are a cousin of tomatoes and peppers. Tomatillos are not spicy; instead, they can taste wonderfully tart, especially when they're firm and bright green. They get a little sweeter and softer as they ripen, when their skins can take on a pretty purple tinge. Tomatillos come in little papery jackets. When you're ready to cook, slip those off and give the fruits a quick rinse – they can sometimes be slightly sticky under the husks.

In some versions of salsa verde, people cook the tomatillos, onion, chilli and garlic before blending it into a salsa. This is the raw (cruda) version. Enjoy it over just about anything, from tacos and quesadillas to huevos rancheros. Or just eat it straight up with corn tortilla chips!

INGREDIENTS

340 g tomatillos (about 6 small to medium-sized), husks removed
1 jalapeño chilli
¼ chopped medium white onion
1 small garlic clove, peeled
4 g fresh coriander leaves
salt

1. Wash and roughly chop the tomatillos and transfer to a food processor or blender.

2. Cut off the stem of the jalapeño and cut it in half lengthways. To make a salsa that's not spicy, you can remove the seeds from the chilli. (Wear gloves so the seeds don't burn your skin.) Slice the chilli halves crossways with or without the seeds and transfer to the processor.

3. Add the onion, garlic and fresh coriander to the processor and purée until you have a chunky salsa. Taste and season with salt.

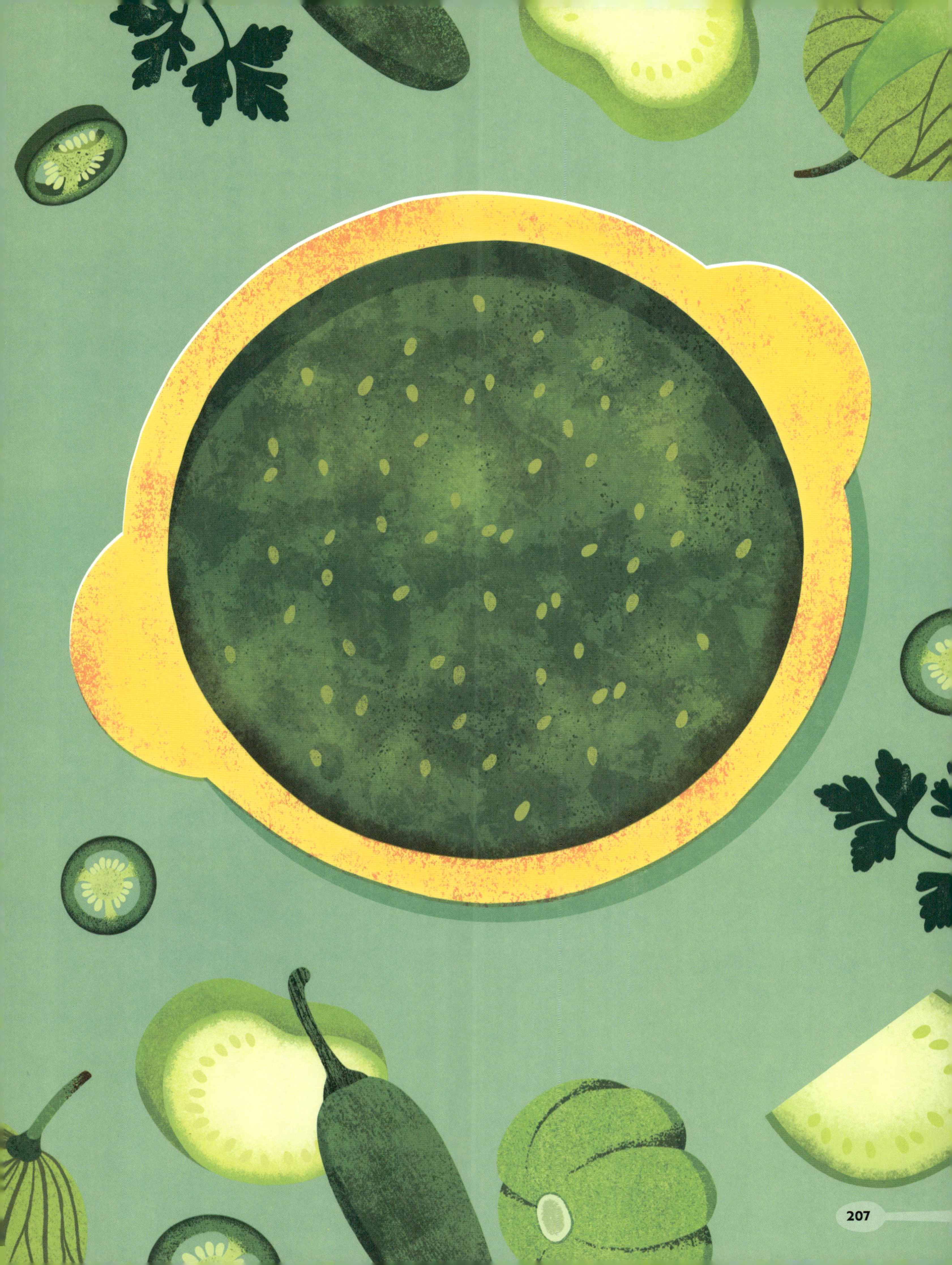

UNITED STATES OF AMERICA

The U.S. is a big, diverse country, with a menu to match! Feast on ancient, indigenous foods – like blueberries, bison, tomatoes, salmon and corn – served alongside steak and fries, gumbo and jambalaya, tacos and empanadas, fried rice and chop suey, fried chicken and mac-and-cheese. Regional specialities range from Alaskan king crab to Wisconsin butter on bread made from Kansas's 'amber waves of grain'. The U.S. is bigger than the fifty states. Its territories include Guam, the U.S. Virgin Islands, American Samoa and Puerto Rico. Favourite Puerto Rican recipes include pork pernil, rice with peas and fried plantains.

BELOVED BARBECUE

The roots of barbecue go back to Native American traditions of smoking and slow-roasting meats over an open fire. Enslaved Africans and their descendants also developed barbecue techniques across the American South. Today, regional variations include vinegary Carolina pulled pork, sweet and tangy ribs in Kansas City and smoked beef brisket in Texas.

THANKSGIVING

This annual American holiday celebrates the autumn harvest. First established by President Lincoln after the Civil War to promote unity, many Americans travel home to their families each November. They give thanks over roast turkey, mashed potatoes, cranberry sauce and pumpkin pie, all of which are made from native ingredients.

TACOS AND NACHOS

Much of the American Southwest was once a part of Mexico. Today, in states like Arizona, Texas, New Mexico, Colorado and California, you can still eat Mexican foods, like carne asada, salsa verde, nachos, quesadillas, burritos and green chillies.

THREE SISTERS

Many Indigenous people here traditionally grew corn, beans and squash together, in companion planting known as the three sisters. Today, they are pillars in the American daily diet and around the world.

STATE-FAIR TREATS

At state fairs across the U.S., you can see award-winning farming, from hogs and goats to tractor shows, jam-making contests and blue-ribbon watermelons. You can also eat all kinds of treats, like corn-dogs in Oklahoma, cheese curds in Wisconsin, deep-fried sticks of butter in Iowa and candyfloss tacos in Texas.

MELTING POT

The U.S. is often called a nation of immigrants – and many iconic American recipes were brought here from around the world. Immigrants brought burgers and frankfurters from Germany, pizza from Italy, and made 'American' apple pie out of fruit native to Afghanistan. Today, people still move here from around the world, mixing foods to create amazing new recipes – like kimchi tacos!

BEEF AND BURGERS

Americans raise a lot of beef cattle and are famous for their love of burgers. Burger toppings can vary from state to state and include Vermont cheddar, Jersey tomatoes, sweet vidalia onions from Georgia, Southwest smoked poblanos and California avocados.

PEANUT PROS

Enslaved Africans brought peanuts to American soils in the 1700s. About 200 years later, an African American man born into slavery named George Washington Carver grew up to be an agricultural scientist who focused on improving the lives of poor Southern farmers. He developed over 300 uses for the peanut, including peanut butter, which is still popular in sandwiches.

FROM SEA TO SHINING SEA

The U.S. is bounded by the Atlantic, the Pacific and the Gulf of Mexico, borders the inland Great Lakes and hosts huge rivers like the mighty Mississippi. All that water means great fishing! People here love Maine lobster, Maryland crabs, New England clam chowder, Rocky Mountain trout, Alaskan salmon and Hawaiian ahi tuna.

209

CHILLI CON CARNE

CHILLI WITH BEEF AND BEANS

PREPARATION TIME	COOKING TIME	LEVEL OF DIFFICULTY	SERVES
15 mins	45 mins	●	4

While its roots go back to Mexico, writers first described chilli con carne in the 1880s, when 'chilli queens' in San Antonio, Texas, sold cauldrons of it from carts at dusk. Today, chilli is eaten daily across the American Southwest, with far too many variations to count. People take chilli very seriously, with chilli cook-offs where opinions run as hot as a habanero pepper. Some people use dried chilli peppers, others add chilli powder; some slow-simmer dried beans for hours, others cook beef, turkey or lamb, and declare that 'real chilli has no beans!'.

INGREDIENTS

2 tablespoons oil
1 medium onion, chopped
2 garlic cloves, thinly sliced
450 g minced beef
1 tablespoon chilli powder
1 400-g tin crushed or chopped
    fire-roasted tomatoes
2 x 400-g tins pinto beans, rinsed
    and drained
475 ml low-sodium chicken stock
    or water
tortilla chips, for serving

1. In a large pot, heat the oil over a medium heat. Add the onion and garlic, season generously with salt, and cook, stirring occasionally, until the onion is translucent: about 10 minutes.

2. Add the minced beef and increase the heat to medium-high. Cook, breaking it up with a spoon, until it is opaque and browned in spots: about 6 minutes. Add the chilli powder and continue stirring, until fragrant: about 1 minute.

3. Add the tin of tomatoes and use a spoon to break them up into smaller chunks if they are large. Add the beans and chicken broth and bring to a boil over a high heat. Reduce the heat to medium-low and simmer until the chilli is thick and flavourful: about 20 minutes.

4. Season with salt to taste and serve the chilli hot with any – or all! – of the toppings and tortilla chips.

Top with any combination of soured cream, chopped fresh coriander, chopped white onion, shredded Monterey jack cheese, pickled jalapeños or diced avocado. Or have them all!

BEANS
AROUND THE WORLD

We've been eating beans throughout human history. There are unique and favourite varieties hailing from cultures across continents. And you may eat even more beans than you realize. Many peas botanically belong to the bean family, and peanuts are technically beans too! Around the world, beans are nutritious, affordable, filling and delicious. No wonder they're eaten at breakfast, lunch, dinner and dessert.

HUMMUS
People have been growing chickpeas for thousands of years in the Middle East. And for thousands of years, they've been simmering the beans and puréeing them with sesame paste to make this delicious dip.

AKARA
This crunchy bean fritter is beloved in West Africa. It's made from black-eyed beans or Nigerian local beans that are peeled, ground into a paste, mixed with onions and spices, and fried into crunchy fritters that are soft on the inside. Enslaved West Africans brought the recipe to Brazil and the Caribbean, where you'll still find akara today.

MUNG BEANS
These little bitty beans are green on the outside, yellow on the inside, and common in many southern, eastern and southeastern Asian cuisines. In India they're made into a fermented paste that people cook into dosa, a thin pancake. In China, mung beans are used for sweet preparations, like in a tong sui, a type of Cantonese dessert. And fresh, crunchy white mung beansprouts are tossed into salads and top dishes from pad thai to Vietnamese pho.

SOY BEANS
These beans are essential in many Asian cuisines, where they're made into soy sauce, soy milk, tofu, miso and more. In Japan, young soy beans – edamame – are eaten straight as a snack. The fuzzy green pods are boiled or steamed, salted, served in bowls and eaten by hand, each little green bean is popped from the pod right into your mouth.

BOSTON BAKED BEANS

People have been growing and eating beans in the United States since long before it was the United States. In the area that would become Massachusetts, Native American people traditionally cooked haricot or yellow-eye beans with fish, venison or bear fat, with a little maple syrup. European colonists learned the recipe, and today savoury-sweet maple-kissed beans are still so popular that some people call Boston 'Beantown'.

MEXICAN FRIJOLES AND REFRIED BEANS

Frijoles is the Spanish word for the most common bean native to Central and South America. There are over thirty varieties, including yellow eye, black, kidney and vaquero, which has black and white markings like a Holstein cow. Beans are a daily staple in Mexican cuisine, where a favourite recipe is frijoles refritos, also known as refried beans.

ADZUKI BEANS

These little reddish-brown beans from Asia are often made into a sweet, sticky paste. In China, red-bean paste is added to steamed buns (baozi and zongzi), as well as to mooncakes for the autumn festival. In Japan, sweet adzuki paste may be used atop ice cream and is a favourite filling inside mochi.

BEANS ON TOAST

One favourite breakfast in the UK features tinned white beans simmered with spices and tomato sauce, served with a thick slice of buttered toast. Introduced to the UK from the United States in the 1910s, baked beans became a filling, affordable staple during World War II.

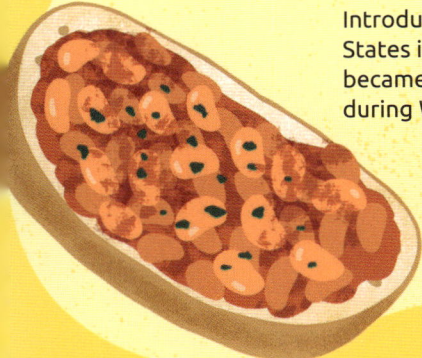

LIMAS

A native bean from the Andes in South America, limas are a white, broad bean named after Peru's capital city. Like other beans, limas sailed to Europe in the sixteenth century. One variety of limas became the gigante or butter beans still favoured in many European cuisines; in Greece, they star in gigantes plaki, cooked in a delicate tomato sauce.

SOUTH AMERICA

Where can you find a rainforest, a pink lagoon (with matching pink flamingos), a desert, the world's largest salt flats, as well as six different types of big felines, a cold-water dolphin, llamas and penguins? In South America. Measuring 7,600 kilometres from the northernmost point in Punta Gallinas, Colombia, to the southernmost tip of Cape Horn, Chile, South America is a region of contrasts and rich natural beauty. Running along the western side of the continent, and crossing seven countries, is the largest mountain range in the world: the Andes. If this were not enough, South America also boasts the largest rainforest in the world: the Amazon. Incidentally, in the largest rainforest is where you can find the smallest monkeys on the planet, pygmy marmosets, which are so small, one would fit in the palm of a hand.

ARGENTINA

Argentina is a land that dazzles, from beaches and flatlands to snow-capped mountains. Its wide grassy, flat pampas are a famously perfect place for raising beef, tended by gauchos – Argentinian 'cowboys'. With a long history of colonialism and immigration, Argentina is second only to the U.S. in the number of immigrants it has taken in from countries including Spain, Italy and Germany, and with a diverse culinary culture that reflects these influences on indigenous traditions. Now mostly urbanized, the country is also home to the Andes Mountains, rich farmland, rolling grasslands, famous vineyards and rugged terrain.

SUBMARINO

The submarino is an indulgently rich, sweet drink sipped here and in neighbouring Uruguay. It's made by melting an entire bar of chocolate into a glass of hot milk. Delicious!

SERIOUS BEEF

Since Spaniards arrived, cattle have thrived on the pampas. Beef is the most important staple in the country's cuisine – in fact, Argentina leads the world (per capita) in both raising and eating beef!

ASADO

Argentinians aren't just famous for raising beef – they've perfected cooking it too! Barbecuing is an art here. *Gauchos* are credited with inventing the Argentinian asado, for which meat is cooked over hot coals on a traditional grill called a *parrilla*.

DULCE DE LECHE

Argentina's iconic confection is made by slowly simmering milk and sugar into a sweet, rich, luscious caramel-like spread. Whether slathered on bread, stuffed in pastries, or sandwiched between alfajores – chocolate or sugar-glazed biscuits rolled in coconut flakes – it is beloved by Argentinians of all ages.

EMPANADAS

Each region has their own favourite but these quintessential, half-moon-shaped pastries are usually stuffed with beef, chicken or lamb mixed with onions, olives and spices, though sometimes they're bursting with veggie options like corn, cheese or spinach. Empanada-making can be a communal activity, with grandparents teaching children to prettily pinch the dough into a frilly edge.

ARGENTINIAN DAIRY

All those cattle aren't just for meat. Their milk is also made into artisanal Argentinian cheese. Among the most popular are queso criollo, a semi-hard cheese with a mild and creamy flavour, popular in sandwiches and empanadas, and aged queso de campo with a more robust taste.

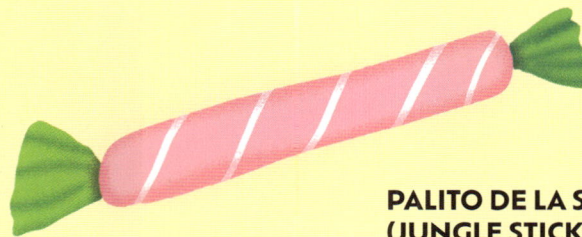

LOCRO

This traditional, hearty stew with white corn and beans is believed to have its recipe roots in Indigenous Andean cultures. Associated with the May Revolution of 1810, which led to the country's independence from Spain, locro is often served on 25 May, celebrated as the National Day of Argentina.

PALITO DE LA SELVA (JUNGLE STICKS)

This classic Argentinian sweet, also known as a jungle stick, has been a beloved treat since its introduction in the 1960s. The chewy, gummy stick-shaped sweets come in vibrant tropical flavours like pineapple and strawberry. Inside the wrapper, you can read about different jungle animals, hence the name.

ARTISANAL GELATO

Introduced by Italian immigrants, dense, smooth, creamy, slow-churned frozen gelato is now on offer everywhere here. Gelato shops, known as *heladerías*, can be found in every corner of Argentine cities and towns, offering a wide variety of flavours, including a rainbow of fruits, plus flavours like dulce de leche and even yerba mate.

HONEY

Argentina is one of the world's leading honey producers. Bees in the country's lush forests, Andean valleys and vast pampas region each visit their area's unique flowers, yielding honey with special character and quality.

CHIMICHURRI

CHILLI AND PARSLEY SAUCE

PREPARATION TIME
25 mins

COOKING TIME
0 mins

LEVEL OF DIFFICULTY
●

MAKES
About 250 ml

This sauce has a name that's fun to say but it's even more fun to eat! Argentina and Uruguay are world famous for their grass-fed beef – and for their delicious grilled steaks. Cowboys and chefs here know how to cook beef to perfection using only fire and salt but this famously tangy green parsley sauce makes it all even better. It's a simple purée of parsley, aromatics, oil and vinegar – some people add oregano or fresh coriander – that only takes a few minutes to prepare but the flavour rewards are huge.

INGREDIENTS

1 small chilli pepper (optional)
2 to 3 cloves garlic, chopped
4 tablespoons red wine vinegar
1 small bunch of parsley
120 ml olive oil
½ teaspoon salt, plus more to
    taste

1. Combine the chilli, garlic and vinegar in a small bowl. Leave to sit for 10 minutes.

2. Meanwhile, finely chop the parsley, including the tender stems. Add the parsley, oil and salt to the bowl and stir to combine. Leave the mixture to rest for 10 minutes, for the flavours to combine.

3. Taste and adjust seasonings as desired.

Spoon it over the top of a perfectly charred steak – or use it as a marinade, basting the steak as it cooks.

No steak? No problem. This zingy sauce is also delicious on everything from beans and eggs to roasted veggies.

SALT

AROUND THE WORLD

Salt is the only rock we eat. It's in every cell of our bodies, helping our muscles and nervous systems work. It also makes food taste even more delicious! Chefs say salt makes food taste more like itself. Salt has been a literal lifesaver throughout history for its magical ability to stop bacteria and preserve perishables. Foods that are salted and dried – like salt cod and beef jerky – can be kept for months or even years. Today, we have new ways to preserve food but traditional salt-making techniques are still practised and prized. People expertly extract salt from saline springs and evaporate seawater into delicious sea salt.

HIMALAYAN PINK SALT

Pink, coarse crystals of Himalayan pink salt are mined from the Himalayan mountains. Believed to be 250 million years old, this ancient mineral has a sweet floral taste. Cooks all over the globe love the rosy, salty sparkle it adds to a dish.

FLEUR DE SEL

This specialty salt is skimmed off the top of shallow evaporation ponds along France's Brittany coast. You might see it sprinkled on caramels and chocolates for a distinct crystalline burst of salty crunch.

MALDON SALT

Flaky pyramids of British Maldon salt are harvested from a briny tidal river and then gently boiled in big vessels. You can crumble the giant flakes between your fingers; they don't taste bitter – in fact, some people think they taste sweet.

CHARCOAL SALT

On the Mediterranean island of Cyprus, flakes of salt are combined with charcoal from local trees to create a black salt. Its soft, fluffy texture adds a light-tasting but dramatic look to salads!

BAMBOO SALT

Korean bamboo salt, or jugyeom, is made by collecting sea salt from the Korean coast, packing it into a piece of bamboo, sealing it with clay, and roasting it nine times until the traditional salt takes on a special, smoky flavour. The slow process takes a lot of effort, which is why this is one of the most expensive salts in the world.

SALAR DE UYUNI

Bolivia's Salar de Uyuni is the largest salt flat in the world – a blinding white expanse dotted with tiny islands covered in cacti. Salt is raked into great pyramids and transported all over the Andes to season foods, from llama steaks to potatoes.

KALA NAMAK

This black salt, popular in India and South Asia, is something of an acquired taste. That's because its natural sulfur content gives this salt a distinctive tangy, pungent, umami-rich sulfurous taste and aroma. While a little pinch can pack a big punch, many people find it irresistible.

PERUVIAN PINK SALT

Popular since the time of the Inca Empire and long harvested from ancient seabeds high in South America's Andes Mountains, this salt's high mineral content gives it a pretty, pink tint.

ROCK SALT

Nigeria is famous for its rock-salt deposits, especially in salty Lake Okposi and Lake Uburu. Some people here still use centuries-old traditional methods of cooking down the brine in enamel basins over wood fires, leaving salt that takes on a deliciously smoky flavour.

BRAZIL

The largest country in South America, Brazil is home to most of the Amazon River basin and its tropical rainforest. There are more species of animals and plants living here than almost anywhere else in the world. Brazilian food and culture is diverse too, as people and customs from the Americas, the Caribbean, Africa and Europe have blended here for hundreds of years. Brazil exports most of the world's oranges and melons, along with all kinds of tropical fruits like pineapple, guava, papaya, mango, avocado, coconut and maracujá.

ALL-YOU-CAN-EAT MEAT

At Brazilian all-you-can-eat steakhouses, waiters bring grilled meats on huge skewers to your table, then use a giant knife to cut the meat right onto your plate. Everybody gets a card where one side is green, meaning bring more meat, and the other side red, meaning you are full!

COFFEE BEANS

Some of the most prized coffee beans come from Brazilian farms that grow coffee plants among the tall trees in the rainforest. It takes a lot longer to grow coffee beans in shade rather than in sunny fields but they taste even better – and are better for the environment too!

BRIGADEIROS

These soft confections are made by cooking condensed milk with butter and cocoa powder, forming the fudge bonbons into little rounds, and rolling the whole thing in chocolate sprinkles. Some say they were named after a brigadier to serve at his rallies.

THE CHRISTMAS CHESTER

For many Brazilians, it's not Christmas without a Chester on the table! What's a Chester? It's a special breed of giant chicken raised for its extra breast and thigh meat.

COXINHA

One of the most popular snacks in Brazil is the coxinha, a golden-fried dumpling shaped like a teardrop or a pyramid. They are filled with creamy cheese and chicken, wrapped in dough, and covered with breading for a very crunchy crust.

SUGAR CANE

Portuguese colonists started growing the tall grass called sugar cane in Brazil more than 500 years ago, and today the country grows more than anywhere else in the world. You can crush sugar cane stalks to get a sweet mild juice or boil the juice down into the sugar we use every day. It can also be turned into fuel – in Brazil, many cars now run on sugar cane!

AÇAÍ

Many tropical fruits grow in Brazil but one of the most unusual is the small, round super-healthy fruit of the açaí palm tree. Now sold worldwide, açaí has been a valuable food for centuries, for those who have lived along the Amazon River.

ACARAJÉ AND CARURU

The cooking in the coastal state of Bahia is often called Afro-Brazilian, and a famous dish here is acarajé, or black-eyed pea fritters, served with a chunky condiment called caruru made from okra, onions, prawns and toasted nuts.

LUCKY BAY LEAF

Some Brazilian New Year's Eve traditions include eating lentils and pomegranates for good luck. You can also put a bay leaf in your wallet and keep it there next to a piece of paper money. Next New Year's Eve, donate the money and throw the bay leaf into a river or stream.

CARNAVAL

The roots of this holiday are religious but today this week-long spring celebration is one of the world's biggest parties, with music, dancing and lots of street food. You can try pastel (a savoury, stuffed, fried pastry), aipim frito (chips made from the tuber called yuca) and espetinhos, also known as meat on a stick!

FEIJOADA

SLOW-COOKED BLACK BEAN AND PORK SOUP

PREPARATION TIME
15 mins, plus overnight
soaking time for beans

COOKING TIME
2 hrs and 20 mins

LEVEL OF DIFFICULTY
● ● ●

SERVES
4

Feijoada, a slow-cooked, earthy black bean soup with wonderful pork flavour, is the national dish of Brazil. It is always made with a smoked and salted meat and can be served with rice, spring greens and farofa, a condiment made from toasted cassava-root flour. It is a mix of influences from Europeans, Native People and Africans – just like Brazil itself!

INGREDIENTS

340 g dried black beans
225 g bacon, diced
2 yellow onions, diced
1 bunch spring onions, roughly
    chopped
2 cloves garlic, chopped
450 g cubed pork or smoked pork
    sausage, sliced
1 smoked ham hock
1 bay leaf
cooked white rice, for serving
1 small bunch fresh coriander
fresh orange slices, for garnish

1. Place the dried beans in a large bowl, cover with plenty of water, and leave to soak at room temperature overnight or for at least 8 hours.

2. In a large pot, cook the diced bacon over a medium heat: about 8 minutes or until crisp.

3. Add the onions, spring onions and garlic, and cook, stirring, until the onions begin to turn translucent: about 5 minutes.

4. Add the pork or sausage and cook, stirring occasionally, until the meat looks brown: about 5 minutes.

5. Drain and rinse the soaked beans and add them to the large pot, along with the smoked ham hock and the bay leaf, and add water until it is 2.5 centimetres above the beans.

6. Simmer, covered, for 2 hours, adding more water if the level goes below the beans. Test beans to be sure they are soft.

7. Serve over rice, garnished with fresh coriander and orange slices.

Starting with dried beans gives you the best flavour and texture but if you're in a hurry, you can use tinned beans instead. Just skip step 1 and omit the water in step 5.

COLOMBIA

Bordering Central America in the north and nestled between the Caribbean and Pacific Ocean, Colombia is one of the most ecologically diverse countries in the world. Covering an area that's almost twice as big as France, Colombia's Amazon rainforest, grassland plains and Andes Mountains hold 10% of the world's biodiversity! In the capital city of Bogotá, restaurants in the Zona G (short for Gourmet) showcase international cuisine, and in the Mercado de la Perseverancia, you can enjoy traditional Colombian flavours.

FRUVER

Walking around Colombia's cities and towns, you may see several stores with the name *fruver*. It's not a chain store, though. *Fruver* is a combination of the first three letters of *frutas* and *verduras* (fruits and vegetables).

COFFEE

Brought to Colombia by the Jesuits, a religious order of clerics, in the eighteenth century, coffee plants thrived in the low Andean region, where mild temperatures and frequent rain offered ideal conditions. Today, coffee is Colombia's most popular produce, and you can not only drink it but also enjoy it in sweets, desserts and even body scrubs!

HORMIGAS CULONAS

When the rainy season starts in April, the people of the north-central state of Santander know it is time for the hormigas culonas, also known as big-butt ants, to appear. Prized as a delicacy, these ants are harvested, toasted and eaten as a high-energy snack that tastes like salty peanuts.

ARROZ CON COCO (COCONUT RICE)

When eating traditional Colombian Caribbean fare, it's likely your order will come with a side of coconut rice. This staple of northern Colombian cuisine is made by cooking rice in caramelized coconut milk. It can be tricky to cook since it can stick to the bottom of the pot! But if you're patient and cook it over a low flame, you will be rewarded.

AREPAS

Round and flat, cooked on a griddle, and usually made of ground cornflour, arepas can be plain or stuffed with cheese, egg or beef. Or you might find rice, yucca or plantain arepas. No matter the flavours or filling, it's Colombia's best-known food.

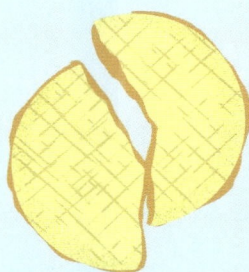

PURPLE PASSION FRUIT

Colombia's greatest treasures include several types of passion fruit, including the supersweet purple variety called gulupa.

'SWEATY' FOOD

Many dishes in Colombia are called sudado (sweaty). While this may make you think that the main ingredient just went for a jog, its name references the little droplets of water that appear on the food as it's cooking, looking like it just finished a workout.

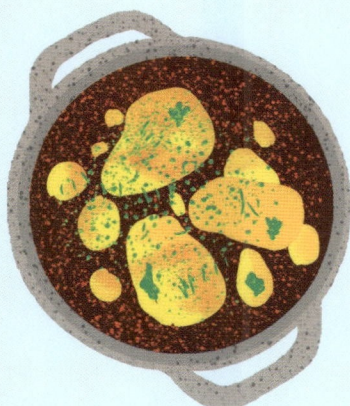

OBLEAS CON AREQUIPE

Sweetened, caramelized milk, known as arequipe, is sandwiched between two thin, giant, foot-wide wafers and eaten as an after-school snack. If you order one, get extra napkins. It's common for the caramel milk to ooze out and stick to your fingers (yum!).

PERRO CALIENTE COLOMBIANO

Colombians have really mastered the art of the loaded hot dog. A common snack after a sports game, movie, or at a fair, regular toppings include pineapple, guacamole, raw onions, crisps and bacon.

CHOCOLATE CON QUESO

For breakfast or a mid-morning snack, many Colombians reach for a mug of hot chocolate in which they dunk a slice of cheese. This combination yields a two-punch of flavour and texture: the chocolate's heat melts the cheese, making it stringy and easy to slurp, and the cheese's saltiness makes the chocolate flavour pop!

SEAFOOD

AROUND THE WORLD

Seafood encompasses a breathtaking variety of edible species, from shellfish and crustaceans like scallops, lobsters and crabs to cephalopods like octopus and squid – not to mention countless kinds of fish! Today, seafood is the world's largest traded food commodity and provides sustenance to billions of people. Unfortunately, you might say we've come to love fish too much – in modern times, we've overharvested some marine species. But there are many sustainable wild choices, including lots of little fishes with big, delicious flavours!

BACALAO

Bacalao is Spanish for dried, salted cod (bacalhau in Portuguese); before freezers, this was the traditional way of preserving the cod catch to eat all year long! When you're ready to cook bacalao, you soak the hard, dried fillets – for hours, or even days – to soften them and remove the salt, changing the water often.

CAVIAR

These yummy, squishy, salty fish eggs are primarily harvested from various species of sturgeon. A luxury food in Europe since at least the fifteenth century, today most caviar comes from the Caspian Sea and the Black Sea, and is produced in Russia and Iran. Caviar is traditionally served with tiny spoons on crackers or on little Russian pancakes called blini, accompanied with lemon wedges, soured cream and chopped chives or dill.

KINILAW

Ceviche is a seafood specialty of Central and South America, made with raw fish, prawns, squid or octopus! Bite-sized chunks of fresh seafood are marinated in lime or lemon juice, and the citric acid 'cooks' and pickles it. A similar dish in the Philippines is called kinilaw.

HÁKARL

One of Iceland's national dishes, hákarl consists of chunks of Greenland shark that have been cured, traditionally by burying the meat in a shallow, sandy hole for six to twelve weeks, then digging it up and hanging it up to dry for months. The results are an acquired taste, with a cheesy texture and a pungent, ammonia-like aroma.

FISH SAUCE

This essential Southeast Asian ingredient is made by fermenting whole little fish (often anchovies) in barrels for up to a year; the resulting liquid brings wonderfully deep, savoury flavours to everything from soups to salads. People call it an 'umami bomb' and often combine it with lime juice, sugar, chillies and fresh coriander in dishes like Vietnamese pho and Thailand's pad thai.

EEL

At least nineteen species of eel are eaten around the world. Freshwater eels are beloved in Japan, where they are called unagi and often served smoked and glazed with a dark, salty-sweet sauce and paired with rice. Other popular eel dishes include smoked eel in the Netherlands and eel soup in Hamburg, Germany.

SEAWEED

Today, diverse, delicious, nutritious seaweeds are enjoyed around the world. Nori is essential in Japan for wrapping sushi; dulse, a reddish seaweed, is used to make soda bread in Ireland and is served as a crispy bar snack in Canada; sweet, silky wakame is often added to miso soup, and kombu is essential in ramen broth. Indigenous people in Chile have been eating cochayuyo, or bull kelp, for at least 14,000 years.

THIEBOUDIENNE

Thieboudienne is a stew-like mix of fish (usually white grouper) cooked with rice, vegetables and tomato sauce. It's both the national dish of Senegal and a symbol of Senegalese hospitality, or *terranga*. Traditionally, it's served in a large communal pot that family, friends, and guests gather around and eat from together.

CEVICHE

CITRUS-PICKLED FRESH FISH WITH JALAPEÑO AND FRESH CORIANDER

PREPARATION TIME	COOKING TIME	LEVEL OF DIFFICULTY	SERVES
1 hr	0 mins	●	4

In this traditional fish dish from Central and South America – especially Peru, Ecuador and Mexico – sparklingly fresh seafood is 'cooked' not with heat but with the acidity of fresh citrus juice. It could hardly be easier or more delicious. Start with the freshest seafood you can find, or catch! Then marinate it in lots of fresh citrus juice and let the acid transform the raw seafood into... ceviche! For added flavour and colour, add fresh chopped tomato, avocado or mango to the finished dish.

INGREDIENTS

680 g fresh, firm-fleshed saltwater white fish fillets (such as grouper, mahi mahi or sea bass) or scallops
salt
175 ml fresh lime juice (from about 6 limes)
60 ml fresh orange juice
1 small red onion, halved lengthways and very thinly sliced crosswise
1 jalapeño, thinly sliced crosswise
14 g fresh coriander, finely chopped

1. Cut the fish or scallops into bite-sized pieces. Place in a bowl and cover with cold water and 1 tablespoon salt. Refrigerate for at least 15 minutes.

2. Meanwhile, in another bowl, toss together the lime juice, orange juice, onion, jalapeño and fresh coriander to create the citrus dressing.

3. Drain the fish, rinse with cold water and pat dry. Add it to the citrus dressing and toss. Cover and refrigerate for 30 minutes, then taste and season with salt and pepper, if desired. Serve chilled.

Some people only let their ceviche take a short bath in lime juice; others prefer a more pickled flavour that results from an hour or more in that tangy citrus.

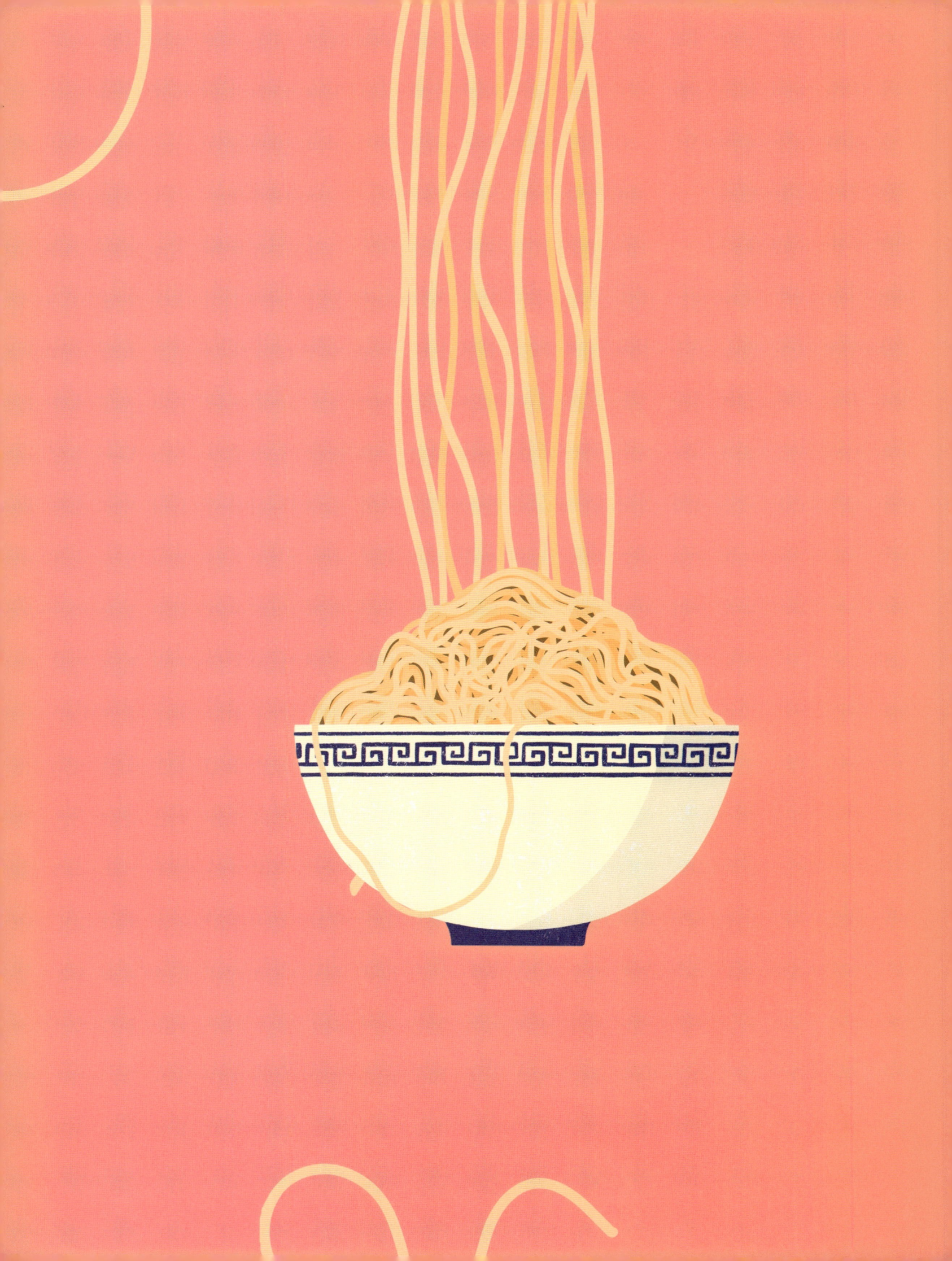

INDEX OF RECIPES

INDEX

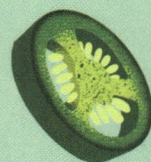

RECIPE NOTES

Here are a few good rules of thumb to keep in mind when shopping and cooking.
Unless a recipe says otherwise, we use:
- Unsalted butter
- Coarse salt and freshly ground pepper
- Fresh herbs, including flat-leaf (not curly) parsley
- Medium-sized eggs
- Full-fat milk
- Large garlic cloves (use two if yours are small)

MEASUREMENT NOTES

- All spoon and cup measurements are level.
- 1 teaspoon = 5 ml; 1 tablespoon = 15 ml.
- Cooking and preparation times are for guidance but individual ovens may vary, so check for doneness. If using a convection (fan) oven, follow the manufacturer's instructions.
- When a recipe doesn't specify an exact amount – like when drizzling oil, seasoning with salt and pepper, garnishing with fresh herbs, or sprinkling with icing sugar to finish a dish – the quantities are flexible. Use the illustration – and your taste – as guides.

NOTE ON SAFETY

This book and the recipes presented in this book are designed for children but assume adult supervision at all times. Although we take care to identify any hazards, we do not take any responsibility for your children during the preparation and cooking of these dishes or for any adverse reactions to ingredients or finished dishes. It is up to parents and caregivers to choose appropriate recipes and ingredients and to ensure the safety of the children under their supervision.